CONSUMERISM

Search for the Consumer Interest

EDITED BY

David A. Aaker and George S. Day

FOURTH EDITION

THE FREE PRESS
A Division of Macmillan Publishing Co., Inc.
NEW YORK

Collier Macmillan Publishers
LONDON

The Free Press
A Division of Macmillan Publishing Co., Inc.
866 Third Avenue, New York, N.Y. 10022

Collier Macmillan Canada, Inc.

Library of Congress Catalog Card Number: 81-69765

Printed in the United States of America

printing number
6 7 8 9 10

Library of Congress Cataloging in Publication Data
Main entry under title:

Consumerism : search for the consumer interest.

Includes bibliographical references and index.
1. Consumer protection--United States--Addresses, essays, lectures. I. Aaker, David A. II. Day, George S.
HC110.C63C6443 1982 381'.3'0973 81-69765
ISBN 0-02-900150-1 AACR2

CONTENTS

PREFACE TO THE FOURTH EDITION

Today consumerism is very different from what it was in 1971, when the first edition of this book appeared, or even in 1978, when the third edition was published. The area continues to broaden, mature, and change its thrust. In Part I, the introduction to this edition, we assess consumerism at this point in time: what is the field's current scope and direction and its probable future?

One hint of present trends comes from the four new sections that are included in this edition. The first is government regulation, an area now undergoing an extensive, healthy, and sometimes rigorous cost-benefit scrutiny. The second is advertising aimed at children, which involves fascinating issues about fairness and the role of government regulation. The third is consumer information systems, especially those entirely or partially in the private sector. We have always thought that consumer information is a key to consumer protection. The efforts of the private sector in this regard are most significant. The fourth new topic is demarketing, or reducing consumption (of tobacco or energy, for example). The ethics, public interest, and effectiveness of demarketing become interesting issues.

Half the selections in the fourth edition are new; only five of the chapters carry over from the second edition and only two from the first. However, those familiar with previous editions will find some similarities. The basic organization of the book, which has been well received, has been retained. We have again attempted to present a balanced treatment of the issues, recognizing that both critics and supporters of current practices in the marketplace have worthwhile points of view and that both groups can learn from each other. Discussion questions are again included to challenge the reader.

Part II reviews historical perspectives, current views, and the special problems of disadvantaged consumers. The following four parts are organized according to the steps of the purchase process—the prepurchase phase, the purchase transaction, and the postpurchase experience. Part III discusses consumer information systems and the debate over information disclosure requirements. Part IV looks at advertising—social issues, advertising and children, and deception in advertising. The fifth part concerns the purchase transaction; chapters deal with selling practices, ecology, demarketing, and antitrust. Part VI, on the postpurchase phase, addresses warranties and service, safety and liability, and consumer satisfaction. Issues associated with business response to consumer problems and with governmental regulation are raised throughout the book. Part VII, however, focuses on these two areas.

We would like to acknowledge the many people in business, government, and academia who have struggled during the past decade to search for the consumer interest. Their efforts have substantially elevated the sophistication with which difficult consumer issues are addressed. It has been a pleasure to watch this process. We owe our greatest debt to the authors who permitted us to include their work in this book. We are also grateful to the many colleagues and students who, having used the book, offered helpful suggestions for improving it. We hope they will find this edition even more useful. Most of all, we acknowledge the encouragement and support of Kay and Marilyn: they are exceptional wives and consumers but nonetheless sometimes need protection.

David A. Aaker
George S. Day

PART I

Introduction

A GUIDE TO CONSUMERISM

David A. Aaker & George S. Day

The term "consumerism" identifies the contemporary consumer movement, launched in the mid-1960s by the concerns triggered indirectly by Rachel Carson[1] and directly by Ralph Nader's auto safety investigation,[2] and by President Kennedy's efforts to establish the four rights of consumers: the right to safety, to be informed, to choose, and to be heard.[3] Consumerism encompasses the evolving activities of government, business, independent organizations, and concerned consumers to protect and enhance the rights of consumers.

From the mid-sixties to the late seventies, the scope of consumerism steadily expanded. This trend was most evident in the rapid growth in expenditures for federal regulatory activities (see Table 1), fueled by the emergence of new issues and the persistence of many long-standing consumer problems. Further impetus for expansion came from the recognition that consumerism was concerned with protecting consumers whenever there is an exchange relationship with an organization, whether a business firm, a government agency, or a hospital. Finally, environmental concerns and consumerism became increasingly interwoven and frequently converged on common issues.

By the end of the 1970s, however, consumerist activity appeared to have peaked out and the consumer movement seemed "everywhere in

---

[1] Rachel Carson, *Silent Spring* (Boston: Houghton Mifflin, 1962).

[2] Ralph Nader, *Unsafe at Any Speed* (New York: Pocket Books, 1966).

[3] For discussion see "Consumer Advisory Council: First Report," Executive Office of the President (Washington, D.C.: U.S. Government Printing Office, October 1963).

TABLE 1.1. EXPENDITURES ON FEDERAL REGULATORY ACTIVITIES (Fiscal Years, Millions of Dollars)

Area of Regulation	*1970*	*1978*	*1980*
Consumer safety and health	$392	$2255	$2467
Job safety and other working conditions	62	496	701
Environment and energy	85	1296	1866
Finance and banking	106	273	373
Industry-specific regulation	125	297	357
General business	96	245	277
	$866	$4862	$6041

Source: Center for the Study of American Business. Cited by Murray L. Weidenbaum, "Public Policy: No Longer a Spectator Sport for Business," *Journal of Business Strategy 1* (Summer 1980), p. 47.

retreat."[4] As evidence, Reich cited a series of reversals that began in 1976:

> Congress has rejected the Food and Drug Administration's proposed ban on saccharin, and several courts and state legislatures have attempted to block the FDA's attack on Laetrile. The Consumer Product Safety Commission's recent ruling that swimming pool slides must carry danger warnings has elicited widespread ridicule, brought a reversal in the federal courts, and contributed to rumors that the Commission itself will be abolished. Congress has rescinded the Department of Transportation's safety-belt/ignition interlock rule, removed its authority to require helmets for motorcyclists, and expressed distaste for its "air bag" regulation. Congress has also rejected the proposed consumer-protection agency.[5] And the Federal Trade Commission's proposal to control television advertising of sugared cereals for children has prompted the *Washington Post* to accuse the agency of becoming the national nanny.[6]

These events coincided with a period of questioning Ralph Nader's effectiveness and power. For example, there was a largely negative reaction to his formation of a group to protect the interests of sports fans—an effort interpreted as evidence that Nader could no longer count on unquestioning public support. This was followed by several widely publicized confrontations between Nader and onetime supporters who had been given

---

[4] Robert B. Reich, "Toward a New Consumer Protection," *University of Pennsylvania Law Review 128* (November 1979), At the time of writing the article the author was director of policy planning for the Federal Trade Commission.

[5] The bill to create an agency for consumer protection was defeated by a vote of 227 to 189. See 124 *Congressional Record* H828 (daily edition February 8, 1978).

[6] "The FTC as National Nanny," *Washington Post,* March 1, 1978, p. 22.

senior positions in the Carter administration.[7] Finally, the 1980 election of Ronald Reagan was viewed by many as conclusive evidence that the consumer movement had lost most of its clout. Not only did Reagan owe little to the traditional constituencies of consumer regulation—unions, environmental interests, and consumer groups—but also he was committed to decreased government intervention.[8]

On the basis of a regulatory or legislative scorecard, the strength of the consumer movement has indeed waned. This would, however, be a premature judgment in light of the considerable momentum of consumerism. For instance, consumer protection is solidly entrenched in the legal system, including provision for private parties to sue to redress violations of regulations, but most of the dissatisfactions that ultimately fuel consumerism have not abated. Indeed, to understand why the contemporary consumer movement has endured longer than similar movements in the 1910s and 1930s,[9] it is necessary to go beyond the issues of the moment and expose the underlying problems and forces. Accordingly, this introduction seeks to clarify the present scope of consumerism—the causal factors and the mechanisms for focusing consumer discontent—and then to use this analysis to suggest what the future likely holds.

THE SCOPE OF CONSUMERISM

At the core of consumerism remain the four rights set forth by President Kennedy. Clearly, the meaning of each of these rights has been broadened considerably to embrace many new concerns. Further, there is a growing recognition that the scope of consumerism now includes the right to redress and the right to an environment that will enhance the quality of life.

The *right to safety* implies protection against the marketing of goods that are hazardous to health or life. Such a right has motivated numerous laws to protect consumers when they cannot be expected to have sufficient knowledge to protect themselves. Thus, laws pertaining to foods, textiles, drugs, cosmetics, and tires demand that the products not endanger health or safety and that if the potential exists for dangerous misuse a clear warning be provided (e.g., on poisonous cleaning liquids).

---

[7] Marc Leepson, "Consumer Protection: Gains and Setbacks," *Congressional Quarterly,* 1978.

[8] "Deregulation: A Fast Start for the Reagan Strategy," *Business Week,* March 9, 1981, p. 62.

[9] For a description of the ebb and flow of consumerism in the past see Chapter 1.

There is little controversy about such a principle; the only question is whether a specific problem will merit legislation and whether the benefits outweigh the costs.

The right to safety has been broadened to include the protection of people from themselves, a policy with which there is more disagreement.[10] It is argued that people should not always be permitted to make decisions that are not in their best long-run interests even when such decisions are deliberate and informed. Thus, people are not permitted to select an automobile without seat belts and other mandatory safety features. The concern is with consumers' long-run interests, not their immediate desires. At one time the paternalism inherent in this argument was generally accepted as legitimate. This acceptance has turned to skepticism as experience reveals the difficulties of limiting government intervention that is paternalistic.[11] So far, however, there has not been serious questioning of intervention when consumer products may have significant adverse effects on third parties.

The *right to be informed* is a fundamental economic interest of the consumer. There is wide agreement that this right implies at a minimum that the consumer should not be deceived. Just what constitutes deception is more controversial and fluid. For example, the FTC has taken the position that an advertising claim should be unique to the advertised product. Thus, Wonder Bread's claim to build "bodies 12 ways" was considered deceptive by the FTC not because the message was false but because other brands could make the same claim and people exposed to the Wonder Bread advertisement could get the impression that the claim was unique. Along the same lines, slogans like "best buy" and "most significant breakthrough," which in the past were regarded as innocent exaggerations, permissible puffery, are now being challenged.[12]

The right to be informed goes well beyond protection against deception to giving the consumer sufficient information to make wise purchase decisions. To this end there has been a great deal of legislation designed to provide useful comparative information—such as the true rate of interest (truth in lending), the cost of food products on a per unit basis (unit pricing), product ingredients, and nutritional quality.[13] Nonetheless, commercial sources, principally advertisements and point-of-sale information, still provide much of the product information upon which the

---

[10] J. Fred Weston, "Economic Aspects of Consumer Product Safety," Presentation to the National Commission on Product Safety Hearings, Washington, D.C., March 4, 1970; also see Chapter 32.

[11] Reich, "Toward a New Consumer Protection."

[12] See Chapter 20.

[13] These disclosure requirements and their probable effects are discussed in Chapter 12.

consumer relies. To what extent are companies responsible for insuring that such sources are informative rather than merely persuasive (effective by conventional standards)? Should firms be required or motivated to tell the consumer about what their products will not do—to reveal product disadvantages as well as advantages even when safety is not at issue?

There is growing interest in protecting the consumer's right to know through means other than legislation to correct specific information problems. Particular attention is being directed to education and independent information systems, encompassing comparative testing and informative labeling,[14] to give consumers a broad capability to make effective decisions and police the market.

Concern over the *right to choose* dates back to the end of the last century, when the Sherman Anti-Trust Act was passed to break the monopoly power of the giant firms of the day. Initially, the focus was on protecting competitors from each other, particularly the small firm from the large one. However, antitrust legislation and enforcement have gradually evolved toward an emphasis upon protecting and encouraging competition. Thus, the major effort is directed at increasing the number of competitors and insuring that competitors do not have understandings that are detrimental to the long-run interests of consumers.

Increasing attention is being paid to the economic role of advertising, especially its potential for raising prices, profits, and barriers to entry, which can reduce the range of choice.[15] In a period of significant inflation, it is not surprising that advertising costs have come under scrutiny for their role in contributing to high prices, particularly in the supermarket. However, it now appears that the most significant threat to the consumer's right to choose is price fixing. Although the U.S. Justice Department has always been concerned with deliberate conspiracy to fix prices, its efforts have not been equal to the surprising prevalence of this behavior during a period of inflation.[16] So far the definition of price fixing has stopped short of including administered pricing, although shared monopolies—a few large companies acting in parallel to block outside competition—have been attacked.[17]

There has recently been a significant move away from the view that the structure of an industry is indicative of anticompetitive behavior and in particular that higher prices characterize the more concentrated industries. Some economists have argued that antitrust policies have been doing more harm to consumers than good, as when strong companies in

---

[14] See Chapter 9.

[15] See pp. 190–219.

[16] "Price Fixing: Crackdown under Way," *Business Week,* June 2, 1975, pp. 42–48.

[17] See Chapter 28.

declining industries protect ailing, inefficient competitors for fear that antitrust enforcers would try to dismantle the efficient companies if they became too big.[18]

President Kennedy indicated that the *right to be heard* involves an assurance that consumer interest will be considered in the formulation of government policy and in regulatory proceedings. The difficulty is that the consumer movement is relatively amorphous and lacks the authoritative spokesmen that labor, business, medicine, education, and other interest groups have.[19] To give the consumer a voice within government, Lyndon Johnson created the Office of Special Assistant to the President for Consumer Affairs in 1964. Many states and cities subsequently established similar offices, as did a number of federal agencies during the Nixon and Ford administrations. This did not satisfy consumer advocates, who campaigned vigorously for an independent agency for consumer advocacy, whose main purpose would be to act as watchdog over regulatory bodies. Business lobbies successfully opposed the agency, arguing that it would only increase the harassment of businessmen and disrupt the work of other government units.

It has become clear, nonetheless, that businesses have difficulty listening to their customers. Thus, many firms have created consumer affairs departments to coordinate consumer programs and to permit a new type of representation of consumer interests.[20] Most of these departments handle customer complaints, but some take a more active role and advocate the consumer interest in the internal policymaking process. However, the political realities of large organizations tend to inhibit such efforts.[21]

It is now generally accepted that there is a fifth right the *right to recourse and redress,* that is, to fair settlement of just claims.[22] A variety of innovations, including free legal services for the poor, consumer class action suits, and arbitration procedures, have substantially enhanced this right. The Magnuson-Moss Warranty Act of 1975 was a major legislative effort to overcome consumer problems with warranties; one provision established incentives for firms to set up dispute settlement procedures. As with much complex legislation based on imperfect under-

---

[18] "Antitrust Grows Unpopular," *Business Week,* January 12, 1981, pp. 90–93.

[19] David Vogel and Mark Nadel, "The Consumer Coalition: Dimensions of Political Conflict," in Robert Katz (ed.), *Protecting Consumer Interests* (Cambridge: Ballinger, 1976).

[20] E. Patrick McGuire, *The Consumer Affairs Department: Organization and Functions* (New York: Conference Board, 1973).

[21] See Chapter 34.

[22] Esther Peterson, "Consumerism as a Retailer's Asset," *Harvard Business Review 52* (May–June 1974), pp. 91–101.

standing of the problem, the ultimate benefits to the consumer are uncertain.[23]

The list of consumer rights has been further expanded to include the *right to a physical environment that will enhance the quality of life.* Indeed, consumerism has been defined broadly as an organized expression for an improved quality of life. A discarded beer can or phosphates from detergents can substantially degrade the physical environment. Advertising cluttering the television screen or the highway can similarly depress the quality of life. Environmental problems differ from other consumer questions in that the decisions of the individual consumer do not create an immediate problem. As a result, individual consumers have little incentive to modify their purchasing patterns because their decisions alone will not have an observable impact.

THE ROOTS OF CONSUMERISM

To understand both the evolution of consumerism and the prospect for the future we must look at the enduring problems, which provide the underlying momentum. Of course, any given issue may represent the convergence of a number of these problems:

- disillusionment with the system
- the performance gap
- the consumer information gap
- antagonism toward advertising
- impersonal and unresponsive marketing institutions
- intrusions of privacy
- declining living standards
- special problems of the disadvantaged
- different views of the marketplace

In this section we examine each of these areas in turn, leaving for the next section the question of how they surface as consumer issues demanding action.

Disillusionment with the System

Consumerism is one manifestation of the societal concerns voiced since the sixties. All institutions—courts, government, universities, church, as well as business—have been subjected to increasing public

[23] See Chapter 29.

scrutiny, skepticism, and loss of esteem. For example, public confidence in big companies fell from 55 percent in 1966 to 27 percent in 1971.[24] Fortunately, polls show that this decline in confidence was arrested between 1975 and 1977 and has been reversed in the early 1980s. Precisely why confidence eroded so far is not clear. An imbalance of power among components of our society may have encouraged this trend. Marketers were among those whose power was resented.[25] As we will see, a number of aspects of the consumer environment support this hypothesis. Indeed, many measures taken to strengthen the consumer's rights can just as readily be interpreted as efforts to strengthen the consumer's bargaining position.

Consumers' perceptions of their bargaining position were documented in a 1977 study of attitudes toward consumerism supported by Sentry Insurance.[26] Some 1500 U.S. adults were asked whether "consumers get a better or worse deal in the marketplace compared to ten years ago." The views were generally negative: 27 percent said consumers got a better deal, while 50 percent said they got a worse deal (16 percent said no change and 7 percent were not sure). However, respondents were optimistic that consumers would get a better deal in the marketplace in the next 10 years.

The Performance Gap

Consumers' expectations of product performance and reliability have been steadily rising, in part because advertising of new products stresses their improvements. However, improvements generally make products more complex,[27] so that even though the basic product may be more reliable (and there is good evidence that such is the case),[28] the added features raise new possibilities for malfunction. Thus, while the failure rate has declined or held constant, the total number of product failures has increased because of the growth in the quantity and complex-

---

[24] "America's Growing Antibusiness Mood," *Business Week,* June 17, 1972, pp. 101–103.

[25] Robert Katz, Introduction to Robert Katz (ed.), *Protecting Consumer Interests* (Cambridge; Ballinger, 1977).

[26] Stephen A. Greyser, "Americans' Attitudes toward Consumerism," *Marketing Science Institute* (October 1977), Similar findings have been reported in other studies, as summarized in Thomas J. Stanley and Larry M. Robinson, "Opinions on Consumer Issues: A Review of Recent Studies of Executives and Consumers," *Journal of Consumer Affairs 14* (Summer 1980), pp. 207–220.

[27] Walter McQuade, "Why Nobody's Happy about Appliances," *Fortune,* May 1972, p. 182.

[28] J. M. Juran, "Consumerism and Product Quality," *Quality Progress,* July 1970.

ity of products. On balance, then, many consumers express broader dissatisfaction with the goods they buy.[29] At the same time, the service industry is having great difficulty providing adequate service in the face of recruiting problems, resistance to the high costs of service, and confusion over warranty protection.

The persistence of this promise-performance gap was revealed in the Sentry study. Some 48 percent of the public said that the difference between manufacturers' claims for products and services and the latter's performance had increased over the past 10 years; 27 percent reported a decrease. It is not clear just how much this gap is contributing to a continuing growth in the level of complaints. The Better Business Bureau reported that there were 9 percent more complaints in 1979 than in the previous year, but most concerned mail-order companies or retail oriented goods and services such as franchised auto dealers, auto repair shops, and home furnishings stores.

The Consumer Information Gap

During the last century, buyers were usually competent to make most of their own buying decisions: the goods were as simple as their needs, at least by today's standards. When buyers did require assistance, they could turn to a merchant, who was either a trusted friend or a proprietor with a reputation for providing reliable information. The marketplace of today is far different. The products from which the consumer must choose have grown enormously in quantity and complexity. A supermarket now stocks 6000–8000 different items; it may add and delete as many as 3500 in a year.[30] Furthermore, products are more complex, requiring evaluation along many more dimensions, some of which are related to new performance and convenience features, others to societal problems such as ecology.

Against the formidable spectrum of products generated by professional sellers, we have an amateur buyer who usually does not have the time, the interest, or the capacity to obtain information needed to make optimal product decisions. In one study of supermarket shopping, 33 women were asked to select best buys in 20 product categories in a 50-minute period; they were correct in only 43 percent of the cases.[31] At the same time that there is more information to process, information

---

[29] The extent of this dissatisfaction is discussed in Chapter 33.

[30] A report by Sales Area Marketing, Inc., cited in the *New York Times,* December 24, 1971.

[31] Monroe Peter Friedman, "Consumer Confusion in the Selection of Supermarket Products," *Journal of Applied Psychology 50* (1966), pp. 529–534.

sources are changing. Knowledgeable salespeople or personal experience are losing their previous significance, while TV, print media, and point-of-purchase displays play an increasing role. The information gap is widened further as people spend less time shopping. Competing activities that accompany the new lifestyles reduce both the time for and the appeal of shopping. The emphasis has turned to doing instead of acquiring, and hours devoted to shopping represent a real cost. The gap also reflects rising aspiration levels with respect to the information on which consumers would like to base purchasing decisions.

Prospects for closing this gap are dim—in part because of the illusory nature of information but also because information is a public good whose universal use is difficult to prevent once the data have been released. This circumstance seriously reduces the incentive for private organizations to create and dispense information.[32]

Antagonism toward Advertising

Although advertising is at the core of the existing information system, there is evidence that consumers are skeptical of the usefulness and truthfulness of such information. In one study respondents categorized advertisements. Only 5.8 percent of those noticed were perceived as informative—"ads that you learn something from that you are glad to know or know about . . . that help you in one way or another because of the information they provide."[33] A number of studies have found that 35–40 percent of the public believe that advertising—especially television advertising—is seriously misleading. In the Sentry study, 46 percent of the respondents said they found all (9 percent) or most (37 percent) television advertising to be seriously misleading; 28 percent found all (4 percent) or most (24 percent) print advertising to be seriously misleading.

Beyond dissatisfaction with the usefulness and truthfulness of the content of advertising, a number of other complaints tend to exacerbate specific consumerism issues:

Intrusiveness and clutter. A major study of television advertising found consumer discontent over intrusiveness to be an important factor leading to a low appraisal of the social value of advertising. Furthermore, an increasing proportion of viewers believe there is more advertising than programs are worth.

---

[32] See Hans B. Thorelli's comments in Chapter 9.

[33] Raymond A. Bauer and Stephen A. Greyser, *Advertising in America: The Consumer View* (Cambridge: Harvard University Press, 1968), p. 183.

Irritation. This occurs when the advertising is irrelevant to an audience and/or does not respect their privacy, values, or intelligence.

Stereotyped role portrayals. These have been a major concern of women and ethnic groups. Ads that perpetuate a minority stereotype or ignore new roles, such as the working wife, are at the center of this debate.

Promotion of unrealistic or unsupportable expectations. The advertisement may associate a product with a certain lifestyle that the product cannot realistically be expected to deliver.

Impersonal and Unresponsive Marketing Institutions

The rise of self-service retailing, the declining knowledgeability of sales employees, the juxtaposition of the computer between the customer and the organization, and the inherent difficulties of dealing with bureaucracies all contribute to this dissatisfaction. Most people cannot identify the chief executives of the largest corporations. The fact that executives maintain a low profile makes it difficult for the organizations to develop a warm personal image. Nearly everyone has had experience with those in organizations who appear to avoid responsibility. When there is a problem with a product or service, it is often not clear to consumers how they can get it rectified. What is worse, it is also often not clear to members of the organization, and consumers may be shuttled from person to person. Prospects for improvement are dim because the benefits of good service and prompt personal attention to complaints are difficult to quantify and consequently are given low priority when investment decisions are made.

Intrusions of Privacy

As computer and telecommunications technologies have exponentially expanded the capacity to store and retrieve data, there has been a corresponding growth in the possibility that the resulting data bases will lead to abuses of the privacy of individuals. Awareness of such abuses has led to greater concern with the protection of private information, including limits on access to personal financial and health records and control over the accuracy of the data that are stored.[34] This concern increasingly manifests itself in other areas, for example, the sale of mailing lists by direct marketing firms.

[34] Robert Ellis Smith, *Privacy* (New York: Doubleday Anchor, 1978).

Declining Living Standards

Early in 1980 *Business Week* proclaimed that the "golden age of the consumer" was over.[35] It was estimated that in 1979 *real discretionary* income per worker (disposable income less expenditures for food, housing, fuel, and utilities) had fallen 16 percent below the 1973 level. Not only were usage increases not keeping pace with the overall inflation rate, but the prices of essentials—especially food, medical care, housing and energy—were jumping much faster than the prices of other goods. These broad averages masked the fact that some households were being disproportionately hurt. A two-tier market had evolved in which one tier, encompassing households with two incomes and no children, was coping, while the working-class household with several children and only one wage earner was not.

For the first time Americans had to admit that they were not going to be better off in the future. This loss of optimism has led to further disenchantment with the economic system, which of course is a major underlying cause of consumerism. At the same time, consumers have attempted to deal with the consequences of stagflation (stagnant growth coupled with double-digit inflation) by seeking better value from their purchases and simplifying their lifestyles.[36] However, their efforts in this direction have heightened perceptions of lack of information and declining product quality. These trends suggest that past consumer protection efforts have been largely ineffective.[37]

The Disadvantaged: The Young, the Old, and the Poor

Whatever problems average consumers face, their capacity to cope is much greater than that of the most vulnerable groups in society. The ghetto poor in particular have suffered from fraud, excessive prices, dependence on costly credit, and poor quality merchandise and services. The atomistic ghetto market structure, coupled with skepticism toward comparative shopping, lack of motivation or ability to seek out the best buys, and general lack of education and mobility, works against programs for improvement of this situation.[38]

The problems of the old and the young are very different. The unprotected status of the young stems from their vulnerability to dangerous

[35] "The Shrinking Standard of Living," *Business Week,* January 28, 1980, pp. 72–78.

[36] Avraham Shama, "The Post Stagflation Consumer," *Journal of Marketing 45* (Summer 1981), forthcoming.

[37] See Chapter 3.

[38] These issues are explored in Chapter 8.

products, such as toys and flammable clothing, and their lack of defenses against television advertising. The aged, on the other hand, who have a lifetime of experience, often lack the income to meet their nutritional, health, and shelter needs. As their strength and faculties decline, they may lose their motivation to overcome these problems or to defend themselves against unfair sales practices.

Different Views of the Marketplace

The analysis of consumer problems frequently suffers from a lack of data both as to the seriousness of the abuses and the costs versus the benefits of proposed solutions. Thus, discussions frequently move into the realm of value judgments; here the potential for confusion is multiplied by the lack of shared meanings of key words. Bauer and Greyser observed that at least two participants in these discussions, who for convenience are labeled businessmen and business critics, have radically different perceptions of several key words.[39]

One of these words is *competition.* The critic of business restricts his attention to price competition. In contrast, the businessman believes that price plays a minor role in the marketplace; he believes that the more important form of competition is product differentiation, which is generated by physical product differences or by distinct brand images created by the marketing program.

Another such word is *product.* The critic views a product as an entity with a primary identifiable function. Thus, an automobile is a transportation device. The businessman is more concerned with a product's secondary functions because they may represent the dimensions upon which product differentiation rests. The automobile's appearance might serve the function of providing a mechanism for the individual to express his personality. High horsepower and superior handling may serve the function of providing an outlet for an individual's desire for excitement.

Third, there are consumer *needs.* The critic sees consumer needs as corresponding to a product's primary function. For example, there is a need for transportation, nutrition, and recreation. In contrast, the businessman takes a much broader view of consumer needs, considering any product attribute or appeal upon which real product differentiation can be based as reflecting legitimate needs—needs that are strong enough to affect purchase decisions.

The other words are *rationality* and *information.* The critic views any decision that results in an efficient matching of product to needs (as he

---

[39] Raymond A. Bauer and Stephen A. Greyser, "The Dialogue That Never Happens," *Harvard Business Review 17* (January-February 1969), pp. 122–128.

defines these terms) as rational. Information that serves to enhance rational decisionmaking is good information. The businessman contends that any decision the customer makes to serve his own perceived self-interest is rational. Information, then, is any datum or argument that will truthfully convey the attractiveness of a product in the context of the consumer's own buying criteria. Clearly the definition of information is central to any discussion of consumer decisionmaking.

Conflicts also arise from basic differences in the models of the marketplace used by marketers and critics. In its most extreme form, the model used by critics portrays marketing's role as basically that of persuading or seducing the less-than-willing consumer to buy. The balance of power is tilted in favor of the marketers. At the other end of the manipulative spectrum is a pro-business model in which success depends on the ability to identify and serve consumer needs. Advertising is seen as facilitating choices made by consumers, who generally know what they want. However, reality is probably best captured by a transactional model that emphasizes the give-and-take of the marketplace relationship.[40]

FOCUSING THE DISCONTENT

Consumer problems characteristically lead to vague discontent with the marketplace, particularly with respect to product performance and safety, the usefulness and truthfulness of advertising, and the responsiveness of organizations. Certainly at any given time some people will be upset by an immediate problem, but in general consumer interest is diffuse and hard to define. Yet the progress of consumerism has invariably come through raising the intensity of a particular discontent to the point where legislation or regulatory action was either threatened or undertaken. Such events require a catalyst—consumer protection advocates like Ralph Nader; legislators such as Warren G. Magnuson, Frank E. Moss, and Benjamin Rosenthal; consumer organizations such as the Consumer Federation of America and Consumers Union; or highly motivated journalists. These individuals and groups have the capacity to isolate issues, raise public awareness, and propose a specific avenue for action. It is clear, however, that there must be a basis of discontent with which the public can identify (such as a spectacular abuse) before specific action will be taken, which is typically not the case with antitrust issues, for example.

In the late sixties pressure for action on a wide range of consumer problems built. At the same time, Congress was no longer so dominated

---

[40] See Chapter 4.

by rural constituencies, who were less interested in such problems; consumer legislation was relatively cheap and appeared to generate goodwill among voters; and various tests of the influence of business lobbyists showed that their power was not so great as had been previously assumed.

The early seventies also brought considerable pressure on the regulatory agencies, notably the Federal Trade Commission[41] and the Federal Drug Administration, to better fulfill their original responsibilities; moreover, the legislature gave them additional tasks and powers. New consumer protection agencies were also established, including the Consumer Product Safety Commission, which became almost overnight one of the most visible, controversial, and powerful regulatory bodies—in part because it inherited some responsibilities from existing agencies.[42] From the burst of legislative and regulatory activity in the consumer's interest came a wide array of mechanisms for focusing and alleviating consumer discontent. For example, since 1970 almost all of the remedies summarized in Table 2 have either been introduced, or the regulatory agencies have been given expanded authority to employ them. Each will be discussed at various points in this book, but at this juncture it might be helpful to distinguish among prevention—eliminating an abuse prior to its introduction; restitution—either the restoration of property rights or the restoration to the former state; and punishment—action either to provide redress for aggrieved consumers or to deter future misconduct.

Not all action on behalf of the diffused consumer interest has been a response to pressure from consumer groups or advocates, legislators, or the public. Perhaps the greatest transfer of power to consumers has come through a series of legal decisions that have vastly expanded the liability

TABLE 1.2. CONSUMER PROTECTION REMEDIES

Prevention	*Restitution*	*Punishment*
Codes of conduct (including cease and desist orders and trade regulation rules)	Affirmative disclosure	Fines and incarceration
	Corrective advertising	Loss of profits
	Refunds	Class action suits
Disclosure of information requirements	Limitations on contracts	
	Arbitration	
Substantiation of ad claims		

Source: Dorothy Cohen, "Remedies for Consumer Protection: Prevention, Restitution, or Punishment, *Journal of Marketing 39* (October 1975), p. 25.

[41] Thomas G. Krattenmaker, "The Federal Trade Commission and Consumer Protection: An Institutional Overview," in Katz, *Protecting Consumer Interests.*

[42] See Paul N. Weaver, "The Hazards of Trying to Make Consumer Products Safer," *Fortune,* July 1975, pp. 109–112, for a discussion of this agency.

of manufacturers for defective and unsafe products. The objective of the reinterpretation of strict liability in tort has been to motivate greater care in manufacturing by imposing severe penalties for distribution of unsafe products. The consequences have been staggering in some industries. In one study of 377 companies, the average number of claims rose from 4.3 per firm in 1971 to an estimated 15 per firm in 1976; in that period the dollar amount of the average claim more than tripled, to $1.7 million.[43]

THE FUTURE OF CONSUMERISM

Is consumerism as a force in society declining sharply? Some observers answer yes. Government regulation has experienced major setbacks; for instance, an open rebellion has occurred with respect to such objects of regulation as car safety and children's advertising. In effect, consumers have indirectly demanded protection from unwanted regulation (in part, this reaction reflects broad distrust of government and resentment of tax burdens) and regulations. Moreover, as Chapter 1 shows, the consumer movements of the 1900s and the mid-1930s eventually faded, suggesting that the process is cyclical. Certainly, many of the problems that sparked the earlier movements have been alleviated by government or business, and consumer activists have moved on to other concerns.

Other observers think the current slowdown is simply a prelude to another burst of activity.[44] This forecast considers the host of laws and institutions already dealing with consumer problems which will not be meaningfully reduced and the enormous backlog of unresolved consumer issues. One estimate made in 1980 identified some 4000 consumer issues that had not been resolved by the federal government. This backlog is symptomatic of the inexorable accretion of knowledge about consumer problems, particularly in the areas of consumer safety and health, and of the persistence of the underlying causes of consumerism. Certainly the performance and information gaps particularly in the growing service sector, antagonism toward advertising, impersonal and unresponsive market institutions, and the presence of disadvantaged consumers support the movement. A severe housing shortage, the crip-

[43] The issues and some of their consequences are discussed in Lawrence Benningson and Arnold I. Benningson, "Product Liability: Manufacturers Beware!" *Harvard Business Review 52* (May–June 1974), pp. 56–65, and in "The Devils in the Product Liability Laws," *Business Week,* February 12, 1979, pp. 72–77.

[44] Graham T. T. Molitor, "Getting Out in Front of Impending Issues," in Frank Feather (ed.), *Through the Eighties: Thinking Globally, Acting Locally* (World Future Society, 1980).

pling impact of inflation on people with fixed incomes, and the difficulty of financing needed public services all provide the potential to create dramatic consumer concerns that serve to accelerate the movement.

It is our opinion, shared by Bloom and Greyser, that consumerism is neither declining sharply nor awaiting dramatic new growth but is rather in a mature, active stage that should continue through the 1980s and beyond.[45] However, the thrust and character of the movement are bound to change, partly in response to evolving issues and partly in response to the mature phase of the product life cycle.

Regulation under Scrutiny

The 1980s should see a much more critical and sophisticated scrutiny of government regulation than has been in evidence in the past. A decade ago government regulation was the accepted solution to a variety of ills. The resulting costs were rarely carefully estimated. Today, political and public support for new regulations is no longer easily obtained; even existing regulations are being challenged. At the same time, measures of benefits and costs are becoming more prevalent and sophisticated.[46]

Although the role of regulation will be examined more carefully, such activity will not be drastically reduced. In some situations regulations are appropriate and justifiable:

- where the product or service has hidden costs that are difficult to detect—this is the case with unnecessary repairs performed by service people or with excessive long-run energy costs due to faulty insulation work;
- where the hidden costs are incurred so long after purchase or consumption that they cannot be traced to a particular product—this is characteristic of carcinogenic effects of food additives;
- where the seller is not concerned about negative word-of-mouth influencing current sales or about poor performance affecting repeat sales;
- where there is a low level of competition or where tacit or explicit collusion is used to achieve profitable sales regardless of performance.

---

[45] Paul N. Bloom and Stephen A. Greyser, "Directions for Consumerism: A Life Cycle Analysis," Working Paper, Marketing Science Institute, Cambridge, Massachusetts, April 1981.

[46] See pp. 460–472 for a discussion of cost-benefit trade-offs.

Consumerism Actors and Institutions

Goverment regulation was never the only or even the dominant aspect of consumerist activities, although it often was the most visible. During the 1980s the relative role of government agencies and legislation will decline and there should be a corresponding growth in the importance of consumer and other private organizations, business firms, and individual consumers.

A host of private organizations presently provide impetus and support to the consumer movement. First, there are national organizations like the Consumer Federation of America. Second, there are local groups such as the "Action Line" efforts of local media and local consumer information programs. Third, there are special interest groups such as GASP (Group against Smoking and Pollution) and ACT (Action for Children's Television). Fourth, there are organizations not identified with the consumer movement that may well play a major role in the 1980s. For example, the AARP (American Association of Retired Persons) took an active part in making generic drugs available. Esther Peterson has predicted that church groups will also develop consumer programs.[47]

Business efforts will likewise assume increased importance. Consumer affairs departments are now well established in many companies. They have proven effective at handling customer complaints and developing consumer information programs but have been less successful at creating a consumer advocacy voice within firms. Self-regulation will take on new significance as government regulation moves toward the sidelines.[48] A key question is whether self-regulation will work.

Individual consumers should also become more of a force. The level of customer complaints is rising,[49] and litigation is increasing dramatically. One unanticipated by-product of reduced government regulation could well be increasing reliance on the courts to obtain redress and to implement policy.

The Sophistication Level

A decade ago the identification of consumer problems and the generation of solutions were rather crude and emotional. There is

---

[47] Stanley E. Cohen, "Peterson Sees New Coalition of Consumers," *Advertising Age*, January 26, 1981, p. 10.

[48] See Chapter 34.

[49] See Chapter 7.

substantial evidence of growing sophistication in approaches to consumer issues. For example, cost-benefit analysis of regulation is much more valid and objective than it was only a few years ago. Much also has been learned about consumer decisionmaking and information processing during the last decade. This body of knowledge is being drawn upon in attempts to develop consumer information programs. New technologies such as interactive cable television and various computer developments may impact significantly on the development of consumer information programs.

. . .

The consumer movement is and should remain a viable force fueled both by persistent problems of the 1970s, such as inflation and the performance and information gaps, and by new ones of the 1980s, such as housing shortages, the elderly and increased demand for costly public services. At the same time, this movement should experience changes in its direction and cast of characters. The following chapters pursue emerging issues and alternative approaches.

PART II

Perspectives on Consumerism

A Historical Perspectives

1 THE CONSUMER MOVEMENT IN HISTORICAL PERSPECTIVE

Robert O. Hermann

The situation of consumers and economic life of the country changed rapidly in the last four decades of the 19th century. Industrial output and employment increased five-fold. The population doubled, and the proportion living in urban areas rose from 20 to 40 percent. During the period, a national network of railroads was completed, creating the possibility of nationwide markets. A few manufacturers of consumer goods recognized the opportunity and began to trademark their wares and to advertise them in the new mass-circulation magazines.

The rapid growth of the cities and industrialization produced a new and unfamiliar set of problems—urban poverty, tenement housing, immigrant ghettos, municipal corruption, hazardous working conditions, sweat shops, child labor and a variety of consumer problems. . . .

A variety of local reform organizations were concerned with local social problems and political reform organizations between 1890 and 1900. . . . The first Consumers' League, formed in New York City in 1891, began its work by preparing a "white list" of shops which paid minimum fair wages, had reasonable hours and decent sanitary conditions. In 1898, the local groups joined in a national federation, the National Consumers' League, the first national consumers organization. By 1903, the national organization had grown to 64 branches in 20 states.

. . .

Reprinted with permission from "The Consumer Movement in Historical Perspective," Department of Agricultural Economics and Rural Sociology, Pennsylvania State University, February, 1970.

The nationwide rail network and the development of refrigerated cars opened a national market to the food processors and meat packers. The packers' and canners' understanding of the principles of food preservation and bacteriology were, however, still rudimentary. Preservatives were used liberally to ensure freshness, or, at least, its appearance. Formaldehyde was added to ensure freshness, or, at least, its appearance. Formaldehyde was added to canned meats, and canned peas were dosed with copper sulphate to produce the proper green shade of freshness. . . .

. . . The first general pure food measure was not introduced until the early 1890's. This bill seems to have elicited some substantial public support. Its sponsor, Senator Paddock, reported that 10,000 petitions supporting it had come to Congress. After amendments, to meet Southern objections, the bill passed the Senate in 1892. The House, however, failed to take action and the bill died.

A second attempt to obtain a Pure Food law was begun in 1902. The bill made little headway, but support for new legislation was gathering. The General Federation of Women's Clubs, the National Consumers' League, and state food and dairy chemists joined together. The muckraker press publicized the dangers of adulterated and dyed food and the hazards of unlabeled patent medicines containing opiates and large quantities of alcohol. Although Pure Food bills twice passed the House, Republican opposition kept the bills from ever coming to a vote in the Senate.

After Theodore Roosevelt was elected in his own right in 1904, an attempt was made to enlist his support for pure food legislation. In his annual message to Congress the following year, Roosevelt urged the enactment of a pure food and drug law. Opposition to the bill in the Senate faded when the American Medical Association threatened a full-scale fight in its behalf. The bill was passed by the Senate on February 21, 1906, and disappeared into committee in the House. That same month, Upton Sinclair's *The Jungle,* an exposé of the working conditions in the Chicago packing houses, appeared. The public was nauseated by the graphic descriptions of adulteration techniques and the unsanitary conditions:

> These rats were nuisances, and the packers would put poisoned bread out for them and they would die, and then rats, bread and meat would go into the hoppers together. . . . Men, who worked in the tank rooms full of steam . . . fell into the vats; and when they were fished out, there was never enough of them to be worth exhibiting—sometimes they would be overlooked for days, till all but the bones of them had gone out to the world as Durham's Pure Leaf Lard!

The President's reaction was similar to the public's. He was, moreover, concerned about the deficiencies in federal inspection detailed in the book. When two independent investigations bore out Sinclair's charges, Roosevelt put all his bulk behind the passage of meat inspection legislation. A rider to the agricultural appropriation bill providing for the expansion of the federal inspection bill was prepared and introduced in the Senate. It passed three days later without debate and without a dissenting vote.

. . .

Sales of meat and meat products had dropped by half and it appeared that important European markets might be lost. Fearful that these losses might be permanent, the packers began to realize that a strengthened system of federal inspection was the only way to save their reputations. A substitute bill passed the House after a brief debate and without a roll call on June 19th. It was signed by the President on June 30th and went into effect the next day. The momentum created by the meat inspection issue had also carried the Pure Food Bill to the floor of the House where it was passed on June 23rd. It also was signed into law on June 30th.

[In 1906] the fight for the pure food law finally [was] won, but only after years of effort, the help of a full-scale scandal and strong pressure from a powerful president.

. . .

THE SECOND ERA: THE 1930'S

Consumer incomes rose gradually in the 1920's, while prices remained relatively stable. . . . Sales of autos, refrigerators, vacuum cleaners, radios and phonographs were brisk. Consumers were flooded with advertising from billboards, electric signs, newspapers, magazines and the new medium of radio. . . .

Although consumer problems aroused little interest among the general public, educators began to recognize the need for more and better consumer education. Consumer problems had been a major concern of Home Economists from the formative years of their association at the turn of the century. In the mid-Twenties, spurred by concern about the "scanty amount of economics in our home economics," they began new research into consumer problems to provide the information needed to improve teaching in the area. . . .

As the decade passed, vague discontent grew among consumers who were deeply involved in purchasing new and unfamiliar consumer durables and a growing array of other new products with little information to go on except that gleaned from the deluge of advertising to which they were subjected. This discontent found expression in 1927 in *Your Money's Worth,* a book by Stuart Chase and F. J. Schlink. The book, subtitled "A Study in the Waste of the Consumer's Dollar," vehemently attacked advertising and high-pressure salesmanship and called for scientific testing and product standards to provide consumers with the technical information they needed to make purchase decisions. The book gave expression to a widely felt concern. . . .

At the close of their book, Chase and Schlink proposed the formation of a consumer-sponsored organization to do product testing and described the testing activities of a local "Consumers' Club" at White Plains, New York. The stream of inquiries from the readers of *Your Money's Worth* soon convinced Schlink that the local Consumers' Club he had organized should be expanded. In 1929, Consumers' Research, Inc. was formed to perform this testing work on a larger scale.

The new organization was only one of a number of new product testing laboratories which appeared in the late 1920's. The potential of scientific testing of consumer goods was accepted widely; several major department stores and trade associations also began testing laboratories about this time. . . .

. . .

The depression gave new immediacy to consumer education. Emphasis was given to identifying the best buys at the lowest cost and to frugal management. Consumers were urged: "Wear it out, use it up, make it do." Inexpensive substitutes for heavily advertised products were suggested and students practiced making their own toothpaste and face creams. Budgeting was taught as a device for cutting down on expenditures.

. . .

Weakened by court decisions and out-dated by new technology, the Pure Food and Drug Act of 1906 was, by the 1930's, badly in need of revision. Early in the 1930's, the New Deal administration did offer a new bill, inspired, as legend has it, by FDR's own reading of Kallet's and Schlink's *100,000,000 Guinea Pigs.* The bill, written in the Food and Drug Administration but often attributed to its administration sponsor, brain-truster Rexford Tugwell, would have extended FDA powers to include not only labeling but newspaper and magazine advertising as well. Cosmetics were to be placed under FDA control along with food and drugs. In addition, definite label information and the grade labeling of food were called for.

The FDA dramatized the need for new legislation with an exhibit of useless and dangerous patent medicines, unsafe cosmetics and adulterated foods. The exhibit, dubbed "The Chamber of Horrors" by the press, showed quack cures for cancer and tuberculosis and included tragic before and after pictures such as the ones of a once pretty matron blinded by Lashlure, an eyelash dye. When hearing began on the bill in 1933, the American Home Economics Association and the National Congress of Parents and Teachers were the only groups actively supporting it. The opposition damned the bill as an interference with consumer choice and "the right of self-medication." The newspapers, cowed by fear of lost advertising revenue, or for other reasons, gave little attention to the bill.

In 1935, FDR sent a message to Congress urging the new legislation but never gave the measure full support, apparently because of a feeling that he should reserve his political clout for more important measures. Nor did the bill get much support from Henry Wallace, in whose department the FDA was housed, since Wallace viewed the proposed legislation as a city-dweller's bill. The battle continued and in 1936, Ruth De F. Lamb's *The American Chamber of Horrors* documented the FDA's case in print and carried it to a wider audience. Gradually opposition to the bill by special interests drew more concerned groups into the fight. By the end of the five year fight, 16 national women's organizations had become involved.

A shocking new tragedy seems to have provided the final impetus for Congressional action. In 1937, a liquid form of one of the new sulfa wonder drugs was placed on the market. *Elixir Sulfanilamide,* proved lethal and nearly 100 died. A new section quickly was added to the proposed bill requiring that manufacturers prove the safety of new drugs to the satisfaction of the FDA before placing them on the market. Substantial changes had occurred in the rest of the bill in the course of five years of hearings and controversy, the grade-labeling provisions had been dropped and the responsibility for control of advertising had been given to the Federal Trade Commission. Business opposition had softened, the newer versions of the bill were much more acceptable than the early ones, and the damage which continuing opposition to the bill could do to public relations was coming to be recognized. Finally in June 1938, a much modified version of the bill, too weak to suit either Tugwell or the militants in the consumer testing organizations, was passed.

By the late 1930's, the impact of the consumer movement had become a subject of increasing concern to the business community. In order to gauge the impact of the movement on public opinion, the Advertising Research Foundation commissioned a national survey by Dr. George Gallup. In 1940 Gallup reported that about a quarter of those questioned in his study had read one of the "Guinea Pig" books and about half of this group said they had changed their buying habits as a result of what they had read. About one-fifth had read research reports of one of the product rating services. While about half favored the idea of compulsory grade labeling, about three-quarters admitted that they were willing to pay more for nationally known brands. About half favored stricter regulation of advertising content. Slightly less than half favored the idea of a new cabinet department to represent the interests of consumers. Gallup found that the movement had developed its greatest strength among teachers, the higher incomes and the more intelligent and among the young. He concluded that the movement had made considerable headway and was likely to continue to grow because of its strength among influential groups.

THE THIRD ERA: THE 1960'S

The tempo of activity in the consumer movement and its impact had increased throughout the Thirties. Consumerism undoubtedly would have gained even greater influence in the next few years if the coming of World War II had not diverted all attention to the problem of national survival. . . .

With the end of the war, [Consumers Union's] circulation began a remarkable upward climb as consumers sought product information to guide them in spending their wartime savings. Circulation grew from 50,000 in 1944 to almost a half million in 1950. There was, however, little activity among grass-roots consumer organizations. . . .

. . .

Despite the relative quiet of the Fifties, flare-ups of consumer concern did occur. One such incident came after the publication of Vance Packard's *The Hidden Persuaders* in 1957. Packard, accepting the ad agencies' and market researchers' claim about their powers at face value, argued that the public was being manipulated without realizing it. The resulting round of charges and counter-charges received extensive press coverage and showed that, given the right issues, there still was public interest in consumer problems.

The beginning of the third era of the consumer movement often is dated from John F. Kennedy's Consumer Message to the Congress in Spring 1962. In fact, Kennedy's influence may have begun even earlier. Arthur Schlesinger, Jr. has pointed out that, in his 1960 campaign, Kennedy "communicated, first of all, a deeply critical attitude toward the ideas and institutions which American society had come in the Fifties to regard with such enormous self-satisfaction." . . .

In the preamble to his Consumer Message to Congress in March 1962, President Kennedy enunciated the now famous Consumer Bill of Rights: (1) the right to safety, (2) the right to be informed, (3) the right to choose and (4) the right to be heard. The main body of the message outlined needed improvements in existing programs and needed new programs. The regulation of food and drugs was one of the areas singled out for special attention. The weaknesses of the existing laws in ensuring that drugs on the market were both effective and safe had become clear in the course of Senator Kefauver's hearings on the regulation of the drug industry. The new legislation was passed only after a new tragedy, as appalling as those which produced legislation in 1906 and 1938, forced action upon the Congress. Word of the thalidomide case reached the public in June; by August, legislation expanding the powers of the FDA had been passed and signed into law.

. . .

About this same time, a new surge of interest in consumer education occurred. Educators and the public both came to recognize that consumer education was an important and useful subject for all students, collegebound and vocational, and boys and girls alike. Consumer education, with its real-life problems, was found to be a useful method of arousing student interest in topics in English, math, social studies and science. The new curricula continued to stress both buymanship techniques and money management, and gave new emphasis to the problems and uses of installment credit. New emphasis also was given to the idea that one's spending should reflect personal goals, rather than someone else's idea of a good budget.

. . .

CU continued to grow rapidly during the Fifties. By its 25th anniversary in 1961, it was publishing nearly a million copies per issue of *Consumer Reports* with an estimated readership of 4 million. CU increasingly came to view itself as an organization to promote consumer education, rather than simply as a product testing agency. It concerned itself with educating consumers about all phases of their relationship with the consumer market: interest rates, guarantees and warranties, life insurance, product safety, and choosing a doctor.

In addition, CU had devoted a significant portion of its budget to the educational and organizational aspects of the consumer movement. It has inspired and financed much of the consumer movement, providing it with a stable organizational base as well as leadership. It has sponsored conferences on consumer problems throughout the country, supplied expert testimony at government hearings and worked with a variety of adult education groups in developing consumer education programs.

. . . CU has attracted chiefly those with higher incomes and better educations. In 1969, the median income of its members was about $14,000.

. . .

In January 1964, President Johnson created the new White House post, Special Assistant for Consumer Affairs, and appointed Esther Peterson to fill it. In Esther Peterson the President had found an experienced publicist and organizer. A strong personality, and outspoken in expressing her views, Mrs. Peterson made the consumer and his problems front-page news. . . .

. . .

After the liberal landslide in the election of 1964, the possibilities for new consumer legislation brightened. In the spring and summer of 1965, hearings were held on tire and auto safety. The hearings revealed to shocked senators the lack of any deep concern over safety problems in either industry. The auto safety hearings, however, ended on an inconclusive note after attention was diverted from the manufacturer's responsibilities for auto safety by arguments which placed the responsibility for auto safety on the driver.

This view was challenged a few months later when Ralph Nader's *Unsafe at Any Speed* presented evidence of the role of faulty engineering, construction and design in auto accidents and injuries. Public concern mounted and, in his State of the Union message in January 1966, President Johnson promised new legislation. In March, hearings began on the administration's Highway Safety Act of 1966. When the news of General Motors' investigation of Nader's background and activities broke, Congressional opinion was thoroughly alienated. The safety legislation passed later that year was significantly stronger than the bill originally proposed by the White House.

The time also was propitious for another important piece of consumer legislation. Senator Philip Hart's "Truth-in-Packaging" Bill was passed and signed into law in late 1966 after 5 years of Congressional inaction.

Consumer prices continued to rise gradually up to the middle Sixties. Food prices and the all items index each increased about 1 percent a year between 1960 and 1965. After this relative stability, the 5 percent increase in food prices in 1966 came as a major jolt to consumers. . . . The buying power of many groups in the population had increased gradually or just kept pace with price increases after the recessions of the early Sixties. Suddenly these groups were faced with an actual decline in purchasing power. Consumer discontent found open expression in October in a wave of consumer boycotts of food stores which began in Denver. Store contests and games, which had been used widely in the previous year, received most of the housewives' blame and were the target of their attack, although the real problem was short supplies of meat and produce.

. . .

. . . In his State of the Union Message and his Consumer Affairs message in February [1968], the President called for passage of a long list of consumer bills. During the course of the year, a "Truth-in-Lending" Bill finally was passed, 8 years after the original bill was introduced by Senator Paul Douglas. Other new legislation on poultry inspection, pipeline safety, fraudulent land sales and hazardous appliance radiation also were passed.

. . .

THE PAST AS PROLOGUE

It seems clear that the consumer movement is destined to be a recurring if not a permanent feature of the American scene. The movement has arisen as a reaction to three persisting problem areas: (1) ill-considered applications of new technology which result in dangerous or unreliable products, (2) changing conceptions of the social responsibilities of business and (3) the operations of a dishonest fringe and the occasional lapses of others in the business community. There is little reason to believe that any of these problem areas will ever disappear completely. Historically, consumers have been most sensitive to these problems in periods when consumer purchasing power is under pressure from rising prices.

The history of the consumer movement demonstrates that new technology frequently has been applied without full understanding of or concern for its potential dangers. The automobile had been around for seventy years before Ralph Nader got general recognition of the fact that autos included unsafe design features and sometimes were ill-engineered. Although the dangers of incompletely understood new technology have been most dramatic in the area of food and drugs, new legislation to control these dangers has come only after some dramatic revelation has focused public opinion on the problem. This legislation often has come long after the problem was first recognized.

The consumer no longer judges business on its products alone, but also on the social costs involved in producing them. The public's ideas of what constitutes a social cost have evolved rapidly in the past 70 years.

The passage of the Pure Food and Drug Act and the Meat Inspection amendment in 1906 recognized the social costs of injurious drugs and adulterated and contaminated food. The work of the Consumers' Leagues brought public recognition that unsafe working conditions, long hours and the exploitation of child and female labor also had social costs. Gradually the public view expanded again to include air pollution and water pollution as social costs. Now a new group of factors, which may seem even less tangible, is coming to be regarded as social costs. These include discriminatory hiring practices, unnecessarily rigid job qualifications, locational decisions which ignore areas of high unemployment, neglect of the needs of the low-income consumer, failure to provide retail competition in ghetto areas and the use of legal tactics and biased laws against poorly educated and powerless installment debtors.

Step by step, the concept of the social responsibility of business has been broadened to include not only its relations with its shareholders, but also with its competitors, its customers, its employees, its neighbors and now is coming to include those who are neither its customers or employees but perhaps could and should be.

A narrow definition of the consumer interest might deal solely with safe, reasonably priced and accurately labeled products. To its credit, the consumer movement has never defined the consumer interest so narrowly, but has come to include more and more aspects of the social cost of business in its considerations.

The business community can and should expect continuing challenge from the consumer movement since there is little reason to believe that the same problems which have perpetuated the movement in [the] past will not continue in the future. The application of new technology will continue to produce problems. The public's concept of responsible business behavior will continue to evolve. And until the milennium arrives, fraud and dishonesty seem likely to persist. Consumer concern with these problems is likely to continue to be especially acute as long as the current period of inflation persists.

In the past, business has fought the consumer movement bitterly, resisting its charges and responding with its own accusations. If Ralph Nader's observation is correct and the consumer movement is moving from ideology to ethics as a basis for action, business' old pattern of response will become less and less appropriate. If the consumer movement is moving from the role of an implacable, ideologically motivated foe to that of a reasonable advocate of a documented case, it, more than ever, deserves a fair hearing. In the future, the business community may be better advised to regard the consumer movement as an early warning system for impending trouble rather than as the unappeasable enemy of the past.

2 THE GREAT AMERICAN GYP

Ralph Nader

Last January a confidential nationwide survey by the Opinion Research Corporation spread considerable alarm among its corporate subscribers. The poll concluded "that seven Americans in ten think present Federal legislation is inadequate to protect their health and safety. The majority also believe that more Federal laws are needed to give shoppers full value for their money." To many businessmen, this finding merely confirmed what speakers had been telling them at trade gatherings during the previous year—that consumers were beginning to fall prey to "consumerism."

"Consumerism" is a term given vogue recently by business spokesmen to describe what they believe is a concerted, disruptive ideology concocted by self-appointed bleeding hearts and politicians who find that it pays off to attack the corporations. "Consumerism," they say, undermines public confidence in the business system, deprives the consumer of freedom of choice, weakens state and local authority through Federal usurpation, bureaucratizes the marketplace, and stifles innovation. These complaints have all been made in speeches, in the trade press, and in Congressional testimony against such Federal bills as truth-in-lending, truth-in packaging, gas pipeline safety, radiation protection, auto, tire, drug, and fire safety legislation, and meat and fish inspection.

But what most troubles the corporations is the consumer movement's relentless documentation that consumers are being manipulated, defrauded, and injured not just by marginal businesses or fly-by-night hucksters, but by the U.S. blue-chip business firms whose practices are unchecked by the older regulatory agencies. Since the consumer movement can cite statistics showing that these practices have reduced real in-

---

come and raised the rates of mortality and disease, it is not difficult to understand the growing corporate concern.

That the systematic disclosure of such malpractice has been so long delayed can be explained by the strength of the myths that the business establishment has used to hide its activities. The first is the myth of the omniscient consumer who is so discerning that he will be a brutal task-master for any firm entering the market. This approach was used repeatedly to delay, then weaken, the truth-in-packaging bill. Scott Paper Co. ran an advertising campaign hailing the American housewife as "The Original Computer": ". . . a strange change comes over a woman in the store. The soft glow in the eye is replaced by a steely financial glint; the graceful walk becomes a panther's stride among the bargains. A woman in a store is a mechanism, a prowling computer. . . . Jungle-trained, her bargain-hunter senses razor-sharp for the sound of a dropping price. . . ." John Floberg, Firestone's General Counsel, has been even more complimentary, arguing that consumers can easily discriminate among 1,000 different brands of tires.

However, when companies plan their advertising, they fail to take advantage of the supposed genius of the consumer. Potential car buyers are urged to purchase Pontiacs to experience an unexplained phenomenon called "wide-tracking before you're too old to know what it is all about." Sizable fees are paid to "motivation" experts like Ernest Dichter for such analysis as this:

> Soup . . . is much more than a food. It is a potent magic that satisfies not only thc hunger of the body but the yearnings of the soul. People speak of soup as a product of some mysterious alchemy, a symbol of love which satisfies mysterious gnawings. . . . The term "pea soup"—mystery and magic—seem to go together with fog. At the same time we can almost say soup is orgiastic. Eating soup is a fulfillment.

A second myth is that most American businesses perform honorably but are subjected to undeserved notoriety because of a few small, unscrupulous merchants and firms. This notion is peddled by so-called consumer protection agencies as well as by the business-dominated Better Business Bureaus. But the detailed Congressional hearings on drug hazards, unsafe vehicles, vicious credit practices, restraints on medically useful or dollar-saving innovations, auto insurance abuses, cigarette-induced diseases, and price-fixing throughout the economy have made it clear that this argument will not hold up.

Most misleading of all is the myth that irresponsible sellers are adequately policed by local, state, and Federal regulatory agencies. Years ago, corporations learned how to handle these agencies, and they have now become apologists for business instead of protectors of the public.

First, the agencies are made to operate on a starvation budget. The combined annual budget of the Federal Trade Commission and the Antitrust Division of the Justice Department in 1968 was $23 million, the highest amount yet appropriated. With this sum, they are suposed to collect data, initiate investigations, and enforce the laws dealing with deceptive and anticompetitive practices of a $350 billion economy.

Secondly, political patronage has undermined local and state consumer protection agencies; it has, for example, helped to make the Federal Trade Commission as ineffectual as it is.

Thirdly, business lobbying—including campaign contributions, powerful law firms, trade associations, and public relations—works against vigorous enforcement.

Finally, so many regulatory officials resign to go into high-paying jobs in the industries they were once supposed to regulate that these government posts are viewed as on-the-job training by cynical appointees.[1] The Federal Aviation Agency, Interstate Commerce Commission and the Federal Communications Commission all carry on a tradition that inhibits officials from action and attracts appointees who are temperamentally reluctant to act.

The increasing irrelevance of these older agencies was made apparent by the unprecedented consumer legislation enacted under the Johnson Administration. After the dismal spectacle of the cigarette labeling act of 1964—which foreclosed action by the states and the FTC in return for a paltry warning on the package that could serve as a company's defense in liability suits—Congress passed a string of important bills and has other legislation near passage. A shift of responsibilities for consumer protection to the Federal government now seems to be taking place: state and local governments have for years defaulted on these obligations to the consumer.

In no other period of history have the safety and prices of marketed products and services recieved remotely comparable legislative treatment. Sensing this climate, President Johnson allowed his consumer adviser, Betty Furness, to speak openly to business groups. In 1964, her predecessor, Esther Peterson, could not get White House clearance even to make a public statement about rigged odometers which misled motorists about the accuracy of mileage traveled, enriched car rental companies to the amount of $4 million a year, and encouraged automobile sales. In 1968, Miss Furness was urging appliance manufacturers to tell their customers how long they can expect their products to last. In 1969, President Johnson established the post of Consumer Counsel in the Justice Department—a first small step toward the creation of a Federal

[1] Two recent chairmen of the Interstate Commerce Commission later became President of the National Association of Motor Business Carriers and Vice-President of Penn-Central. Both industries are supposedly regulated by the ICC.

office which would have powers to intervene in cases before the courts and regulatory agencies as the representative of consumer interests.[2] In July, 1968, Vice-President Humphrey said he favored enlarging the counsel's powers to include making complaints about dangers to public health. He also became the first government official to endorse public disclosure of information about consumer products now in the files of the General Services Administration and the Department of Defense. These agencies test hundreds of consumer products—from light bulbs and bed sheets to washing machines—in order to determine which have the best value. But they have refused thus far to release the data that would rank products by quality—a refusal naturally supported by the business community.

The business world, meanwhile, has become increasingly adept in dealing with the rising pressures for consumer legislation. Tutored by their well-connected Washington lawyers, the large corporations and their trade associations can sense the critical moment at which it is wise to stop opposing a bill and begin to cooperate with Congressional committees in order to shape legislation to their liking. For example, after opposing the passage of any auto safety bill whatever, the auto manufacturers relented in the spring of 1966 and hired Lloyd Cutler, an experienced Washington lawyer, who succeeded in weakening the disclosure provisions of the bill and in eliminating all criminal penalties for willful and knowing violations of the law.

Although consumer measures may be weakened in this way, they do at least commit the government to the idea of consumer protection and they lay the groundwork for the stronger legislation that may be feasible should the consumer movement gain more strength. The attack on corporate irresponsibility which produced the recent flurry of legislation in Congress has not, it must be said, been the work of a broad movement but rather of tiny ad hoc coalitions of determined people in and out of government armed with little more than a great many shocking facts. They have gotten important support from Senator Warren Magnuson, Chairman of the Senate Commerce Committee, whose interest in consumer problems set in motion a little-noticed competition with the White House to promote legislation.

What has taken place during the last few years may be seen as an escalating series of disclosures. The charges made by independent Congressmen and people like myself almost always turn out to be understatements of the actual conditions in various industries when those industries are subsequently exposed in Congressional hearings and investigations. As these charges get attention, demands for new legislative action increase. This, at least, has been the case with the exposure of defects in

[2] The first appointee to this job was Mr. Merle McCurdy, who died in May, 1969.

vehicles, industrial and vehicle pollution, gas pipelines, overpriced or dangerous drugs, unfair credit, harmful pesticides, cigarettes, land frauds, electric power reliability, household improvement rackets, exploitation in slums, auto warranties, radiation, high-priced auto insurance, and boating hazards. How many people realized, for example, that faulty heating devices injure 125,000 Americans a year or that poorly designed stoves, power mowers, and washing machines cause substantial injury to 300,000 people annually? Or that, as Rep. Benjamin Rosenthal recently revealed, the food rejected by Federal agencies as contaminated or rotting is often rerouted for sale in the market? These abuses are now starting to be discussed in the press and in Congress.

One result of the detailed Congressional hearings has been a broader definition of legitimate consumer rights and interests. It is becoming clear that consumers must not only be protected from the dangers of voluntary use of a product, such as flammable material, but also from *involuntary* consumption of industrial by-products such as air and water pollutants, excessive pesticide and nitrate residues in foods, and antibiotics in meat. A more concrete idea of a just economy is thus beginning to emerge, while, at the same time, the assortment of groups that comprise the "consumer's movement" is moving in directions that seem to me quite different from the ones that similar groups have followed in the past. Their demands are ethical rather than ideological. Their principles and proposals are being derived from solid documentation of common abuses whose origins are being traced directly to the policies of powerful corporations.

This inquiry is extending beyond the question of legal control of corporations into the failure of business, labor, and voluntary organizations to check one another's abuses through competition and other private pressures. It is becoming apparent that the reform of consumer abuses and the reform of corporate power itself are different sides of the same coin and that new approaches to the enforcement of the rights of consumers are necessary. There are, I would suggest, at least ten major forces or techniques that now exist in some form but greatly need to be strengthened if we are to have a decent consumer society.

1. Rapid disclosure of the facts relating to the quantity, quality, and safety of a product is essential to a just marketplace. If companies know their products can quickly be compared with others, the laggard will be goaded to better performance and the innovator will know that buyers can promptly learn about his innovation. On the other hand, buyers must be able to compare products in order to reject the shoddy and reward the superior producer. This process is the great justification for a free market system. Manufacturers try to avoid giving out such information and instead rely on "packaging" or advertising. Auto companies refuse to tell the motorist the safety performances of his car's brakes and tires, and concentrate on brand-names—Cougar, Barracuda, Marauder—and vehicle "personality": "Mustang makes dull people interesting. . . ." From cosmetics to soaps and detergents, the differences emphasized are emotional and frivolous and have no relation to functions. This practice permits the producer with the largest advertising budget to make matters very difficult for a smaller competitor or potential entrant into the market who may have a superior product. The anti-competitive effects of such advertising led Donald F. Turner, the former head of the Anti-trust Division of the Justice Department, to suggest that the government subsidize independent sources of consumer information. Senator Philip Hart has gone a step further in proposing a National Consumer Service Foundation to provide product information to consumers at the place of purchase. Computers could help to assemble such information cheaply and quickly. One can, for instance, imagine machines dispensing data on individual products at shopping centers, a plan which Consumer's Union has begun to study,

2. The practices of refunding dollars to consumers who have been bilked and recalling defective products are finally becoming recognized as principles of deterrence and justice. More than six million automobiles have been recalled since September, 1966—the date of the auto safety law. The Food and Drug Administration now requires drug companies to issue "corrective letters" to all physicians if their original advertisements were found to be misleading. Nearly 30 such letters were sent out by drug companies during the first 20 months of FDA action. The threat of liability suits and the willingness of the press and television to mention brand and company names in reporting on defects are causing companies to recall products "voluntarily" even where no law or regulation exists. Earlier this year, for instance, Sears-Roebuck recalled some 6,000 gas heaters after public health officials warned of lethal carbon monoxide leakage. After similar warnings by U.S. Public Health officials and the threat of disclosure by a major newspaper, General Electric made changes in 150,000 color TV sets which had been found to be emitting excessive radiation. Some insurance companies are beginning of offer "defect recall" insurance.

The duty to refund remains even less well recognized than the duty to recall a product because of defects. Orders to "cease and desist," the usual decree of the Federal Trade Commission after it catches swindlers, at best stop the defrauder but do not require him to pay back the funds. Without this sanction, a major deterrent is lost. The mere order to "go and sin no more," which replaces it, is easily evaded.

The only enforcement action made by the FTC is pertinent here. For 30 years, the Holland Furnace Company used scare tactics and routinely deceived the public. Its salesmen were encouraged to pose as "safety inspectors" and were trained to be merciless: one elderly and ailing woman was sold nine new furnaces in six years, costing a total of $18,000. Following up on complaints beginning in the Thirties, the FTC secured a stipulation from the company that it would stop its misleading advertising. This had little if any effect. A cease and desist order was entered in 1958 but it was not until January, 1965, that the company was fined $100,000 for violating the order and an ex-president was sent to jail. At that point, the Holland Furnace Co. decided to file a petition for bankruptcy. But as Senator Warren Magnuson said: "In the meantime, Holland Furnace at the height of its business cost the American public $30 million a year." The FTC's ponderous procedures and anemic enforcement powers (it has no power of preliminary injunction, no criminal penalties, and no power of its own to fine, assess, or award damages) encourage the unscrupulous businessman to continue his abuses; if he is caught later on, he will merely be told to stop.

Two developments in recent years have strengthened private actions against malpractices by established corporations with large assets. The first is the growing practice of filing treble damage suits against violators of anti-trust laws. In the early Sixties, corporate and government customers of G. E., Westinghouse, and other large companies collected about $500 million in out-of-court settlements after these companies and their officers were convicted for carrying on a criminal antitrust price-fixing conspiracy. Although such punitive damage payments were tax-deductible as "ordinary and necessary business expenses,"[3] the deterrent was an effective one. Cases brought by both private and government procurement agencies have multiplied in many other industries recently —from drugs to children's books—and these will increase, especially with tougher antitrust action by the Justice Department and by the states.

The second development is in the use of "class actions" in which suits are filed on behalf of large numbers of people who have been mistreated in the same way. In modern mass merchandising, fraud naturally takes the form of cheating a great many customers out of a few pennies or dollars: the bigger the store or chain of stores, the greater the gain from gypping tiny amounts from individuals who would not find it worthwhile to take formal action against the seller. Class actions solve this problem by turning the advantage of large volume against the seller that made predatory use of it in the first place. Poverty lawyers, supported by the U.S. Office of Economic Opportunity, are just beginning to use this important technique.

A case of great potential significance for developing broad civil deterrence has been brought in New York City against Coburn Corp., a sales finance company, by two customers who signed its retail installment con-

[3] Starting in 1970, only one-third of such damages are deductible.

tracts. They are being assisted by the NAACP Legal Defense and Educational Fund. The plaintiffs charge that Coburn violated Section 402 of the New York Personal Property Law by not printing its contracts in large type as specified by law. They are asking recovery of the credit service charge paid under the contracts for themselves and all other consumers similarly involved. If the plaintiffs win, consumers in New York will be able to bring class actions against any violations of law contained in any standard form contracts.

3. Disputes in courts and other judicial forums must be conducted under fairer ground rules and with adequate representation for buyers. Here the recent appearance of neighborhood legal service attorneys is a hopeful sign. These poverty lawyers—now numbering about 2,000 and paid by the Office of Economic Opportunity—are representing the poor against finance companies, landlords, auto dealers, and other sellers of goods and services. Because of their work, the law of debtors' remedies and defenses is catching up with the well-honed law of creditors' rights that generations of law students studied so rigorously. These lawyers are bringing test cases to court and winning them. They are gradually exposing the use by slum merchants of the courts as agents to collect from poor people who are uninformed or cannot leave their jobs to show up in court. For the first time, poverty lawyers are challenging the routine contract clauses that strip the buyers of their legal defenses in advance, as well as those involving illegal repossession, unreasonable garnishment, undisclosed credit and financing terms, and a great many other victimizing practices.

But even many more poverty lawyers could handle only a few of the cases deserving their services. What is important is that recent cases are documenting a general pattern of abuses and injustices in the legal system itself. This is beginning to upset influential lawyers; it may prod law schools to more relevant teaching as well as guide legislatures and courts toward much-delayed reform of laws, court procedures, and remedies. At the same time, wholly new and more informed ways of resolving conflicts are being considered—such as neighborhood arbitration units which are open in the evenings when defendants need not be absent from their work. However, if such developments seem promising they must not obscure the persisting venality of the marketplace and the generally hopeless legal position of the consumer who is victimized by it.

4. The practice of setting government safety standards and periodically changing them to reflect new technology and uses is spreading, although it is still ineffective in many ways. Decades after banking and securities services were brought under regulation, products such as automobiles (53,000 dead and 4½ million injured annually), washing machines and power lawn mowers (200,000 injuries annually), many chemicals, and oil pipeline systems did not have to adhere to any standards of safety performance other than those set by the companies or industries themselves. With the passage of the auto safety law in 1966, other major products have been brought under Federal safety regulation. To avoid continuing a piecemeal approach, Congress in 1967 passed an act establishing the National Commission on Product Safety to investigate many household and related hazards, from appliances to household chemicals. Moreover, the Commission must recommend by this year a more detailed Federal, state, and local policy toward reducing or preventing deaths and injuries from these products.

The Commission's recommendations will probably go beyond household products to the problem of a safer man-made environment. So far, most state and Federal efforts to set meaningful safety standards and enforce them have failed miserably. The only organized and effective pressures on the agencies responsible for setting standards have come from the same economic interests that are supposed to be regulated. Two illustrations of this failure have been the Flammable Fabrics Act of 1953 and the Oil Pipeline Safety Act of 1965. In both cases, little has happened because the laws have not been administered. It took three-and-a-half years before the Federal government even proposed oil pipeline standards, and these were taken almost verbatim from the pipeline industry's own code. Similarly, when the General Accounting office recently reviewed the enforcement of the pesticide law by the Department of Agriculture it found that repeated mass violations of the laws between 1955 and 1965 were never reported to the Department for prosecution. This is a typical example of how consumers are deprived of legal protection in spite of a statute intended to protect them.

5. If the government is to impose effective standards, it must also be able to conduct or contract for its own research on both the safety of industrial products and possible methods of improving them. Without this power, the agencies will have to rely on what is revealed to them by industry, and their efforts will be crippled from the start. They will, for example, be unable to determine whether a better vehicle handling system is required or to detect promptly the hidden dangers in apparently harmless drugs. The government could also bring strong pressures on business by using its own great purchasing power and by developing its own prototypes of safer products. The existing safety laws, however, do not even permit the government to find out quickly and accurately whether industry is complying with the law. The National Highway Safety Bureau, for example, had little idea whether or not the 1968 automobiles met all the safety standards since no Government testing facilities existed.

But full enforcement of the law also depends on the existence of effective penalties, and in this respect the recent safety laws are feeble, to say the least. There are no criminal penalties for willful and knowing violation of the auto safety, gas pipeline, radiation control, and similar laws. The civil fines are small when considered against the possibility of violations by huge industries producing millions of the same product. Of course, the Washington corporation lawyers who lobby to water down the penalties in these safety laws have no interest in the argument that stronger sanctions would not only act as a deterrent to industry but make enforcement itself cheaper.

6. In the ideology of American business, free competition and corporate "responsibility" are supposed to protect the consumer; in practice both have long been ignored. Price-fixing, either by conspiracy or by mutually understood cues, is rampant throughout the economy. This is partly revealed by the growing number of government and private antitrust actions. Donald Turner, the former head of the Antitrust Division, has despaired of effectively enforcing the law against price-fixing with the existing manpower in the Justice Department. Price-fixing, of course, means higher prices for consumers. For example, the electrical price-fixing conspiracy, broken by the Justice Department in 1960, involved not only G. E., Westinghouse, Allis Chalmers, but several small companies as well; the overcharge to the direct purchasers of generators and other heavy duty equipment was estimated at more than a billion dollars during the ten-year life of the conspiracy that sent several executives to short jail terms.

Even greater dangers arise when the failure of large industry to compete prevents the development of new products that might save or improve the lives of consumers. When such restraint is due to conspiracy or other kinds of collusion, it should be the task of antitrust enforcement to stop the practice of "product-fixing." Traditional antitrust enforcement has been slow to grasp the fact that the restraint of innovation is becoming far more important to big business than the control of prices. New inventions—steam or electric engines, longer lasting light bulbs and paints, and cheaper construction materials—can shake an industry to its most stagnant foundations. For 18 months the Justice Department presented to a Los Angeles grand jury its charges that the domestic auto companies conspired to restrain the development and marketing of vehicle exhaust control systems. When and if it files its complaint, a pioneering case of antitrust enforcement in a health and safety issue could reveal much about this as yet unused weapon for public protection.

Ideally, one of the most powerful forces for consumer justice would be the exercise of corporate responsibility or private "countervailing" and monitoring forces within the corporate world. Unfortunately for believers in a pluralist economic system, recent decades have shown that the economics of accommodation repeatedly overwhelms the economics of checks and balances.

The casualty insurance industry is a case in point. Logically it should have a strong interest in safer automobiles. In fact it has chosen to raise premiums instead of pressuring the auto industry to adopt safety measures that have been available for a long time. The casualty insurance industry has not demanded legislation to improve the design and inspection of motor vehicles; nor has it encouraged the rating of vehicles according to their safety. It has been equally indifferent to the need to reform methods of fire prevention (where the U.S. is far behind Japan and England) or standards of industrial safety and health. What the industry has done instead is to spend large sums on advertising assuring the public it is concerned about the consumer safety it has declined to pursue in practice.

7. Professional and technical societies may be sleeping giants where the protection of the consumer is concerned. Up to now, such groups as the American Society of Mechanical Engineers, the American Chemical Society, and the American Society of Safety Engineers have been little more than trade associations for the industries that employ their members. It is shocking, for example, that none of these technical societies has done much to work out public policies to deal with the polluted environment and with such new technological hazards as atomic energy plants and radioactive waste disposal. Except in a few cases, the independent professions of law and medicine have done little to fulfil their professional obligations to protect the public from victimization. They have done less to encourage their colleagues in science and engineering to free themselves from subservience to corporate disciplines. Surely, for example the supersonic transport program, with its huge government subsidies and intolerable sonic boom, should have been exposed to careful public scrutiny by engineers and scientists long before the government rather secretively allowed it to get under way.

The engineers and scientists, however, had no organization nor procedure for doing this. None of the professions will be able to meet its public responsibilities unless it is willing to undertake new roles and to create special independent organizations willing to gather facts and take action in the public interest. Such small but determined groups as the Committee for Environmental Information in St. Louis, headed by Professor Barry Commoner, and the Physicians for Automotive Safety in New Jersey have shown how people with tiny resources can accomplish much in public education and action. If such efforts are to be enlarged, however, the legal, medical, engineering, and scientific departments of universities must recognize the importance of preparing their graduates for full-time careers in organizations devoted to shaping public policy; for it is clear that professionals serving clients in private practice will not be adequate to this task. Had such organizations existed two or three decades ago, the hazards of the industrial age might have been foreseen, diagnosed, exposed, and to some extent prevented. During the recent controversy over auto safety I often speculated that the same kind of reform might have occurred 30 years ago had a handful of engineers and physicians made a dramatic effort to inform politicians about scandals that even then took more than 30,000 lives a year and caused several million injuries. Instead the doctors were busy treating broken bones and the engineers were following corporate orders, while their technical journals ignored a major challenge to their profession. For all the talk about "preventive medicine" and "remedial engineering," this is what is happening now.

8. During the past two decades, the courts have been making important if little noticed rulings that give injured people fairer chances of recovering damages. These include the elimination of "privity" or the need to prove a contractual relation with the person sued; the expansion of the "implied warranty" accompanying items purchased to include not only the "reasonable" functioning of those items but also the claims made in deceptive advertising of them; and the imposition of "strict liability" which dispenses with the need to prove negligence if one has been injured through the use of a defective product. At the same time, the laws of evidence have been considerably liberalized.

This reform of the common law of "bodily rights"—far in advance of other common-law nations such as Great Britain and Canada—has been followed by some spectacular jury verdicts and court decisions in favor of the injured. These are routinely cited by insurance companies as a rationale for increasing premiums. The fact is, however, that these victories still are rare exceptions, and for obvious reasons. Winning such cases requires a huge investment in time and money: the plaintiff's lawyers must collect the evidence and survive the long and expensive delays available to the corporation defendant with its far superior resources. But now the rules give the plaintiff at least a decent chance to recover his rights in court or by settlement. It remains for the legal profession to find ways to cut drastically the cost of litigation, especially in cases where a single product, such as a car or drug, has injured many people.

However, the law of torts (personal injuries) still does not protect the consumer against the pollution of the environment which indiscriminately injures everyone exposed to it. Pollution in Los Angeles is a serious health hazard, but how may the citizens of that besmogged metropolis sue? A group of eighty-eight residents of Martinez, California, is suing Shell Oil's petroleum refinery for air pollution and its "roaring noises, recurring vibrations and frightening lights." In an increasingly typical defense, Shell claims that it meets the state's mild pollution-control regulation. But such standards are largely the result of political pressures from corporations whose profits are at stake. Thus, increasingly, justice in the courts must be paralleled by justice in the legislatures. However, there are some signs that the courts are beginning to take account of the right to a decent environment in cases against industrial pollutants. In 1967, a lady in Pennsylvania recovered about $70,000 for injuries sustained from living near a beryllium plant which emitted toxic fumes daily. (The case was appealed.)

9. One of the more promising recent developments is the growing belief that new institutions are needed within the Government whose sole function would be to advocate consumer interests. As I have pointed out, the Johnson Administration has done no more than create in 1968 an Office of Consumer Counsel in the Justice Department. The Executive Branch has been hostile to a proposal by Congressman Rosenthal and others for a new Department of Consumer Affairs on the Cabinet level. This proposal has been criticized by Federal officials on grounds that it would duplicate what government agencies are now doing. The fact is, however, that most of the government agencies that are supposed to be concerned with the health and safety of consumers are also promoting the interests of the industries that cause the consumer harm. The U.S. Department of Agriculture represents the farmers and processors first and the consumer second—whether in controversies over the price of milk or over the wholesomeness of meat and poultry. The regulatory agencies themselves at best merely act as referees and at worst represent business interests in government.

Clearly it would be useful if a new bureau within the Government itself could expose these regulatory agencies and challenge them to take more vigorous action. Senator Lee Metcalf has introduced legislation to create an independent Office of Utility Consumer's Counsel to represent the public before regulatory agencies and courts. This approach is different from that of Congressman Rosenthal and it remains to be seen which scheme can best avoid the dangers of bureaucratization and atrophy. What is not generally appreciated however is that if they are to succeed, such new governmental units will badly need the vigorous support of organizations outside the government which would have similar concern for the consumer and would also be able to carry on their own research and planning.

10. I have already pointed out the need for independent organizations of professionals—engineers, lawyers, doctors, economists, scientists, and others—which could undertake work of this kind. But they do not as yet exist. Still, we can draw some idea of their potential from the example of people like Dr. Commoner and his associates who have managed to stir up strong public opposition to Government and private interests while working in their spare time. Similarly, other small groups of professionals have saved natural resources from destruction or pollution; they have stopped unjust increases in auto insurance rates; they have defeated a plan for an atomic explosion to create a natural gas storage area under public land, showing that excessive safety risks were involved.

Is there reason to hope that the high energy physicists who lobbied successfully for hundreds of millions of dollars in public funds might be emulated by other professionals seeking to improve the quality of life in America? Certainly there is a clear case for setting up professional firms to act in the public interest at Federal and local levels. While thousands of engineers work for private industry, a few hundred should be working out the technical plans for obtaining clean air and water, and demanding that these plans be followed. While many thousands of lawyers serve private clients, several hundred should be working in public interest firms which would pursue legal actions and reforms of the kind I have outlined here. Support for such firms could come from foundations, private gifts, dues paid by consumers and the professions, or from government subsidies. There is already a precedent for the latter in the financing of the Neighborhood Legal Services, not to mention the billions of dollars in subsidies now awarded to commerce and industry. In addition, groups that now make up the consumers' movement badly need the services of professional economists, lawyers, engineers, and others if they are to develop local consumer service institutions that could handle complaints, dispense information, and work out strategies for public action.

Notwithstanding the recent alarm of industry and the surge of publicity about auto safety and other scandals, the consumer movement is still a feeble force in American power politics. The interests of consumers are low on the list of election issues; the government's expenditures to protect those interests are negligible. Some would argue that this situation will inevitably prevail in view of the overwhelming power of American corporations in and out of government. But, as I have tried to show, new approaches to judging and influencing corporate behavior have begun to emerge in the last few years. It seems possible that people may begin to react with greater anger to the enormity of their deprivation—each year consumers lose half a billion dollars in securities frauds and a billion dollars in home repair frauds, to name only two of thousands of ways in which their income is being milked. The current assault on the health and safety of the public from so many dangerous industrial products, by-products, and foods has resulted in violence that dwarfs the issue of crime in the streets. (In a recent three-year period, about 260 people died in riots in American cities; but every two days, 300 people are killed, and 20,000 injured, while driving on the highways.) What the consumer movement is beginning to say—and must say more strongly if it is to grow—is that business crime and corporate intransigence are the really urgent menace to law and order in America.

B *Current Perspectives*

3 THE CONSUMER'S REAL NEEDS

Sidney Margolius

The unusual opportunity I have is to discuss what I consider to be the consumer's real needs. The fact is, there are no more important and urgent needs than those of the consumer. The consumer's problems are the nation's problems, and the waste of consumer resources that has become so flagrant in our time has been proven to be the waste of the nation's resources. It is responsible for many of the energy and environmental problems and the teetering inflation and recession that plague our country and frighten our people today.

In recent years consumer problems have become a matter of national attention and tension. The high costs of food and auto insurance; high borrowing costs; repair and service complaints; the growing problems of landlord-tenant relations; hazardous appliances; flammable fabrics; and many other problems including even the nutritional value of breakfast cereals all have been under scrutiny. Currently at least eight Congressional committees are investigating various consumer problems.

I have tried to examine the consumer's position today after the last fifteen years of intensified efforts at consumer protection. I can only conclude that much of the purported consumer protection falls short of the consumer's real needs. Our gains mostly have been some lessening of deceptive selling methods, some reductions in product hazards, and slow but useful reforms in the pricing and merchandising of prescription drugs and over-the-counter medicines. Other gains for which consumers had to fight every inch of the way include truth-in-lending and a few

From *Journal of Consumer Affairs* (Winter 1975), pp. 129–138. Reprinted [as amended] by permission of the American Council on Consumer Interests.

other credit reforms; clearer labeling of net weights; unit pricing and open dating although still incomplete; and a truth-in-packaging law which did not, however, even return us to the standard pounds and quarts of 20 years ago. We now also have a new federal warranty law which may be useful in improving the durability of goods as well as the reliability of guarantees.

These reforms certainly have been useful and have benefited the nation as a whole as well as consumers. But effective consumer protection has been almost wholly absent in defending the public against the real problem of the day—the relentless inflation which has already seen a transfer of billions of dollars from consumers to the pockets of oil companies, mining companies, banks, and food processors. For food alone the nation's bill has gone up 30 billion dollars in just two years. As you know, oil company profits went up 40 to 300 percent in just one year. Profits of sugar refiners are up as much as 1,100 percent. And so on for many other industries.

The result is a great deal of bitterness among consumers and a noticeable skepticism of the federal administration's weak anti-inflation efforts. Up to now the administration has given little real help to consumers except a childish and soon-forgotten offer of a lapel button with the word WIN.

To understand the public's bitterness, you need only realize that the rise in living costs actually has wiped out all the wage gains made by the average worker in the past seven years. Most moderate-income families literally have been spinning their wheels. In 1967 the average worker with three dependents had spendable earnings after taxes of $91. By 1972 his spendable earnings in terms of 1967 dollars had risen to $97. But as a result of inflation, by early 1975 those spendable earnings in terms of 1967 dollars had dropped to $87. So the average worker who now makes $157 in gross earnings, compared to $102 in 1967, now has $10 less in actual purchasing power after taxes and after adjusting those dollars for the inflation.

SIX NEEDS

There are six overriding problems today for which consumers need serious help. Presently little or no help is available, and there is no way to solve these problems simply by consumer education. Too much of our so-called consumer education today is occupied with such advice as telling consumers not to go shopping when they are hungry and to buy day-old bread. At least the government should ask the bakers to make more day-old bread.

The real problems are:

1. The high cost of food. As you know well enough, food prices have gone up 72 percent since 1967 and 9 percent just in the past 12 months.
2. Booming medical costs and inadequacies of present private medical insurance, causing real anxieties in many families and encouraging high-pressure promotions of low-value insurance plans seeking to capitalize on these anxieties.
3. High housing and operating costs, including mortgages of 8 to 9 percent and a nationwide increase in fuel oil costs of 107 percent since 1970, utility rates of 50 percent and 16 percent in the past twelve months alone and more to come.
4. The widespread effects of high interest rates, coupled with collection laws stacked on the side of the sellers. These high rates affect consumers directly in financing homes, cars and other needs and also lead to high property and other taxes as government and municipal agencies also pay more on their borrowings.
5. Serious quality problems which have led to high repair costs especially for cars and household appliances and which even create safety hazards as shown by the investigations of the Commission on Product Safety. The lack of quality standards and the further deterioration of quality in a period of inflation have caused an increase of complaints—about furniture and clothing now as well as cars and appliances.
6. The big jump in costs of car ownership due to the increase in gasoline prices, plus the lofty prices of cars, the already high cost of auto insurance, and the big increase in charges for maintenance and repairs.

Food Prices

High food costs are perhaps the most basic problem. Food costs affect all other costs. One-fourth of the labor cost of manufacturing steel or building a house actually is the cost of the food required to feed a worker's family. Food and housing take about 55 percent of a typical moderate-income family's budget.

The particular need is to eliminate some of the waste that has characterized the marketing of food in recent years. One of the prevailing myths is that we have the most efficient food distribution system in the world. What we really have is the most elaborate and sometimes the costliest. Any industry that takes 15 cents' worth of cracker meal and other ingredients, packages it as a product called Shake 'n Bake and sells it at the rate of $1.92 a pound is hardly efficient. An industry that goes in for such manic proliferation as 151 different brands, sizes and types of breakfast cereals, as you may find in just one supermarket, certainly is not efficient. What would you call an industry that takes 25 cents' worth of noodles, adds a one-ounce package of dry sauce and sells it as Hamburger Helper for 73 cents? I can cite hundreds of examples of such wastes of family and national resources in our overelaborate, consumer-fooling food industry.

The fact is, the growing *waste* in distribution is one of the main causes of the increasing farm-to-market price spread. Before World War II and up to about the 1950's, farmers traditionally got 50 cents of the retail food dollar and the distributors got 50 cents. In recent years, distribution and processing have been taking 60 cents and the farmer has been getting only 40—sometimes a little more but sometimes also a little less. The growing marketing margin is a major reason for the discontent of both farmers and urban consumers.

One of the most pervasive stumbling blocks to reducing some of the tremendous waste in food marketing is the constant propaganda of the food industry and the Department of Agriculture that food is a bargain and takes only 17 percent of income. This allegation is enough to make any housewife bang her head against the wall as she tries to think of new ways to stretch a meatball.

A representative family with two children under 14 and an after-tax income of about $11,000 to $12,000 a year more likely spends about 30 percent of after-tax income on food. With more than two children, the food bill may well take 35–40 percent of income. That's the way the government's own cost-of-living specialists figure it in the official Bureau of Labor Statistics estimates of moderate-cost budgets for a family of four.

The BLS estimate is based on surveys of actual *family* expenditures. In contrast, the 16 percent figure used by the food industry is an estimate by the U.S. Department of Commerce of how much of the *national* income goes for food. The Commerce Department figure includes institutions, the Armed Forces and rural families who produce some of their own food. These groups of course pay less for food and spend a lower percentage of their income for food.

Still another piece of sophistry is that food costs more nowadays because of built-in maid service and that the public wants this convenience. The truth is that the public wants, at least for a while, what it has been sold on TV the week before. One out of every four dollars now spent for TV advertising is for food products.

Actually what the public is getting is a lot of pseudoconvenience. One manufacturer sells an instant oatmeal that takes only one minute to prepare four servings. This company now has brought out what I can only call an "instant instant" oatmeal. It takes a half a minute to prepare four servings but costs more. The housewife pays for this time saving at the rate of $4.90 an hour while her husband, the average wage-earner, is earning at the rate of $4.35 an hour. Sometimes I think the poor fellow would be better off staying home and stirring oatmeal for his wife, sprinkling sugar on his children's cereal and mixing water into their orange juice.

Housing Costs

The average wage-earner has been effectively priced out of the new housing market. The national median sales price of new homes currently is approximately $37,000. A family needs an income of $20,000 a year to afford this at current mortgage rates. In fact with rising property taxes and mortgages in the 8½–9 percent bracket, it now takes over $400 a month to finance and operate the median new house today including mortgage payments, maintenance and utilities. Only one family in five can afford that kind of housing expense.

Just as one example of how this inflation takes dollars out of the pocket of consumers, note that for a $30,000 30-year mortgage at 8¼ percent you have to repay a total of $81,000. A typical wage-earner earning $11,000 a year after taxes would have to work almost five years just to pay the $51,000 in interest.

Consumers are going to need even more mortgage protection. Some lenders want to increase terms to as long as 40 years with a balance at the end of 25 years which the homeowners would have to refinance at the current rate. This is called a balloon mortgage. Another dangerous device mortgage lenders and government agencies now are pushing is variable-rate mortgages in which the rate moves up or down with the general level of interest rates.

While labor costs often are blamed for high prices of homes, the fact is that construction costs, which include both labor and materials, have risen less sharply than the price of land, interest and other contractor costs and overhead. Construction costs rose 22 percent from 1964 to 1970 compared to the increase of 29 percent in the median sales price of houses in that period. Construction costs of publicly-owned housing have gone up even less—about 14 percent in the same period.

Health Care

Because of the critical nature of rising health-care costs, several plans for national health insurance have been formulated. The experience of Medicare as well as that of other medical insurance is that insurance alone is not enough. Medical fees tend to rise to meet the available insurance. One proposal supported by the administration would try to use private insurance. A proposal supported by consumer groups would provide not only health insurance but encourage more economical delivery of health care through prepaid group care and an increased supply of health-care personnel.

Consumer officials and leaders will need to pay close attention to the problems of medical costs and adequate health insurance in the years immediately ahead. Since 1967 medical costs have gone up 60 percent nationally and are still rising. The increase has been led by hospital room charges and physicians' fees. They have gone up 110 percent and 60 percent respectively in that period. We need to keep in mind that the only safe way a family can protect itself against an inflation in medical costs is through economical insurance and efficient delivery of health services.

Insurance

Auto insurance is another consumer dilemma. The increase in the cost of auto insurance in recent years and sometimes the difficulty in getting insurance at all create a critical problem for families in areas without adequate public transportation. There is no single gimmick to alleviate this problem. Many consumer organizations have oversimplified the needed cures by seizing on the so-called no-fault plan. But no-fault insurance would eliminate only part of the claim and legal expenses that add to insurance premiums, and it does nothing about the insurance industry's large selling and administrative expenses or the fact that earnings on reserves are not credited against payments and expenses.

Quality Standards

There are many more consumer needs than I can cover here, of course. In my own experience, one of the most urgent needs is the development of quality standards for consumer goods in order to stem some of the present huge waste of family money on faulty goods and service problems.

Pending the development of quality standards, consumers at least have the right to know what they are buying. While the Food and Drug Administration and the food industry have been willing to go into nutritional labeling, which tells you the relative amounts of protein, vitamins and minerals in food products, they resist percentage ingredient labeling which would tell you, for example, actually how much sugar there is in presweetened cereals, how much water in canned drinks, and how much meat and gravy in canned meat stew.

After a long debate the FDA finally required that canners say how much fruit juice there is in big selling canned drinks such as Hi-C, Hawaiian Punch and so on; for example, that they have 10 percent orange juice. But what was left out of this new regulation is an honest, frank declaration that the rest of these drinks are mainly flavored water; in fact, they are 90 percent water and sugar plus a few additives and artificial coloring. These products are actually just flavored water with a little inexpensive synthetic vitamin C.

As for the widely sold presweetened cereals, they are 25 to 50 percent sugar. Typically, I estimate, the consumer pays for the sugar in these products at the rate of $1.60 a pound. At least the consumer has the right to know what the actual percentage of sugar is in these cereals.

I use these two products only as examples to show the need for more information than merely nutritive labeling. The same problem occurs in the amount of fat and water added to franks, bologna and salami, and often to other meat products. These fillers are listed on the label in order of descending importance. But nowhere does it say, for example, that these products usually contain 28% fat and 10% water.

What especially concerns me is the bandwagon syndrome that has appeared in the consumer movement with many people jumping on such bandwagons as no-fault insurance and nutritional labeling without making realistic, even skeptical appraisals of such proposals. We already have nutritional labeling of breakfast cereals and watered fruit drinks and the result is merely more exploitation of consumers. Some cereal manufacturers now advertise "100 percent of your daily needs of vitamins and minerals." The manufacturers can make this claim by adding inexpensive additional synthetic vitamins. I figure that the added vitamins and minerals in fortified cereals are worth about a penny per serving if you bought them in capsule form. Yet consumers pay 5 to 7 cents more per serving than for ordinary cereals. In the watered fruit juices the addition of synthetic vitamin C costs the canners only one-fourth of 1 cent for a 46-ounce can. But consumers pay at the rate of 37 cents a quart for this flavored water, or almost as much as for milk.

CONSUMER EDUCATION AND REGULATION

I cannot emphasize too strongly that the public's consumer awareness and skepticism are growing, and that people no longer will accept merely generalized or lip-service consumer education and legislation. Often, in truth, the public knows more than its teachers and political leaders about its needs. If consumer educators do not want to be ignored they must avoid games and keep in touch with the real needs and interests of working families and search out honest, frank and truly informative answers to their problems.

Consumer educators also can serve a vital role in evaluating various proposals purporting to help the consumer. Some of the programs advanced even by well-meaning consumer advocates have no true relation to the consumer's real needs and even serve to divert attention from necessary basic remedies. One proposal advocated by two of the most prominent consumer advocates seeks to have all buying information computerized so a consumer could pay a few dollars and get a compilation of data on various makes of all products on the market from autos to zucchini. But in an age when there are 1400 different brands and types of tires, and in textile fabrics several thousand fiber blends, weaves and finishes, to try to solve the consumer's buying problems by collecting, computerizing and constantly updating all this information would keep half our population busy collecting facts for the other half.

The real need, of course, is for mandatory quality standards that would assure consumers basic serviceability no matter what the brand plus truly informative labeling that would give consumers basic facts needed to select suitable and efficient products. We now have a few such standards as in air conditioners. We need many more to stop the present huge waste of resources.

Curiously, some of the most fervent advocates of consumer education today are businessmen. But the business corporations are really calling for consumer education as an alternative to legislation. Many corporations now are loading up schools and colleges with their versions of educational materials. At best much of it is so generalized as to be of limited usefulness, and some of it is openly self-serving.

There also is an outpouring of publications, film strips and other classroom materials by commercial publishers seeking to cash in on the publicity given consumerism. Much of it is repetitive and all of it is high priced and seeking to soak up government and school funds. Even organizations with little real consumer background such as Time-Life and Readers Digest have gotten into the act with slick-looking materials that rehash already published materials. Interestingly, a good 15 years ago I heard Colston Warne himself warn against this very development.

At the same time the consumer materials offered by the U.S. government often now are platitudinous rehashes and sometimes even nakedly serve commercial interests as in the distorted surveys tending to show that convenience foods often cost less than basic foods.

We not only suffer a dollar cost in the millions of dollars spent on some of the government consumer services but also the opportunity cost—the lost opportunity to give students truly useful and honest materials. We need more detailed research and more experienced and critical evaluation so that publishers, writers and educational TV producers do not simply turn out collages of already published materials.

Even genuine consumer education cannot, of course, solve consumer problems by itself. If all meat prices go up it's little help to tell consumers to buy the lower-price cuts. These usually go up the most. Nor can consumer education help much in restraining high mortgage interest rates or high medical and hospital fees.

But modern consumer education can take some interesting forms. A battle for consumer legislation itself is educational. I think more people were educated to understand the true annual rates on installment purchases by the fight for truth-in-lending legislation than by all the articles and classroom discussions by the most dedicated teachers. Picketlines in front of supermarkets by boycotting housewives were another effective form of consumer education outside the classroom. The picket-lines even finally educated some of the retailers to understand that the housewives really prefer lower prices to trading stamps. Increasingly, too, some regional consumer groups are using picket-lines in front of stores, car lots and finance companies to secure redress for members who feel they have been treated unfairly.

In a rolling recession as now consumer educators and officials may have an even more urgent task. This is the need to inform and protect moderate-income consumers, especially the younger families, against foreclosures, repossessions, wage garnishes, loss of health insurance in a time of joblessness and other disasters. Young families especially tend to push the panic button and give up possessions, even abandon homes, as in earlier recessions. We should be aware that nationally bankruptcies are expected to reach a historic high of 225,000 in 1975 compared to about 195,000 last year and 207,000 in the previous high year of 1967.

4 PUBLIC POLICY AND THE MARKETING PRACTITIONER—TOWARD BRIDGING THE GAP

Stephen A. Greyser

Many . . . are addressing themselves to identifying, describing, and defining the gaps between public policy interests and marketing practice. My purposes are to try to understand what underlies those gaps, and to suggest ameliorative actions on the parts of marketers, public policy officials, and researchers. In so doing, much of my attention will be devoted to issues involving advertising, for this is the area where most of my own research work has been done. Much of the presentation also will focus particularly on what we can logically expect from marketers themselves in bridging the gap.

WHY THE GAP?

[Why is it] that a problem exists if marketing is the practice of varying responses by firms to the heterogeneous demands of the marketplace? The matter of trying to understand the conflicts between marketers and critics of marketing has been a long-standing interest of mine. I see three different sets of phenomena involved. One has to do with ways different groups and individuals view the *mechanism of the marketplace*, i.e., the inter-

---

Reprinted [as amended] from Fred Allvine (ed.), *Public Policy and the Marketing Practitioner*, pp. 219–223, published in 1973 by the American Marketing Association.

face between marketers' actions and consumers. (For example, how does advertising work—in terms of the consumer behavior it is intended to affect and how that influence occurs.[1]) A second is the conflict within us (individually and communally) between "citizen" and "consumer," a dilemma for both the *marketer* and *marketplace*. A third is the consequence of the realities of segmentation. Let us look at each in more detail.

Marketplace Models

How one views the marketer-consumer interactions as taking place is one's model of the marketplace. And the fact that different people have different models of the marketplace underlies some of the conflict between marketer and public policy groups. In a recent *Harvard Business Review* article, I described three different overall models, and set forth a set of questions to enable one to define his own model.[2] While no single model applies to all situations, one's *basic* view of the marketplace will generally fit one of the following overall models:

1. Manipulative—a critic's model that portrays marketing's role as basically that of persuading/seducing less-than-willing consumers to buy. Consumers are seen as pawns struggling in an unequal battle against their adversaries, the marketers, who use advertising as an important and powerful one-sided weapon.

2. Service—a pro-business model that (a) portrays as successful marketers only those who serve consumers best and (b) predicts failure for those who do not so serve. Consumers are seen as rather more intelligent and less seduced than in the manipulative model. A credo of the service model is: "Consumers cast their ballots at the cash register every day . . . and besides, we know what they want via market research." Advertising is seen as helping to facilitate choices made by consumers who generally know what they want.

3. Transactional—a model derived from communications research that portrays the marketplace relationship in more of a give-and-take fashion. Consumers trade time and attention to advertising for the information and entertainment in the ads; consumers trade money for products that provide them with functional and/or psychological satisfactions. The transactional model posits a somewhat sophisticated consumer, at least in terms of his or her individual buying criteria.

---

[1] For a more detailed treatment of this concept see Raymond A. Bauer and Stephen A. Greyser, "The Dialogue That Never Happens" (Thinking Ahead), *Harvard Business Review,* November–December, 1967, p. 2.

[2] Stephen A. Greyser, "Advertising: Attacks and Counters," *Harvard Business Review,* March–April, 1972 from which the models and questions are repeated.

To try to define your own model of the marketplace, let me suggest a self-administered test of your thinking. Thus:

- What is your basic view of how the marketplace mechanism operates?
- What really constitutes "consumer needs" and "rational" choice?
- How intelligent are the choices made by the typical consumer?
- Where does the emphasis lie between adversary and friend in the marketer's role toward the consumer?
- How does advertising work?
- What is the perceived "seduction quotient" in advertising?
- How sophisticated or defenseless are consumers in their ability to screen the advertising and its content that comes their way?

After you have determined your marketplace model, then ask yourself whether your model grows from your view of how consumers do behave or your view of how consumers should behave. I suspect that how consumers *should* behave is the premise for what most critics of advertising and marketing believe, whereas how consumers *do* behave perforce is the premise for what most marketers believe. From answering the foregoing questions, you should be able to understand why you view certain issues regarding advertising's social impacts as you do.

Consumer versus Citizen

Each of us faces a set of moral dilemmas as individuals, the understanding of which may help further to explain the gap. And as a community or society, we face the same dilemmas. For example, as citizens we may want to hold in check the use (depletion) of energy; yet as consumers we may wish to have air conditioners, electric appliances, and the like that consume such energy. Indeed, the Electric Companies of New England have recently been running an advertising program spawned by this dilemma. The ads show "two faces" of the same person debating the personal desire for more appliances and the societal interest in fewer power plants.

Another example is the consumer use of throw-away bottles and the citizen concern for the environment. The extent to which we, as individuals, are willing to trade off additional inconvenience or additional cost (e.g., in cars for safety or anti-pollution equipment) is a measure of our individual resolutions of the citizen-consumer conflict. My impression is that the *citizen* in us is affected first by new directions in broad societal thinking, witness Ford's experience in the 1950's with "safety doesn't sell."

As some . . . have noted, particularly George Fisk, certain situations seem so serious that societal resolution, affecting us all, is the eventual resolution. Mandatory safety and anti-pollution equipment on cars is one example, as would be a ban on the manufacture of cigarettes, Until such mandatory actions occur, however, the brunt of the dilemma for the typical marketer is far more serious than for the typical consumer. The reason: a marketer typically aims at only *part* of the marketplace; thus he is extremely vulnerable, in serving one subset of heterogeneous demands, to having all his eggs in an unsteady basket. This is not to plead for those marketers; it is to explain in part how voluntary action can go only so far. What, pray tell, would a liquor manufacturer do—by way of voluntary restriction—in the face of arguments to restore Prohibition?

Realities of Segmentation

This leads us to the third factor that helps us to understand the gap between practitioner action and perceived community interest, namely the realities of segmentation. That ever more refined segmentation—in products and premises addressed to subgroups of consumers—is the trend seems undebatable. Whether this trend reflects improved marketer *service to* or *power over* consumers is very debatable (based largely on one's view of the marketplace mechanism!)

The realities of segmentation create a host of ''fallout'' problems. Here are a few illustrations drawn from just one area of marketing, namely advertising:

Irritating Advertising

The current mass media structure represents a relatively narrow channel through which most of the segmented consumer products are promoted to their intended consumer subgroups. Despite the existence of segmented magazines, more use of direct marketing, and some clear audience segmentation in TV (e.g., daytime audiences predominantly women), the bulk of consumer product is done via TV at times when much of the audience may *not* be in the segment being directly addressed. The result is increased annoyance on the part of the *non*-target members of the audience. Further, the apparent acceleration of diversity in life styles within our society, and the vigorous affirmation of that diversity, seems to me to strengthen the likelihood of more such annoyance in the future.

Role Portrayal

How advertising portrays different groups in our society is another ''fallout'' issue in advertising. The portrayal of women and of ethnic groups in ads has been a topic of concern and complaint. For example, ads in which women are portrayed in a particular manner may individually be defensible in terms of management's view of the majority of its market.

Yet the cumulative effect of all such ads (for a given brand, product, or in general) may not reflect present-day roles of women.[3] Value judgments are again distinctively involved—e.g., should ads show society as it is or as someone (the advertiser?) thinks it should be?

The reality of segmentation here lies in large part in the kind of people to whom the product and advertising are geared . . . and how the portrayal of *these particular people* is perceived by others who *aren't* like them.

Miscommunication in Advertising

The availability of media advertising, particularly in TV, leads to yet another problem. The *opportunity* for miscommunication—or, better, misreception of intended communication—particularly on the part of a minority of the audience, is enhanced. Our growing societal sensitivity to the importance of such miscommunication and misreception creates a salient new question for advertisers and public policy people: Is there a "normal minimum" proportion of people who take away an incorrect impression from marketing communications? (Perhaps rephrased more pungently as "What is the consumer equivalent to the legendary military 10% who 'never get the word'?") Whatever one's view on what constitutes miscommunication, this question is relevant.

[3] For an analysis of this subject, see Alice E. Courtney and Sarah Lockeretz, "A Woman's Place: An Analysis of the Roles Portrayed by Women in Magazine Advertisements," *Journal of Marketing Research,* February, 1971, p. 92.

5 THE THEORY AND PRACTICE OF SWEDISH CONSUMER POLICY

J. K. Johansson

The institutions and practices which make Sweden a welfare state have often been discussed and analyzed, but few studies have considered the influence of the welfare state on consumer issues. Although Thorelli[1] has discussed consumer information policies in Sweden, there have been a number of important new developments in this field which call for an updated discussion. More importantly, Swedish consumer protection and information policies need to be analyzed in their broadest possible context in order to make their relevance to other societies most clear.

This paper reviews both the theory and practice of recent Swedish consumer policy. At present both have features which will already be familiar to the American consumer movement or contain provisions that could easily be extended to it. However, there are new and very radical consumer theorists in Sweden, who, in the name of comprehensive consumer protection, are advocating unprecedented types of reforms which reject some of the premises on which a free market system is based.

---

[1] H. B. Thorelli, "Consumer Information Policy in Sweden—What Can Be Learned?" *Journal of Marketing,* Vol. 35, January 1971, pp. 50–55; and H. B. Thorelli and S. V. Thorelli, *Consumer Information Handbook; Europe and North America,* New York: Praeger, 1974.

From *Journal of Consumer Affairs* (Summer 1976), pp. 19–32. Reprinted by permission of the American Council on Consumer Interests.

THE PARADIGM OF THE WEAK CONSUMER

Although Sweden is often called a socialist country, its economy remains one which is based on the competitive free-enterprise system. Over 94% of industry is privately owned, and manufacturers compete for customers in a fundamentally free market.[2] At present, however, Swedish consumer policy is based upon the premise that consumers are weak and must be protected, while most producers are powerful and must be watched carefully. The operating plan of the government's National Board for Consumer Policy states:

> The purpose of the Consumer Policy is to support the consumer and improve their position in the marketplace. . . . The starting point for this work is that the individual consumer occupies a weak position relative to producers, distributors, and marketers. The consumer needs active support from the society to get his and her interests considered in the marketplace.[3]

Americans familiar with the idea of the manipulated consumer or the work of Nader will find nothing strange or unfamiliar about these beliefs. Some consumer legislation in America has been based implicitly on similar assumptions even though the enforcement and legal interpretations vary.[4] What makes Sweden noteworthy is that the government has officially adopted this theory of consumer/producer relations and overtly sided wth the "weak" consumer.

More importantly, not only does the weakness of consumers spring from their manipulation by propagandistic advertising but it is considered inherent in their decision-making under severe constraints, notably a scarcity of time, income and generally limited resources.[5] Swedish microeconomists who take the consumer/household rather than the firm as their basic unit of analysis attempt to identify and define the constraints operating upon the consumer in different segments of the total market so as to indicate opportunities for and obstacles to improved consumer decisionmaking. But this identification process has yet to be carried out on any large systematic basis.

At present most energy has been spent trying to more fully inform

---

[2] R. Link, "The Sociomobile," *Sweden Now,* December 1970.

[3] Swedish National Board for Consumer Policies, *Konsumentverket-Verksamhetsplan,* Stockholm, June 26, 1973, p. 1.

[4] I. Preston, "Reasonable Consumer or Ignorant Consumer? How the FTC Decides," *The Journal of Consumer Affairs,* Vol. 8, no. 2, Winter 1974, pp. 131–143.

[5] Swedish Ministry of Commerce, *Synpunkter på den framtida konsumentpolitiken,* Stockholm, December 1969; and Swedish National Board for Consumer Policies, *Konsumentverket—Verksamhetsplan.*

and educate consumers about the products presently available. Several positive effects are anticipated once consumers have been more fully informed about planned purchases. The most immediate benefits are those which accrue to the consumer in terms of greater material satisfaction. Generally, stronger and more sophisticated consumers are expected to lead to a cleaning up of the market, for example through the gradual elimination of undesirable product alternatives. Ideally, manufacturers should be forced to upgrade their products automatically through the workings of competitive pressures in the market. But if big firms possess manipulative powers the pressure for change could be eliminated or resisted for a long time before resulting in any net positive improvement in the overall quality of goods produced. As a consequence, the argument goes, there are not automatic mechanisms through which even strong, better educated consumers could force the development of newer and better products than those currently available.[6]

Because of these considerations, Swedish consumer policy further approves of certain forms of direct action which interfere with the right of the manufacturer to produce whatever will sell in the market. Government agencies in charge of consumer welfare feel justified in eliminating certain products from the market by negotiation and (threats of) blacklisting in order to protect the weak consumer.[7]

CONSUMER POLICY INSTITUTIONS

These general policy considerations are now embodied in a complex series of institutions. In some respects the administration of official consumer policy has yet to fully institutionalize the theory of the weak consumer in contrast to many other countries in which existing practices only later get a coherent theoretical justification. Several advances have taken place in the last few years however. The basic consumer agency at the governmental level is the newly established National Board for Con-

---

[6] In this context it is not suprising to find that the desirability of relying on the entrepreneurial instincts of the Swedish businessmen for desirable new products is a hotly contested question in the current consumer discussion. See G. Claesson, *Visionen om en Konsumentpolitik,* Helsingfors, Askild & Karnekull Forlag AB, 1972; and F. Ölander and H. Lindhoff, *The Interests of Consumers and Business: In Harmony or Conflict?,* Paper presented at the Second Workshop in Marketing, Berlin, May 2–5, 1973.

[7] R. Back, Marknads- och Konsumentchef, Sveriges Industriförbund (The Association of Swedish Industries), Personal interviews, July 20, 1973 and September 23, 1974; H. Berggren, Byråchef för Informationsavdelningen, Konsumentverket (The National Board for Consumer Policies), Personal interview, July 2, 1973; and Swedish Ministry of Commerce, *Bakgrundsmaterial-Konsumentpolitik,* Stockholm, April 2, 1973.

sumer Policies which incorporates three previously separate agencies concerned with labelling, product testing and consumer information. In addition to these activities the Board is charged with broader investigations of products and markets and relaying of information to consumers via pamphlets and training seminars. Furthermore the Board carries the responsibility for the producer contacts that might be deemed necessary. Presently there is no legal way of making manufacturers adhere to the Board's views on particular products. However if considerable difficulty in producer cooperation is encountered such legislation will be initiated.[8] The Board also incorporates a Public Complaints Office through which consumers' complaints about faulty products are processed.[9]

The Board is mainly a regulatory agency; it does not implement any particular piece of legislation. This is in contrast to the Consumer Ombudsman, whose basic responsibility it is to enforce two laws. One is a law against unwarranted claims in advertising, deceptive packaging and certain home selling methods. The other law concerns standard buyer/seller contracts with the purpose of protecting the buyer against contracts which improperly favor the seller.

A third government agency, the National Price and Cartel Office, has as one of its tasks the introduction of unit pricing. In this work it attempts to develop comparable prices for varying sizes of packages, for alternative brands and even for alternative "need satisfying units." Thus, for example, different breakfast menus with equivalent nutritional value are developed and priced. In the introductory stage, however, the stores' unit pricing has been confined much as in the U.S. to package sizes and alternative brands, covering basically food products.[10]

These are the three main consumer policy institutions. Several smaller agencies as well as sections of larger agencies are charged with enforcing other laws of relevance to the consumer policy area; as in the U.S. the total effort is spread out over a considerable number of institu-

---

[8] Kungl, Maj:ts Proposition nr. 33 år 1972, *Proposition med förslag till riktlingèr för och organisation av sämhällets konsumentpolitik m.m.*, Stockholm, Riksdagstrycket, 1972.

[9] With regard to the Board's activities related to the market offerings its operating plan says: "*Market supervision*—protect against dangerous and functionally unsatisfactory products; watch over the effects of consumer protective legislation; watch over the adherence to the norms of informative labelling; test the products in the market" (Swedish National Board for Consumer Policies, *Konsumentverket-Verksamhetsplan,* p. 4). Further, on the producer contacts work: "The producer contacts have been divided as follows: 1. *Information*—inform firms, trade organizations, etc., of results from investigations undertaken by the Board; marketing of informative labelling. 2. *Negotiations*—influence producers, importers, and distributors to change their products/their market conduct. 3. *Other contacts*—e.g., gather experiences and viewpoints from a certain industry or a certain firm" (*Ibid.*, p. 4).

[10] B. Brolund, Byrådirektör, Statens Pris- och Kartellnämnd (National Price and Cartel Office), Personal interview, July 5, 1973.

tions. It is up to the National Board of Consumer Policies to coordinate these different activities.

How do these institutions avoid losing contact with the consumers they are supposed to serve? Several formal as well as informal channels of communication are available. For one, in contrast to the usual bureaucratic model the institutions are open for direct contacts with any consumers who approach them. This has worked particularly well for the Consumer Ombudsman who dealt with 4500 cases during 1972, 75% of which came from such outside sources.[11] In addition, through their own investigations the institutions uncover undesirable situations. The impetus to such investigations might come from the consumers, from the Public Complaints Office or from other institutions, government as well as private. At the more local level the home consultants (similar to the county extension services in the U.S.) and voluntary county consumer groups provide feedback on situations in need of correction.

How successful the institutions will be in keeping track of consumers' needs remains to be seen. Judging from the Ombudsman experience, however, the Swedish consumer is becoming increasingly militant and willing to exert some individual effort to get things changed. Such an attitude seems a necessary prerequisite for the successful working of these institutions.

In what follows a brief list of examples of actions taken by the institutions will be given. In accordance with the theoretical discussion the presentation will be divided into two subsections. One section will cover actions that are directly related to the betterment of the weak consumer as a decision-maker. The other section will deal with actions that tend to restrict producers and their products directly.

ACTIONS ASSISTING THE CONSUMER

Many of the actions designed to assist the consumer in his/her decision-making resemble similar actions here in the U.S. but have perhaps gone further. Most of the product information is made available through product labelling, disclosing contents of the product (for most foods, chemical products and textiles), and also indicating the characteristics of the product in use. Thus, for example, the stretchability, fire resistance and durability characteristics of various products such as teddy bears,

---

[11] Y. De Geer, Informationschef, Konsumentombudsmannen (The Consumer Ombudsman), Personal interview, July 5, 1973; Swedish Ministry of Commerce, *Annual Report on Consumer Policy 1972,* Stockholm, March 8, 1973; and Claesson, *Visionen om en Konsumentpolitik.*

women's dresses and children's clothes are often indicated.[12] The labelling is still voluntary although very much adopted as a competitive tool. A new investigation recently completed will probably lead to some obligatory labelling as well as the introduction of minimum standards.[13] In addition the emphasis is shifting towards information specifically dealing with the product in use. This is exemplified by the furniture and shoe industries where informative labelling has gone furthest.[14] Here, elaborate classifications of alternative product uses have been developed with each single product classified into one type of usage. The product is given a set of ratings along several dimensions deemed to be of importance in the particular use category. Thus, for example, leisure shoes are rated on resistance to water and paint, hill and mountain climbing as well as more simple endeavors such as long walks.[15] Most of this information does not appear directly on the label but can be asked for in the store, and access to the ratings is provided. Only a few summated ratings appear on the label.[16]

In order that the consumer may avoid a costly trial-and-error learning procedure in regard to the use of this product information a considerable educational effort is taking place. Consumer textbooks for school children are being prepared.[17] Local chapters of countrywide organizations long active in the labor movement are carrying out grass roots seminars on selected consumer problems.[18] Radio and television, both operated under government supervision, are used for short programs on various consumer issues. These programs, incidentally, are often made possible and necessary by the empty slots in American TV-programs presented without commercials. At the county level the home

---

[12] R. Johansson, Redaktör, Kooperativa Förbundet (The Consumers' Cooperatives), Personal interview, July 4, 1973; and Statens Offentliga Utredningar (SOU) 1971:20, *Verudeklaration—ett medel i konsumentpolitiken,* Stockholm, 1973.

[13] R. Back, Personal interviews; H. Berggren, Personal interviews; and *Verudeklaration—ett medel i konsumentpolitiken.*

[14] Statens Offentliga Utredningar (SOU) 1971:37, *Konsumentpolitik-organisation,* Stockholm, 1971, pp. 56, 209.

[15] R. Back, Personal interviews.

[16] It should perhaps be noted that nobody opposes these detailed ratings as such, but their probably restrictive effect upon exports and imports is emphasized by producer organizations (R. Back, Personal interviews; and *Varudeklaration—ett medel i konsumentpolitiken,* pp. 136–79). Also, it should be emphasized that the practical implementation of informative labelling is yet far from complete.

[17] H. Berggren, Personal interview; and Swedish Ministry of Commerce, *Annual Report on Consumer Policy 1972.*

[18] L. Hillbom, Utredningssekreterare, Landsorganisationen (The Organization of Labor Unions), Personal interview, July 26, 1973; and Swedish National Board for Consumer Policies, *Konsumentverket-Verksamhetsplan.*

consultants are charged with the responsibility of informing the local consumers of new products and other information. This activity sometimes takes the form of exhibitions where a set of products related to some particular use category—such as back-to-school clothes—are displayed together with product ratings.[19]

In addition, many stores—particularly the consumers' cooperatives—feature sections where product information and test results relating to many product areas are available. Here one will often find copies of the government test reports, for example, as well as other test information.[20]

ACTIONS AGAINST THE PRODUCERS

The actions designed to eliminate undesirable products and product features also have their counterparts in this country, but again Sweden has probably advanced further. A few examples will provide a picture of the comprehensive nature of the undertaking.

Only very recently did consumers in Sweden receive the opportunity of buying a tumble dryer. Although automatic washing machines have been on the market a long time, the government testing institute found that the tumbling activity of the dryer tore clothes and made sheets and similar textiles difficult to fold.[21] No firm introduced a tumbler on the market because of the perceived negative effects of this test report. Instead a kind of cabinet dryer was invented and serves now as the dryer in most Swedish homes. It is cheaper than the tumble dryer but lacks its speed. After the recent introduction of more acceptable tumble dryers, the Swedish consumers are now faced with a greater array of choices than their American counterpart.

The lemon-scented washing detergent introduced here in the U.S. not so long ago also made a brief appearance on the Swedish market, but it was argued that its package similarity to certain soft drinks made repackaging necessary. The importer argued that several factors prevented any injury to consumers: the products were presumably stored in different areas of the kitchen, an initial taste of the detergent would tell anyone to stop drinking, and finally even if a child drank it all no harm would be done. The outcome, however, was to waive a blacklisting of the detergent only after its repackaging.[22]

---

[19] R. Johansson, Personal interview, July 4, 1973; and *Konsumentpolitik-organisation.*

[20] R. Johansson, Personal interview.

[21] R. Back, Personal interviews.

[22] R. Back, Personal interviews; and Hillbom,Personal interview.

Several actions have been directed against advertising. In general when a product is advertised the important features from a consumer standpoint are to be exhibited prominently. Thus, for example, if a food product contains some artificial ingredient—such as some juices and other soft drinks—this should be clearly communicated even to a consumer who is only briefly exposed to the advertisement.[23]

Cigarette and liquor advertising might be completely banned in the near future—an investigation is currently pondering that question.[24] The rule so far allows for such advertising in magazines and newspapers, but in the advertisements no human being can be portrayed; foreign magazines and newspapers are exempted for obvious reasons.[25]

Although pollution controls for automobiles are not as advanced as in some places (for example, California), Sweden's safety standards have long been a model for other countries. Among the newer developments are laws which require used cars to be inspected at the seller's expense and warranties extended.[26] Furthermore, there probably will be a right-of-return for the buyer in case the car does not perform according to road and safety standards.[27] As for new cars, one future development might be the development of more easily repaired cars. The argument is that repair costs are high partly because the basic engineering design does not take into account future repairs but could do so at very little extra cost and without major design changes.[28] Since such a development will probably be supported by the big insurance companies, who are now reducing premiums for cars with less expensive repairs, chances are that it will come about. Overall, however, one can say that automobiles (especially new cars) have come under less attack in Sweden than in this country. Part of the explanation might lie in the role of the automobile as a status symbol which to a casual observer still seems strong in Sweden relative to the U.S. Another reason lies perhaps in the fact that the smaller cars of Sweden leave less to criticize than their larger American counterparts.

The travel agencies in Sweden that organize charter flights to other countries—there are many of them, especially active in the summer—are obliged to establish collateral with a government agency to be

---

[23] R. Back, Personal interviews; and De Geer, Personal intervies.

[24] Swedish Ministry of Commerce, *Bakgrundsmaterial-Konsumentpolitik,* Stockholm, April 2, 1973.

[25] De Geer, Personal interview.

[26] *Proposition med förslag till riklinjer för och organisation av sämhällets konsumentpolitik m. m.*, p. 20.

[27] Hillbom, Personal interview.

[28] K. Blomqvist, Marknadschef, Folksam Försäkringsbolag (Folksam Insurance Company), Personal interview, July 12, 1973; and *Baksgrundsmaterial-Konsumentpolitik,* p. 8.

used for customer compensation in case something goes wrong.[29] As is well known such mishaps can be very frequent, and in several cases the travelers have been reimbursed for their actual outlays as well as opportunity costs.

OTHER PROJECTED LEGISLATION

Looking to the future it seems quite likely that the Swedish consumer will get a general "open purchase" law that enables him/her to return a product within one week and receive the money back. This would provide additional protection against deficient products and fast-talking salesmen. The law could clearly not cover products such as perishables but would specifically exclude those and similar goods, the rule applying unless excluded. One reason why the passage of such a law is probable is that many private retailers favor it; the consumers' cooperatives are the major stores featuring a trial week now, and the competitive effect has hurt the independents.

It is also probable—and has been legally enforced in a few cases already—that advertising claims will have to accurately represent actual product performance.[30] Thus not only will claims have to be substantiated once and for all to a government agency as in the U.S., but any user of the product could use the claims when legally establishing a divergence between expectations and actual performance.

The regulations pertaining to installment payments for consumer durables have been subject to intensive study. Two probable future developments are, one, the imposition of a minimum down payment possibly as high as 30% of sales price, and, two, an enforced limit on the length of the contract, the limit set perhaps as low as 18 months. One reason for the probable passage of these regulations is the support given them by the big labor unions. The unions have developed an active interest in the consumer movement as an extension of their traditional labor concerns.[31]

These are, then, some of the developments in Swedish consumer policies as they have taken place over the last three to four years. It is clear that during these years one of the main concerns of the well-established Swedish welfare state has been with consumer welfare. Although one might think that this state of affairs would change in case of a possible transition of the party in government, this does not seem very likely. Any

[29] *Ibid.*, p. 34.

[30] De Geer, Personal interview; and *Baksgrundsmaterial-Konsumentpolitik*, p. 16.

[31] Hillbom, Personal interview.

governing political party will have to reckon with the politically strong unions and their proconsumer stand. In addition the center party and the liberal party whose coalition would make up the most probable alternative to a social-democratic government are both pushing proconsumer measures strongly, and there is no particular reason to assume they would stop doing so after being given a governing mandate.

It is clear that in Sweden the consumer welfare state is here to stay. However, it is also true that none of the existing laws and institutions seem to aim for or project an elimination of the private sector of the economy or the free market as we know it. But among the many advocates of consumer reforms in Sweden are a group of radical thinkers (both inside and outside official government positions) who want to see the capitalist basis of producer/consumer relations fundamentally altered.[32] They base their demands for radical change on a collection of ideas which might be called the paradigm of the ignorant (or naive) consumer.[33] Since seemingly radical ideas have a way of becoming institutionalized in Sweden much as in the U.S., it is worthwhile to consider the ideas of the most vocal and extreme advocates of consumer reform now active in Sweden.[34]

THE PARADIGM OF THE IGNORANT CONSUMER

When the National Board for Consumer Policies carried out a set of interviews of retired people on their problems as consumers they found that to a large extent the senior citizens were content with their lot.[35] Radical consumer advocates were apppalled at these findings and took the stand that these aging consumers clearly exhibited too low levels of aspirations in terms of overall living standards.[36]

As a consequence consumer radicals began to develop an informal theory of the consumer not as a capable and rational being in need of

---

[32] Ölander and Lindhoff, *The Interests of Consumers and Business;* and Swedish Ministry of Commerce, *Synpunkter på den framtida konsumentpolitiken.*

[33] The term "ignorant" is adopted following Preston ("Reasonable Consumer or Ignorant Consumer" How the FTC Decides"). Much of Preston's discussion of the role of the ignorant consumer paradigm in U. S. courts provides a very relevant parallel to the Swedish development.

[34] It should be emphasized that these newer lines of thought are still very much contested and hardly the views of all Swedish economists (Back, Personal interviews). Also, recent interviews indicate that this more radical program is yet far from being implemented (Back, Personal interviews; and Odhnoff, Personal interview).

[35] Back, Personal interviews.

[36] Swedish Ministry of Commerce, *Synpunkter på den framtida konsumentpolitiken.*

more information and better product guarantees but as an "ignorant" or "naive" judge of his/her own best interests as a purchasing agent for a household.

First, the radicals begin with the postulate that the goal of society's economic activity is the physical, social and psychological well-being of the consumer. The wording is based on the charter of the United Nations' World Health Organization.[37] Second, the theory asserts that the individuals' subjective contentment is not necessarily an adequate indicator that their real or objective needs are being met and their well-being truly assured.

In support of this second proposition a few empirical illustrations are given. For example many people around the world report that they are satisfied with the kind and amount of food which they consume daily. But dieticians and doctors often argue that their basic nutritional needs are not being met. Since there appear to be objective standards for judging whether or not the food eaten by an individual or group contains sufficient amount of different essential nutrients, these standards, radicals argue, should take precedent over subjective contentment in judging whether or not an individual's needs are being met by the market.[38] In this and similar situations the opinions of individuals will have to be dismissed and the consumer protected from himself/herself as it were.

In other words, many people have aspirations or material expectations which are too low to satisfy their real needs, and there is room for improvement. The radicals argue, third, that the individuals' motivation toward this kind of self-improvement is low precisely because of the subjective contentment generated by the low levels of aspiration. As a consequence the initiative rests with the government whose actions can and should be taken even in the absence of manifested support from the consumers themselves.

The forced elimination of the discrepancy between subjective satisfaction and objective well-being can be handled in two ways. On the one hand levels of aspiration which are too low can be pushed upwards through education and training in problem solving.[39] In support of this proposal the radicals use findings which show that people with higher education tend to have higher, more beneficial aspiration levels. On the other hand product offerings might be supervised so that only products

---

[37] Claesson, *Visionen om en Konsumentpolitik;* and *Synpunkter på den framtida komsumentpolitiken,* p. 2.

[38] Berggren, Personal interview; Hillbom, Personal interview; and *Synpunkter på den framtida konsumentpolitiken.*

[39] *Synpunkter på den framtida konsumentpolitiken,* p. 3; and H. Lindhoff, Civilekonom, Ekonomiska Forskningsinstitutet (The Economic Research Institute), Personal interview, June 21, 1973.

which fulfill the more stringent requirements of the objective standards are allowed to remain on the market. Then, of course, the consumers simply cannot suffer even if, paradoxically enough, for some the sense of subjective contentment might be lowered.

Obviously one can argue that it would be difficult to develop correct definitions of the objective criteria for need satisfaction even in the relatively easy case of physical well-being. To the radical consumer reformers, however, this is mainly an empirical question, and as we have seen attempts have already been made at defining rating scales for product performance in actual use.[40] Against this background there should be little wonder at the fact that there is presently much discussion in Sweden concerning the desirability of forcibly eliminating those products whose ratings are below certain levels. An interesting example which institutionalizes such screening is provided by the work at the consumers' cooperatives where children's toys, for example, are carefully examined and tested before allowed into the stores.[41] Increasingly, even government officials view such screening and forced elimination as highly desirable.[42]

One implication of the theory of the ignorant consumer is that the notion of the demand curve as an indicator of consumer needs is thoroughly discredited. The demand functions used by more traditional economists are considered a reflection of the amount of collective buying power, not the real need or desire for the product among the general populace. Since some desires might even be judged objectively inappropriate, Sweden's radical advocates of consumer reform prefer to base their analysis of demand primarily on the material needs, not the expressed desires which are often psychological, of the consuming public.

Because of this preoccupation with where the consumers' real interests lie, another integral part of the theory argues for the importance of generic product purchase decisions as opposed to brand decisions.[43] The

---

[40] Statens Offentliga Utredningar (SOU 1971:37, *Konsumentpolitik-organisation;* and Statens Offentliga Utredningar (SOU) 1973:20, *Varudeklaration—ett medel i konsumentpolitiken.*

[41] Blomqvist, Personal interview; and Johansson, Personal interview.

[42] Cases exist where such direct market actions of the government would seem less controversial. Thus, for example, when both the subjective and the objective criteria are unsatisfied the actions will have clear justifications. Similarly, where both are satisfied, no action is necessary. Furthermore, although subjectively dissatisfied many individuals might find no government action forthcoming where objective criteria are fulfilled. This will occur especially where the dissatisfied consumers belong to the economically and educationally favored groups. The emphasis of the effort is upon disadvantaged consumer groups (Berggren, Personal interview).

[43] Ölander and Lindhoff, *The Interests of Consumers and Business;* and *Synpunkter på den framtida konsumentpolitiken.*

brand choice research very common earlier in Sweden is dismissed as focusing upon a very minute, unimportant and relatively simple decision process from the consumer's point of view.[44] Rather the focus of research should be on what type of goods to buy, what type of products to acquire for one's transportation needs, what kinds of home entertainment equipment to buy and so on. It is for these kinds of decisions that the consumer is especially badly equipped and where the amount of guiding information from any source is severely lacking.

Accordingly some research is being undertaken into the questions as to what alternative means of satisfying the needs in a broad sense are available and how they stack up against one another.[45] As noted earlier food menus can be acquired from local government authorities. The private consumers' cooperatives have developed apparel lines covering womens' and mens' basic designs and colors. Analyses of the insurance needs of the average citizen have also been published.[46]

Just as the paradigm of the ignorant consumer leads to a new conceptualization of demand it also leads to a redefinition of the concept of competition. Obviously if government officials are to be allowed—even encouraged—to purge the market of some brands or some products little faith remains in the ability of competitive mechanisms to meet the real needs of consumers. The idea that product proliferation at the brand level is necessary for freedom of competition is rejected by the advocates of radical consumer legislation.[47] If a particular brand of product X is judged as the one which best meets the real needs of the consumer it is unnecessary to have alternative brands on the market, particularly since they must be inferior. To paraphrase, if Volvos are best everyone who wants a car should drive a Volvo. Competition is not banished entirely, however, since it will take place between types of products which strive to fill similar, general needs.[48] The makers of Volvo, for example, would compete with other types of transportation (trains, subways, buses, taxis) rather than other auto makers. In this way competitive benefits including low prices would still accrue to the consumer.

---

[44] As for freedom of choice at the brand level, the insignificance of this choice allows a considerable reduction in the number of alternatives without substantially lessening the freedom, according to the Swedish framework.

[45] Swedish National Board for Consumer Policies, *Konsumentverket-Verksamhetsplan.*

[46] Blomqvist, Personal interview; Johansson, Personal interview; Swedish Ministry of Commerce, *Bakgrundsmaterial-Konsumentpolitik;* and Statens Offentliga Utredningar (SOU) 1973:20, *Varudeklaration—ett medel i konsumentpolitiken.*

[47] *Synpunkter på den framtida konsumentpolitiken.*

[48] Berggren, Personal interview.

CONCLUSION

On the surface it seems clear that the logical extension of the paradigm of the ignorant consumer is a centralized, economically totalitarian state in which the means of production are controlled by the state. Moreover if the consumer is to be treated as a child who can only be trusted to make relatively few decisions in the market place the consumer-as-voter can neither be expected to make mature political decisions as expected in basically democratic institutions. Unless Sweden abandons its historically successful mating of political democracy, economic capitalism and socialist welfare state, it seems unlikely that the philosophy of the ignorant consumer will be fully institutionalized. On the other hand it cannot be denied that some Swedish reformers and officials are willing to go to greater lengths than the present system would seem to allow to purge the market of undesirable products based on paternalistic decisions about what is good for the consumer. Since Sweden has historically opted for the middle way, however, it seems most probable that those in charge of extending the welfare state to the Swedish consumer will continue to find ways to preserve a good deal of freedom of choice for the individual while seeking ways to minimize the hidden dangers which come with such freedoms. In this sense their efforts should be of continued interest to the American consumer movement.

6 AXIOMS FOR SOCIETAL MARKETING

Philip Kotler

Some years ago, Charles Malik, the Lebanese philosopher-statesman representative to the United Nations, threw out the challenge:

> Technique, efficiency, management, results! . . . Nobody asks the fundamental question as to what is the whole blooming thing for. Nobody cares to find out what spirit pervades the whole thing. Nobody has the time to ascertain whether Man, in his freedom and in his fullness, exists at all (Malik, 1963).

Malik was voicing a concern over the growing uncritical acceptance of Western industrial ideology and values. His pleading is appropriate today as the problems created by industrial society come into clearer focus. We may well raise this concern about current marketing institutions and ideology and ask what they are all about.

The field of marketing has the distinction of being singularly uncontroversial within its ranks and endlessly controversial outside of its ranks. Its leading contemporary critics—John Kenneth Galbraith, Ralph Nader, Vance Packard, and others—are outsiders—economists, lawyers, journalists. The overwhelming majority of marketing practitioners have defended rather than questioned the premises underlying their profession.

This is in dramatic contrast to other fields which have, during the last turbulent decade, bred splinter groups that have challenged the deepest

---

Reprinted, with permission, from George Fisk, Johan Arndt, and Kjell Gronharg (eds.), *Future Directions for Marketing* (Boston: Marketing Science Institute, 1979), pp. 33-41.

premises of their discipline. Today there are active insurgent groups of radical economists, radical political scientists, radical sociologists, and even radical therapists. They are disputing the basic thought patterns of their respective fields, and in the process, stimulating fresh, long overdue dialogues. By inquiring into "what is the whole blooming thing for," they precipitate an intellectual crisis in their discipline and lay the groundwork for intellectual regeneration and advance.

The marketing profession, in contrast, has no well-established native son radicals. A price is paid for this. Marketing doctrine grows soft and less relevant to new conditions. Research grows stale and repetitive. A sense of challenge and excitement is missing. Ultimate issues are forgotten. One could argue that if marketing radicals do not exist, they should be created.

CONVENTIONAL MARKETING AXIOMS

Cynics within marketing have suggested that the marketing discipline lacks heresy because there is no doctrine to rebel against. This is incorrect. There is a conventional marketing wisdom that is taken for granted by its practitioners and academics. It consists of five axioms.

> *Axiom 1:* Marketing is essentially a seller science. Its major purpose is to assist business decision-makers in determining what to produce and how to sell their output.

The popular image of marketing is that it is a discipline designed to help sellers solve problems posed by the market. Since the major marketing problem of business firms in the last twenty years has been that of finding enough customers, marketing has been viewed primarily as the task of building demand for company products and services. The advent of major shortages in recent years has created new tasks for the seller, such as reducing demand and allocating scarce supplies to customers. This has led to the suggestion that the true generic task of marketing is to help sellers *manage* demand (Kotler, 1973). This is consistent with Axiom 1 and not a contradiction.

> *Axiom 2:* Sellers should be relatively free of constraints in designing their marketing mix.

Sellers instinctively rebel against interferences by government and consumer organizations in their freedom to set their marketing mix and effort level. Sellers want to determine the products they will produce, the prices they will charge, the channels they will use, and the promotion they will develop, subject to the normal consideration of viable competition and consumer welfare. There is the wish to protect property rights; the high costs of complying with outside imposed requirements; and the sincere belief that companies and their customers would only be worse off if there is outside intervention. The auto industry, through its delays and opposition to recent laws regulating product safety and pollution control, illustrates how hard an industry will fight to preserve its ancient prerogatives.

> *Axiom 3:* Sellers will be effective to the extent that they study and serve the needs and wants of the buyers.

Modern marketing thought is dominated by the *marketing concept,* the doctrine that the most successful firms will be those that design their products and marketing program out of a real understanding of the needs and wants of their buyers. The marketing concept requires active consumer research, integrated marketing, and consumer satisfaction. The question that is being increasingly used, however, is whether the marketing concept is a *sufficient* guide for company success in the marketplace.

> *Axiom 4:* Sellers should vary their offerings as much as possible to match the varying wants of different buyer segments.

Axiom 4 follows from Axiom 3. If effective marketing calls for satisfying consumer wants, then different wants will require the development of different products. This is the philosophy of *market segmentation.* At one time, this was a heresy, because sellers felt that the only way to bring down costs and prices was to resort to mass production of standardized items. Henry Ford's famous dictum "People can have any color car they want, as long as it is black," was based on the sound proposition that automobiles would be cheaper to make if they were all one color. Over time, the marketing ideal swung to the other extreme, with companies vying to offer minuscule refinements of their products to serve every discernible variation in desire.

> *Axiom 5:* The well-being of consumers will be maximized under the marketing concept.

The great importance of the marketing concept to the marketing profession is that it gave its practitioners a basis for believing that there is a direct harmony of interests between the buyers and the sellers. Their critics were always complaining that business is self-serving and even exploitative. The marketing concept offered a ground for believing that business gained only through the consumer's gaining. The marketing concept reduced the need for conflict, legislation, and regulation.

THE CHANGING ENVIRONMENT

Although the axioms of current marketing thought are individually and collectively attractive, they impress the writer as being increasingly fragile as a guide to future marketing practice. They were formulated for a particular economic setting at a particular point in its history. The axioms received their quintessential development in the United States in the 1950s and 1960s, a period characterized by (1) surplus capacity, (2) affluence, (3) growing competition, and (4) the illusion of boundless resources.

The existence of surplus capacity meant that producers were anxious to find buyers for their goods. The nation's affluence meant that the buyers had the funds if they could be coaxed into spending them. Growing competition meant that sellers had to be sensitive to what consumers wanted and what satisfied them. The illusion of boundless resources meant that producers and consumers had no qualms about the energy or material used up in the acts of production and consumption.

The marketing dogma that was formulated during this earlier period prevails today. It fails to take cognizance of major new factors in the environment that were not present in the earlier period. These new factors are:

1. *Energy and material shortages* that signal the eventual exhaustion of key nonrenewable resources and their imperfect replacement by higher cost substitutes.
2. *Worldwide inflation* precipitated by a worldwide growth in demand and growing scarcity of resources to satisfy this demand.
3. The specter of *economic stagnation* suggested by the dearth of major innovations and fields for investment.
4. The rise of *consumerism* in the form of active citizen and government effort to increase the rights and power of buyers vis-à-vis sellers.
5. The rise of *environmentalism* in the form of active citizen and government effort to limit the despoliation of the environment.
6. Increased *government regulation* going beyond consumer and environmental protection to promote competition, price stability, and even selective deconsumption.
7. Increased *international barriers* in the form of trade regulation, antimultinationalism, and currency instability.
8. *High cost of borrowed money* and its dampening effects on capacity expansion and new product development.
9. *Changing consumer life styles* in response to shortages, inflation, and quality-of-life considerations.

The sum of these developments poses a substantial challenge to current marketing practice and dogma. They form the basis of an incipient revolution in marketing thought whose full force will not be apparent for many years.

SOCIETAL MARKETING AXIOMS

Marketing dogma admittedly constituted a progressive philosophy in its day. Under the new conditions, however, the prevailing marketing dogma may succeed only in delaying solution to the problems facing modern society.

I would like to advance a set of five axioms that individually and collectively challenge the five axioms of conventional marketing wisdom. They are offered in the spirit of encouraging a much needed dialogue on the fundamentals of marketing thought and practice in the interest of improving marketing's contribution to the welfare of producers, consumers, and society as a whole.

> *Axiom 1′*: The essential purpose of the marketing discipline is to assist sellers to sell better, buyers to buy better, and government to perform better.

Up to now, marketing has been primarily a tool of the sellers. Academic researchers spend their time studying the consumer buying process not primarily to help consumers buy better but to help sellers sell better. They study the marketing practices of leading manufacturers and retailers to evaluate not the social impact of these practices but rather their profit impact on the firm.

A case can be made for expanding the mission of marketing to include helping buyers to buy better. Marketers would join in the work being shouldered primarily by consumer economists, educators, and media. This work takes the form of finding effective ways to expand consumers' information, education, and protection. Marketers would undertake such studies as:

1. How concerned are consumers with the safety and health aspects of different categories of products and what cues do they use to judge safety and health aspects? How much information do consumers need or want and what are the most effective ways to make this information available?
2. How aware are consumers of appeals and devices used by advertisers and salesmen to motivate purchase? What is the most effective way to train consumers to recognize these devices and be less vulnerable to them?

3. How informed are buyers of price and quality differences in different product categories? What are the best information devices for improving their awareness?

The mission of marketing should also be expanded to help government perform better in the marketplace. The government carries on informational, legislative, and regulatory activity in the marketplace that is not always well-conceived or effective in reaching its aims. Laws are passed requiring manufacturers or retailers to provide information to consumers without studying how consumers attend to or use this information. Regulatory commissions take steps to limit the pricing or promotion discretion of sellers without understanding the role of pricing and promotion from either the seller's or buyer's point of view or the consequences of their regulations. Government actions are largely conceived by lawyers or economists who are chronically naive about consumers' and producers' needs, perceptions, preferences, and behavior.

Axiom 2′: Outside parties should be represented in seller decision-making.

The American tradition of private enterprise holds that the seller should be as free as possible to make all decisions connected with his product, such as its design, price, promotion, and channels of distribution. If the seller fails to satisfy the consumer, the consumer will "vote" against the product and the seller will lose his capital. This is especially true when there is active competition. The fact that the seller is risking his capital will lead him to study consumer wants, as well as society's needs, and he can be depended upon to do a responsible job of product development and marketing.

This logic of the "invisible hand" has to be reexamined today in the light of the growing size and power of today's enterprises. A small number of giant corporations make decisions in terms of their own interests that affect millions of people throughout the world. The question is being raised more widely whether the production and marketing decisions of giant enterprises should be subject to public review and accountability. For example, did the American auto industry behave in the public interest by continuing to "push" large gas-consuming automobiles well after a growing portion of the public registered an interest in smaller automobiles? Should the public review the amount of the nation's resources going into alcoholic beverages, pet foods, convenience packaging, and so on, in the light of growing world problems of hunger, pollution, and crime?

The issue is one of how to make giant enterprises more responsive to consumer and societal needs without "overkill," that is, without compromising their efficiency and flexibility. Today, the modern firm researches the market's wants but makes the final decisions entirely on its own. A wide variety of mechanisms have been suggested to bring the consumers' interest closer to the decision-making process: consumer advisory boards, consumer directors, consumer review boards, consumer ombudsmen, and so on. Some of these mechanisms are being tried by some companies and it is too early to tell what the gains and costs of these mechanisms are. More radical experimentation is occurring abroad. In Sweden, the government's Consumer Agency has power to lean against manufacturers who are not making well-designed products or who are building too much psychological differentiation into their products. In the Philippines, manufacturers of certain staple products are required to follow "social pricing," that is, to price a part of their output at the lowest possible prices so that the poor can afford them and not have to pay for brand and advertising costs.

> *Axiom 3′*: Sellers will be effective to the extent that they attempt to serve consumers' interests in addition to their desires.

Most marketers are of the opinion that their responsibility ends with giving consumers what they want. If consumers want cigarettes, alcohol, fattening foods, and large cars, they shall have them. Consumers usually know the risks of various products and should be free to consume what they want.

This marketing philosophy has a noble ring because it centers choice and responsibility on consumers, denying the right of others to impose their tastes. *De gustibus non disputem est.* Any other point of view would establish an elite who will tell consumers what they can have or should have.

Unfortunately, unmitigated consumer sovereignty is growing less tenable in the face of the emergent social forces enumerated earlier. Consumers do not always know what is best for themselves, especially as products get more complex. Nor do they always take the interests of society into account. Consumers can hurt themselves by being unaware of or indifferent to the impact of certain products on their health or safety; they can hurt those near them, such as family or neighbors; and they can hurt society at large by being wasteful or polluting. We are beginning to see conflicts between consumers themselves growing out of antagonistic life styles.

The question is whether the firm has a responsibility to help consumers consume more intelligently. It can be argued that the firm not only has a responsibility but would be a more effective marketer if it focused on the consumers' long-run interests. As consumers grow more educated and perceptive, they will favor the firms that are trying to enhance the quality of their lives rather than those that only cater to their appetites.

Axiom 4′: Sellers should vary their offerings primarily in response to basic differences in needs.

Under today's marketing philosophy, marketers are concerned with finding any differences that would give their brand an edge over competition. They are prepared to offer any sizes, colors, and features that will appeal to the fancies of buyers. Marketers do not bother to judge whether the differences are basic or trivial.

Marketers will take homogeneous product categories and create differences where none formerly existed. Such commodities as sugar, salt, flour, gasoline, and cigarettes become subject to a brand differentiation process which leads consumers to believe in brand differences and the validity of paying more for these brands than would be commanded by these commodities qua commodities. This process, known as "decommodization," is accomplished by heavy seller investment in packaging and advertising for which the consumer ultimately pays. The price-sensitive consumer notices one day that he can no longer buy a brand of "just plain soap" or "just plain cereal."

No marketing advantage lasts very long. A marketing innovation that is successful is quickly imitated and even outdone. The marketer's quest for marginal differentiation is never-ending and the product category eventually balloons into endless variety, a condition known as *product proliferation.* Product proliferation creates or contributes to three major social problems.

The first is the problem of *inflation.* Every departure from mass production creates additional costs in production set-up time, inventory carrying cost, administration, and advertising. The consumer gets more choice but at higher cost. The plain inexpensive brand disappears from the market, leaving the price-conscious consumers no choice but to buy a brand with "built-ins." This persists until some nonvested new producer notices a marketing opportunity to launch a basic brand again. In this sense, marketing practice is inflationary.

The second problem is *overchoice.* Consumers have to spend more time studying the different brands, weighing their attribute differences, and arriving at a confident decision. Not only do they spend more time, they often experience anxiety arising out of the great amount of choice. Ironically, the amount of real choice is never as great as the amount of brand choice, since many brands are essentially the same.

The third problem is *advertising bombardment.* Every brand must be touted to the target markets through the mass media. The mass media turn into tools of advertising rather than vehicles for genuine information, edification, and entertainment. Consumers are assaulted by hundreds of product messages during their waking hours and lose the pleasures of wholeness and simplicity in their life experiences.

There is no simple solution to the problem of product proliferation. In the first place, it is an inevitable consequence of adopting *economic growth* as a societal goal. Unless the society finds a way to live with less economic growth, product proliferation and its social consequences will continue. In the second place, government intervention or regulation would create other, probably worse problems for consumers. No one wants inferior products, inadequate choice, or insufficient information. The ultimate answer may come from changes in consumer life styles which lead consumers to want more basic products at lower prices. This would lead to the recommodization of certain basic product categories which have moved too far in psychological differentiation and cost inflation.

Some marketers will begin to review whether they have pushed brand differences and market segmentation too far. Some will recognize a market opportunity in going after fewer and larger segments representing major differences in consumer desires rather than going after many and smaller segments representing minor differences in consumer desires. In over-segmented markets, sellers will be giving serious thought to desegmentation as a way to bring down their costs and consumer prices.

> *Axiom 5*: The well-being of consumers will be maximized under the societal marketing concept.

The marketing concept calls upon companies to design those products that individual consumers want or find appealing. The existence of enough consumers with the same want is considered sufficient justification for producing the product. The company normally does not raise any questions about the consequences of the product on the consumers' well-being or society's welfare. The company is satisfied that the product is wanted and will yield a profit.

The emerging issue is whether sellers in a technologically complex society can ignore social cost fallouts in their pursuit of profit. Does satisfying the wants of individual consumers result in maximizing their well-being? There is a growing feeling that the effort of companies to cater to the full range of consumer desires does not maximize consumers' well-being in the long run. A society of high consumption speeds up processes of environmental deterioration, economic insecurity, and psychological maladjustment. The planet's resources are reduced at an accelerated rate, thus threatening the well-being of present and future generations. The landscape is despoiled and air and water is polluted by careless or wanton industrial activity. Jobs are created on the fragile ability of sellers to continuously stimulate new wants. People define their goals and values in terms of high earnings and consumption, and when they fail, they feel bitter and angry.

When this happens, consumers take out their frustrations on business. Business is pictured as selfish and irresponsible. The ground is laid for more legislation and regulation. As consumers get more concerned with the social costs of business, they also become more aware of those firms that are trying to behave responsibly. Their patronage shifts to sellers who introduce social criteria in their decision-making and attempt to respond to the consumers' interests as well as wants.

This possibility calls for a new concept of effective company marketing. The proposed concept is the societal marketing concept:

> The societal marketing concept calls for a *consumer orientation* backed by *integrated marketing activity* aimed at generating *consumer satisfaction* and *long-run consumer well-being* as the key to achieving *long-run profitable volume.*

The objective of the marketing system is not to maximize *consumption, consumer satisfaction,* or *consumer choice.* The objective is to maximize the *quality of life.* Life quality is made up of a person's satisfaction of his basic material needs, his satisfaction with the average quality and availability of goods, his satisfaction with his physical environment and surroundings, and his satisfaction with his cultural environment. There is too much of a tendency to rest the case for the current marketing system on its ability to produce a high level of goods and services, and not to consider the total impact of the marketing system on life quality.

CONCLUSION

The revised axioms will strike many marketing practitioners and academics as heresy. They challenge traditional "frontier-style" marketing practices. Sellers want unlimited freedom to deal with customers. They want to view transactions as a private matter. Anything less is regarded as containing the seeds of totalitarian control. The axioms, because they introduce societal considerations and responsibilities, compromise the model of the free and private transaction.

It is easy to perceive the issue as one of *freedom* versus *bureaucratic control.* Posed this way, most people would prefer the present marketing practices. The real issue, however, is that private transactions have social consequences which feed back on the welfare of those who participate in private transactions, as well as on nonparticipants, often making them worse off in the short or long run. Somehow the social consequences of private marketing activity must be taken into account by the parties. Sellers bear the heavier burden because they have more of the power and take more of the initiative in defining and affecting the life quality of the society.

The marketing discipline is not serving the long-run interests of the sellers if it fails to research and represent the long-run interests of the buyers. Students of marketing must expand the vision of their work to that of forging useful theory to help the sellers sell better, the buyers buy better, and the government perform better.

REFERENCES

KOTLER, PHILIP, "The Major Tasks of Marketing Management," *Journal of Marketing* (October 1973), pp. 42–49.

MALIK, CHARLES, Speech reported in *Fortune* (November 1963), p. 72.

7 CONSUMERISM LIVES! ...AND GROWS

E. Patrick McGuire

Several years back a news magazine, examining the state of religion in America, asked on its cover: "Is God Dead?" (*He* was not.) A few years later another magazine wondered, on its cover, whether consumerism was dead. (It *is* not.)

It has been the belief among many senior executives, however, that consumerism, if not yet dead, is certainly moribund. And the 1977 defeat of the Consumer Protection Act seemed to support that point of view. Indeed, Edie Fraser, president of Fraser Associates, one of the country's top consumer consulting firms, advised her corporate clients that

> Carter Administration hopes for legislative consumer initiatives in 1977 have gone up in smoke. . . . No *major* piece of consumer legislation has been passed since the Magnuson-Moss Act and the Medical Device Act of 1976. . . .* Despite the leadership of consumer grande dame Esther Peterson, all the consumer organizations could not muster forces to overcome major opposition by business and many Congressional leaders.

But a new picture, obtained from a Conference Board survey of nearly 100 consumer affairs and customer relations executives and interviews with the directors of a number of consumer advocate organiza-

---

* The Magnuson-Moss Act, 1975, mandates the standards and performance of consumer warranties; the Medical Device Act regulates the testing and marketing of such equipment.

Reprinted, with deletions, from *Across the Board,* January 1980, pp. 57–62, by permission of the publisher, the Conference Board.

tions, indicates that the movement remains remarkably healthy—and influential. Consumerism, in fact, is here to stay.

How, then, have so many senior managements come to misjudge the situation? Consumer affairs managers believe it is because some business executives, despite all that has been written to the contrary, still view consumerism primarily as the expression of what is wanted by advocates—not by consumers as a class—and that these wants are translated into new legislation and regulations. Thus, in their minds, the legislative scorecard became all-important in assessing the strength of the movement. When the score declined—i.e., fewer laws, more emphasis on deregulation—they assumed that consumerism had spent its momentum.

Such a misperception bemuses some consumer affairs specialists. Mary Gardiner Jones—formerly an FTC commissioner, now a vice president of Western Union—says, "Some businessmen have never understood consumerism—perhaps never will. They just can't seem to grasp the breadth of the movement." Consumer affairs executives, however, know the truth of the situation.

These executives are confronted by an increasing number of customer complaints. Their legal departments, they report, are "inundated with lawsuits" by consumer plaintiffs. According to the results of the Board's survey, consumer affairs executives, by two to one, believe that consumer advocates are having an increasing impact on the public and government. And several major companies report that the number of customer complaints has jumped by more than 50 percent during the past two years.

Moreover, the number of Americans complaining to regulatory agencies has increased—in some cases, dramatically—over the past two or three years. Complaints to the Comptroller of the Currency about banking policies and practices have doubled in three years. Calls on the Consumer Product Safety Commission's hotline—a direct line for reporting or inquiring about unsafe products—have doubled in the last year. And the consumer complaint rate—complaints per population—has climbed notably at the Food and Drug Administration, Civil Aeronautics Board, Federal Trade Commission and other agencies.

Consumer advocates, because they are often among the first recipients of consumer complaints, are well aware that the tide of consumer dissatisfaction is still rising. But who are the consumer advocates, and what do they want?

Organizations include a dozen or more umbrella-type groups—such as Ralph Nader's Public Citizen, The Consumer Federation of America, The Conference of Consumer Organizations, The National Consumer League—that tend to deal with a broad range of consumer issues, from financial services to truth in advertising. To a great extent, there is general agreement among these groups on various issues. On the other hand, there are many consumer groups that focus narrowly on specific issues, and their impact on business can be quite substantial.

GASP (Group Against Smoking and Pollution), for example, is concerned almost exclusively with smoking pollution and its reputed harm for nonsmokers. But this focus certainly affects many sectors of the economy other than cigarette manufacturers, particularly when government agencies decree that separate facilities must be provided for nonsmokers in planes, restaurants, trains. ACT (Action for Children's Television) concerns itself with advertisements aimed at young television watchers. But their efforts also reach the manufacturers of the products being advertised. And the impact on these companies may be more serious than that of some of the broader range advocacy organizations.

Consumer affairs executives like to stay in touch with those groups that have an influence on their companies' businesses, and about half of those surveyed say they make regular contact with them. Identifying consumer advocate organizations, however, isn't always easy. And simply concentrating on the "traditional" advocates won't fill the corporation's needs, since there is increasing evidence that organizations previously not thought of as "consumer advocates" are very much in the forefront of consumer issues.

Consider the American Association of Retired Persons (AARP), a group whose membership totals more than 12 million Americans over the age of 65. The AARP took on the issue of generic versus trade-name drug prescriptions. Although the over-65 members of our population account for only 11 percent of the total population, they purchase 25 percent of all the prescription drugs sold—more than $2 billion worth each year. By not having the option of substituting generic drugs for brand-name ones, they were paying more than they would have, had they been able to buy generic drugs. Unable to effect a change at the national level, AARP lobbyists adopted a grass-roots strategy and took their case to the state legislators.

The result? Since 1970 more than 40 states have adopted laws allowing—and in some states requiring—pharmacists to substitute generic drugs for brand names. Some companies, with a large investment in brand-name drugs, have fought an unsuccessful guerrilla war against AARP lobbyists. In terms of media visibility AARP may not rank with some of the Nader organizations, but it certainly has clout—ask the drug companies.

Also getting into the act are various health organizations—e.g., the American Heart Association, the Lung Association and the like. They may support the regulation—or even the abolition—of specific products or services, or urge government intervention on behalf of consumers in the sale and distribution of certain goods (such as artificial sweeteners).

And any attempt to identify the most influential consumer advocates must take into account certain government officials who perform advocacy functions. In the insurance sector, for example, Herbert Denenberg, former insurance commissioner for the state of Pennsylvania, is regarded as a pioneer in exposing insurance abuses and in drafting remedial action.

Or take California Gov. Jerry Brown, who joined such notables as Ralph Nader, Jane Fonda, Gray Panther founder Maggie Kuhn, and Dr. Benjamin Spock this past May in Washington, D. C., to participate in the antinuclear rally. The rally brought together an unlikely alliance of such groups as the Communist Party, the International Association of Machinists, the Union of Concerned Scientists, the Clamshell Alliance, the Gay Liberation Movement—if only momentarily—to protest nuclear power.

Jane Fonda and her husband, Tom Hayden, are in the forefront of the protest against nuclear power, and, in addition, advocate "consumer control of the massive corporations." Hayden, who helped found Students for a Democratic Society in the Sixties, heads a movement he calls the Campaign for Economic Democracy.

. . .

. . . Many of the consumer advocates have become as disillusioned with government regulation as the business community has been. The picture that emerges from interviews with the advocates is that too many of the regulations are vague, unequally applied, arbitrary—even counterproductive. As a whole, they are *not* in favor of fueling the regulatory engine; some, in fact, believe that the nation has all the laws it needs to protect the health and safety of its citizens. It's not additional laws we need, these advocates say, but effective enforcement of existing laws.

"Laws work best only when people believe they will be enforced, and when the price of transgression is greater than the benefits obtained by violating the law." says one advocate. "But the problem is that when industry starts to disregard some of the most inane regulations, it is likely to be tempted to expand its disobedience into other areas, into laws and regulations that do directly affect consumers' health and safety."

But if regulations alone can't do the job, what other strategies are consumerists likely to espouse? The advocates interviewed favor a number of approaches.

Ralph Nader, who has had more than a few opportunities to observe "Federal policemen" in action (agencies such as the Consumer Product Safety Commission and the National Highway Traffic and Safety Administration), judges the regulators to be, often, more intractable foes than the companies he opposes. While it may come as a surprise to some of his adversaries, Nader continues to have considerable faith in a free (and responsible) enterprise system. It is his belief that a more rigorous enforcement of statutes that foster competition, such as antitrust laws, would go a long way toward correcting abuses that result from "product oligopolies"—dominance by a few suppliers.

Nader also subscribes to the theory that civil litigation—particularly the class action suit—is a powerful deterrent to corporate transgressions. Abuses of individual consumers, he points out, often amount to only a few dollars per customer. But millions of customers may be involved. He would like to see the rules of procedure changed to make it easier for class action suits to be filed in the Federal courts on behalf of consumers. And he would oppose significant alterations in tort liability statutes—such as a statute of limitations on claims or the use of state-of-the-art defenses—that would result in reducing the consumer's access to product liability litigation.

Arlie W. Schardt, former executive director of the Environmental Defense Fund, agrees with Nader that the best way to get something done is through litigation. The targets of the Fund's suits, however, are the regulatory agencies themselves. The Fund has been involved as a plaintiff in cases ranging from porpoise protection to Federal coal leasing—in suits aimed at getting Federal agencies to do what the law already empowers them to do. And the advocates point out that in some instances the agencies may actually welcome such suits. For a variety of reasons (including political considerations), regulators may be hesitant to enforce the letter of the law. But if an agency is sued and loses a court decision, it can evade the (political) responsibility of its activities by pointing out that their actions have been court-mandated.

. . .

Recently the president of an appliance manufacturer, vexed by attacks upon his company by consumerists, asked his consumer affairs director: "What conceivable good do they [the advocates] do? Wouldn't we have done many of the things that the advocates want, even if they weren't looking over our shoulders?" The answer, sadly, is no.

Most corporate consumer affairs specialists acknowledge that businesses would seldom have moved as fast—or as far—in improving their products. Several of the consumer affairs executives say that consumerism can produce significant dividends for the company that "works with it instead of against it." (Most agreed with this position, by more than 20 to 1.) The corporate specialists credit the advocates for helping in three prime areas:

1. Promoting improvements in product and service quality.
2. Helping to sensitize managements to the importance of consumer concerns.
3. Delineating the positions of consumers on various product, service, and economic issues.

Ned Smith, owner-relations manager at Ford Motor Company, while concerned with the inflationary impact that product regulations have had, says: "Their [the advocates] watchdog role, while sometimes painful, has resulted in measurable [product] improvement." And his counterpart at General Motors, customer-relations manager Glen Warren, agrees: "Consumer advocates have caused all manufacturers to do certain things that competitive pricing considerations would have otherwise precluded."

A recently published report from the Committee for Economic Development ("Redefining Government's Role in the Market System," a statement by the Research and Policy Committee, July 1979) points out that "although there is currently no accurate estimate of the overall cost of regulation, evidence about the cost of specific regulations shows that they are substantial." One of the conclusions drawn in the report—a conclusion that many senior managements would support—is that some of the goals sought by the government have "imposed enormous costs on the market system. Some of these costs have been borne by consumers and workers. The pursuit of unrealistic mandatory standards has therefore raised costs of production, reduced productivity, and contributed to inflation."

A majority of the consumer affairs executives surveyed believe that the actions of advocates have helped to make products safer and easier to use. "They have made us more critical of ourselves, of the products we make, of the services we provide," one appliance industry executive says. The advocates are seen as providing one very valuable contribution: a viewpoint not available from inside the corporation. "As hard as we try to market 'perfect' products," says Nell W. Stewart, director of customer relations at Texize, "we cannot always determine all of the possible effects of them in day-to-day use."

Perhaps one of the most significant areas of service improvement, according to the service executives, is in complaint handling. "Consumer advocates don't solve complaints," points out R. H. Janssen, director of consumer affairs for Culligan USA, "but they do force companies to take measures to solve individual problems."

. . .

From the standpoint of both strategy and policy, companies may have more difficulty dealing with a grass-roots consumer movement than with one whose primary focal point is Washington, D.C. In fact, many of the companies surveyed say that local consumer advocate groups are often more important to them than some of the national organizations. Several of those questioned say that although their companies are national in scope, they now have to devote a major part of their resources to "fighting a brush fire in one state or region, rather than dealing with issues of national import."

This development, executives say, has significant implications for staffing the consumer affairs function, as well as for developing corporate responses to consumer issues. Companies may be more adept at responding to national issues than they are at coping with local ones, but the local issues can be just as influential on a firm's operations as the national ones. For example, companies that have committed substantial resources to the planning and development of production facilities at various sites around the country only to encounter stubborn local opposition to these plants—from local environmentalists, public interest groups, and so on—can testify to the importance of learning to deal with local issues.

Many professionals in the consumer movement, including the corporate consumer affairs managers, the advocates, and the regulatory agency staff members, expect that the movement will gain further strength in the early 1980s. There are certain issues that a majority of those surveyed expect to be of primary concern in the years immediately ahead:

Public participation and intervention in regulatory decision-making, including public funding for such participation.

Renewed pressure for the establishment of a Federal agency for consumer advocacy.

Standards for complaint processing and settlement, including mandatory use of third-party arbitration.

Measures to protect consumers against economic abuses such as utility cutoffs, invasion of privacy, credit discrimination, unfair debt collection, the continuing issue of unsafe products.

More precise definition of the rights of consumers to sue for damages, with particular emphasis on easing the entry barriers to Federal class action suits.

Deregulation of the trucking, communication, and insurance industries—and extension of the successful deregulation efforts of the Civil Aeronautics Board.

Reform of antitrust statutes to allow consumers to recover damages from antitrust violations, and new legislation to inhibit conglomerate mergers.

Most of these issues can only be resolved at the Federal level. But some can be realized by state or county governments. First priority will be given to those issues that will effect cost reductions (i.e., tax savings), and it will come as no surprise to find that consumerists and business are once again at odds. But consumer advocates are beginning to realize that business is not a monolith—that it is often possible to find allies within the business community.

As for companies, some have already perceived trends in the consumer movement and are moving in the same direction. Dwight Johnson, corporate consumer affairs specialist for American Telephone and Telegraph, says: "Companies are going to have to decentralize their consumer relations efforts. They're going to be even more dependent on consumer-conscious local managements. At AT&T we're trying to develop that kind of consciousness—and responsibility—at all levels of our company."

What happens to consumerism in a recession; is it put on hold? Looking back at previous recessions, one finds indications that consumer disaffection rises as economic activity falls. That makes sense. When people have less money to spend, their expectations about products and the services they do purchase tend to rise. But reality falls short of expectations—as it inevitably must. "We're hip deep in complaints right now," one appliance company executive said, "but the really high water is yet to come."

C *Disadvantaged Consumers*

8 THE DIFFERING NATURE OF CONSUMERISM IN THE GHETTO

Alan R. Andreasen

Two generally accepted propositions about the consumerism movement in the United States in the mid-1970s are:

1. The consumerism movement is now in a stage of consolidation in numbers of supporters, media coverage, academic interest and, most importantly, political influence;
2. Among those whom the movement ought to benefit, residents of our urban ghettos—the poor, the elderly, and the racial and ethnic minorities—are presently our most seriously disadvantaged consumers.

Three corollaries would seem to follow from these propositions: (1) inner-city consumers ought to be active supporters of the consumerism movement; (2) organizations in the movement ought to be devoting a considerable proportion of their efforts to alleviating the problems of inner city consumers; and (3) we ought by now to be seeing some tangible improvements in the lot of inner-city consumers. My own experience in the field suggests that none of these corollary propositions is substantially true at the present time.

Three principal theses are offered in this paper to explain this dilemma. First it is asserted that consumerism is essentially a white, middle-class movement. Second it is argued that the consumer problems of the disadvantaged are *qualitatively* not just quantitatively different from

---

Alan Andreasen, "The Differing Nature of Consumerism in the Ghetto," *Journal of Consumer Affairs* (Winter 1976), pp. 179–190. Reprinted by permission of the American Council on Consumer Interests.

those of the white middle class. Finally it is concluded that these differences make it very likely that, without what are literally extraordinary efforts, the consumerism movement is destined to have relatively limited impact on the consumer problems of the disadvantaged over the near, and perhaps long, term.

THE CONSUMER MOVEMENT AS WHITE AND MIDDLE CLASS

Elizabeth Drew, among others, has argued that consumerists such as Ralph Nader are "leading essentially white middle class movements."[1] This is a proposition, I assume, few would debate. Indeed, it is a problem well recognized by the movement. In its 1973 policy resolutions the Consumer Federation of America recognized its current lack of impact on these problems:

> We urge all consumer groups to solicit membership among the poor and to develop programs to alleviate their problems. . . . We further urge that low income consumers be involved in CFA efforts to expand consumer organizations and that special funds be made available by CFA affiliates . . . *to organize low income consumers.* (emphasis added)[2]

More relevant to the present paper is the argument that it is precisely in the interest of disadvantaged consumers that the consumer movement be dominated by the white middle class. Again, to quote Elizabeth Drew:

> It is a simple historical fact about the way America works that until the middle class is organized around a significant social change, it doesn't happen. Take any of the important movements of the last decade. . . . I don't recall our political leaders talking about the problem until it moved out of the ghetto and into the suburbs.[3]

This relocation of the problem will of course be beneficial to the disadvantaged if either:

1. Middle class problems are essentially the same as those of the disadvantaged—that is, if the latter are only different in degree; or
2. If middle class problems are *different,* middle class consumers recognize these differences, understand them thoroughly, and can have major impact upon them.

---

[1] Elizabeth Drew, Review of *Citizen Nader, The New York Times Book Review,* March 19, 1972, p. 10.

[2] *Policy Resolutions of the Consumer Federation of America,* Washington, D.C., July 21, 1973, p. 8.

[3] Drew, Review of *Citizen Nader,* p. 10.

It will be argued below that the problems of the disadvantaged are in important respects qualitatively different, and while the middle class may think they recognize these differences they do not understand them well and it may be impossible for them to have much direct impact on them anyway.

DIFFERING PROBLEMS OF DISADVANTAGED CONSUMERS

It has been asserted by consumerist writers that the disadvantaged do not behave very rationally in the market place. As Richards concludes: "How do consumer practices of the poor compare with the recommended rules of financial management? On almost every count, we have found that the poor fail to use what many would call the rational solution."[4] Yet it can be shown that much of what Richards considers irrational may well be rational given the unique barriers disadvantaged consumers face in their own marketplace. As I have outlined elsewhere[5] the sources of their difficulties are threefold:

1. First, there are problems relating to the disadvantaged consumers' own characteristics, age, race, income, and the like, as well as the attitudes and values associated with these characteristics.
2. Then, there are problems related to the market structure in which they generally shop; and
3. Finally, there are problems related to the exploitative practices of merchants in the outlets they patronize.

To understand how these barries operate, we shall explore two types of irrationality specifically mentioned by Richards. First, she points out that the poor too often buy more than they can afford and so undertake too much debt. Second, most of the poor "do not use more deliberation, consult more sources, or shop more widely, to get the best buys."[6] As I have summarized elsewhere, there is considerable, probably conclusive, evidence to support these contentions.[7] Many ghetto consumers do take

---

[4] Louise G. Richards, "Consumer Practices of the Poor," in Lola M. Irelan, Editor, *Low-Income Life Styles,* Washington, D.C., U.S. Department of Health, Education and Welfare, 1966, p. 82.

[5] Alan R. Andreasen, *The Disadvantaged Consumer,* New York, The Free Press, 1975.

[6] Richards, "Consumer Practices of the Poor," p. 82.

[7] Alan R. Andreasen, "Consumerism in the Inner City," paper presented at the Brookings Institution Conference on Consumerism, Rochester, New York, June 10, 1972.

on credit at frightening levels,[8] and they do cast about more narrowly for purchase information.[9] While agreeing to these facts, I specifically do not agree with the implicit charge of irrationality this behavior is supposed to evidence.

Credit Usage

Take for example the use of credit. Perhaps 70 percent of the take-home income of the poor is spent on necessities. Yet we find that they allocate their incomes to discretionary expenditures in about the same proportion as middle income families.[10] This fact, together with the finding that the poor spend more than they take in, suggests that their need for the standard American package of durable goods is only different in degree from that of middle class consumers. Given these needs and their low incomes, it is inevitable that the poor have low or negative savings and high installment debt.

One may ask then: why do the poor not further scale down their discretionary needs? One possible answer lies in the fact that the incomes of the poor and especially those who are poor and black are not only low but also highly unstable. In 1970 only about one in five poor families had full time jobs fifty or more weeks compared with about two in three non-poor families, with poor blacks having more unstable incomes than poor whites.[11] Thus while typical white middle class families only rarely are seriously concerned about whether their incomes will continue at least somewhere near their present level, this is a very serious and constant fear for inner city families. For such consumers a critical piece of information for following "the recommended rules of financial management" is missing. How then might the disadvantaged cope with this uncertainty?

Undoubtedly the psychological and behavioral response to this greater uncertainty varies across ghetto consumers. Some may adopt a highly conservative minimax strategy, minimizing the maximum calamity that could befall them in the event of a substantial decline in income by spending only cash, buying only the barest essentials, engaging in considerable home production of food and clothing, and thus saving modest amounts for future emergencies. This strategy would undoubtedly seem to most middle class consumers to be highly rational. It is one

---

[8] George Katona *et al, 1969 Survey of Consumer Finances,* Ann Arbor, Survey Research Center, University of Michigan, 1970, p. 25.

[9] David Caplovitz, *The Poor Pay More,* New York, The Free Press, 1963.

[10] Andreasen, *The Disadvantaged Consumer, pp. 32–37.*

[11] *Ibid.*

of several highly plausible explanations of empirical findings of why blacks dissave less than whites at low income levels.[12]

An alternative strategy given high uncertainty about future incomes would be a maximax strategy that takes the course of action that would yield the best outcome if the most favorable future circumstances prevailed. It is entirely possible that many of the poor may see the undertaking of debt as a commitment of hope. As Irelan and Besner put it in another context: "A lower-class youngster has more urgent, material reasons for wanting an improved future. His present is painfully unsatisfactory. His urge toward better, stabler occupations is not so much drive for achievement as flight from discomfort and deprivation."[13]

The final, and probably most common, alternative is a strategy of maximizing expected value. This requires that the household assume neither the best nor the worst future but estimate realistically the likelihood of each possibility and choose the course of action that would lead to the maximum weighted average outcome given all possible circumstances. This strategy could lead to high debt accumulation under several conditions:

1. Some poor blacks, those whom Bauer and his colleagues characterize as strivers,[14] may believe that the odds of a substantial increase in income are very high.
2. Others who are temporarily well off may, given what Martineau sees as their short time horizon, see this as permanent.[15]
3. Others among non-strivers may perceive the costs of being wrong (that is, of not securing a substantial increase in income to pay for the debts) as being relatively minor. This could occur for two reasons:
   a. Because of limited education and market sophistication they may actually know less about the likely consequences of default, effects on credit ratings, effects on future employment prospects, court costs and the like.
   b. Although knowing the nature of the consequences, they may estimate the potential dollar losses to be small, arguing that they will have few possessions to repossess or wages to gar-

---

[12] Marjorie Galenson, "Do Blacks Save More?" *American Economic Review,* Vol. 62, March 1972, pp. 211–16.

[13] Lola M. Irelan and Arthur Besner, "Low Income Outlook on Life," in Lola M. Irelan, Editor, *Low Income Life Styles,* Washington, D.C., U.S. Department of Health, Education and Welfare, 1966, p. 5.

[14] Raymond A. Bauer and Scott Cunningham, *Studies in the Negro Market,* Boston, Marketing Science Institute, 1971.

[15] Pierre Martineau, "Social Classes and Spending Behavior," *Journal of Marketing,* Vol. 23, October 1958, pp. 121–30.

nishee and, if worse comes to worse, they have no good jobs or careers keeping them from skipping out on their debts.

To summarize, while the absence of critical information on future disposable income undoubtedly leads some ghetto consumers to adopt a minimax strategy which would seem perfectly sensible to middle class families, it also leads others for various reasons *that are sensible to them* to adopt strategies that do not conform to what Richard calls "common-sense rules of financial management." To the extent that others in the consumer movement share Richards' perspectives this suggests a serious misunderstanding of the motives and goals of ghetto consumers, a problem of intellect and empathy that may explain some of the movement's lack of impact in the area.

"Irrationality" in Shopping Behavior

As Richards suggests, the disadvantaged shop less widely for bargains. Studies by Bauer and Cunningham[16] and Feldman and Star[17] have found that blacks do indeed mention low price as their major shopping goal more often than do whites even with income controlled. Yet a number of studies have shown that blacks are less likely to read newspaper ads or to shop widely for product alternatives, strategies which a majority of shoppers use to minimize price. Again, are there plausible, rational explanations for this behavior?

The less frequent use of newspaper ads parallels findings by Bauer and Cunningham,[18] Oladipupo[19] and others that blacks in general are less often readers of newspapers and magazines but more avid viewers of television and listeners to radio. In part, this is because newspapers are of limited interest as sources of general news because of their scant coverage of activities in the black community. Two possible further explanations for limited use of newspaper ads are:

1. For reasons we shall note below many black consumers carry out most of their convenience shopping and much of their nonconvenience shopping in their neighborhood market where large city-

[16] Bauer and Cunningham, *Studies in the Negro Market.*

[17] Laurence P. Feldman and Alvin D. Star, "Racial Factors in Shopping Behavior," in Keith Cox and Ben M. Enis, Editors, *A New Measure of Responsibility for Marketing,* Proceedings of the American Marketing Association National Conference, June 1966, pp. 215–226.

[18] Bauer and Cunningham, *Studies in the Negro Market.*

[19] Raymond O. Oladipupo, "How Distinct Is the Negro Market?" New York, Ogilvy and Mather, Inc., 1970.

wide outlets (for example, supermarket and discount chains and department stores) which are heavy newspaper advertisers are less frequently found or entirely absent;

2. For many black consumers, when shopping for durable goods the critical piece of information needed is the cost and availability of credit, data which are typically not available in newspaper advertisements.

Restricted Shopping Scope

The principal explanations for the findings of Caplovitz[20] and others that blacks have more restricted shopping scope are that ghetto blacks have neither the opportunity nor the motivation to shop extensively for needed goods and services and in many cases have positive motivations for shopping locally.

Opportunity for Extensive Personal Shopping

Opportunity for personal shopping is a function of available time, access to transportation, and/or access to a range of alternative outlets within a reasonable travel radius. Available shopping time for ghetto consumers is restricted by several sociological factors:

1. Larger family size puts more time burdens on the adults in ghetto families.
2. In the broken homes that occur more frequently among black families there are simply fewer adults to meet these burdens.
3. Often all adult heads are working, meaning fewer hours for family responsibilities including shopping.

Compounding the problem of time scarcity is the fact that fewer blacks have automobiles which means that they must take more time simply to get to a given number of outlets. This problem is in turn aggravated by the fact that the major alternative to private automobiles, public transportation, in almost all urban areas is designed primarily to bring people into the center city for employment, entertainment and shopping and not to take ghetto consumers to outlying shopping areas.[21] As a consequence downtown shopping centers are rapidly becoming the shopping plazas of the poor.

---

[20] Caplovitz, *The Poor Pay More.*

[21] C. B. Notess and R. E. Paaswell, *The Mobility of Inner City Residents,* Department of Civil engineering, State University of New York at Buffalo, July 1969.

Motivation for Extensive Personal Shopping

Obviously one of the strongest disincentives for blacks to shop outside the ghetto is the problem of racial discrimination. In the late 1950's Martineau first identified the fact that blacks were very sensitive to their treatment as individuals in stores.[22] A more recent study by Campbell and Schuman in fifteen northern U.S. cities found that about one in three blacks felt that black customers were being treated less politely than white customers in downtown stores, a perception much more frequently found among younger blacks.[23]

A second factor inhibiting black motivation to shop outside the inner city may be a belief that assortments in some categories (for example, clothes, foods) or services (for example, beauty, barber shops) may not be appropriate to their preferences. The existence of differences between blacks and whites in consumption expenditures and brand preferences is well attested to in the work of Alexis,[24] Gibson,[25] Sawyer,[26] Larson,[27] and others, although the effect of these differences on store preferences is at present unknown.

The third additional inhibiting factor is the earlier mentioned need for credit. Blacks with large families and unstable incomes need access to credit even for food. Many such families undoubtedly believe that the probability of getting credit outside their area is low enough to make comparative shopping trips to the suburbs not worth the effort in time and expense.

In addition to these disincentives to shop outside the inner city there are other traditional motivations to stay within the area, particularly the time and place conveniences available there and the opportunity to use delivery services. These conveniences are especially important to ghetto consumers since:

---

[22] Pierre Martineau, "The Personality of the Retail Store," *Harvard Business Review,* Vol. 36, January–February 1958, pp. 47–55.

[23] Angus Campbell and Howard Schuman, *Racial Attitudes in Fifteen American Cities,* Ann Arbor, Institute for Social Research, University of Michigan, 1968.

[24] Marcus Alexis, "Some Negro-White Differences in Consumption," *American Journal of Economics and Sociology,* Vol. 21, January 1962, pp. 11–28.

[25] D. Parke Gibson, *The $30 Billion Negro,* New York, The Macmillan Company, 1969.

[26] Broadus E. Sawyer, "An Examination of Race as a Factor in Negro-White Consumption Patterns," *The Review of Economics and Statistics,* Vol. 44, May 1962, pp. 217–220.

[27] Carl M. Larson, "Racial Brand Usage and Media Exposure Differentials," in Keith Cox and Ben M. Enis, Editors, *A New Measure of Responsibility for Marketing,* Proceedings of the American Marketing Association National Conference, June 1966, pp. 208–215.

1. With lower incomes often paid on a weekly or daily basis they must shop more frequently, which would greatly increase the transportation cost per item purchased if they regularly left the area.
2. With all adults working and with large family responsibilities children more often do much of the shopping. Safety considerations prompt patronage of nearby outlets.

There are, finally, two other motivations that encourage important segments of the minority community to shop locally:

1. For many low income householders living impoverished lives in deteriorated and crowded housing and lacking the income and transportation for many diversions away from home (and barred by discrimination from many others), the opportunity to escape briefly each few days for a shopping excursion may make the experience a major social occasion, a time for seeing new things, talking with friends, socializing with storekeepers and the like.
2. While most blacks would argue that price and quality are more important than race of store ownership in store and product selections, Gensch and Staelin's research in Pittsburgh found that a substantial minority of blacks, particularly the younger blacks, considered black ownership an important secondary consideration in choosing where to shop.[28]

SUMMARY

There are differences between ghetto and non-ghetto consumers which lead them to behaviors that many middle class consumerists consider irrational. Yet we have shown that this may very well be far from a fair conclusion. There are in fact other seemingly irrational acts of poor blacks—for example their less frequent use of formal consumer redress systems despite being more often deceived and defrauded—that also can be explained by looking at the unique characteristics of disadvantaged consumers.

This analysis permits the formulation of two major theses. First, although many of the barriers faced by ghetto blacks are only quantitatively different from those faced by middle class white consumers, a great many of those barriers are in fact *qualitatively* different. I have proposed elsewhere that the most significant of these qualitative differences

---

[28] Dennis H. Gensch and Richard Staelin, "The Appeal of Buying Black," *Journal of Marketing Research,* Vol. 9, May 1972, pp. 141–148.

are their place of residence, their color, and the stability of their incomes.[29] Place of residence subjects ghetto consumers to an undercapitalized, fractionated, poorly managed, high cost market structure and a set of exploitative merchant practices that are major barriers to effective consumption. Color is a direct source of disadvantage because it acts as a signal to merchants that blacks are consumers who:

1. *can* be charged higher prices because they have less physical and psychological mobility;
2. *ought* to be charged higher prices when they buy on credit because "their kind" are bad risks; and
3. *can* be deceived because they are typically "unsophisticated" and, even when they are not, they have little power or motivation to secure legal redress.

Finally, unstable incomes make it infinitely more difficult for ghetto consumers to plan purchases carefully. This difficulty leads many consumers to a strategy of incurring heavy consumer debt which may seem irrational to many non-poor consumers.

These socioeconomic characteristics in turn lead to attitudes and values that further inhibit effective consumption. Many ghetto blacks with low and unstable incomes have a fear of being discriminated against which discourages shopping excursions to lower priced outlets beyond their area. Further as merchants have often sensed, ghetto blacks often have a sense of powerlessness and persecution which discourages price comparison and legal pursuit of deceptive sellers.

More fundamentally the analysis has suggested the possibility that shopping itself may perform a different role for ghetto consumers than for white middle class families. For many ghetto consumers shopping constitutes a social event making important contributions to their well-being and self-definition. In addition for many patronage of black outlets is a means for asserting ethnic identity and participating in community-building in a small but presumably personally satisfying way.

IMPLICATIONS FOR THE CONSUMER MOVEMENT

The second principal thesis developed in the previous section is that those who see the behavior of ghetto consumers as irrational may not understand their unique circumstances and problems very well. This then

[29] Andreasen, "Consumerism in the Inner City."

raises questions about the relevance of a middle class consumer movement to ghetto consumer problems. One must ask:

1. whether white middle class consumer activists can truly understand and empathize with inner city consumers' needs and world view sufficiently well to be able to develop really effective programs to help them;
2. whether, if middle class consumers cannot develop programs for them, ghetto consumers will feel enough empathy for their problems within the consumer movement to want to join and work closely with existing activists to mutually develop and implement needed solutions; and
3. whether, even if they sense such empathy, the most disadvantaged blacks with their sense of powerlessness and discrimination will believe that the consumer movement is nothing more than another white ego trip or imaginative new plan to "rip off" more of the wealth of the black community.

Further, there is a question of whether an attack on more narrowly defined consumer issues is really relevant to what we have seen are ghetto consumers' major sources of difficulty. The fact that blacks live in ghettos, are indeed black, and/or have unstable incomes clearly suggests that programs that would have *most* impact on their problems would be those designed to (1) promote residential desegregation; (2) reduce racial prejudice among the white middle class (particularly those in retailing); and (3) improve job opportunities and increase income stability among black heads of household.

Clearly such goals are well outside the main thrust of the consumer movement. One might argue, however, that these are general societal problems and at best are solvable only in the very long run. If then not much can be done in the short run to get these consumers out of the ghetto marketplace, one must either make them better able to cope with it as it exists or change the marketplace. Remedies directed at the former usually involve consumer education, and the problems of empathy already mentioned militate strongly against the success of middle class efforts there. With respect to improving the marketplace, stronger efforts could be made by middle class consumerists to try to stop exploitation through more market regulation and better enforcement. However, the localized nature of these problems and the slipperiness of the transgressors makes prospects again unpromising.[30] And even if some effect were achieved,

[30] Recent changes in the Federal Trade Commission's mandate permit it to intervene in local business. However, the Commission's resource constraints and present philosophy are likely to preclude active movement in this direction.

blacks pay more *more often* because of the undercapitalized, fractionalized, badly managed retail system which they must patronize in ghetto markets.

It is my own judgment that improving these markets is probably the best way to bring short run relief to ghetto consumers. It will not only help bring prices down but through the force of increased competition also will have major impact on the practices of exploitative merchants. Again however solutions in this domain are outside the traditional thrust of the consumer movement.

Given these difficulties, how should the movement proceed? I have outlined elsewhere one specific approach, that of trying to develop an indigenous black consumer movement by linking it with black economic development efforts.[31] Beyond that, it may perhaps be the most useful advice to suggest that the consumer movement reconcile itself to a low-impact role in ghetto areas, that it consider lending its weight to the long-term solutions discussed above, that it encourage blacks to organize their own consumer movement, and finally that until they understand more fully the qualitative differences suggested here middle class consumerists recognize that white involvement in ghetto consumer problems may make the situation *worse* not better.

A. HISTORICAL PERSPECTIVES

1. For each of the three consumer movements identify the causes or problems upon which they were based. Distinguish among fundamental concerns, symptoms of these concerns, and catalysts of the movement. Which causes were common to all and which were unique? Project these causal variables into the future. What can you predict about the future of the current consumer movement?
2. Show how the rights of consumers have evolved. Project this trend. What will consumer rights be in 1990?
3. How would you define consumerism? How does your definition differ from the one that Nader attributed to business spokesman?
4. In 1968, Nader proposed that the casualty insurance industry try to pressure the automobile industry into developing safer cars. Is this a realistic proposal in today's environment? How could the insurance industry apply pressure? At the same time, Nader argued that professional societies should take an active role in consumer protection. Do you agree? How should these societies proceed?

[31] Andreasen, "Consumerism in the Inner City."

B. CURRENT PERSPECTIVES

5. In the mid-seventies, Margolius identified six real needs of the consumer. If he were to write a similar article today, would the real needs be the same? Are there any important needs he overlooked? Were his recommendations for dealing with these needs appropriate? What else could be done in each of the six problem areas?
6. How would you define the consumer interest? Compare and contrast pluralist theory with economic models of politics. Which, in your opinion, explains the consumer movement? Who represents the consumer? Is consumer representation adequate? What might be done to enhance it?
7. Use Greyser's self-administered test to determine your model of the marketplace. Identify some conflicts that you have in roles as consumer and citizen.
8. Some observers of international trends in consumerism have argued that events in Sweden are often a precursor of similar activity in North America. Is this a reasonable approach to forecasting consumerist activity? Have the developments described by Johansson taken place in the United States yet?
9. Do you agree that consumers are usually unable to judge their own best interests? What are the arguments for and against this premise? What are some of its implications?
10. Is the marketing concept an inappropriate or irrelevant guide to marketing practices in an era of pervasive shortages, inflation, environmentalism, economic stagnation, and international trade barriers? Will the revised axioms of marketing proposed by Kotler alleviate the problems? In particular, will they lead to greater recognition of the social consequences of private marketing activity?
11. Comment on the opinion that the consumer should be required to do what is good for him even at the expense of some individual rights. Is paternalism a legitimate policy of business or government? Should all people be required to buy and use seat belts even if they make a reasoned decision that they don't want to?
12. McGuire concludes that unless advocates continually apply pressure, companies will not do the things that consumer advocates want. Why should companies be unresponsive?

C. DISADVANTAGED CONSUMERS

13. Why do disadvantaged consumers buy more than they can afford and why is their shopping scope restricted? How can the consumer movement be more responsive to the disadvantaged consumer?

14. What are the similarities and differences between the ghetto consumer and other disadvantaged consumers such as the aged, the young, and the non-native English speaker?
15. Does the ghetto consumer pay more for food? For durables? Why? What are the basic problems? What are the symptoms or results of these problems?
16. How do the shopping patterns of ghetto consumers differ from those of middle-class consumers? What about their exposure to advertisements? What about the type of goods they buy?

PART III

The Prepurchase Phase: Consumer Information

INTRODUCTION

It has been argued that an informed consumer is a protected consumer. Certainly, providing timely, accurate, and useful consumer information is one way to alleviate or eliminate consumer problems. During the past decade three broad approaches to providing information have been pursued with varying degrees of intensity:

independent consumer information programs
business sponsored consumer information and education programs
information disclosure requirements

Independent consumer information systems are sponsored by organizations that have no direct commercial interest in the involved consumer decisions. The sponsor could be a government agency or an association like **Consumer's** Union. Thorelli, in Chapter 9, discusses the European experience with comparative testing, labeling, and quality certification, three activities performed to aid consumers. In comparative testing, performance tests of competitive products are conducted and the results may or may not be categorized in terms of relative recommendability. Labeling involves a testing organization establishing norms as to the range and depth of information about product characteristics to be declared on a label; manufacturers are permitted to use the labels to rate their brands according to these norms (e.g., colorfastness, wool content). Quality certification indicates that the product carrying the seal of certification meets a minimum standard. Thorelli projects what consumer information systems might look like when they get integrated into computerized cable television systems. In Chapter 10 Dunn and Ray discuss the issues involved in the development of local consumer information services, such as how they might obtain information and how they can become self-supporting.

In Chapter 11 Aaker examines corporate consumer information programs. Why and how should a firm develop such a system? What benefits will result to the firm? What steps are needed to insure that the program will be effective?

Information disclosure requirements proliferated at an amazing rate in the 1970s. The intent of most are to help consumers compare performance and efficiency or to warn consumers about products or product use contexts that are dangerous or unhealthy. In Chapter 12 Day discusses the stream of disclosure requirements and isolates recurring issues and patterns of effects. He indicates how and under what conditions such regulations influence consumer decisions.

The Cunningham and Cunningham selection, Chapter 13, suggests that the public is woefully uninformed as to their rights under current laws designed to safeguard consumers from deceptive trade practices. They conclude that wider dissemination of information about consumers' rights may be more beneficial than proliferation of consumer protection legislation.

Finally, in Chapter 14 Tyebjee examines in detail one area in which a substantial amount of disclosure regulation has occurred, nutritional information. This area is also of interest because it has attracted considerable amount of empirical research on the need for consumer information and the effectiveness of disclosure requirements.

A *Consumer Information Systems*

9 THE FUTURE FOR CONSUMER INFORMATION SYSTEMS

Hans B. Thorelli

Consumer information systems constitute a vital area of consumer policy, private and public. Conceptually, if not always practically, such systems also have a vital role to play in any policy aimed at maintaining and strengthening the open market economy. The mission here is to retain (or create) workable market transparency in an era of increasing product complexity and proliferation and consequent consumer information gap.[1]

Our concern is strategic planning for the consumer information systems of the future. After a brief diagnosis of the present, more attention is given to forecasting and, finally, to programmatics. The latter dicussion is based on a set of values capsuled in the epigraph of the essay. Our time horizon may be anywhere from five years to the end of this century.

---

[1] This paper builds upon the last chapter of Hans B. Thorelli and Sarah V. Thorelli, *Consumer Information Systems and Consumer Policy* (Cambridge Mass.: Ballinger, 1977), the last volume in a trilogy also comprising Hans B. Thorelli, Helmut Becker and Jack Engledow, *The Information Seekers—An International Study of Consumer Information and Advertising Image* (Cambridge, Mass.: Ballinger, 1975) and Hans B. Thorelli and Sarah V. Thorelli, *Consumer Information Handbook: Europe and North America* (New York: Praeger, 1974). For a detailed analysis of the existing consumer information gap, see Ch. 1 of the first mentioned work.

From Jerry C. Olson (ed.), *Advances in Consumer Research 7* (Ann Arbor, Mich.: Association for Consumer Research, 1980), pp. 227–232. Reprinted with permission.

THE PRESENT CONSUMER INFORMATION SYSTEM: A BRIEF DIAGNOSIS

All the sources of information about market offerings available to consumers, as well as the actual flows of such information, constitute the elements of what we shall call the consumer information system (CIS). Sources are generally divided into *commercial, personal,* and *independent.* Of the many commercial sources (including owner's manuals, warranties, fairs, demonstrations, etc.) advertising is by far the most important. Although many would say that the subjective (persuasive) component of advertising is too prominent, it is nevertheless probably true that due to its enormous volume advertising constitutes by far the most important single source of objective information about products. Nevertheless, research has demonstrated that advertising falls far short of satisfying those savvy consumers in Western industrial democracies whom we have identified as the Information Seekers (IS) (Thorelli, Becker, Engledow 1975). We also know that consumers in most of these countries consider misleading advertising as the single most objectionable feature of the marketplace.

Personal information sources include our own past experience of market offerings, personal examination of them, and advice by relatives, friends, neighbors and other individual consumers. Independent consumer information programs (hereafter CI programs) is the third major set of product information sources. CI programs have no direct commercial interest in the promotion of the offerings about which they provide consumer information.

CI programs are of course less well known than commercial and personal information sources. Many of these programs are narrow-scope, in that they relate only to a single characteristic (energy consumption, wool contents) or only to a single product or related group of products (life-vest certification, food nutrition labels). The great problem with such programs is that their proliferation tends to add to the "noise" characteristic of Western cultures, thereby tending to enhance rather than to reduce consumer confusion and frustration. Of much greater principal (and, we believe, in the future also practical) interest are multiproduct, multi-characteristics programs. Currently, there are some fifty broad-spectrum CI programs in the twenty-nation North Atlantic community (Thorelli and Thorelli 1974 and 1977). As all such programs are based on the testing of products and services our collective term for them is The Testmakers. Sponsorship of such programs may be quite diverse: consumer groups (Association des Consommateurs in Belgium, Consumers Union in the U.S.), government (Stiftung Warentest in Germany, Institut National de la Consommation in France) or pluralist (DVN—the Danish information labeling institute, Association Française de l'Etiquetage d'Information). At present, comparative testing (CT) programs as run by the four first-named organizations dominate the field, followed by informative labeling (IL) programs as illustrated by DVN and AFEI.

Less attention has been given to quality certification (QC) programs. The pioneering group in this area is Qualité France. AFNOR, the French standards organization, also has a quality marking scheme, with its NF symbol, as does the British Standards Institute with its Kitemark. In its pure form a QC program involves the marking of products with a symbol (such as a star), indicating that products thus marked have been tested and found equal to or better than a certain minimum standard or threshold defined by the certifying organization. Clearly, this represents a stark simplification of information dissemination as compared to CT reports (IL is in a middle position in this regard). Yet there are many indications there is a need for simplified point-of-purchase information.

We note in passing that almost by definition voluntary IL and QC programs require the cooperation of industry for their success. Another passing remark of great practical significance is that CI programs themselves must be given *large-scale* advertising and promotion in order to be successful.

The CIS of any given country, then, consists of a certain "mix" of commercial, personal and independent information sources and flows. It would carry us too far here to inquire into the determinants of the local mix in any given environment. We may merely observe that at the present time there is very little effort made anywhere in the world in the direction of conscious coordination of the elements of the local CIS.

FUTUROLOGY

The view of the future environment relevant to CIS to emerge here is based in part upon analytical material from our own research, in part derived from other sources. In several instances we are projecting and evaluating trends already at work. However, many pieces of the puzzle are necessarily based on mere assumptions, whose credibility must be left to the reader to evaluate. At least we have tried to make them explicit.

. . .

Future of Commercial, Personal, and Independent Information Sources

The current product information system is dominated by sellers. No one could seriously question the legitimacy of advertising and sales promotion in an open market economy. Nor is there much doubt that advertising in various forms will remain the most important single source of product information in such economies. Personal experience—be it our own or that of our friends—seems likely to continue its relative demise, assuming that the pace of change and proliferation will remain brisk. It is important to note, however that rising standards of education will make everyone both more information-conscious and more capable of evaluating data, regardless of source.

The future of CI programs will be bright. Their core audience of Information Seekers will grow. Their natural advantage—saving the consumer time in comparative shopping—will be increasingly important. The need for greater transparency in the marketplace will be recognized in ever wider circles. As average consumers become more information-minded, and as IS become more harried, simplified, point-of-purchase oriented CI programs will be especially vital. If CI programs can be given a local anchorage (see below), they may even supersede commercial and personal information sources as the most important element in the product information system at the community level as regards such vital matters as local prices and availability of offerings, the after-sales service of various dealers, etc.

We think the media will become more interested in product information. There will be market overviews (based on producer specifications) and independent product reviews in the daily press, as we already find them in some hobby magazines. In affluent countries where the daily and/or specialized press fails to seize this kind of opportunity to serve consumers, CI groups will themselves fill the void. *Handyman Which?*, *Holiday Which?* and *Money Which?*, published by Consumers' Association in Britain, and specialty issues produced by several continental CT programs, demonstrate that this is no idle talk.

Technology Assessment; Computerized CI Utility; Localized CI

We need only think of the role of TV advertising in countries in which sellers are free to use this medium to realize that technology impacts the product information system. The makings of a technological revolution in the CI area are already on hand; the problems in harnessing these technical advancements are primarily economic and institutional.

Saving time by buying from the home will be greatly facilitated by such developments as the picture-phone and by two-way cable TV. Sales presentations may also be made on videocassettes, using the TV set as screen. It will soon be economical for individual households to be linked to large central computer facilities by means of input-output terminals attached to their telephone or TV. Most of these developments also provide new opportunities for the consumer to "talk back" to sellers in market surveys, product tests, and satisfaction studies. All of these communications technology has tremendous potential for the creation of new types of CI programs. From a CI point of view, however, even more important is the capability of large computers to store, and instantly retrieve, astronomical quantities of data.

We predict that the next breakthrough in CI programs will be the computerized CT utility. Independently of each other, this grand vision was conceived by Consumers' Association of Canada (CAC) and Sweden's VDN in 1968. Large-scale experimentation is currently going on both in Britain and France.

We confidently foresee a bright future for a properly conceived computerized CI utility as a supplement to existing programs due to some powerful inherent advantages. The greatest of these is the dialog feature, which literally makes possible information—and advice, if so desired—tailored to the personal needs and preferences of the individual consumer. Even the exploratory Consumer Enquirer Program module developed at Indiana University a decade ago (Thorelli and Thorelli 1977, App. F) demonstrates two other important advantages. It incorporates basic consumer education about the exemplary product involved (tape recorders), not merely brand comparisons. The consumer who already has sufficient background knowledge can simply bypass the educational routines. The program also carries data about local availability of various brands of tape recorders and corresponding service facilities in Bloomington, Indiana, thus combining education and product information with highly desirable local data. Pending the everyday availability of home computer terminals and similar communications devices, access to a CI utility might be arranged by calling an intermediary operator at a time-sharing terminal from any telephone.

Obviously there are also certain weaknesses in the idea. At present there is no easy way for the computer to arrange an actual viewing of the product. The logic of computers is also to focus on one characteristic (buying criterion) of the offering after another in staccato fashion, leading the prospect down an orderly decision path. However, in this way the consumer may lose sight of the forest for the trees. Like so many other phenomena, a product has Gestalt, that is, it may appear different when viewed as a whole from the impression gained by examination characteristic by characteristic. Care must also be taken to achieve a distinct separation between factual information and buying recommendations.

One may wonder why we do not already have a computerized CI utility system. There are at least two good reasons. First, no data bank can be any better than the information which is fed into it. Even assuming the willingness of The Testmakers to cooperate, it is a formidable effort to prepare all their information in a format suitable to the computer, not to speak of attendant programming of education and dialog routines for all products involved. It is also a fact that for hundreds of products the requisite data do not yet exist. Here one would have to make do with market overviews based on manufacturer catalogs pending neutral testing data. It will also be a very big—and costly—job to keep the information up to date. There would be some scale economies, in that product information would have national—in some markets international—validity. Yet it is self-evident that to be successful a CI utility system would have to be extensively decentralized, so that in any given community it would include local availability, price, service and perhaps even complaint data.

Second, the economics of this kind of venture is still highly uncertain. The CAC (1966) speaks of a nonprofit, nongovernmental venture (which philosophically has our own preference), while E. Scott Maynes (1975) talks in terms of either user or local government financing. The main point in favor of the latter alternative would be the public-goods (externality) nature of the information provided by the utility.

PROGRAMMATICS

Having thus attempted to forecast the operating environment we turn to the policy conclusions part of our exercise in strategic planning for CI systems.

Attending to the Information Seeker

The Information Seekers identified in our and related research are generalists, i.e., their interest in market information is transferable from one product to another. Indeed, to a fair extent their information-mindedness is independent of any given buying situation. We know that in the open market democracies these IS are the shock troops in the perennial struggle to maintain and increase consumer sovereignty. Being vigilantes of the marketplace the IS will, more than average consumers

personally enforce consumer rights
personally exercise consumer responsibilities
keep suppliers on their toes by pinpointing poor service, deficiencies in products, out-of-stock conditions, misleading advertising and other malpractices

voluntarily financing CI programs
disseminate information and advice to fellow consumers
serve as proxy purchasing agents for many less information-conscious and planful consumers

Everyday observation indicates that there are also *specialty-IS,* that is, average (or even underprivileged) consumers with a strong information-seeking propensity for a single type (or limited range) of product, such as autos, records, or "soul" food. Little research has been done on this group, but there is reason to believe it is quite numerous—possibly several times larger than the generalist-IS category. It is also likely that in the markets of particular interest to them the specialty-IS perform some of the consumerist functions associated with IS in general.

The IS are most effectively assisted in their public functions in the marketplace by greatly enlarged and diversified CI programs of the variation discussed in this paper. But in a democracy everyone must be free to become an Information Seeker. An indispensible part of this upward thrust is a comprehensive set of policies aimed at the emancipation of underprivileged consumers. Average consumers are most readily helped along the way by consumer education and simplied CI programs.

What Business Can Do

The number of transactions between sellers and individual consumers in the affluent democracies of the world may well exceed one billion per day. It appears that in a clear majority of these transactions consumers are at least fairly well satisfied. To say that the open market system is a failure seems to us grossly unfair. Yet we are singling out business, among all consumer-policymaking groups, for separate discussion here as there is so much more that it can do that is yet undone, or done to much less than perfection. Much of this can be accomplished by voluntary action. A further reason for such a discussion is a conviction that individual firms in the future may secure an important differential advantage by adopting superior information as a competitive strategy. Finally, it seems clear that business in general stands to gain by being proactive rather than merely reactive in dealing with the modern consumer, his needs, aspirations and problems.

Business should make *advertising and sales promotion more informative.* An excellent way of making ads and mailorder catalogs more informative is to use material from CI programs to the extent this is permissible (e.g., referring to test reports and reprinting informative labels as done by the German mailorder house Quelle). Let the package inform, not deceive. Facilitate comparability by *sensible* and fair comparative advertising, by unit pricing, by providing an assortment that offers real choice, by participating in fairs, collective displays and multi-brand outlets. Most retailers could vastly improve sales training, to *upgrade clerks into consumer consultants.* Owner's manuals and assembly instructions could be markedly improved. *Warranties* could be made more specific and yet more understandable.

This brings us to some of the things business could do *in cooperation with others, notably consumers.* In the past decade or two of consumerism we have witnessed a kind of "fighting on the barricades" in most affluent countries. We firmly believe the time has now come when both business and consumer groups are ready to sit down for problem-solving of mutual interest, just as management and labor have learned to do after an initial period of mutual suspicion. As part of this process consumer affairs management must be given much more weight in corporate affairs.

Whether in the interest of long-term survival of the open market system, or as a matter of social responsibility, or as an element of a superior competitive information strategy, it behooves business to do what it can to promote voluntary CI programs together with consumers and perhaps other interested parties, such as independent experts and government. The most crying current need among average and underprivileged consumers is simplified point-of-purchase information of the IL and QC varieties. We are firmly recommending *a combined voluntary IL-QC program* open for all consumer products and services. Participating firms (be they producers or distributors) would themselves decide whether they would like the tags attached to their products to carry only the label, only the quality mark, or both. Separate committees—composed on a pluralist basis—should decide on the characteristics and measurements to be declared on the label and on the minimum performance threshold required for the quality mark. Other circumstances equal, consumers will naturally be served best when a seller uses both the label and the seal on his tag (and in his advertising).

A hypothetical example of a combined label and seal is shown in Figure 9-1. The scales used in communicating performance data is in line with Swedish research a decade ago aimed at optimal combination of information and intelligibility. The thickened part of the scale indicates the range of performance of this type of cleaners currently being marketed. The arrow indicates this model. The star (or other simple symbol of a quality seal) should be in a striking color for those interested only in the simplist type of information. Incidentally, there is evidence from the Netherlands that even information-shy consumers may appreciate a double-decker quality seal plan. A green OK star may stand for "suitable for everyday reasonable use", while the gold EXTRA star may stand for extra high quality. Labeling is to be preferred to any additional complication of the quality seal.

FIGURE 9–1. COMBINED INFORMATIVE LABEL (IL) AND QUALITY CERTIFICATION (QC) LOGO

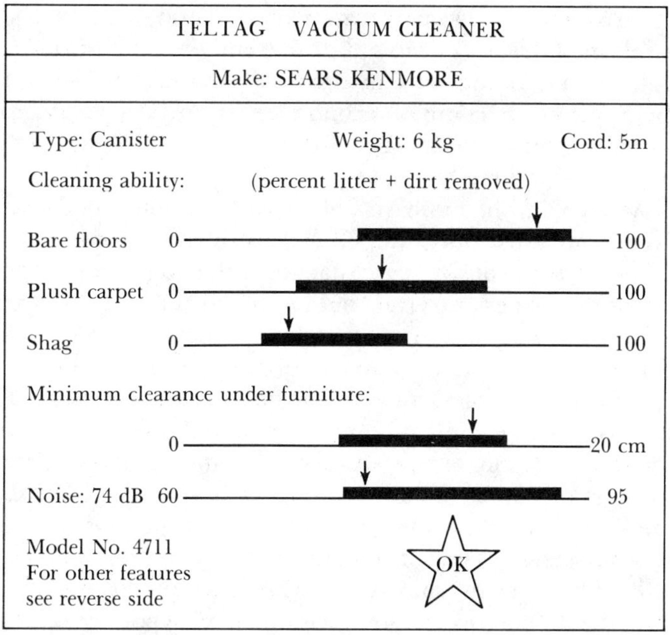

As only a few germane characteristics can find room on a label, and as the label is not to be construed as a damper on innovation, producers should be free to inform consumers about other features of their product on the reverse side of the label. To facilitate comparative shopping at home it is desirable to publish an annual catalog of all labels in force.

Apart from the fact that a common, easily identified type of tag would be used whether a product would be given a label, a mark or both there are three other areas in which major gains will be obtained by a combined IL-QC program. Great common economies may be secured by joint testing, joint performance control, and joint promotion. Testing is an expensive and yet indispensable activity for both IL and QC. Even if most performance control is delegated to producers themselves, any independent CI agency must occasionally conduct performance control audits by repeat testing and/or a review of the quality control procedures at the factory level among participating producers. This is also costly. Promotion of the CI program itself to both consumers and producers requires a great deal of money. Our research indicates that a prime reason for the failure of many IL and QC programs in the past has been insufficient promotional and educational effort. A single promotional program for IL and QC is a major economic advantage.

Industry, consumer groups and independent laboratories should cooperate much more intensively than at present in the development of standard methods for measuring performance (SMMP). This is also an expensive activity. Decentralized experimentation in the development of testing methods is desirable, but presently a great deal of unnecessary duplication is taking place in almost all countries as well as internationally. Some of the common economies for an IL–QC program we have pointed to here would also benefit the proposed CI computer utility, both directly and indirectly.

A payoff from more straightforward product information will be fewer complaints. But better CI will also increase consumer satisfaction. In the long run, consumer satisfaction is the single most important determinant of business survival, both at the firm and at the system level.

Business may elect not to engage in the kinds of CI and consumer policies illustrated here, or do it only in a perfunctory way. If so, we have to put aside our programmatics and go back to prognostics. The scenario then likely will be quite different. It will probably involve obligatory information requirements, counter-information programs, mandated corrective information, an advertising tax to finance government CI programs, etc.—all these measures adopted in an atmosphere of animosity toward business. Some of these things may come anyway, but then likely in less severe form, and with business-proposed amendments incorporated with due respect for a legitimate viewpoint.

Further away on the horizon of that type of scenario are such prospects of questionable merit in an open market system as censorship of new products, mandated economy models, minimum quality standards, and such hamstringing regulations at every step of managerial activity that we shall have to accept zero growth whether we want it or not.

Wanted: Decentralized Pluralist CI Systems

CI Part of Consumer Policy

It is important to view CI as part of overall consumer policy. The numerous trade-off and reenforcement opportunities between education, information and protection should be especially considered. So, it should be emphasized, should the trade-offs and reenforcements between different types of CI programs and different groups of consumer policymakers. Related areas of private and public consumer policy include the following:

consumer education	standardization
advertising	sales training
complaints handling and redress	product safety
antitrust and competition policy	environmental protection

SYSTEMS DEVELOPMENT

The need of viewing CI programs as parts or extensions of consumer policy, marketing communications, education and other social systems has been emphasized. But there is also need to think of all sources of consumer product information existing in a given culture as constituting a CI system (CIS). The opportunities for synergy and reenforcement are great—as are the somewhat opposite needs of independence and experimentation. We are convinced that in a pluralist, decentralized system the benefits of both competition and cooperation can be obtained without incurring an overdose of either.

CONSUMER'S LIBERATION

The rationale of CI programs is simple. It is the liberation of the citizen in his role of consumer. That role is a major one, whatever our interests or stations in life. CI is in and of itself an instrument to enrich the quality of life. It helps us free time and resources for other concerns than purely material ones. It helps us save on material resources for society as a whole. It has virtually nothing to do with inculcating or reenforcing materialism as such.

Incompatible it is with the idea of a free society to prevent anyone from spending his money foolishly, but it is quite within the scope of this ideal to assist people in spending their money less ignorantly. The costs of doing this are miniscule relative to the costs of everyday commercial information.

In the end it may well be that the principal effect of such programs is not the dissemination of information in itself, but rather the renewal of consumer trust in business, of consumer faith in the integrity of products and their makers. Inevitably, CI programs will tend to reward the purveyors of "value for money." Thus they are an instrument of perfecting the open market system. Let it not be forgotten that in a free society the market itself is the greatest comparative testing agency of them all.

REFERENCES

Consumers' Association of Canada (1969), *A Community Information Network* (Mimeographed, Ottawa).

MAYNES, E. SCOTT (1975), "The Local Consumer Information System: An Institution-to-be?" in *Proceedings of the Second Workshop in Consumer Action Research,* April 9-12, 1975, Berlin: Wissenschaftszentrum.

SCHERHORN, GERHARD (1973), *Gusucht: Der Mündige Verbraucher,* Düsseldorf: Droste.

THORELLI, HANS B., BECKER, HELMUT, AND ENGLEDOW, JACK (1975), *The Information Seekers—An International Study of Consumer Information and Advertising Image,* Cambridge, Mass.: Ballinger.

__________, AND SVENTELL, GERALD D., *Consumer Emancipation and Economic Development: The Case of Thailand* (forthcoming).

__________, AND THORELLI, SARA V. (1974), *Consumer Information Handbook: Europe and North America,* New York: Praeger.

__________, AND __________ (1977), *Consumer Information Systems and Consumer Policy,* Cambridge, Mass.: Ballinger.

10 A PLAN FOR CONSUMER INFORMATION SYSTEM DEVELOPMENT, IMPLEMENTATION, AND EVALUATION

Donald A. Dunn & Michael L. Ray

The basic concept of improving the operation of markets through the provision of better information to consumers is at least as old as Consumers Union, which was founded in 1936. Consumers Union has built a successful, self-supporting information service that provides both general information and comparative ratings on nationally advertised products and some other items of general interest to consumers. The question posed here is, can this concept be extended to local services, such as retail sales, auto repair, medical care, and real estate? If a financially self-sustaining service were to be developed, what would its effects be on local service markets?

These are the questions which drove a several year study of the potential of local consumer information systems which was conducted at Stanford with the support of the National Science Foundation.

Our tentative answers to these questions are as follows. The concept can be extended to local services, but it will not be easy. It has not yet been done in a systematic or comprehensive way. The concept should be developed if possible, because the benefits to consumers and to the economy are likely to be favorable and large, of the order of a hundred

---

From Jerry C. Olson (ed.), *Advances in Consumer Research* 7 (Ann Arbor, Michigan: Association for Consumer Research, 1980), pp. 250–254.

billion dollars per year (Dunn and Ray, 1979). The costs should be a small fraction of the benefits, because only a small fraction of consumers need to be given improved information in order to induce providers to lower prices or improve the quality of their service. Non-users as well as users of the information service will benefit from the operation of the service.

THE INFORMATION AVOIDANCE PHENOMENON

We conducted a survey of consumer organizations that might offer services to consumers that would include pre-purchase information in the form of comparative ratings of local service providers, similar to those of Consumers Union on manufactured products. Out of 600 listed organizations, we found 15 active local consumer information services in the U.S. in 1977, but only about half of these provided any pre-purchase information and only a few of these provided a regular systematic coverage of any local service market. None provided a comprehensive service covering a range of local services. It is evident that, if it were easy to provide such a service on a financially self-supporting basis, there would be far more operating services of this type than there are today. Similar results have been reported by the Thorelli's (1977).

The basic concept from economic theory that consumers are made "as well off as they can be" through the operation of a competitive market only has validity if consumers have perfect information with respect to both prices and the quality characteristics of the services being provided. The contrast between perfect information with respect to what a consumer needs to know to make a good decision in choosing local services and the information that is presently available in the market is extreme. In such areas as auto repair, medical services, and legal services the consumer usually confronts the need for a decision at a time of crisis. The costs and terms of the purchase are often vague and not resolved until after the choice as to which provider to use has been made.

Comparative information regarding costs, honesty and competency of local service providers is usually totally lacking. In this type of situation, when a consumer is offered information that might be of assistance, the consumer often rejects it, perhaps on the assumption that it will be too technical to understand. Choices with respect to major service decisions are made infrequently and little learning by individual consumers can take place. Thus, very little information processing takes place in many of these situations, even though the decisions being made may be very important ones. A majority of consumers in these cases can better be characterized as "information avoiders" than as "information seekers" (Ray & Dunn, 1978). Perhaps this pattern of information avoidance is rational, in complex markets with very little trustworthy information available. But whether it is rational or not, we should not expect to find a large, eager group of consumers waiting to purchase information with respect to local services as soon as it is put on the market. Perhaps the market for information will grow when it is found that useful information can be acquired, but as an initial assumption, it seems reasonable to project a startup market for a consumer information service in the range of only one to ten percent of the local consumers who would be potential users of the service. Therefore, the consumer information service should, in our opinion, be designed to serve, and to break even financially serving, the small group of information seekers in any market. The much larger group of information avoiders may also be served indirectly by such as service, as will be explained below, but cannot be expected to become users. This business strategy is exactly the strategy followed by Consumers Union which has as subscribers less than one percent of American consumers. In our study of various specific markets, we have found that there are information seekers in every market. In most markets information seekers tend to be near the upper end of the national income distribution; they have a high value of time and are accustomed to pay for services that save them time. In the auto repair market, information seekers are likely to be patrons of an auto diagnostic service, if one is available. In the health field, information seekers are likely to go outside the medical establishment for information on nutrition, exercise, and various self-help medical aids. The design of a consumer information service should take into account these aspects of information seeker behavior.

THREE TYPES OF INFORMATION NEED

The types of information that a consumer normally wants and needs are closely related to the three levels of information need that seem to be common to any type of decision making: (1) problem recognition; (2) search for alternatives; (3) choice and implementation of decision. After the decision has been made, the consumer may want assistance with complaints. At the problem recognition stage, the consumer needs to be alerted to the characteristics to look for in a service and ways of getting information about a service. In searching for alternatives, the consumer needs comparative information on alternative sources of service, presented in a way that facilitates comparison. Honesty and competency are obviously key characteristics of any provider. At the choice and implementation stage, the consumer needs information on business practices and assistance in actually making a purchase.

TWO BROAD SOURCES OF INFORMATION

Consumer information services can acquire information in two fundamentally different ways. First, tests and experiments can be performed to acquire a sample of a service provider's honesty and competency. For example, test vehicles known to be in excellent condition except for a loose wire on the distributor have been taken to a number of auto repair shops in tests of this type. Some shops make no charge for reconnecting the wire. Others run up bills for hundreds of dollars.

Second, the accumulated experience of consumers can be sampled and the results of the sample analyzed and combined to present a picture of consumers' opinions about honesty, competency, price and other characteristics of a local service provider. Maynes, Morgan, Vivian, and Duncan (1977) have proposed a design for a system of this type using telephone interviews. A properly conducted sample of this type avoids the bias inherent in a complaint-oriented system, because it samples satisfied users as well as dissatisfied users. However, this approach has the limitation that it can only learn what consumers know from their own experience. In some cases, the knowledge gained by experts through tests or other investigations would also be extremely helpful. In most cases the two approaches can provide useful complementary data. Consumers Union now uses consumer opinion surveys to supplement its test data in some cases. A consumer information service can expect to obtain useful information from its customers who use recommended service providers and report back their experience to the information service.

BUSINESS AND ECONOMIC EFFECTS

Once the information has been acquired, a consumer information service encounters the usual difficulty of all information service providers in recovering the costs of information creation from users. Once the information is made available to some users, copies can be made and either resold or shared with other users. The price charged per user by the information service cannot therefore exceed the cost of sharing by very much. Of course, copyright law is intended to encourage the creation of information products by protecting the provider from large-scale resale competition. But copyright protection is limited and has a negligible effect on sharing.

A variety of delivery techiques are available, ranging from magazines or newsletters to computer data bases and cable television. For many uses and many classes of information, a magazine or newsletter like Consumer Reports, combined with a book that summarizes and classifies past data by subject matter, like the annual Consumers Union buying guide, provides an adequate delivery system. However, some users need, and are willing to pay for, a personalized consultation on their information needs on major purchases like real estate. Consultants may want and be willing to pay for access to continuously updated computer data bases. Telephone-based consulting could probably be provided at a fairly modest cost per inquiry, such as $5, for a simple request for information.

Once an information service is in operation, it can be expected to have two effects. First, it will provide benefits to its users, both in the form of savings of time formerly used in search and as a result of obtaining the best price/quality combination available in the market. Consumers Union has sometimes been criticized for not reaching a larger cross-section of American consumers; most of its subscribers are in the upper-middle income range. While it would, of course, be desirable to have a broader spectrum of income groups among its subscribers, this criticism ignores the second (and most important) effect of a consumer information service, its effect on provider behavior in the market. In our view, this second effect is likely to produce consumer benefits much greater than the direct benefits conferred on subscribers. A provider, faced with a low quality rating or a report that its prices are above those of other providers in a consumer information service, is quite likely to alter its price and/or quality to bring it in line with the market, even though the number of information service subscribers represents only a small percentage of the consumers in the market. One reason for such a response is the potential danger that a provider's poor performance will become news and reach a much wider audience than the information service users.

An example of the effect of comparative rating information on provider behavior is presented by a shopping guide to banking services in the San Francisco area prepared by Consumer Action, a San Francisco consumer group (1976). This shopping guide was sold for $3 as a booklet, and it was available in both bookstores and magazine stands. The banking industry purchased a number of booklets, and one of the low rated banks changed its practices in response to the booklet, benefiting all of its customers. For whatever reason, the market is likely to respond to an information service report, and the resulting price and quality variances will be smaller than before.

Even more significant is the potential role of a consumer information service in increasing innovation in the local service market. For example, new products and services that receive favorable ratings can experience a growth rate far in excess of normal, because of the trust that subscribers have in the information service. Consumer Reports sometimes rates the product of a new small firm a best buy and causes the small firm to become established much more rapidly than would be the case in the ordinary course of events. Thus, the market can both respond more rapidly to new products and act to eliminate overpriced and poor quality providers more effectively in the presence of an information service than without it. The market's behavior in this case benefits both subscribers and non-subscribers, and if subscribers represent only a few percent of the consumers, it is evident that the benefits to non-subscribers far outweigh the benefits to subscribers.

This favorable result has only one negative aspect. If the market is functioning well, as a result of the operation of the information service, the incentive to subscribe to the service is reduced. Consumers can receive the benefits without paying the price of a subscription. If the service went out of business, market practices would then become less competitive, and eventually a new information service could enter the market and obtain enough subscribers to survive. This prospect of working itself out of a job is a problem that should be faced by any information service initially, and a business plan should be developed that takes this possibility into account. In our opinion, there are business strategies that can be adopted that will protect a consumer information service in this situation. The basic concept that underlies a sound strategy is simply diversification, i.e., the provision of information regarding a wide range of local markets rather than a single market. Diversification can work, both because of the substantial and different time delays for different markets to adjust and because of the different kinds of provider responses to be expected in different local service markets. Local service markets differ widely, both in market structure and in the nature of the services offered. The role of consumer information in these markets may also vary widely, which suggests that a careful study of each type of service market is an appropriate first step in the design of an information service for that market.

. . .

REFERENCES

Biehal, Gabriel J. (1978), "The Effects of Prior Information and Information Search Costs on External and Internal Information Search Behavior," Ph.D. Dissertation and Technical Report No. 63, Stanford, California: Graduate School of Business, Stanford University.

DUNN, DONALD A. and RAY, MICHAEL L. (1979), "Local Consumer Information Services," *Report No. 16, Program in Information Policy,* Stanford Engineering-Economic Systems Department, Stanford University.

KRUGHOFF, ROBERT (1979), *Washington Consumer Checkbook,* Washington, D.C.: Center for the Study of Services.

MAYNES, E. SCOTT; MORGAN, JAMES N.; VIVIAN, WESTON; and DUNCAN, GREG, J. (Summer 1977), "The Local Consumer Information System: An Institution to Be?" *J. Consumer Affairs,* 11, 17–33.

MOFFITT, DONALD (November 27, 1978), "Your Money Matters," *Wall Street Journal.*

OWEN, BRUCE M. (1977), "Kickbacks, Specialization, Price Fixing, and Efficiency in Residential Real Estate Markets," *Stanford Law Review,* 29, 931–967.

RAY, MICHAEL L. and DUNN, DONALD A. (1978), "Local Consumer Information Systems for Services: The Market for Information and its Effects on the Market," in *The Effect of Information on Consumer and Market Behavior,* Mitchell, A. A., ed., Chicago: American Marketing Association.

SAN FRANCISCO CONSUMER ACTION (1976), *Break the Banks, A Shopper's Guide to Banking Services,* San Francisco: San Francisco Consumer Action.

THORELLI, HANS B. and THORELLI, SARAH V. (1977), *Consumer Information Systems and Consumer Policy,* Cambridge, Massachusetts: Ballinger.

11 DEVELOPING CORPORATE CONSUMER INFORMATION PROGRAMS

David A. Aaker

Shell Oil has prepared a series of "answer series" booklets on car use and care and has employed a major consumer advertising campaign to distribute 600 million of these booklets to consumers during a three-year period.

PG&E provides consultants to come to your home to consult on home improvements that will save energy.

Whirlpool pioneered the much imitated "cool line" service by which 150,000 consumers annually call directly to the factory for help on using, installing, and repairing appliances.

Corning provides spokespeople who present information about such topics as kitchen safety and microwave cooking to group meetings and on radio and television.

The Christian Brothers winery explains on their label how to serve the wine.

Dayton-Hudson runs advertising explaining how to buy carpeting.

These organizations and others have developed some form of consumer information program. There are several advantages to both the organization and to society in making consumers more informed. Yet many companies openly admit that they have no consumer information program or have just allowed an apparently successful program to lapse.[1]

---

[1] The illustrative examples and observations presented in the paper are drawn, in part, from correspondence with a sample of eighty consumer affairs professionals.

Reprinted with permission from *Business Horizons,* November 1981.

The approaches of those that do have a consumer information program vary enormously in scope, commitment and effectiveness.

What is useful consumer information and how does it relate to advertising and promotion? What is the value, if any, of consumer information programs to the firm? How should consumer information programs be developed, implemented and evaluated? Each of these questions will be addressed in turn.

WHAT IS USEFUL CONSUMER INFORMATION?

Useful consumer information is information that will help consumers buy or use a product or service. It will improve the consumer's purchase or use experience. An implication is that an external standard exists to which a purchase decision and or use experience can be compared. Useful consumer information should by definition move the consumer toward the external standard.

To fix concepts it is helpful to consider the difficulties of measuring the consumer information content of a communication. One approach is to use content analysis. Resnick and Stern [1977] did a content analysis of 387 television commercials and found that less than half could be coded as having any information content. However, such objective measures control neither for what consumers need to know nor for what consumers already know nor for their motivation to process information. To be useful, information needs to be actually used and to potentially influence purchase and use decisions.

Another approach is to measure the consumer satisfaction with the purchase and use experience. An effective information program might reasonably be expected to increase consumer satisfaction. The problem is that consumer satisfaction could have been artificially high because of misinformation and accurate consumer information could then have the effect of making it lower.

Still another approach is to let the consumer be the judge. For example, General Motors found that 89 percent of those exposed to a car buying advertising campaign found it to be interesting and informative. However, consumers may not be competent to evaluate the information content because they are simply unable to evaluate the truthfulness, the completeness or the relevance of the information. Thus, the concept of external standards as to how consumers ought to make purchase and use decisions is introduced. In some cases, it might be desirable and feasible to have people expert in the product or service and its use evaluate a communication's informativeness with such standards as a reference point.

For consumer information to be useful to an audience segment, several conditions should exist. First, the information should be potentially relevant to the consumer. Second, it should contribute something which the consumer does not already know. Third, this contribution should be substantial enough to motivate the consumer to process the information. Fourth, the information as perceived by the consumer should be truthful, complete and intelligible [Howard and Hulbert, 1973].

Consumer Information Types

Consumer information can take several forms such as:

1. Providing brand/attribute information.
2. Structuring the decision process.
3. Focusing on the use system.

The first type of consumer information involves the communication of brand information and/or the association of brands with attribute information. Most advertising and other promotion fits into this category. The information content of such communications can vary widely. If the communication involves a new brand, a new product attribute, the results of a relevant government study or a helpful presentation of information as in comparative advertising, it could be very useful. For example, the Pontiac advertisements which compare their gas mileage with that of competitive imports, involve brand/attribute information that may be helpful to some audience segments.

Some brand/attribute oriented advertising contains little information not already known to the audience. In this category would be reminder advertising involving a well known brand name and most advertising that attempts to associate an existing brand with an established product attribute. For example, many deodorants attempt to indicate superiority at removing moisture. The information content of such advertising is very likely low.

Another type of consumer information, sometimes termed consumer education, involves efforts to help the consumer structure the decision process. One approach is to suggest product attributes that consumers should consider in their choice decisions. For example, Smith-Corona suggests nine portable typewriter attributes to consider before buying. The communication could, however, also attempt to discuss the interaction between the attribute and the use context. For example, a General Motors advertisement explains how to select the appropriate engine size by discussing use contexts. In each case the goal of the information program is at least in part to help the consumer structure the decision process.

The third type of consumer information, also sometimes termed consumer education, involves information on using the product or service. Further, the focus can be the context in which the product is used. Thus, a shampoo brand may have an information program focusing upon the care of the scalp or a detergent company might become involved in the care of clothing.

The information could be involved with a context that is only indirectly related to the purchase or use of a product and still qualify as consumer information. For example, the Shell Oil booklet on road hazards may be only indirectly related to contexts surrounding the purchase and use of oil products. However, as the contexts become less related, the associated information program should be considered a public service program rather than a consumer information program. For instance, the Shell booklet on protecting the home from burglaries is so far removed from the purchase and use of oil products that it would be much more of a public service than a consumer information program.

Information vs. Persuasion

Of practical and theoretical interest is the distinction between persuasive communication and consumer information. For example, to what extent does or should the advertising effort contribute to the consumer information program?

As Hunt [1976] has observed, the distinction between information and persuasion in advertising is highly artificial. The reality is that all advertising and indeed all corporate communication is nearly always justified by its direct or indirect potential to persuade, to ultimately affect choice. Thus, the issue is not whether the communication is "to persuade" but rather how informative is it and what role does it have in the total consumer information program. Certainly some communication programs that are informative are also "persuasive." An example might be the advertising and promotional effort of the Armstrong Cork Company, makers of flooring products, which is oriented toward providing decorating suggestions and to provide installation and maintenance information. Fortunately, for Armstrong, the best way to generate interest in their products and their advertising is to provide good consumer information. Their expertise in decoration led to a "decorating" magazine selling for $1.75 which reached a circulation of 300,000 after eighteen months.

POTENTIAL BENEFITS TO THE FIRM OF CONSUMER INFORMATION PROGRAMS

In determining if consumer information programs should be developed or continued, it is useful to consider the possible ways in which they can provide value to the organization. As Figure 11-1 notes, there are at least five possible rationales for consumer information.

First, a consumer information program has the potential to improve customer satisfaction. When consumers buy a product attuned to their needs and use it properly, their chances of becoming dissatisfied later will be reduced. A satisfied consumer in the long run will generate loyalty and thus profitability.

Second, a well-developed consumer information program that is truly effective is likely to help generate a positive consumer image. In the early 1970s the Giant Food Store chain gained market share from a consumer image which was, in part, due to a series of consumer information programs. More recently, the overall image of Shell increased during the first two years of the "answer man" campaign while that of its four major competitors fell during the same period.

Third, the process of developing a consumer information program can provide consumer insights which can stimulate new products and marketing programs. Most organizations are concerned with consumers' reactions to elements of the marketing program, but few actually consider such questions as: How should the consumer buy? What information would be helpful? Do consumers use the product or service effectively and appropriately? What problems are associated with the purchase and use of the product? Yet such questions can lead the firm to the discovery of consumer problems which can represent substantial opportunities. A formal consideration of consumer problems associated with product use has been credited with the development of many new products and advertising themes [Norris, 1975].

Fourth, the inclusion of useful information into advertising has the potential to make that advertising more effective. David Ogilvy has observed that informative, long-copy print advertisement, such as those for Rolls-Royce and Good Luck Margerine, have been extremely effective [Ogilvy, 1964]. Further, consumer information can sometimes involve a consumer attribute that represents a competitive advantage. Examples include the use of the EPA objective automotive mileage measure and FTC tar and nicotine content measures. Of course, it is possible to turn such advertising into misinformation by selectively deleting some models from comparisons or by otherwise distorting the information.

A fifth justification of consumer information programs is that they will collectively help the market mechanism work better [Stigler, 1961;

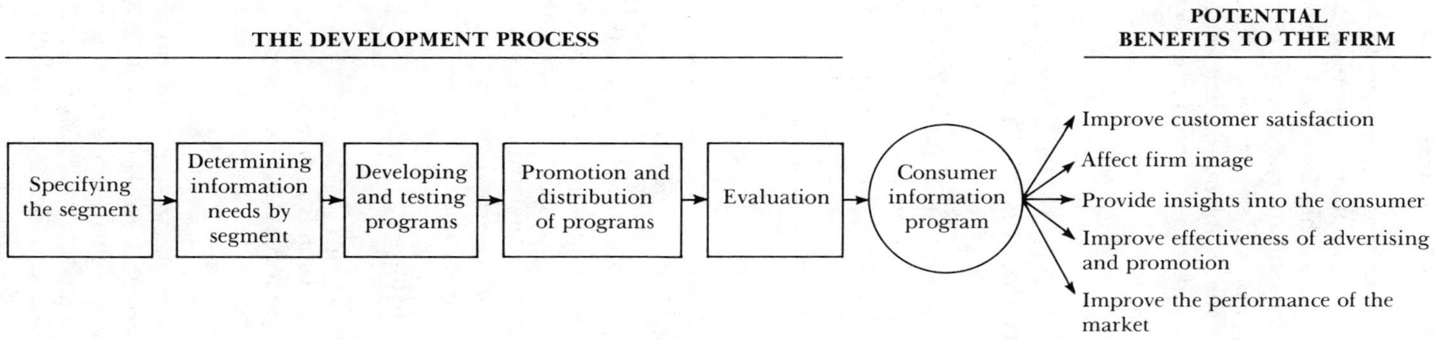

Figure 11–1. Consumer Information Programs

Beales and Salop, 1979]. The free market system is based upon informed economic choices. When information is absent or distorted or rendered impotent by pressure selling, then the market system will be handicapped and becomes vulnerable to criticism and regulation. Further, an informed consumer is a protected consumer [Thorelli and Thorelli, 1977]. In many cases, the problems that underlie the consumerism movement of the past decade can be traced to inadequate or faulty consumer information.

ON DEVELOPING AND IMPLEMENTING CONSUMER INFORMATION PROGRAMS

Developing effective consumer information programs is really no different than developing other aspects of the marketing effort. As Figure 11–1 suggests, there are five stages in the process. In many cases some or all of these stages are omitted, sometimes appropriately so but more often because the process had not received the management effort that is warranted.

Specifying the Segments

The reality is that people differ enormously in their motivation, need, and ability to process consumer information. A recognition of this fact will usually lead to the development of consumer information programs that are tailored to the needs of particular segments of the potential audience. Segmentation variables particularly useful in consumer information program development include:

information-seeking behavior
age
level of current information
whether a purchase decision is imminent
involvement in the product or service
education and income
opinion leadership

The potential audience for consumer information often contains a small segment of ''information seekers'' such as Consumer Reports users who tend to have higher education and income than others [Thorelli, Becker, and Engledow, 1975; McEwen, 1978]. Such information seekers will have greater motivation and ability to process information. Conversely, those who are not information seekers may actually have the greatest information need but will be the most difficult to reach.

Another relevant segmentation variable is age. Certainly, the very young and the very old have special information processing needs and constraints [Calder, Robertson, and Rossiter, 1975; Phillips and Sternthal, 1977]. School-age students represent a particularly relevant segment. Efforts directed at students are sometimes necessary because the facts and concepts to be communicated really require a course of study, or because it is necessary to reach young people before they have a chance to develop bad habits and before they lose interest in the subject matter. Many firms have developed such programs. Montgomery Ward, for example, has educational programs on microwave cooking techniques, energy conservation in households, and using consumer information (an instructional unit based upon the Ward's catalogue).

There are, of course, many other possible segmentation variables. The level of current information is a variable that is often of use in segmenting audiences for any communication program. The attempt to generate motivation can lead to consideration of those facing an imminent purchase decision, to those with high product involvement, or of working through opinion leaders.

Determining Information Needs

The determination of the optimal content of a consumer information involves comparing how consumers make purchase and use decisions with how those decisions should be made. In particular, it is of interest to determine the:

consumer information used
information sources accessed
decision process employed
way the product was used
perceived consumer problems

and to compare the findings with normative judgements.

One source of information is the consumer. For example, the Confectionary Industry Association in Japan uses three sixty-member consumer advisory panels. These panels, which comment monthly on various consumer problem areas and actually meet every other month, have generated several informational programs.

Employees represent another information source. For example, one firm has employee groups systematically consider the consumer purchase-and-use process and its associated problems and information needs. Those handling consumer complaints can develop unique perspectives on consumer problems. Such a source was used by MACAP

(Major Appliance Consumer Action Panel), a panel of eight independent consumer experts who process complaints from appliance owners, to develop one of the better consumer handbooks. MACAP's handbook included general information concerning credit, legal recourse, and warranties and provided a list of buying considerations and recommendations on proper use and care of fourteen major appliances.

Outside sources, such as independent product experts, taking the perspective of a "consumer consultant" may be particularly helpful in determining the normative judgments relating to how consumers ought to make purchase-and-use decisions. Employees and sometimes even knowledgeable consumers may be too familiar with the existing situation to recognize that consumers should be receiving and processing information differently than they now do. A consumer consultant would be a person assigned to improve the buying-and-use decisions of consumers. The "client" would be consumers representing various segments.

It could be worthwhile to move beyond product specific consumer problems. For example, inflation and the resulting impact upon the food budget has for some time been a prime consumer concern [Margolius, 1975]. Hunt-Wesson's "Low Cost Cookery" program of the late 1960's was responsive to such concerns. The $2.5 million campaign helped consumers plan more nutritious, low cost meals in part, by distributing two million "Low Cost Cookery" cookbooks.

Developing and Testing Programs

In developing a consumer information program, a wide variety of approaches and vehicles should be considered. Too often, a single vehicle, like a booklet, will dominate the planning. Although a booklet can cover in depth product purchase and use, it is not always easy to motivate its use. In contrast, a simplified point-of-purchase message will potentially reach the consumer motivated by an immediate purchase decision. Sometimes a live or media spokesperson is needed to communicate concepts because a demonstration is appropriate or because target segments do not learn well by reading. Among the companies with a field staff giving demonstrations and educational programs is Sunbeam. If a dialogue is necessary, a toll-free telephone number or a training program for retail salespeople may be useful. The key is to consider a wide variety of approaches selecting those that match the specific communication task involved.

Many information format alternatives seem to have little impact upon the communication effectiveness. McNeil and Wilkie [1979], for example, found that variations in presentation of refrigerator energy consumption information made little difference. However, communication effectiveness may be sensitive to whether information is organized by brand, by attribute, or in matrix form. Information organized by brand is certainly the most common way for a manufacturer to provide information since it avoids problems of obtaining and including specific information on competitors. However, several have argued that information in matrix form as *Consumer Reports* does, for example, is the most useful [Bettman, 1975[. Others have suggested that information organized by attribute is more useful than information organized by brand. Russo [1977] showed that unit-price information was effective when it was posted on a list including all brands instead of on individual shelf tags. Comparative advertising where information is organized by attribute, is encouraged by the FTC. However, the hypothesis that such advertising will be more informative has yet to be confirmed [Pride, Lamb, and Pletcher, 1977; Wilkie and Farris, 1975].

Retailers are usually in a better position than manufacturers to provide consumer information on purchase alternatives and guidance on decision process because they often are indifferent as to the ultimate selection. Thus, the supermarket could pursue a variety of information programs that a manufacturer would find difficult such as presenting information across brands. Thus, Safeway could present comparative nutritional information across products and brands.

Testing

Most consumer information programs will benefit from testing if testing expenditures can be justified. A minimal test is to ask consumers via a survey or focus group about their reactions to the program. However, consumers sometimes claim to want consumer information but then fail to use it when it becomes available [Jacoby, Chestnut, and Silberman, 1977; Day, 1976]. Another approach is to ask those knowledgeable about consumers' reactons to provide judgments. The best test, however, is usually either a laboratory or field experiment. A laboratory experiment [i.e., McNeill and Wilkie, 1979] can be relatively inexpensive and fast and allows several alternative versions of the program to be compared under highly controlled conditions. The field experiment, more realistic but also more costly [Bloom and Ford, 1979], can uncover unanticipated program benefits. Federated Department Stores developed a series of in-store experiments with tel-tags on small appliances and learned that tel-tags were of considerable value to salesclerks.

The development of a consumer information program could benefit from a sequence of tests such as AT&T used to help develop an improved telephone directory customer call guide. After an improved call guide developed, reactions were obtained from several consumer groups. The next step was a laboratory "look-up test" experiment involving the old and improved versions. Finally, a field experiment provided a final test of the improved call guide.

Promotion and Distribution

To be of value, a consumer information program must directly or indirectly reach consumers. Kraft provides a good illustration of a variety of ways to achieve substantial distribution of informational material. They estimated that over 1.4 million informational booklets on such topics as food and nutrition terms, packaging and labelling, and food-buying considerations have been distributed in a three- or four-year period. Included in their efforts to publicize the booklets are:

a. A four-page newsletter providing coverage of current events and issues is sent to 8,000 educators and consumer, health, government, and industry professionals and calls attention to the booklets.
b. One-page fact sheets summarizing the contents of a booklet and explaining how to get one are sent to consumer affairs representatives of supermarkets for distribution.
c. News releases highlighting the information covered in the newsletters and booklets are sent to consumer, food, and business editors of major newspapers and magazines. The intent is to get the consumer information into editorial copy and to offer the booklets to the readers. A similar collection of feature stories is sent to newspapers with less than 20,000 circulation.
d. A series of thirty-second radio and television public service messages inform the public about the booklets. In addition, 130 public services radio spots on nutrition, meal planning, etc., have been produced and distributed to more than 1,000 radio stations.

Evaluation

Program objectives can include measures of:

1. behavior related to the product use context
2. the firm's consumer image, loyalty, and sales
3. consumer awareness, understanding, attitude toward, and use of the information program.

Some programs focus upon the product use context. For example, the drunk driving campaigns of Allstate Insurance could use numbers of drunk driving accidents as a program measure, although it would be a demanding one. Similarly, the Hunt-Wesson low-cost cookery program could measure the use of their menus. Staelin [1978] suggests evaluating consumer product safety education by using reported safety use behavior rather than injury history, because injuries are rare events influenced by uncontrollable environmental events.

The firm's consumer image, loyalty, or sales provide natural objectives for those whose information program is backed by a large-scale advertising program for which consumer tracking data are collected. For example, Shell tracks overtime advertising awareness and customer attitudes. Shell found that their image as a company that provides useful information for consumers went from 31 in January 1977 to 33 in May 1978, while their closest competitor fell from 26 to 12 in the same period. Other measures such as purchases, loyalty and letters from consumers and other influential people also indicated that the campaign was successful and still effective after more than two years.

Consumer awareness, understanding, and use of the communication program provide an evaluation basis for some utility companies who distributed via newspapers an "energy" magazine offering a combination of pure energy stories, do-it-yourself projects, recipes, and a puzzle page. A readership poll concluded that 100 percent of newspaper readers recalled the magazine, 65 percent had unaided recall of specific articles, and 74 percent recalled details from the lead article.

Some consumer information programs necessarily and appropriately are too small to justify spending monies on evaluation. Yet even these programs can often measure usage levels. For example, Armstrong Cork estimated that 225,000 saw a motion picture on flooring that featured decorating, shopping, installation, and maintenance advice. As a result of an advertising campaign in New York and Pittsburgh, Bristol-Myers in three months distributed 100,000 copies of a consumer guide containing basic information on buying, using, and storing forty common household products.

When a consumer information program is formalized, it is useful to consider objectives for the total program in addition to evaluating its components. The objectives for the Corning program include several programmatic objectives such as:

1. Direct media visits to fifty major markets and secondary media markets. (A media visit could be a visit by a Corning specialist to consumer-oriented radio or television shows or segments of shows.)
2. Develop communications programs with educational kits and special-event aspects to emphasize kitchen safety as a means of reducing accidents in the kitchen and improving Corning's position in product liability cases.
3. Plan at least four tie-in projects with food companies.

The objectives of Kraft's "Consumer Right to Know" program are more general·

1. To establish a rapport and continuing dialogue with consumer educators and communicators.
2. To reach the general public through diverse media with information and materials directed toward the development of informed consumers capable of making intelligent, independent, purchasing decisions.
3. To address consumer concerns in an open, constructive manner.
4. To convey information on current issues, trends, and legislation concerning the food industry.
5. To convey Kraft's commitment to better-informed consumers.

SOME MISCONCEPTIONS

There exist several potentially influential explicit or implicit beliefs about consumer information that, upon close examination, usually turn out to be false. It is worthwhile to mention a few of these misconceptions.

A Consumer Information Program Is Not Appropriate for My Firm

Clearly, there are products and contexts in which a consumer information program is most easily justified with a consumer cost-benefit analysis. The benefits will tend to be higher when:

the purchase size or purchase frequency is high
there exists uncertainty about the product and its use
first-hand experience is lacking, a "search" product is involved
the alternatives are perceived to have potentially meaningful differences
health or safety is involved

[Bucklin, 1965; Holton, 1969; Miller, 1979; Nelson, 1970; Stigler, 1961]. The cost of processing information will depend upon the:

required investment of time and money
mental effort involved
annoyance of being exposed to uninteresting or distasteful information

[Capon and Lutz, 1979, p. 62].

There are managers claiming to be supportive of consumer programs in general, who will use these cost-benefit factors to argue that a consumer is not appropriate to their ''special'' context. However, in many of these ''special'' situations, a little creative effort would result in a very worthwhile consumer information program, especially if the consumption system in which the product is imbedded is considered. A deodorant company could easily become involved in skin care and hygiene or a refrigerator company in food preservation. Gillette became involved in grooming, Corning in safety in the kitchen, and Shell in car care. The ''doesn't-apply-to-me'' syndrome may represent a valid judgment but only after a thorough appraisal of possible alternative consumer information programs.

A Successful Program Will Survive

Consumer information programs have payouts that are difficult to quantify, that are often indirect, and that do not necessarily materialize in the short run. Because of these characteristics they are vulnerable to organizational fluctuations and pressures. Several years ago a division of the Gillette Company created several information kits on grooming (hair and skin care, use of deodorants, etc.) for elementary and high schools. The kits, which included film strips, records, booklets, and product samples, were popular and generated considerable publicity. However, a division merger and the transfer of a key person combined to terminate the program despite its apparent ''success.''

The More Information the Better

Too often the government has made decisions and developed policies based upon the faulty assumption that the consumer wants and will use as much information as possible, or ''the more information the better.'' Consumer information programs sometimes appear to be guided by the same erroneous judgment. The reality is that most consumers are usually not motivated to process and use large amount of consumer information [Wilkie, 1974b]. Even when consumers express motivation they will not necessarily actually use it [Jacoby, Chestnut, and Silberman, 1977; Day, 1976[. The potential improvement in decision making may not justify information processing costs [Hagerty and Aaker, 1980]. In addition, there are limits as to the number of information chunks that can be processed by the consumer [Bettman, 1979b, p. 41; Simon, 1974]. It has even been hypothesized that information overload can actually lead to inferior choice decisions, especially if there is a time constraint.

However, efforts to support this hypothesis [Jacoby, Speller, and Kohn, 1974a and 1975b] have been inconclusive [Russo, 1974; Wilkie, 1974a; Summers, 1974].

There are two implications of the observation that more information is not necessarily better. First, effective consumer information should be concerned with motivation to process information, identifying the motivated consumers and contexts. Second, the information content need not be exhaustive. On the contrary, it is sometimes better to communicate a few points rather than attempt to be comprehensive. The results should be judged, not on the communication itself, but rather on its impact.

IN CONCLUSION

In evaluating consumer information programs consider that:

1. Potential program payoffs include improvements in customer satisfaction, image, consumer insight, the free market systems, and the advertising and promotion effort.
2. The development of a consumer information system involves segment specification, need determination, product development and testing, promotion and distribution, and evaluation.
3. Misconceptions can exist such as it is not appropriate for our "special case," a successful program will survive, and more information is always better.

REFERENCES

Beales, Howard, and Salop, Steven. 1979. "Selling Consumer Information." Paper delivered to the Conference of the Association for Consumer Research, San Francisco, October 28.

Bettman, James R. 1975. "Issues in Designing Consumer Information Environments." *Journal of Consumer Research* 2 (December): 169–177.

———. 1979a. *An Information Processing Theory of Consumer Choice.* Reading, Mass.: Addison-Wesley.

———. 1979b. "Memory Factors in Consumer Choice: A Review." *Journal of Marketing* 43 (Spring): 47–53.

Bloom, Paul N., and Ford, Gary T. 1979. "Evaluation of Consumer Education Programs." *Journal of Consumer Research* 61 (December): 270–279.

Bucklin, Louis P. 1965. "The Informative Role of Advertising." *Journal of Advertising Research* 5 (September): 11–15.

CALDER, BOBBY J.; ROBERTSON, THOMAS S.; and ROSSITER, JOHN R. 1975. "Children's Consumer Information Processing." *Communication Research* 2 (July): 307-316.

CAPON, NOEL, and LUTZ, RICHARD T. 1979. "A Model and Methodology for the Development of Consumer Information Programs." *Journal of Marketing* 43 (January): 58-67.

DAY, GEORGE S. 1976. "Assessing the Effects of Information Disclosure Requirements." *Journal of Marketing* 40 (April): 43-52.

HAGERTY, MICHAEL and AAKER, DAVID. "A Normative Model of Consumer Information Processing," presented at the conference of the Association for consumer Research, October, 1980.

HOLTON, RICHARD H. 1969. "Business and Government." *Daedalus* (Winter): 47-58.

HOWARD, JOHN A. and HULBERT, JAMES. *Advertising and the Public Interest.* Chicago: Crain Communications, 1973.

HUNT, SHELBY D. 1976. "Information vs. Persuasive Advertising: An Appraisal." *Journal of Advertising* 5 (Summer): pp. 5-8.

JACOBY, JACOB; CHESTNUT, ROBERT W.; and SILBERMAN, WILLIAM. 1977. "Consumer Use and Comprehension of Nutrition Information." *Journal of Consumer Research* 4 (September): 119-128.

JACOBY, JACOB; SPELLER, DONALD E.; and KOHN, CAROL A. 1974a. "Brand Choice Behavior as a Function of Information Load." *Journal of Marketing Research* 11 (February): 63-69.

————. 1974b. Brand Choice Behavior As a Function of Information Load: Republican and Extension." *Journal of Consumer Research* 1 (June): 33-42.

MARGOLIUS, SIDNEY. 1975. "The Consumer's Real Needs." *Journal of Consumer Affairs* (Winter): 129-138.

MCEWEN, WILLIAM J. 1978. "Bridging the Information Gap." *Journal of Consumer Research* 4 (March): 247-251.

MCNEILL, DENNIS L., and WILKIE, WILLIAM L. 1979. "Public Policy and Consumer Information: Impact of the Energy Labels." *Journal of Consumer Research* 6 (June): 1-11.

MILLER, JOHN A. 1979. Product/Service Characteristics—Signals for Consumer Education/Information Program Success." Paper presented at the Conference of the Association for Consumer Research, San Francisco, October 28.

NELSON, PHILLIP. 1970. "Information and Consumer Behavior." *Journal of Political Economy* 78 (March-April): 311-329.

NORRIS, E. E. 1975. "Your Surefire Clue to Ad Success: Seek Out the Consumer's Problem." *Advertising Age,* March 17.

OGILVY, DAVID. *Confessions of an Advertising Man.* New York: Atheneum, 1964. Pp. 108-110.

PHILLIPS, LYNN W. and BRIAN STERNTHAL, "Age Differences in Information Processing: A Perspective on the Aged Consumer." *Journal of Marketing Research* 14 (November 1977), pp. 444-457.

PRIDE, WILLIAM M.; LAMB, CHARLES W.; and PLETCHER, BARBARA A. 1977. "Are Comparative Advertisements More Informative for Owners of the Mentioned Competing Brands than for Nonowners?" In *1977 Educator's Proceedings.* Edited by Barrett A. Greenberg and Danny N. Bellenger. Chicago: American Marketing Association, pp. 298-301.

RESNIK, ALAN, and STERN, BRUCE L. 1977. "An Analysis of Information Content in Television Advertising." *Journal of Marketing* 41 (January): 50–53.

RUSSO, J. EDWARD. 1974 "More Information is Better: A Reevaluation of Jacoby, Speller, and Kohn." *Journal of Consumer Research* 1 (December): 68–72.

———. 1977. "The Value of Unit Price Information." *Journal of Marketing Research* 14 (May): 193-201.

SIMON, HERBERT A. 1974. "How Big is a Chunk?" *Science* 183 (February): 482–488.

STAELIN, RICHARD. 1978. "The Effects of Consumer Education on Consumer Product Safety Behavior." *Journal of Consumer Research* 5 (June): 30–40.

STIGLER, GEORGE J. 1961. "The Economics of Information." *Journal of Political Economy* (June): 213–225.

SUMMERS, JOHN O. 1974. "Less Information is Better?" *Journal of Marketing Research* 11 (November): 467–468.

THORELLI, HANS B.; BECKER, HELMUT; and ENGLEDOW, JACK. 1975. *The Information Seekers.* Cambridge, Mass.: Ballinger Publishing Co.

WILKIE, WILLIAM L. 1974a "Analysis of Effects of Information Load." *Journal of Marketing Research* 11(November): 462–466.

———. 1974b. "Public Policy and Product Information: Summary Findings from Consumer Research." Cambridge, Mass.: Marketing Science Institute.

WILKIE, WILLIAM L., and FERRIS, PAUL W. 1975. "Comparison Advertising: Problems and Potential." *Journal of Marketing* 39 (October): pp. 7–15.

B Information Disclosure Requirements

12 ASSESSING THE EFFECTS OF INFORMATION DISCLOSURE REQUIREMENTS

George S. Day

One continuing manifestation of consumerism is the increase in legislative and regulatory requirements for disclosure of product information. The pressure for additional information shows no sign of abating,[1] although the focus of the pressure is certainly changing. For the past five years the greatest emphasis has been on information about ingredients, relative prices, safety, and the useful life of products. The future will see greater attention paid to disclosures of efficiency and comparative performance information[2] on a much broader array of products. Table 12-1 illustrates the scope of present and probably future requirements.

---

[1] See generally, Hans B. Thorelli, "Consumer Information Systems of the Future" (Distinguished Lecture in Marketing, York University, 1972); William L. Wilkie and David M. Gardner, "Marketing Research Inputs to Public Policy: The Case of the FTC," *Journal of Marketing,* Vol. 38 (January 1974), pp. 38-47; William A. French and Hiram C. Barksdale, "Food Labeling Regulations: Efforts Toward Full Disclosure," *Journal of Marketing,* Vol. 38 (July 1974), pp. 14-19; William C. Whitford, "Functions of Disclosure Regulation in Consumer Transactions," *Wisconsin Law Review* (No. 2, 1973), p. 403; and Gwen Bymers, "Seller-Buyer Communication: Point of View of a Family Economist," *Journal of Home Economics,* Vol. 64 (February 1972), p. 59.

[2] George S. Day, "Full Disclosure of Comparative Performance Information to Consumers: Problems and Prospects," *Journal of Contemporary Business,* Vol. 4 (January 1975), pp. 53-68.

Reprinted with deletions from *Journal of Marketing* 40 (April 1976), pp. 42-52, published by the American Marketing Association.

TABLE 12-1. RECENT OR PROSPECTIVE INFORMATION DISCLOSURE REQUIREMENTS

TYPE OF DISCLOSURE	IMPLEMENTED IN PAST FIVE YEARS[a]	PROBABLE IN THE FUTURE[b]
1. Comparative prices	Truth in lending Unit pricing Automobile list prices	Prescription prices Truth in life insurance Costs of operation of appliances and automobiles Truth in consumer leasing
2. Comparative performance and efficiency	Nutrition labeling of food products Lumen and life data for bulbs Stereo amplifier power output Octane labeling Automobile performance (vehicle stopping distance, acceleration and passing ability, and tire reserve load)	Automobile gas mileage Appliance energy consumption and comparative efficiency Appliance performance Tire mileage, stopping ability, and high speed resistance to heat Carpet and upholstery wear characteristics Quality grade labels for food products Sun screen efficacy of suntan preparations Standards of drug efficacy Detergent efficacy Vocational school drop-out rate
3. Ingredients (including additives)	Cosmetics Food Liquor Phosphate content of detergents	Labeling of fat content in food Presence of pesticides Pigment content of paint Labeling to explain purpose of food ingredients and additives
4. Life/perishability	Open dating of foods	Appliance durability and life Expiration dates for drug potency Automobile damage susceptibility and repair costs
5. Warnings/ clarifications	Cigarette health hazards Lack of efficacy of vitamins Flammability (children's sleepwear)	Flammability of cellular plastic insulation
6. Form and usage of product terms of contract and warranties	Size standards (i.e., TV screens and refrigerators) Truth in warranties and service contracts Tire construction and load rating	Standards specifying amount of product to use (i.e., detergents) Care labeling for clothing Terms of land sales contracts Truth in imports (country of origin) Truth in savings (interest payments) Disclosure of manufacturer, packer, and distributor of food products Net and drained weights of canned and frozen food

[a] Many of the disclosure requirements in this column will be the subject of future legislation designed to xtend coverage (especially from state to federal jurisdictions) or clarify implementation problems. Some are rimarily in existence as voluntary industry standards motivated by the threat of government involvement.

[b] As of the second quarter of 1975, none of these requirements had been implemented federally although erious proposals were being considered in virtually all cases.

A curious feature of the growing demand for more information is the paucity of concrete evidence that past disclosures have made significant differences in consumer or market *behavior*. And if the future is like the past, there will be little or no programmatic research available to help decision makers forecast the impact of new disclosure requirements.[3]

The lack of evidence on the behavioral effects of information disclosures is due to the relative newness of most requirements and the inherent difficulties of designing and implementing the appropriate evaluation research.[4] These factors are compounded by a lack of conceptual bases for understanding how buyers use information[5] and confusion as to the objectives to be served by providing additional information. Without specific agreed-upon objectives there is no basis for a subsequent determination of success or failure. Yet there is seldom agreement among proponents as to whether new requirements should simply enhance the consumer's "right to know," improve the quality of products and competition, facilitate value comparisons, enable buyers to better match products and needs and thus increase purchase satisfaction, or pursue broad educational aims such as creating general public interest in nutrition or sensitivity to energy conservation.

The knowledge void has been partially filled by a recent spate of studies dealing primarily with grocery product information (notably unit pricing, open dating, and nutrition labeling) and truth in lending. Although the types of disclosure examined in these studies are not entirely representative of the requirements expected in the near future, and there is an overemphasis on intermediate (cognitive and affective), rather than behavioral, effects, they do contribute to a cumulation of knowledge about probable effects.

This article reviews the available evidence in the context of our present knowledge of buyer behavior in order to identify recurring patterns of effects that can be used to assess the value of future disclosure requirements. A second objective is to define more sharply future research directions and priorities. Finally, the management implications of the available evidence will be considered.

The probable direct and indirect effects of information disclosure

---

[3] The major exceptions to this pattern have been the research on nutrient labeling and open dating. See Monroe Peter Friedman, "Consumer Responses to Unit Pricing, Open Dating and Nutrient Labeling," in *Proceedings of the Association for Consumer Research*, M. Venkatesan, ed. (Chicago, 1972), pp. 361–369.

[4] George S. Day and William K. Brandt, "Consumer Research and the Evaluation of Public Policy: The Case of Truth in Lending," *Journal of Consumer Research*, Vol. 1 (June 1974), pp. 21–32.

[5] William L. Wilkie, "Assessment of Consumer Information Processing Research in Relation to Public Policy Needs" (Report to the National Science Foundation, 1974).

requirements will be summarized in a series of hypotheses covering the following issues:

The existence of a hierarchy of effects (H 1)
The determinants of the effectiveness of the information (H 2)
Segment differences in the extent of the effects (H 3)
The extent of indirect effects on manufacturer and retailer behavior (H 4)

To make this process manageable, only information disclosed at the point of sale will be considered. This does not exclude situations where the information is provided at both the point of sale and in media advertising or educational materials. This limitation is directed primarily at the special cases of counteradvertising and corrective advertising.

THE HIERARCHY OF EFFECTS

HYPOTHESIS ONE: There is a hierarchical ordering of possible effects of a disclosure of information such that prior cognitive effects are a necessary condition for subsequent changes in attitude and behavior.

The hierarchy in Figure 12-1 summarizes the hypothesized direct effects of a specific disclosure requirement. A change in a prior stage is presumed to be a necessary (although not sufficient) condition for a change in subsequent stage; the corollary of this hypothesis is that the observed impact will be greatest in the initial stages of the hierarchy. Feedback from past experience is included because it is unlikely that after a positive experience with the new information a buyer will repeat the preliminary cognitive stages with subsequent purchases.

Two parallel, but not necessarily simultaneous, hierarchies are portrayed in Figure 12-1. The righthand side describes the possible *specific* effects and hypothesizes that awareness, comprehension, and consideration of the information must produce a change in attitude before choice behavior can be changed. Lack of a specific behavioral change may be a consequence of a lack of change in any or all of the prior stages. On the left-hand side are the hypothesized *general* effects; notably, that an information disclosure requirement will improve attitudes toward the state of product information and will also increase the buyer's confidence in both the specific choice decision and the relevant industry (including retailers).

Although the specific and general effects may be independent, they are both hypothesized to increase satisfaction with the purchase decision process by reducing predecision conflict. To the extent that the information also helps the buyer better match the product or service to his needs,

FIGURE 12–1. A HIERARCHY OF POSSIBLE EFFECTS OF INFORMATION DISCLOSURE REQUIREMENTS

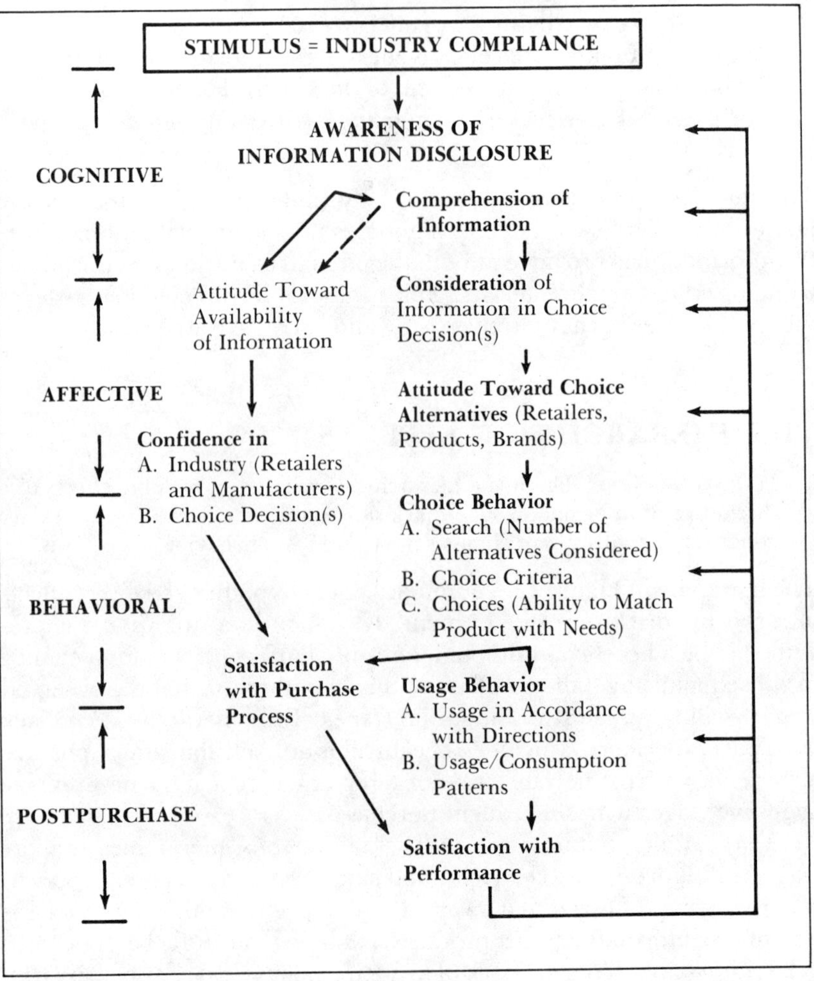

or use and maintain it properly, there will also be an increase in post-purchase satisfaction.

Evidence Supporting the Basic Hierarchy

Evidence on the effects of five disclosure requirements is summarized in Table 12–2. Two features of these results should be noted. First, there is broad support for the basic hierarchy notion across the five examples: characteristically there is much less than full awareness, and even less

Evidence of Effects of Selected Information Disclosure Requirements
(Unless noted, proportions refer to entire sample)

Effect	Disclosure Requirement: *Nutrition Labeling*[a]	*Unit Pricing*[b]	*Truth in Lending*[c]	*Buying Guide Tags*[d] *(small appliances)*	*Open Dating*[e]
1. Awareness of information	26% saw label	60% to 70% awareness of concept	57% of all credit buyers noticed some credit information	50% noticed tag	65% noticed
2. Comprehension of information	16% understood label	50% understood meaning of concept	34% correctly reported interest rate on a recent purchase	—	36% knew that the pull date was used
3. Confidence in judgments	N/A	—	54% felt better knowing rates and charges	—	N/A
4. Satisfaction	—	—	—	—	Higher degree of satisfaction with freshness
5. Claimed use of information (one or more times)	9% used labels at least once	30% to 50% used in a buying decision	10% of all credit buyers used in last durables purchase	28% found tag helpful	39% used open dating on one or more products during last trip
6. Impact on behavior (a) Self-report	—	5% to 38% of claimed users said some element of a shopping trip was influenced	—	—	50% reduction in report of spoiled food
(b) Other evidence	—	—	Negligible relationship of knowledge and shopping behavior, choice of credit source, or decision to use cash or credit	No evidence of effect on pattern of sales for specific models	—

[a] R. J. Lenahan, J. A. Thomas, D. A. Taylor, D. L. Call, and D. I. Padberg, "Consumer Reaction to Nutritional Labels on Food Products," *Journal of Consumer Affairs,* Vol. 7 (Spring 1973).

[b] Summary conclusions from a recent review of unit pricing studies. Ivan Ross, "Applications of Consumer Information to Public Policy Decisions," in *Marketing Analysis for Societal Problems,* Jagdish Sheth and Peter Wright, eds. (Urbana, Ill.: University of Illinois, 1974).

[c] George S. Day and William K. Brandt, *A Study of Consumer Credit Decisions: Implications for Present and Prospective Legislation* (Washington, D. C.: National Commission on Consumer Finance, 1973).

[d] Federated Department Stores, Inc., *Buying Guide Tag Pilot Program,* February 1970.

[e] R. C. Stokes, R. Haddock, W. J. Hoofnagle, and E. F. Taylor, *Food Dating: Shoppers' Reactions and the Impact on Retail Foodstores,* Report No. 984 (U.S. Department of Agriculture, Economic Research Service, January 1973).

comprehension of the meaning of the information, while the behavioral effects are usually negligible or nonexistent.[6] Second, these results emerge despite significant gaps and shortcomings in the data. Virtually all the research on disclosure requirements suffers from some or all of the following defects:

Short duration (i.e., three months or less).
Little or no control over competing explanations for observed changes.
Absence of before-after comparisons.
Only a few of the possible effects are investigated; particularly lacking are measures of confidence and satisfaction.
Weak behavioral measures; heavy reliance on self-reports and virtually no investigation of brand or product type switching.[7]

The Role of Confidence and Satisfaction

There is sketchy but encouraging support for the more general hypothesis that mere availability of information increases buyer confidence. This is evidently the case with nutrition labeling, which has otherwise had little apparent effect. One interpretation for this effect is that

> consumers see informative nutritional labels as a part of general food industry accountability rather than an input to the purchase decision. . . . [they] see themselves benefiting from nutritional labeling because of the way it affects others—through advertising and through the accountability of food manufacturers for the nutritional quality of their food products.[8]

More specifically, there are indications of increased confidence in the freshness of all food in a store when open dating is used.[9] Similarly, while

---

[6] The exception to the pattern is open dating. While some behavior change did occur, there was a great deal of inaccurate reporting of use. If the data are suitably corrected, the basic hierarchy is present. See R. C. Stokes, R. Haddock, W. J. Hoofnagle, and E. F. Taylor, *Food Dating: Shoppers' Reactions and the Impact on Retail Foodstores* (U.S. Department of Agriculture, Economic Research Service, January 1973).

[7] For more specific comments, see James M. Carman, "A Summary of Empirical Research on Unit Pricing," *Journal of Retailing,* Vol. 48 (Winter 1972–1973), pp. 63–72. An interesting exception to the general pattern is discussed in Karl E. Henion, "The Effect of Ecologically Relevant Information in Detergent Sales," *Journal of Marketing Research,* Vol. 9 (February 1972), pp. 10–14.

[8] R. J. Lenahan, J. A. Thomas, D. A. Taylor, D. L. Call, and D. I. Padberg, "Consumer Reaction to Nutritional Labels on Food Products," *Journal of Consumer Affairs,* Vol. 7 (Spring 1973).

[9] Raymond C. Stokes, "Consumerism and the Measurement of Consumer Dissatisfactions" (Paper presented to the American Marketing Association Conference on Attitude Research Bridges the Atlantic, Madrid, Spain, February 1973).

18% of credit buyers who noticed credit information said they used the information in making a recent purchase, 54% said that they did not have a specific use but felt better knowing the rates and charges.[10] In general, information seems to enhance confidence by assuring buyers of the correctness of their choice.

The grestest weakness in the available data concerns the linkages of satisfaction and confidence. In several laboratory studies, Jacoby and his associates found that as the amount of information was increased, subjects made "poorer" purchase decisions but felt more satisfied and certain regarding their selection.[11] Although these results are difficult to generalize to field environments, they do suggest that enhanced confidence and satisfaction may be the principal outcomes of most disclosure requirements.

INFORMATION EFFECTIVENESS

> HYPOTHESIS TWO: A disclosure requirement will have maximum effect when the buyer (a) has easy access to the information at the point of sale, (b) can readily comprehend and process the information, and (c) can use it to make direct comparisons of the choice alternatives along relevant attributes—in short, when the information is easy to use and relevant to the choice process.

An extreme case, in which none of the hypothesized conditions appears to have been satisfied, is the disclosure of automotible performance data in the areas of braking power, tire wear, and engine efficiency. This technical information is provided, separately for each car, in a sealed envelope in the glove compartment. In many cases the salespeople are not even aware of the existence of the envelopes. Thus, every possible barrier to the use of the information has been placed in front of the consumer.

Is the Information Accessible?

In general, the closer the information display is to the point of decision, in a form that permits easy comparison of alternatives, the greater the effectiveness of the information. This notion casts doubt on the effec-

---

[10] Same reference as footnote 4. This was in response to an open-ended question on the use of the information.

[11] Jacob Jacoby, Donald E. Speller, and Carol A. Kohn, "Brand Choice Behavior as a Function of Information Load," *Journal of Marketing Research,* Vol. 11 (February 1974), pp. 63–69; Jacoby et al., "Brand Choice Behavior as a Function of Information Load: Study II" (Purdue Paper in Consumer Psychology No. 131, 1973); and Jacob Jacoby, "Consumer Reaction to Information Displays: Packaging and Advertising," in *Advertising and the Public Interest,* Sal Divita, ed. (Chicago: American Marketing Assn., 1975).

tiveness of any disclosure requirement in which the information is only presented after the effective agreement—the oral agreement—is concluded.[12] Yet this is precisely the procedure for providing truth-in-lending (TIL) information. Not only does the buyer not get the correct information when it is needed, but there is compelling evidence that many sellers are (incorrectly and illegally) quoting the lower add-on interest rate. Thus the implementation of TIL requirements suffers from both *design* and *execution* problems.

All disclosure requirements are subject to execution problems, whose role in diminishing the effectiveness of the requirements is typically understated. For example, unit pricing would appear to be relatively easy to execute in view of the systems and procedures already in place for posting prices. Yet a survey of grocery stores in Washington, D.C. (presumably the showcase of unit pricing), found significant problems in most stores with respect to extent and uniformity of coverage within the store, legibility and understandability of labels, and "a virtual absence of in-store promotional or explanatory material to call attention to or aid consumers in the use of unit pricing information."[13]

Can the Information Be Comprehended?

Information availability does not mean comprehension.[14] The barriers to comprehension involve issues of communication and education, notably the potential for misinterpretation and the ability of the buyer to absorb the information.

Potential for Misinterpretation

The likelihood that a buyer will correctly interpret a new piece of information depends on:

1. The number of possible interpretations. One of the problems with open dating is that the date can be variously interpreted as the pull date, expiration date, pack date, or display date.[15]
2. The extent to which variability in product characteristics influences the interpretation. For example, variations in concentra-

---

[12] Whitford, same reference as footnote 1, p. 443.

[13] Office of Consumer Affairs, "Unit Pricing Survey" (Washington, D.C., April 7, 1972). Similar execution problems have been encountered with mandatory posting of consumer drug prices; see Boston Consumer's Council, "The Report on the Effect of Boston Drug Price Posting Regulation," July 1972.

[14] Bymers, same reference as footnote 1, p. 60.

[15] Same reference as footnote 6.

tion, density, and active ingredients influence unit price comparisons.[16]

3. Whether the new disclosure requirement provides completely new information or represents a modification of previous practices. Thus, many buyers appear to treat the annual percentage rate (APR) required by TIL as an add-on rate and simply estimate the dollar credit charges by multiplying the principal by the APR.[17]
4. Prior expectations. A study of the Swedish VDN system (which involves the voluntary disclosure of product information according to government standards) found that 65% of Swedish consumers think of a VDN label as a stamp of quality when in fact there is no minimum quality standard.[18]

The seriousness of these problems will depend on the effectiveness of the education program used to introduce the disclosure requirement. Too often, it appears, these efforts do not recognize the existence of the alternative explanations and interpretations.

. . .

Is the Information Relevant?

There are several reasons why behavior changes may not occur, even though the information is available and comprehended. First, the buyer may not have any choices. For example, a store may stock only a very limited selection of a certain size of product. An extreme case of this problem is beef grading. As many retail outlets adhere to a "one-grade policy," the buyer is limited to "U.S. Choice" beef.[19] Thus, the grading system conveys no information because it cannot be used to differentiate among alternatives. There is some evidence that manufacturers will anticipate a new information requirement by withdrawing poorly rated

[16] Lawrence Lamont, James Rothe, and Charles Slater, "Unit Pricing: A Positive Response to Consumerism," *European Journal of Marketing,* Vol. 6 (1972), pp. 223–233. See also, Raymond C. Stokes, "Unit Pricing, Differential Brand Density and Consumer Deception" (Working paper, Consumer Research Institute, June 1973).

[17] William K. Brandt, George S. Day, and Terry Deutscher, "The Effect of Disclosure on Consumer Knowledge of Credit Terms," *Journal of Consumer Affairs,* Vol. 9 (Summer 1975).

[18] Information provided author by Dr. Melvin Meyerson, chief of the Product Evaluation Technology Division, National Bureau of Standards, Washington, D.C.

[19] Robert A. Mittlestaedt, "Consumer Protection and the Value of Information," in *Proceedings of the Association for Consumer Research,* M. Venkatesan, ed. (Chicago, 1972), pp. 101–106.

products. Buyer behavior patterns will thus have been changed before the new requirement is implemented, and a before-after study will show no behavioral effects.

Second, the previous choices may have been "correct"; that is, the product matched the buyer's needs. There is some evidence that brand loyalty is based on a periodic analysis of all the alternatives in the consideration class and the choice of the one that best meets the buyer's needs.[20] This is one explanation for the limited effect of unit pricing; even without this information, buyers were in fact periodically making judgments about relative cost versus other attributes.

Third, the information may not be relevant. Information on an unimportant attribute will have little effect. Thus, a buyer is unlikely to be swayed by the fact that a television set is certified as being in compliance with UL safety requirements, FCC broadcast requirements, and federal regulations on radiation.

SEGMENT DIFFERENCES

> Hypothesis Three: Information disclosure requirements have the least effect on those buyers who have the greatest need for consumer protection.

Information disclosure requirements have been aptly described as protection for the middle class. Low-income buyers, who have the greatest need for protection or assistance in making more informed choices, are more likely to lack the characteristics that will allow them to take advantage of the information:

1. Low-income consumers are often unaware of the benefits of comparative shopping.
2. They lack the education and knowledge necessary to choose the best buy, even if it were available.
3. They often lack the freedom to go outside their local community to engage in comparative shopping.
4. Nothing in their experience has reinforced the benefits of seeking better value for their money; consequently, the low-income buyer lacks the motivation to make improvements in his situation.[21]

By contrast, the subscriber to *Consumer Reports* is well equipped to use any additional information: "he is part of an educational and income

---

[20] George S. Day, "A Two-Dimensional Concept of Brand Loyalty," *Journal of Advertising Research,* Vol. 9 (September 1969), pp. 29–35.

[21] Eric Schnapper, "Consumer Legislation and the Poor," *Yale Law Journal,* Vol. 76 (1967), pp. 745–768.

elite. . . . he is information-sensitive in general and consumer information-sensitive in particular. . . . he is a 'rational' buyer in the traditional sense . . . uses more utilitarian, performance-related choice criteria in shopping."[22]

The implication of these and other, comparative analyses of income groups is that observable differences in awareness and use of information can be largely attritubed to education. However, this explanation ignores the possibility that low-income buyers don't pay attention to additional information because they know they can't use it. For example, the level of rate awareness for installment credit transactions of respondents in poverty areas rose only from 9.7% to 16.1% in the fifteen months following the implementation of TIL, while in other areas rate awareness rose from 14.5% to 38.3%.[23] One reason for this lack of effect is that low-income buyers are primarily influenced by the availability of credit and the size of the monthly payment, rather than by the APR or the total cost of the credit.[24] Their economic circumstances put severe constraints on their choice of credit sources and credit plans, which makes the TIL information of little relevance. Yet low-income buyers have been found to be quite well informed as to the relative rates and ease of borrowing from alternative credit sources.[25]

Whether economic constraints or educational differences are the explanation for the lack of use of new information, the fact remains that information disclosure requirements mainly benefit the middle class.

INDIRECT EFFECTS ON PRODUCER AND RETAILER BEHAVIOR

An information disclosure requirmement is not simply a net addition to the information environment of the buyer. It also changes the environment of manufacturers and retailers who must decide how to adjust their marketing programs to minimize the perceived adverse effects on their market position, or possibly to exploit an opportunity. In any event, a

[22] Jack Engledow, "The Consumer Reports Subscriber: Portrait of an Intense Consumer," *Indiana Business Review,* Vol. 47 (July/August 1972), pp. 32–40.

[23] R. Shay and M. Schober, "Consumer Awareness of Annual Percentage Rates of Charge in Consumer Installment Credit: Before and After Truth in Lending Became Effective," National Commission on Consumer Finance, Technical Studies, 1973.

[24] Same reference as footnote 4.

[25] Homer Kripke, "Gesture and Reality in Consumer Credit Reform," *New York University Law Review,* Vol. 44 (March 1969), pp. 1–52.

disclosure requirement that promises to have any relevance to buyers will certainly affect the relationships and balance of power in the channel. The question is: How will the buyer fare?

> HYPOTHESIS FOUR: On balance, the consumer will also benefit from the indirect effects of the disclosure requirement on retailer and producer behavior.

As we will see, some of the most significant effects may be indirect, but the data are incapable of supporting definite conclusions about consumer welfare.

Positive Effects

These are known or forecasted indirect effects where the consumer clearly benefits. One of the best examples comes from a study of buying guide tags for small appliances which found that more complete point-of-sale information helps buyers overcome the inadequacies of salespeople.[26]

Buyers may also benefit from anticipatory changes in marketing strategies, including active adoption and promotion of the requirement before it becomes mandatory. Carman notes that "manufacturers can respond to an increased ability to make price comparisons (afforded by unit pricing) by increasing quality, facilitating quality comparison or lowering prices"[27] All these consequences are beneficial to the consumer. Unfortunately, there is no evidence that manufacturers have made such changes.

Negative Effects

Some side effects of disclosure requirements are clearly not in the consumer interest. Some are a consequence of changes in pricing and merchandising practices designed to minimize the effect of disclosure requirements. As a consequence of the truth-in-lending legislation, for example, most retailers simply note that credit is available in order to bypass the space-consuming disclosure of annual percentage rates and

[26] Federated Department Stores, *Buying Guide Tag Pilot Program,* February 1970. A similar result was also noted in a less formal buying tag program conducted by J. L. Hudson in Detroit.

[27] Carman, same reference as footnote 7, p. 70.

credit charges. Also, there is some evidence that credit sellers who do not compete for cash business (those in low-income areas primarily) are simply burying their credit charges in the total purchase price.[28]

There may also be adverse effects from changes in consumer behavior. For example, the requirement that a manufacturer attach to all new cars a label showing the suggested retail price has apparently weakened the bargaining position of the buyer. In this case, the effect has been to encourage retail price maintenance.[29] The new Real Estate Settlement Procedures Act has apparently reduced comparative shopping for mortgage rates. Because of the penalties associated with the information disclosure procedure, lenders are unwilling to quote rates over the phone.[30]

Likewise, the consumer will not benefit if the effect is to raise barriers to entry to small manufacturers. For example, it is felt that ingredient labeling requirements will put processors of regional price brands at a competitive disadvantage because a large portion of the costs of compliance are fixed (e.g., food analyses, label changeovers, and product certification tests).

More generally, whenever the costs of compliance or implementation exceeds the benefits, the consumer will suffer a welfare loss. As we noted earlier, however, the objectives and hence the benefits of disclosure requirements are seldom stated precisely, much less quantified, and the costs are difficult to assess. The issue of cost-benefit ratios promises to become critical in the future as disclosure requirements increasingly emphasize comparative performance information involving complex standard-setting and testing procedures.

Ambiguous Effects

In some situations, the judgment as to whether the effect will be beneficial to consumers depends on the perspective of the analyst. This is particularly apparent in the differences in the reactions of business and consumer advocates to proposed disclosures of comparative performance information. One type of industry forecast is that "producers [would] tend to emphasize the characteristics identified as significant and they may become standard (i.e., uniform) throughout the

---

[28] Whitford, same reference as footnote 1.

[29] Marshall C. Howard, "Government, the Retailer and the Customer," *Journal of Retailing,* Vol. 48 (Winter 1972–1973), pp. 48–62.

[30] "The Decline and Fall of a New Consumer Law," *Business Week,* October 13, 1975, p. 40.

industry . . . thus discouraging innovation and limiting consumer choice."[31] By contrast, consumer advocates tend to see standardization as a desirable outcome since it reduces product proliferation and, hopefully, increases price competition.

Another contested effect of comparative disclosure requirements concerns the shift in the balance of power between manufacturers and retailers as a consequence of making the private labels more competitive with national brands (perhaps leading to a reduction in the number of national brands). Whether this outcome is desirable depends on one's judgment as to whether retailers are more responsive to consumer needs than manufacturers.

SUMMARY AND IMPLICATIONS

Proposals for new information disclosure requirements continue to emerge as the buyer's "right to know" takes on new meaning. Many such proposals have been or will be implemented for this reason alone, in the absence of relevant research on actual or possible effects on consumer, producer, or retailer behavior.

This article has reviewed a number of studies of existing disclosure requirements in order to isolate recurring issues and patterns of effects that can guide future policies and research. Many of the aspects examined are so situation specific, arguable, or devoid of relevant research as to defy generalization. This is particularly true of the possible benefits to consumers of indirect effects of changes in producer and retailer behavior, and of differences between immediate and long-run effects.

On the central question of the direct effects of information disclosures on buyer behavior an interesting pattern emerged. First, there is a hierarchy of effects in which prior cognitive effects are a necessary condition for subsequent changes in attitude and behavior. One of the most difficult thresholds in this hierarchy is from availability to awareness and comprehension of the information. Second, there is little evidence of significant effects on buyer behavior (including search, choice criteria, or actual choices of brands or models). But just as consistent is the finding that more information enhances confidence in the choice, and possibly satisfaction with the purchase, through assuring the buyer that the product is correct, that mistakes have not been made, and that the price is justified. Moreover, the manufacturer and retailer are felt to be more accountable, contributing to greater confidence in the entire marketing system. Finally, it is clear that the design and execution of the disclosure

---

[31] Summary of industry opinion given in same reference as footnote 2.

requirement are of crucial importance in achieving even the intermediate cognitive and affective changes.

. . .

Implications for Management

Despite the voids in knowledge of effects, the existing evidence does have immediate implications for the response of companies and trade associations to new information disclosure requirements. The first step is to accept the inevitability of further disclosure requirements for most consumer goods and services. The consumer's "right to know" is an effective argument supporting this trend and will be skillfully employed by increasingly powerful regulators.

The next step must begin with the recognition that while most of the requirements in existence have had little direct effect on buyer behavior, they frequently enhance confidence in the choice process and, to some extent, in the entire marketing system. Other beneficial indirect effects may also accrue, through helping sales personnel for example. Thus, it is important to question the posture that a new disclosure requirement will simply impose new costs and will create few benefits for either buyers or sellers. The danger of an excessively negative response is that the requirement, as implemented, will be either unworkable or unnecessarily restrictive. One way to avoid this outcome is to undertake studies of alternative designs and executions before the requirement is implemented. Because of the "negative halo" around industry-sponsored or conducted research, government participation in the design of such research is essential to ensure that the results are not ignored.

The best way to avoid the loss of flexibility inherent in any mandatory disclosure requirement is to voluntarily provide the information. In most stiuations, this will require trade association leadership to define the need and initiate the process, perhaps in conjunction with the relevant government agencies.

Finally there is increasing recognition that the quality of execution of existing (and proposed) disclosure requirements may vary greatly, thereby drastically diminishing their effectiveness. Thus, it is important to periodically evaluate implementation to ensure compliance.

13 CONSUMER PROTECTION: MORE INFORMATION OR MORE REGULATION?

William H. Cunningham & Isabella C. M. Cunningham

The legal aspects of marketing have been a continuing concern of marketing scholars and practitioners. The objective of this research was to determine how much individuals in various sectors of society know about the consumer protection laws and their rights as consumers.

RESEARCH PROCEDURE

The research was broken down into two substudies. The first dealt with the consumers' knowledge of ten areas of the law. These included: false or deceptive advertising, false or deceptive retail advertising, credit regulations, credit reporting, door-to-door selling, automobile sales, credit cards, labeling, truth in lending, and deceptive retail practices.

The consumer respondents were divided into six income segments to determine if their knowledge of consumer protection law differed according to income level. Caplovitz and Sturdivant have both indicated that lower-income segments of our society are vulnerable to abuses by the distribution system partially because they have virtually no understand-

---

Reprinted with deletions from *Journal of Marketing* 40 (April 1976), pp. 63–68, published by the American Marketing Association.

ing of their rights.[1] Caplovitz states further that low-income consumers should be treated differently from the rest of society because they are no match for the sophisticated marketer.[2] This portion of the research was designed to determine if the low-income consumer is any less capable of dealing with sophisticated marketing appeals than are middle- or upper-income individuals.

The second half of the study consisted of asking a sample of lawyers the same questions that were administered to the consumers. Although very few, if any, of the attorneys interviewed specialized in consumer protection law, these individuals do represent an educated elite of society who should have a sound knowledge of the law. The responses of the attorneys were compared with those of the consumer sample. (Table 13-1).

TABLE 13-1. EXAMPLES OF STATEMENTS USED TO TEST CONSUMERS' KNOWLEDGE OF TEN AREAS OF THE LAW *

AREA OF THE LAW	STATEMENTS
False or Deceptive Advertising	
	1. A children's commercial for toy race cars which exaggerates the speed of the cars is *legal.*
	2. An advertisement which claims that an automobile will get good mileage because its motor runs cool is *legal* even though there is no relationship between a car's mileage and how hot its motor runs.
False or Deceptive Retail Advertising	
	3. It is *not legal* to advertise a low-priced item and then only stock enough for the first few customers who enter the store.
	4. It is *legal* for a store to have a going-out-of-business sale even though in reality is is NOT going out of business.
	5. It is *legal* to advertise a television set as being ''original'' if it has been totally reconditioned.
Credit Regulations	
	6. It is *not legal* for debt collectors to make annoying telephone calls to the consumer or his family.
	7. It is *legal* to deny a female college student a credit card on the basis of her sex.
Credit Reporting	
	8. If you have been denied credit you have the *legal* right to be told the name and address of the consumer reporting agency responsible for preparing the report that was used to deny the credit.
	9. If you have been denied credit you have the *legal* right to know the nature and substance of the information (except medical) collected about you by a credit reporting agency.

[1] David Caplovitz, *The Poor Pay More* (Toronto, Canada: Free Press, 1963), pp. 170-178; and Frederick D. Sturdivant, ''Better Deal for Ghetto Shoppers,'' *Harvard Business Review,* Vol. 46 (March-April 1968), pp. 130-139.

[2] Caplovitz, op. cit., p. 190.

TABLE 13-1, cont.

AREA OF THE LAW	STATEMENTS

Door-to-Door Selling

10. When you purchase a vacuum cleaner from a door-to-door salesman, and on the following day you change your mind and want to return it, the salesman may *legally* refuse to refund 100% of your purchase.
11. A door-to-door salesman is *not legally* required to furnish the purchaser with a fully completed contract until 24 hours after the sale has taken place.
12. It is *legal* for a salesman of encyclopedias to give you a special discount on your purchase if you refer him to three of your friends for a sales presentation.

Automobile Sales

13. When selling a car it is *not legal* to turn the odometer (mileage meter) back on the car to show that the vehicle has less miles on it than it actually has.
14. Automobile dealers are *not legally* required to display on their new cars' windows a ticket by the manufacturer listing the basic price, the price of federal tax, factory installed accessories, and the retailer's service and delivery charges.

Credit Cards

15. You are *legally* responsible for a credit card which has been mailed to you which you did not request.
16. If one of your credit cards is stolen you are *legally* responsible for all unauthorized charges until you have notified the company which issued the card.

Labeling

17. A manufacturer which produces merchandise which is subject to cleaning, such as clothing, is *legally* required to have a label in plain sight which tells the consumer how the product is to be laundered or dry cleaned.
18. It is *legal* for a manufacturer to make clothing out of textile products without a label which indicates what the product is made of.

Truth in Lending

19. Banks and other lending institutions are *legally* required to state the true interest rate and all other costs of a credit transaction.
20. Retail stores are *legally* required to state the true interest rate and other costs of credit transactions.

Deceptive Retail Practices

21. It is *not legal* for a gasoline company to have a game or raffle without posting the odds of winning.
22. It is *legal* for a store to tell you that you have won a free gift of an oil painting if you have to pay $15.00 for the frame to receive the gift.

* For correct responses see Editor's Note, page 174.

FINDINGS

The results of the research are presented in Table 13-2. Significant differences between the different income groups were found only in the area involving truth-in-lending legislation. In this case, the respondents in the lower-income groups appeared to be somewhat less familiar with the law than did those individuals in the higher-income families. In the remaining nine consumer protection areas, no significant differences were

TABLE 13.2. MEAN CONSUMER AND LAWYER SAMPLES

AREA OF THE LAW	TOTAL CONSUMER SAMPLE	TOTAL LAWYER SAMPLE
	% *Correct*	% *Correct*
False or deceptive advertising	33.5	46.5
False or deceptive retail advertising	35.1	51.5
Credit regulations	63.7	75.2
Credit reporting	60.6	80.0
Door-to-door selling	29.4	38.8
Auto sales	77.5	85.5
Credit cards	44.5	77.0
Labels	64.5	52.5
Truth in lending	83.5	94.5
Deceptive retail practices	37.8	50.6
Total N	(607)	(175)

found in the amount of knowledge shown by the different consumer groups.

Table 13–2 also indicates that the amount of information that the consumer respondents had varied a great deal among the ten areas of law that were investigated. As an example, in the area of door-to-door selling, none of the six consumer groups had more than 31% of the responses correct. In the areas of false or deceptive advertising, false or deceptive retail advertising, and deceptive retail practices, none of the six income groups had more than 40% of the responses correct. In contrast, in the areas of credit regulation, auto sales, labeling, and truth in lending, the consumer respondents seemed to have a better understanding of the law. In each of these cases, 60% or more of the responses in all of the six income groups were correct.

The differences between the lawyer and the consumer samples in their knowledge of each area of the consumer protection law were statistically significant, although the magnitude of the differences in responses was not as large as might have been anticipated. As an example, in the area of false or deceptive advertising, 33.5% of the consumers' responses and 46.5% of the lawyers' responses were correct. With the exception of credit card regulations, for which 44.5% of the consumers' responses were correct compared with 77% of the lawyers' responses, the spread between the correct answers of the two samples averaged 12.2%. Only in the area of labeling did the subjects in the consumer sample have a better knowledge of consumer protection regulation than the lawyer sample. In this case, 64.5% of the consumers' answers were correct, compared to 52.5% for the lawyers.

DISCUSSION AND IMPLICATIONS

Two aspects of the findings are particularly interesting and merit further discussion. First, the overall percentage of correct responses is relatively low for both the consumer sample and the attorney sample. This is particularly meaningful when one takes into consideration that some respondents surely tried to "guess" the correct answers. If an individual took this approach, he or she should have gotten 50% of the answers correct by mere chance alone. Although every effort was made to ask the subjects not to guess, some of this was inevitable.

Second, there are several reasons why the lawyers' results were not as good as might have been expected. As was stated previously, most of these individuals were not specialists in consumer protection law; the sample represented a broad spectrum of legal expertise. Also, consumer protection law is one of the most rapidly changing areas of the legal profession. The Texas Deceptive Trade Practices Act and Consumer Protection Act were hardly two years old at the time of this investigation. Finally, many lawyers do not take the time to learn about the law unless they are hired by a client interested in such matters. Since lawyers are prohibited from soliciting business by the Bar Association, and since consumers often do not know that they have been taken advantage of and, therefore, do not contact an attorney, there is little incentive on the part of attorneys to study this particular legislation.

The research also has several implications for those individuals in the public sector who are responsible for enacting legislation designed to protect the consumer, as well as for those people in the public and private sectors who are charged with enforcing rules designed to safeguard consumers from unscrupulous businesspeople.

The most important implication derives from the lack of information demonstrated by all income segments of the consumer sample. This situation suggests that what is needed is not more and tougher laws, but rather more information made available to more individuals concerning their rights as consumers. Texas has one of the toughest consumer protection laws in the United States, yet many of its citizens go unprotected. This problem can be solved only if ways are established to spread the truth about consumers' rights and about the means available to them to enforce such rights. This could be accomplished by programs sponsored at the local level by the Bar Association. Attorneys who are specialists in consumer protection law could speak to organizations such as church groups and P.T.A.'s. In addition, programs that clearly spell out what the consumers' rights are and what should be done when the rights of consumers have been violated could be designed for use in high schools.

A second implication of the research is that the spread of information must be designed to reach all levels of society. The findings indicated that there was very little difference between the income groups as to their understanding of the law. This would seem to negate Caplovitz's statement that low-income consumers need to be treated with special care; apparently all consumers need to be treated in a special way if they are to be fully protected. There is certainly ample evidence to indicate that the only difference between how wealthy people and poor people are swindled is that wealthy people lose more money. A classic example of executives who have been misled by unethical practices is the current Home-Stake Production Company scandal, in which the chairmen of the board of General Electric, Western Union, and New York's First National City Bank all apparently lost large sums of money.[3]

Third, even though the general level of understanding of the law was not as high as might have been hoped, it is clear that the subjects had a better understanding of some areas of the law than others. Unfortunately, the respondents seemed to have the least knowledge in those areas of illegal activities in which they are most directly affected on a day-to-day basis: false or deceptive retail advertising, door-to-door selling, and deceptive retail practices. This would imply that those individuals who are responsible for informing people of their rights must direct their efforts to specific areas of consumer protection law if they are to have the maximum impact.

Lastly, it is critically important that individual businesspeople and organizations such as local Better Business Bureaus, national trade associations, and local retailers' groups realize that consumers do not know as much about the law as they should. As a result, these individuals and organizations should join the effort to help communicate to consumers their rights and to monitor trade practices in their own markets. If this is not done, one response to the problem will be the passage of more and more government legislation designed to regulate the activities of the marketplace. Although this may bring the unscrupulous businessperson under control, it is also likely to substantially increase the cost of doing business for the vast majority of businesspeople who are trying to provide a good product at a reasonable price for the consumer.

CONCLUSIONS

There are a number of reasons why private citizens frequently do not avail themselves of the legal remedies that are available to them under local, state, and federal consumer protection laws. Often the consumer

---

[3] David McClintok, "Home-Stake's Trippet Emerges as a Complex, Unpredictable Person," *Wall Street Journal,* May 30, 1975, p. 1.

does not feel that the issue is important enough, or he does not want to take the time to pursue the defendant, or he feels that he could not win his case without a high-priced attorney. The present research has demonstrated that one other variable is important: with the exception of a few areas of the law, both consumers and attorneys know very little about their rights as consumers. This was particularly true in areas such as door-to-door selling, false or deceptive advertising, false or deceptive retail advertising, and deceptive retail practices.

Several implications of the research for individuals in the public and private sectors were mentioned. Most importantly, more and better information concerning consumers' rights must be provided to individuals of all economic strata. This can best be accomplished through an alliance of individuals in the educational, legal, and business communities. The only alternative to this approach is increased government regulation. Although this might help solve the consumer protection problem, it would add substantially to the cost of doing business for the great majority of honest businesspeople.

Editors' Note: In Table 13-1, statements, 3, 6, 8, 9, 13, 17, 19, 20, and 21 are true. All other statements are false.

14 AFFIRMATIVE DISCLOSURE OF NUTRITION INFORMATION AND CONSUMERS' FOOD PREFERENCES: A REVIEW

Tyzoon T. Tyebjee

The relationship between food advertising and the nutrition status of consumers has recently become a major public policy issue. Two large scale surveys, the Ten State Nutrition Survey and the Health and Nutrition Examination Survey, found that, in spite of the relative affluence of American society, a significant number of Americans had nutrition-related problems or were at high risk of developing them [1, 2, 33, 34]. Part of the blame for these problems has been placed on food advertising and marketing practices. The Panel on Popular Education at the White House Conference on Food, Nutrition and Health stated that "the gaps in our public knowledge about nutrition, along with actual misinformation carried by some media, are contributing seriously to the problem of hunger and malnutrition in the United States" [35]. A variety of consumer activist groups, including Ralph Nader, Action for Children's Television, and the Center for Science in the Public Interest, have criticized the marketing practices of the food industry for fostering, if not encouraging, poor dietary practices. These various developments in the early seventies were some of the factors which were responsible for a

---

Reprinted, with deletions, by permission of the University of Wisconsin Press. From *Journal of Consumer Affairs* (Winter 1979), pp. 206–223.

trade regulation rule proposed by the Federal Trade Commission. This proposed rule is designed to enhance the availability of nutritional information in food advertising and to protect consumers from the potentially deceptive claims about the nutritional qualities of an advertised food product [13].

The proposed regulation, as currently framed, has two objectives. The first is to stringently define certain nutrition-related claims such as "organic" or "loaded with vitamins" so that a food product which makes such a claim would have to meet certain criteria in terms of its nutrient composition and method of cultivation or processing. This aspect of the regulation attempts to define the meaning of several descriptors about food. A methodology for examining the semantics of advertising claims from a public policy perspective has been developed by the author elsewhere [32] and, hence, this aspect of the trade regulation rule will not be the focus of this paper. The second facet of the proposed regulation would require the affirmative disclosure of the nutrient composition of an advertised food if a nutrition-related claim were made. The form and content of such disclosures would be prescribed by the FTC. The regulation, in effect, would extend the 1973 FDA regulation regarding food labeling to also encompass food advertising. Currently, affirmative disclosure of nutrient content is required on labels of all processed foods which make nutritional claims or are fortified with nutrients (it is voluntary for other food items). It is the affirmative disclosure of nutrition information in food advertising and its anticipated effects on consumers which is the dominant interest of this paper.

. . . The following [section reviews] studies which have focused on the cognitive, attitudinal and behavioral effects of food advertising and nutrition information. Next, the communication effects of the format and content of the affirmative disclosure requirement are evaluated. Finally, two scenarios of industry response to the regulation are developed to assess some of the secondary effects on consumer nutrition status which may result from the proposed regulation.

CURRENT PRACTICES IN FOOD ADVERTISING

. . .

[Some] general conclusions are possible about the content of food advertising on the basis of [several] studies. . . . First, food advertising makes up a major portion of television advertising. Second, a large portion of the foods advertised are high-sugar foods. Third, commercial practices in food advertising place a higher emmphasis on sensory satisfaction and immediate gratification the food provides, than upon its ability to provide the nutrients essential for good health. Fourth, the kinds of food products most frequently advertised and the contextual settings of the ads encourage snacking and between-meal eating. Fifth, more food advertising is directed toward children than adults; as a result, the audience for food ads has a significant number of viewers who have limited information processing capabilities, are more susceptible to deceptive practices, and are at a period of development where food habits and attitudes are in a formative stage.

. . .

NUTRITIONAL INFORMATION AND DIETARY HABITS

The proposed FTC trade regulation of food advertising has as its explicit purpose the protection of the consumer from deceptive or misleading advertising. By providing nutritional information in advertising to the consumer, the meaning of vague nutritional terms such as "high in nutrition" and "loaded in vitamin C" will, one hopes, be clarified. However, the extent to which the rule will have a positive impact on the dietary practices of American consumers depends on the answers to several important questions. Do consumers need or want nutritional information? Will the consumer comprehend the nutritional information? Finally, will the consumer use the nutritional information in selecting foods and, if so, will their nutritional intake be improved by this information?

Jacoby, et al [20] have reviewed a variety of studies which asked consumers whether they would use nutritional information if available. In all the studies reviewed more than 60 percent of consumers responded affirmatively. Jacoby and his colleagues, however, point out that this self-reported desire for nutritional information is likely to be substantially higher than actual use of such information. In support of this conclusion, they cite several studies of information acquisition behavior which found that actual information search behavior demonstrates a far lower interest in nutritional information than do surveys of self-reported desire for such information. Moreover, the extent to which nutritional information was sought declined substantially as the number of product categories on the consumer's shopping list increased. Hence single purchase experimental studies of nutritional information acquisition are likely to overestimate the use of such information, and have poor external validity for predicting behavior during multiple purchases in the supermarket. One survey of 1,664 consumers found that 63 percent reported that they did not use any nutrition labeling [14].

In a study by Asam and Bucklin [4] it was found that when consumers were provided nutrition information on canned pea labels there was no impact upon their attitude or preference toward the product. Their perceptions of wholesomeness and tenderness were, however, positively influenced. It also was found that non-nutritional claims about the peas, specifically claims about their sweetness and succulence, provided many consumers with a quality assurance comparable to that of more detailed nutritional information.

On the other hand, one of the few studies which has evaluated the impact of nutrition information on behavior, as opposed to attitudes, reports that when such information was posted at food vending machines in a university dormitory, consumption, as measured by sales, shifted away from less nutritious foods such as cookies and candies to more nutritious ones such as milk, fruits, and yogurt [22].

One explanation of the inadequate utilization of nutrition information could be that most consumers do not understand such information. Lenahan, et al report that only 16 percent of 2,150 consumers they surveyed in 1972 claimed to understand nutrition information [24]. Similarly, Jacoby, et al found that consumers intercepted in a shopping mall scored low on a test of nutrition comprehension [20]. From a policy perspective, it is important to ask whether the provision of nutrition information whenever a nutrition claim is made will reduce the ambiguity of the meaning of the claim. Many consumers find nutrition claims such as "nourishing" and "wholesome" to be ambiguous [26]. Similarly, 291 members of the Society of Nutrition Education, presumably experts in the field, could not agree about the meaning of several comparative claims about nutritional qualities of advertised food products [29]. The mere provision of nutritional information may clear up ambiguities about the meaning of advertising claims in the case of the experts who are equipped to interpret such information. However, for most consumers this information is not likely to alleviate the ambiguity, and may even aggravate it, unless other measures are taken to facilitate the comprehension of this information. This points to the necessity of consumer education programs as a key to the success of programs which regulate the consumer information environment.

. . .

NUTRITION INFORMATION DISPLAY: FORMAT AND CONTENT

The effectiveness with which affirmative disclosure of information in advertising is communicated to the consumer will depend upon the format in which it is presented and the kind of information included. The FTC proposed regulation prescribes two broad options in the case of television commercials which are 30 seconds or less, which includes most television advertising. The first option requires the display of the names and percentages of the U.S. Recommended Dietary Allowance of at least four of eight nutrients (protein, vitamin A, vitamin C, thiamine, riboflavin, niacin, calcium, iron) if they are present in amounts of 10 percent of the USRDA or more. If there are less than four nutrients at these levels they should all be displayed, and if no nutrient is present in a quantity of at least 10 percent USRDA a simultaneous audio and video message must so state. Calories per serving must also be displayed. The second option is to display the nutrient information appearing on the label for at least 15 seconds. In the case of either option, an audio message must direct the consumer to the label for more information. Sixty second commercials must follow the same requirements except that, in the case of the first option, the information must be displayed for at least 15 seconds.

Bettman has conducted an information processing analysis of the FTC proposal [7]. Among his conclusions are:

1. Consumers may not attend to the video display of the information unless an audio message directs their attention to it, and news media publicity evokes interest in such information.
2. The short length of time the information will be presented, especially in the case of the first option, creates a stressful information environment for the average consumer who may not be able to process such information.
3. The information is more likely to be processed in terms of satisfactory vs. unsatisfactory relative to some threshold level, as this allows the consumer to chunk the information into a decision about acceptance or rejection of the advertised brand.
4. The information is more likely to increase awareness of the availability of such information, with the actual processing of the information occurring at the store.
5. The presentation of a single brand's nutrient levels in a commercial does not provide any basis for comparing different brands, and even less for comparing different food categories.
6. The regulation should direct attention to in-store nutrition information displays as these uncouple the memory system from the processing system, and information is presented at the time and place closest to the purchase decision.

The information load placed on consumers is particularly high in the case of advertising in the broadcast media. Here the rate at which information is received is usually high, and more importantly, is controlled by the advertiser. This differs from the case for print media where the audience controls the rate at which information is processed. Early studies of information load conclude that more information does not necessarily result in better choices by consumers [19].

Methodological artifacts, however, may have been largely responsible for the conclusion that the above studies reached [27, 31]. Scammon considered these criticisms in designing an experimental study of the impact of the amount and format of nutrition information on consumer response [28]. Thirty-second commercials for two peanut butter brands were modified to include nutrition information in the last six seconds of each commercial. These were shown to audiences of television show previews in a Los Angeles theatre. A factorial design manipulated the amount of information (four vs. eight nutrients) and the format of the information (percentage of Recommended Daily Allowance vs. adjectival descriptions of each nutrient). A control group saw the unmodified version of the commercials with no nutrition information. Though the nutrition information was accurately processed as measured by recall measures, an analysis of attitude and intention-to-buy measures showed that the information had not switched preferences away from the more popular brand even though it had been portrayed to be nutritionally inferior.

Scammon found with respect to the format of the information, that the adjectival format (excellent/good/fair/none ratings for each nutrient) resulted in more accurate recall but the percentage format provided more consumer satisfaction. Increasing the number of nutrients about which information was conveyed in the six seconds of the commercial allotted to the display significantly reduced the accuracy with which the information was recalled. The main conclusions of the study are that simpler formats and restricted amounts of information increase the accuracy with which this information is recalled. Even these formats, however, have little or no impact on preferences and behavior, at least in the case of a single exposure to the information.

The conclusions of the information processing research need to be qualified. First, all the studies have measured the impact of a *single* exposure to the information. It is not possible to generalize their results to the long term effects of repeated exposure to such information. The reinforcing effect of repetition would probably make the effect of information disclosure on attitudes and behavior stronger than indicated by the above studies. Second, the experimental studies facilitated the comparison of the nutrient levels across brands because the information for various brands is made available either simultaneously or sequentially within a short interval of time. Hence, conclusions of these studies may be limited to instances when information processing occurs primarily from short term memory. In natural settings, the nutrition information in a particular brand's advertising is received in relative temporal isolation from similar information about other brands. Thus, how this information is processed into and later retrieved from long term memory becomes crucial to the nature and extent of the impact of the information at a time when brand choices are made.

INDUSTRY RESPONSE: SOME SECONDARY EFFECTS

Up to this point we have concerned ourselves with consumer response to the proposed regulation requiring affirmative disclosure of nutrition information in food advertising. The manner in which the food industry responds to such a regulation will also affect consumer nutrition status. Industry spokespersons have been particularly adamant in pointing to two possible consequences of the regulation if it should come into force.

Scenario 1

Industry will comply to the regulation and pass on the costs associated with this compliance to the consumer, thereby resulting in higher food prices and detrimentally affecting consumer nutrition status.

A study sponsored by CBS had lawyers evaluate whether 175 food commercials on network television and 80 non-network commercials broadcast during a typical week of CBS programming conformed to the guidelines in the proposed regulation [17]. Sixty-nine network commercials and 19 non-network commercials were found to come under the provisions of the proposed rule. Half of these did not conform to the provisions and there was some ambiguity about another one-fourth. Moreover, an additional ten network and three non-network commercials came under the reserved provisions which are yet to be specified. In summary, somewhere between 15 percent and 33 percent of current food advertising would have to be changed to comply with the proposed regulation. The changes in advertising copy would undoubtedly be costly. The industry argument completely ignores the fact that competitive pressures would reduce each advertiser's ability to pass on the resulting costs to consumers. Also, the advertising industry is accustomed to frequently changing advertising copy. As a result, changes to meet regulatory standards could be incorporated at little incremental cost, especially if the FTC provided some time for industry to adapt to the new regulation.

Scenario 2

Industry will avoid coming under the provisions of the proposed regulation by abandoning any mention of nutrition in its advertising claims.

The proposed regulation applies only to those ads which make a nutrition-related claim; food processors may choose to protect themselves from the uncertainties of regulatory action by avoiding nutrition as a selling point altogether. Again, this argument ignores the effect of competitive pressure. To the extent that consumer wants and needs justify nutrition in the marketing strategy of a brand, the proposed regulation will give competitive advantage to the brand which can rise to this opportunity by marketing a product which meets the standard associated with the claim accompanying it. The author conducted an informal positioning analysis of 29 national brands of cereals. Even though the proposed regulation has been on public record for over four years, the claims currently made on the package front panels of 24 of the 29 brands continue to make nutrition claims.

In the opinion of this author, the reaction of the food industry to the proposed regulation reflects its traditional view of regulators as adversaries. It fails to recognize that the proposed regulation can be beneficial to industry in that information disclosure often enhances consumer confidence in and satisfaction with the marketing practices of the industry as a whole [11]. These in turn would protect the food industry to some extent from consumer activism, which in the long run may be more detrimental to its health than the proposed regulation.

. . .

REFERENCES

1. ABRAHAM, S., F. W. LOWENSTEIN and C. L. JOHNSON, *Preliminary Findings of the First Health and Nutrition Survey, United States, 1971–1972: Dietary Intake and Biochemical Findings,* DHEW Publication No. (HRA) 74-1219-1 (Washington D.C.: U.S. Government Printing Office).
2. Ad Hoc Committee to Review the Ten State Nutrition Survey, "Reflections of Dietary Studies with Children in the Ten State Nutrition Survey," *Pediatrics,* Vol. 56 (August 1975), pp. 320–326.
3. *Advertising Age,* "USDA Food Plan Hits Responsive Chord" (October 23, 1978), p. 114.
4. ASAM, EDWARD H. and LOUIS P. BUCKLIN, "Nutrition Labeling for Canned Foods," *Journal of Marketing,* Vol. 37 (April 1973), pp. 32–37.
5. AXELSON, JULIEN M. and DIANA S. DELCAMPO, "Improving Teenagers' Nutrition Knowledge Through the Mass Media," *Journal of Nutrition Education,* Vol. 10 (January-March 1978), pp. 30–33.

6. BARCUS, F. EARLE, "Television in the After-School Hours," and "Weekend Children's Television" (Working Papers, Action for Children's Television, Boston, Massachusetts, October 1975).

7. BETTMAN, JAMES R., "Issues in Designing Consumer Information Environments," *Journal of Consumer Research,* Vol. 2 (December 1975), pp. 169–177.

8. BROWN, JUDITH, "Graduate Students Examine T.V. Ads for Food," *Journal of Nutrition Education,* Vol. 9 (July–September 1977), pp. 120–122.

9. CLANCY-HEPBURN, KATHERINE, ANTHONY A. HICKEY and GAYLE NEVILL, "Children's Behavior Responses to TV Food Advertisements," *Journal of Nutrition Education,* Vol. 6 (July–September 1974), pp. 93–96.

10. CUOZZO, PETER F., "An Inquiry into the Image of Food and Food Habits as Presented by Television Food Advertising," Master's Thesis, Annenberg School of Communications, University of Pennsylvania, 1971.

11. DAY, GEORGE S., "Assessing the Effects of Information Disclosure Requirements," *Journal of Marketing,* Vol. 40 (April 1976), pp. 42–52.

12. EPPRIGHT, ERCEL S. et al., "Nutrition Knowledge and Attitudes of Mother," *Journal of Home Economics,* Vol. 62 (May 1970), pp. 327–332.

13. Federal Trade Commission, "Food Advertising: Proposed Trade Regulation Rule and Staff Statement," *Federal Register,* Vol. 39 (November 11, 1974), pp. 39642–39862.

14. FUSILLO, ALICE E. and ARLETTA M. BELOIAN, "Consumer Nutrition Knowledge and Self-Reported Food Shopping Behavior," *American Journal of Public Health,* 67 (September 1977), pp. 846–850.

15. GIFFT, HELEN H., MARJORIE B. WASHBON and GAIL G. HARRISON, *Nutrition, Behavior and Change.* Englewood Cliffs, New Jersey: Prentice-Hall, 1972.

16. GOLDBERG, MARVIN E., GERALD J. GORN AND WENDY GIBSON, "TV Messages for Snack and Breakfast Foods: Do They Influence Children's Preferences?" *Journal of Consumer Research,* Vol. 5 (September 1978), pp. 73–81.

17. GOLDBERG, R. E. and ANNE M. DAVIS, "Comments of C.B.S., Inc.: Proposed Food Advertising Trade Regulation Rule" (C.B.S., Inc., New York, 1976). Also on record of the Federal Trade Commission hearings on the proposed food advertising trade regulation rule held in San Francisco, July, 1976.

18. GUSSOW, JOAN, "Counter-nutritional Messages of Television Ads Aimed at Children," Testimony before the Subcommittee on the Consumer of the Senate Commerce Committee, March 2, 1972. Excerpts of this testimony are reprinted in *Journal of Nutrition Education,* Vol. 4 (Spring 1972), pp. 48–52.

19. JACOBY, JACOB, DONALD E. SPELLER and CAROL A. KOHN, "Brand Choice Behavior as a Function of Information Load," *Journal of Marketing Research,* Vol. 11 (February 1974a), pp. 63–69.

20. JACOBY, JACOB, ROBERT W. CHESTNUT and WILLIAM SILBERMAN, "Consumer Use and Comprehension of Nutrition Information," *Journal of Consumer Research,* Vol. 4 (September 1977), pp. 119–128.

21. KASSARJIAN, HAROLD H., "Content Analysis in Consumer Research," *Journal of Consumer Research,* Vol. 4 (June 1977), pp. 8–18.

22. LARSON-BROWN, LORA BETH, "Point of Purchase Information on Vended Foods," *Journal of Nutrition Education,* Vol. 10 (July–September 1978), pp. 116–118.

23. LEAMAN, F. A., "Nutrition: Television's Fruitless Image. A Cultivation Analysis of Children's Nutritional Knowledge and Behavior," Master's Thesis, Annenberg School of Communications, University of Pennsylvania, 1973.
24. LENAHAN, R. J. et al., "Consumer Reaction to Nutritional Labels on Food Products," *Journal of Consumer Affairs,* Vol. 7 (Spring 1973).
25. LEWIS, CHARLES E. and MARY ANN LEWIS, "The Impact of Television Commercials on Health-Related Beliefs and Behaviors of Children," *Pediatrics,* Vol. 53 (March 1974), pp. 431–435.
26. Response Analysis Corporation, "A Survey of Consumer Responses to Nutrition Claims: Summary Report," A Report Prepared for the FTC, Response Analysis Corp., Princeton, New Jersey, November 1975.
27. RUSSO, J. EDWARD, "More Information is Better: A Reevaluation of Jacoby, Speller, and Kohn," *Journal of Consumer Research,* Vol. 1 (December 1974), pp. 68–72.
28. SCAMMON, DEBRA, "Information Load and Consumers," *Journal of Consumer Research,* Vol. 4 (December 1977), pp. 148–155.
29. SCHWATZBERG, LYNDA, CLAIRE GEORGE and MARGARET C. PHILLIPS, "Issues in Food Advertising: The Nutrition Educator's Viewpoint," *Journal of Nutrition Education,* Vol. 19 (April–June 1977), pp. 60–63.
30. SHIMP, TERENCE A., ROBERT F. DYER and SALVATORE F. DIVITO, "An Experimental Test of the Harmful Effects of Premium-Oriented Commercials on Children," *Journal of Consumer Research,* Vol. 3 (June 1976), pp. 1–11.
31. SUMMERS, JOHN O., "Less Information is Better?" *Journal of Marketing Research,* Vol. 11 (November 1974), pp. 467–468.
32. TYEBJEE, TYZOON T., "Measuring the Meaning of Advertising Claims: A Public Policy Perspective," Working Paper, School of Business, University of Santa Clara, October 1978.
33. U.S. Department of Health, Education and Welfare, *Ten State Nutrition Survey 1968–1970,* DHEW Publication No. (HSM) 72-8134, Washington, D.C., U.S. Government Printing Office, 1972.
34. WHITE, P. L., "National Nutrition Survey," *Journal of the American Medical Association,* Vol. 223 (March 1973), pp. 1272–1273.
35. White House Conference on Food, Nutrition and Health, *Final Report,* 1970, U.S. Government Printing Office, Washington, D.C.
36. WINICK, CHARLES et al., *Children's Television Commercials: A Content Analysis.* New York: Praeger, 1973.

A. CONSUMER INFORMATION SYSTEMS

1. What is your view of the future of consumer information systems? What form will they take? How will they be financed?
2. How would you develop a databank for a computerized, interactive consumer information system covering audiotape recorders?

3. Comment on the label (Figure 9–1) shown in Chapter 9. Is it understandable and helpful? How would you change it?
4. What is an information seeker? How does such a person differ from an information avoider? Can a person be both? Give examples.
5. Design a self-supporting consumer information system to provide information on automobile repair shops.
6. Design a self-supporting consumer information system to provide information on homes that are being sold by their owners and are not listed with a multiple listing service.
7. What is useful consumer information? How could you determine whether information actually helped the consumer? Consider a carpet store brochure telling consumers how to buy carpets. How would you determine whether that brochure actually improved consumer decisionmaking? What about a factual advertisement for a particular automobile model?
8. How would you assess the value of the Shell "answer man" campaign to Shell?
9. Advise Bank of America on designing a consumer information system.

B. INFORMATION DISCLOSURE REQUIREMENTS

10. One commentator on truth in lending has argued that "the use the consumer makes of information is peripheral to the main issue of right to know." What are the reasons behind this statement? Do you agree?
11. Would you expect the immediate effects of a disclosure requirement on consumer behavior to be greater or less than the long-run effects? Will this be the case for all types of disclosure requirements?
12. Select two different disclosure requirements that have been proposed for future implementation. What are their likely costs? How would you measure costs and benefits of these plans?
13. Spokesmen for low-income consumers tend to dismiss efforts to improve the quality and adequacy of consumer information on the ground that such efforts mainly benefit the middle class. Do you agree? Can the perceived problems be overcome?
14. In a survey of 200 people, 90 percent recognized the *Good Housekeeping* seal, 50 percent relied upon it in purchasing decisions, and 29 percent believed that the product met federal quality and safety standards, but no one interviewed recognized that

the seal was given only to advertisers. Should such a seal be continued? What role does it have in consumer decisionmaking?

15. How would you formulate a regulation governing nutrient labeling? What information should be provided on the label? In what form? For what purpose?
16. The 1969 White House Conference on Food, Nutrition, and Health concluded that a large segment of the population followed bad diets (e.g., too many hamburgers and French fries) and that a smaller segment was too poor to eat well. Nutritional labeling, it has been argued, might be one way for food companies to help alleviate these problems. Do you agree? What else might a company like Del Monte or General Foods do to address such problems? How would they measure results? How could programs of this nature be justified?

PART IV

The Prepurchase Phase: Advertising

INTRODUCTION

Because advertising is the most visible and perhaps the most important source of consumer information, this area is highly controversial. In Chapter 15 Aaker structures and positions the consumer issues raised by advertising—manipulation, taste, deception, effects on social values, and economic effects. Chapters 16 and 17 are vigorous commentaries on the social issues surrounding advertising. Jones, a highly vocal, former Federal Trade Commission member, discusses materialism and role stereotyping in the context of television advertising. Kendall, president of Pepsi-Cola, explores these and other advertising issues from the perspective of a user of advertising.

Social issues in advertising and questions of deception take on tremendous significance when the audience is children. In Chapter 18 consumer researchers who have studied children's reaction to advertising summarize their findings and opinions. Chapter 19 presents the views of government, industry, consumer spokespersons.

In Chapter 20 Aaker looks at the legal definition of deceptive advertising and the judicial interpretation of laws governing deception in advertising. Finally, Wilkes and Wilcox review the regulatory environment, examining various FTC remedies for deceptive advertising. They suggest guidelines for designing advertising programs in that environment.

A *Social Issues In Advertising*

15 THE SOCIAL AND ECONOMIC EFFECTS OF ADVERTISING

David A. Aaker

For decades, indeed centuries, broad social and economic issues have been raised concerning the role of advertising in society. In 1759, Dr. Samuel Johnson suggested that advertisers had moral and social questions to consider:

> The trade of advertising is now so near to perfection, it is not easy to propose any improvement. But as every art ought to be exercised in due subordination to the publick good, I cannot but propose it as a moral question to these matters of the publick ear. Whether they do not sometimes play too wantonly with our passions.[1]

Since then advertising has been studied, analyzed, defended, and attacked by individuals representing a wide spectrum of professional interests, including economists, sociologists, politicians, businessmen, novelists, and historians.

The role of advertising in society is a controversial one, largely because opinions associated with it are heavily interwoven with more fundamental values and beliefs about how a society does and should operate. Some will view a product advance as making an important con-

---

[1] *The Works of Samuel Johnson, LL.D.*, IV (Oxford: Talboys and Wheeler, 1825), p. 269.

Excerpt from David A. Aaker and John G. Myers, *Advertising Management,* © 1975, pp. 535–553. Reprinted by permission of Prentice-Hall, Inc., Englewood Cliffs, New Jersey.

tribution to a valued life style, increasing the range of choice and standard of living. Others who prefer a different life style will view the same product as adding to product clutter and decreasing the quality of life. Supporters of advertising argue that it is a form of "speech," analogous to the news and entertainment components of mass media and that it should be kept entirely free of government interference. Critics often argue that government should be involved to protect the "public interest," to keep consumers from being duped by the power of advertising, and to protect the interests of competitive firms whose performance or existence could be affected by unfair advertising practices. There is little agreement about whether or not advertising has the power to "manipulate" an unwilling consumer. Since people can be influenced to a considerably different degree, there is undoubtedly some truth in both sides of the argument regarding the persuasive power of advertising. Because value judgments and basic assumptions are involved and much depends on the perspective of a particular consumer, the debate is often highly subjective.

A STRUCTURING OF THE ISSUES

A discussion of the social and economic issues of advertising can be divided into three categories, as depicted in Figure 15–1. The first category represents the nature and content of the advertising to which people are exposed. Is advertising performing an informative role or a deceptive one? Are appeals used that manipulate consumers against their will, par-

FIGURE 15–1 STRUCTURING THE ISSUES

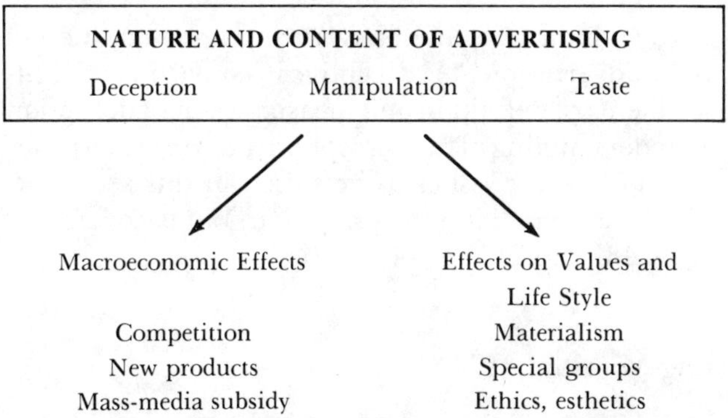

Source: Adapted from Stephen A. Greyser, "Advertising Attacks and Counters," *Harvard Business Review,* 50, March–April 1972, p. 3. See, also, John G. Myers, "Social Issues in Advertising," American Association of advertising Agencies Educational Foundation, 1971.

ticularly certain groups such as children or the economically disadvantaged? Finally, there are a variety of issues associated with taste. Is advertising too repetitious, too silly, too preoccupied with sex? Does it irritate or offend the audience member? In essence, this category considers the means rather than the ends of advertising, the means being the copy and media tactics used.

The remaining two categories represent the aggregate effects of advertising on society as a whole. One of these is the effect on society's values and life styles. There are those who believe that advertising competes with or dominates such other socialization agents as literature, plays, music, the church, the home, and the school; that it fosters materialism at the expense of other basic values; or that it may serve to reinforce sexual or racial discrimination. The second is the effect of advertising on society's economic well-being and on the efficiency of the operation of the economic system. To what extent can the power of advertising lead to the control of the market by a few firms, which will weaken competition and raise consumer prices? What is the economic value of advertising as an efficient mechanism for communicating the existence of new products? To what extent does it subsidize mass media? Because the analysis is concerned with the economic health of the economy as a whole, as opposed to that of individual consumers, it focuses on the macroeconomic rather than microeconomic effects of advertising.

THE NATURE AND CONTENT OF ADVERTISING

Deception

A primary concern with the content of advertising is the question of the degree to which the advertisement is deceptive in conveying the selling message. The problems of definition and measurement of deception are closely tied to an understanding of the perception process. Such problems are implicit in many of the issues to be raised in this selection. (Deception is not discussed in detail in this selection, but is covered in Chapters 20 [pp. 239–248] and 21 [pp. 249–257].)

Does Advertising Manipulate?

Perhaps the essence of a free marketplace and a free society is the freedom to make decisions of various kinds, or in this context, the freedom to select or not select a particular brand. There are those who fear that this freedom is circumscribed by the "power" of advertising—

that advertising is so effective it can manipulate a buyer into making a decision against his will or at least against his best interests in allocating his financial resources.

The argument takes several forms. First, there is concern with the use of motivation research, the appeal to motives at the subconscious level. Second, there is the use of indirect emotional appeals. Finally, there is the more general claim of the power of scientific advertising to persuade —to make people believe things and behave in ways that are not in their own or society's best interests.

In each of the three forms there are simple misconceptions of how advertising decisions are made, how the communication process works, and the role of advertising in the total marketing program and the consumer buying process. There also exist, however, serious questions of fact and judgment that legitimately need to be raised.

Motivation Research

Motivation research is an approach that draws on the Freudian psychoanalytic model of consumer decision making. It assumes that important buying motives are subconscious in that a respondent cannot elucidate them when asked his opinion of a brand or a product class. Thus, a person may dislike prunes because of a subconscious association of prunes with old age or parental authority but may not consciously realize the existence of this association and its relevance to his purchasing decisions. A consumer may actually prefer a cake mix that requires the addition of an egg because it subconsciously satisfies her need to contribute to the baking process, although she consciously believes that the only reason is that a fresh egg adds quality.

Motivation research made a strong impact on marketing in the 1950s; many saw it as a decisive and powerful marketing tool. Furthermore, it received widespread attention beyond marketing professionals by such books as Vance Packard's *The Hidden Persuaders.*[2] The result was a feeling that advertising could indeed identify subconscious motives and, by playing on these motives, influence an unsuspecting public. The result was an Orwellian specter of the consumer's subconscious exposed and manipulated without his knowledge. Packard discusses

> the large-scale efforts being made, often with impressive success, to channel our unthinking habits, our purchasing decisions, and our thought processes by the use of insights gleaned from psychiatry and the social sciences. Typically these efforts take place beneath our level of awareness, so that the appeals which move us are often, in a sense, "hidden." The result is that many of us are being influenced and manipulated, far more than we realize, in the patterns of our everyday lives.[3]

---

[2] Vance Packard, *The Hidden Persuaders* (New York: Pocket Books, 1957).

[3] Ibid., p. 1.

The concept of the consumer being manipulated at the subconscious level reached its zenith with a well-publicized subliminal advertising experiment by James Vicary. In a movie theater, he flashed the phrases, "Drink Coke" and "Eat popcorn" on the screen every five seconds.[4] The phrases were exposed for 1/3,000 of a second, well below threshold levels. The tests, which covered a six-week period, were reported to have increased cola sales by 57 percent and popcorn sales by 18 percent. The concept of subliminal advertising operating at the subconscious level really suggested manipulation. However, this test did not employ even rudimentary controls and has not been replicated. Other tests of subliminal communication have had negative results.[5] There is additional evidence that suggests there is an ability to screen out unwanted advertising subliminally. Engel and his associates concluded:

> Vicary's findings should merely be regarded as an interesting historical event. Indeed, if anything, the evidence suggests more strongly that subliminal perception in no way eliminates perceptual defense. While there seems to be little or no support for truly unconscious perceptions, stimulus presentation below threshold does not necessarily circumvent an individual's power to perceive selectively.[6]

We now know that motivation research, for better or worse, was oversold and that motivation research knowledge does not give an advertiser anything approaching total control over an audience. There are fundamental difficulties in applying the technique. It usually involves some kind of relatively lengthy, unstructured interview. Thus, the interview itself is necessarily subjective and highly dependent on the interviewer. The analysis is even more subjective. It is not uncommon for two motivation research groups to address the same situation and arrive at widely different conclusions. Furthermore, controlled experimentation is usually precluded because of the small samples. Thus, it is difficult to place much confidence in the result. Finally the implementation of the conclusions, whatever they may be, is almost never obvious.

On the contrary, implementation can also take a variety of directions, and the nature of the conclusions usually provide no guidance in selecting among these directions. How does one reach a person, for example, who dislikes prunes because of an association with parental authority? Furthermore, any approach can be neutralized by competing senders and other forces acting on brand choice.

---

[4] James F. Engel, David T. Kollat, and Roger D. Blackwell, *Consumer Behavior* (New York: Holt, Rinehart & Winston, 1968), pp. 108–110.

[5] See J. J. Bachrach "The Ethics of Tachistoscopy," *Bulletin of the Atomic Scientists,* 15, 1959, pp. 212–215.

[6] Engel, Kollat, and Blackwell, *Consumer Behavior,* p. 110.

Motivation research does have a role to play in developing effective advertisements, however. It has been particularly useful in providing insight, in suggesting copy alternatives, and in helping creative people avoid approaches that will precipitate undesirable reactions. However, as suggested earlier, the power of advertisers to manipulate consumers by using motivation research has been vastly overstated. Most people probably make choices most of the time for reasons they are aware of, particularly in situations in which real economic risk is involved. Unlike the situation of having the receiver totally under the control of the persuader, popularized in brainwashing experiments, advertising does not control a receiver's options. Although marketing professionals have accepted the reduced scope of motivation research, the layman is still haunted by the specter of the "hidden persuaders."

Although it does seem clear that the motivation research user does not have absolute power over consumers, there are still ethical questions associated with its use—indeed, with the use of many forms of market research that are most relevant. Is the practice of conducting depth interviews to attempt to isolate hidden motives acceptable? It is one thing to probe in an analyst's office for medical reasons but another to do so in the home or laboratory for commercial reasons. Can interviewers be sure that such an experience will not do psychological harm? And what about the common situation wherein a respondent is not told the actual purpose of the interview? These issues really focus on the research effort itself. The concern with using the results brings to the surface issues that are raised in the following section wherein emotional appeals are discussed.

Emotional Appeals

The communication of factual information about a product's primary function is usually accepted as being of value to the consumer. However, when advertising utilizes appeals or associations that go beyond such a basic communication task, the charge of manipulation via "emotional appeals" is raised. Scitovsky declared:

> To the extent that it [advertising] provides information about the existence of available [buyer] alternatives, advertising always renders the market more perfect. If advertising is mainly suggestive and confined to emotional appeal, however, it is likely to impede rational comparison and choice, thus rendering the market less perfect.[7]

The implication is that consumers will be led to make less than optimal decisions by such emotional appeals.

. . .

[7] Tibor Scitovsky, *Welfare and Competition* (Chicago: Richard D. Irwin, 1951), pp. 401–402.

This observation is related to issues of deception. The line between artistic license and deception is sometimes hard to draw. Is an advertisement an innocent, entertaining exaggeration that few will take seriously, or is it really capable of deceiving?

. . .

Another relevant question is, given a decision to restrict the use of emotional appeals, how such restrictions might be formulated. Exactly what emotional appeals should be banned? How could codes be adopted so that the communication of factual information is not also inhibited? Should all animation, for example, be prohibited? The question of implementation, too often ignored, can crystallize basic issues and aid the analysis process.

THE POWER OF MODERN ADVERTISING

There also exists a somewhat more general claim that advertisers have the raw power to manipulate consumers. Many companies have the capacity to obtain large numbers of advertisement exposures. Furthermore, some observers believe that these companies can utilize highly sophisticated, scientific techniques to make such advertising effective.

. . .

The reader should by now be painfully aware of the limitations of the most sophisticated approaches available. The fact is that consumer-choice behavior is determined by many factors in addition to advertising—the advice of friends, decisions and life styles of family members, new stories, prices, distribution variables, and on and on. Advertising is but one of many variables, and it has a limited role. It can communicate the existence of a new automobile and perhaps induce a visit to a dealer, but it can rarely make the final sale. It can explain the advantages of a toothpaste and perhaps be influential in getting some people to try the brand, but it has little impact on their decision to repurchase it. There is an inexhaustible number of examples of huge promotional efforts for products that failed, such as the Edsel. If advertising had the power that some attribute to it, many of these products would still be with us.

Taste

Some critics feel that advertising is objectionable because the creative effort behind it is not in good taste. This type of objection was explored in a massive study conducted in the mid-1960's.[8] More than 1,500 people

---

[8] Raymond A. Bauer and Stephen A. Greyser, *Advertising in America: The Consumer View* (Boston: Division of Research, Graduate School of Business Administration, Harvard University, 1968).

were asked to list those advertisements that they found annoying, enjoyable, informative, or offensive. Of the more than 9,000 advertisements involved, 23 percent were labeled as annoying and 5 percent as offensive.[9] Although a portion of these advertisements irritate respondents because they were considered deceptive, the majority were so categorized for reasons related to questions of taste.

Advertising may not be omnipotent, but many contend that it is too omnipresent or intrusive. More than 42 percent of the annoying advertisements in the foregoing study were considered too loud, too long, too repetitious, or involved unpleasant voices, music or people.[10] Another 31 percent had content that was considered silly, unreal, boring, or depressing.[11] In some cases, it was the product advertised that was the source of objection. More than one-fourth of the advertisements regarded as offensive involved such products as liquor or cigarettes, which the respondents did not like to see advertised.[12] Another problem concerned the appeal used; those using sex were particularly singled out for criticism. Nearly one-fourth of the offensive advertisements were considered inappropriate for children.[13] Several of these dimensions will be examined in more detail in the following sections.

THE APPEAL

In an open letter to the *Detroit News* entitled, "You Dirty Old Ad Men Make Me Sick," a reader took issue with the use of sex in advertising. In making her case, she described several advertisements:

> A love goddess runs down the beach, waves nibbling at her toes, her blond streaked hair sweeping back behind wide, expectant eyes. A flimsy garment clings to every supple curve. She runs faster, arms open, until finally she throws herself breathless into HIS arms. . . .
>
> Where's this scene? Right in your living room, that's where.
>
> Wild and passionately aroused, she can't stop herself. She runs her fingers through his hair, knocks his glasses off, and kisses him and kisses him again. . . .
>
> Who's watching? Your nine-year-old daughter as she sits on her stuffed panda bear and wipes jelly off her face.[14]

The letter received considerable response from advertising professionals. Some argued that advertisements, as long as they are not obscene, reflect society and its collective life styles. They observed that

[9] *Ibid.*, p. 183.

[10] *Ibid.*, p. 217.

[11] *Ibid.*

[12] *Ibid.*, p. 223.

[13] *Ibid.*

[14] Kathy McMeel, "You Dirty Old Ad Men Make Me Sick," *Advertising Age*, December 1, 1969, p. 28.

nudity and the risqué are part of the contemporary world in which advertising is imbedded. Others agreed that sex is overused and suggested that effective advertising can be created without titillating.

One problem is that television commercials have to create attention and communicate a message—and accomplish all this in sixty or even thirty seconds—a demanding task, indeed. Another problem is that television reaches large, broad audiences. It is one thing to use a risqué approach in *Playboy* magazine and quite another to use it on prime-time television when the likelihood of offending is much greater.

Fear appeals have also been criticized. The intent of the fear appeal is to create anxiety that can supposedly be alleviated by an available product (insurance against a fire or a safe tire to prevent accidents) or action (stop smoking). There exists the possibility that such appeals may create emotional disturbances or a long-run anxiety condition in some audience members. The cumulative effects of such advertising may be highly undesirable to some although it can also be argued that they quickly cease to have any significant degree of emotional impact, and the audience soon becomes immune to the messages.

Intrusiveness

To some people, advertising, especially television advertising is often like a visitor who has overstayed his welcome. It becomes an intrusion. Greyser postulates a life cycle wherein an advertising campaign moves with repetition from a period of effectiveness, and presumably audience acceptance, to a period of irritation.[15] The cycle contains the following stages:

Exposure to the message on several occasions prior to serious attention (given some basic interest in the product).
Interest in the advertisement on either substantive (informative) or stimulus (enjoyment) grounds.
Continued but declining attention to the advertisement on such grounds.
Mental tune-out of the advertisement on grounds of familiarity.
Increasing re-awareness of the advertisement, now as a negative stimulus (an irritant).
Growing irritation.

The number of exposures between the start of a campaign and the stage of growing irritation is obviously a key variable. On what factors

[15] Stephen A. Greyser, "Irritation in Advertising," *Journal of Advertising Research,* 13, February 1973, p. 8. © copyright (1973) by the Advertising Research Foundation.

will it depend? An important factor, of course, is the intensity of the campaign itself. Bursts of advertising that generate many exposures over a short time period will undoubtedly run a high risk of irritation. A second factor involves other advertising to which the audience is exposed. The cycle will be shorter if different brands and even different product classes use similar approaches. Advertisements involving similar demonstrations, spokesmen, jingles, or animation may be difficult to separate in the mind of an audience member. Campaigns for menthol cigarettes, for example, have been perceived as being highly similar.

Product usage and brand preferences are two additional factors affecting the cycle time period. Greyser noted that:

> Consumers dislike only 21 percent of the advertisements for products used (19 percent annoying, 2 percent offensive), whereas they dislike 37 percent of advertisements for products they don't use (29 percent annoying, 8 percent offensive) For brand preferrers the tendency is even more marked; only 7 percent of advertisements for one's favorite brand are disliked compared with 76 percent of the advertisements for "brands I wouldn't buy" (only product users included).[16]

Still another factor is the entertainment value of the advertisement. Campaigns using advertisements with high entertainment value have demonstrated their ability to survive heavy repetition. An important issue is the determination of the link between liking and effectiveness. There is some evidence that the very pleasant and the very unpleasant advertisements are more effective than those in between. A British study found that commercials that were either well liked or especially disliked did not differ markedly in their effectiveness.[17] However, hard data on this issue are sparse. The nature of the relationship will undoubtedly depend on the audience, the product, and other variables. Furthermore, there are severe definitional and measurement problems involved.

One difficulty is that advertisements tend to be evaluated by advertisers in isolation, whereas the audience reacts to the totality of the advertising to which they are exposed. This reaction, when it is negative, therefore tends to apply to some extent to all advertising. The result is a decrease in the long-run effectiveness of advertising. It is in the best interests of advertisers to be concerned not only with the irritation caused by specific campaigns, but also with that caused by the impression of advertising in general. Twenty- or thirty-second television spots may be cost-effective for the brand but less so when the total impression of a cluttered medium is considered.

---

[16] *Ibid.*, p. 6.

[17] John Treasure and Timothy Joyce, *As Others See Us,* Institute of Practitioners in Advertising, Occasional Paper 17 (London: 1967).

Advertising to Children

Issues relating to the nature and content of advertising are magnified when the audience is made up of children. It is argued that they are more susceptible to deception, that they lack the perceptual defenses of adults, and that they cannot objectively evaluate advertisements. It is therefore assumed by some that the potential for manipulation is greater with children. Furthermore, the use of sexual appeals is particularly offensive when there is the possibility that children will be in the audience. Critics like ACT (Action on Children's Television) argue that advertising directed to children should be banned entirely; others have proposed special restrictions on this type of advertising. Supporters contend that children have a right to consume, that they are affected most by their parents and peers, and that advertising does much to educate them about the uses of products and goods and the role of selling techniques.

An exploratory study of young children's perception, judgments, and explanations of television advertising provides some data that can help evaluate the various positions and proposed remedies.[18] Focused group interviews were held with children from kindergarten, second, fourth, and sixth grades the day after they were exposed to a videotape of a typical Saturday morning's television program for children. The children's responses, which fell into eight conceptual categories, are summarized in Table 15-1. The striking thing about the findings is the dramatic differences in the children's reactions to commercials on the basis of age.

EFFECTS ON VALUES AND LIFE STYLES

Advertising by its very nature receives wide exposure. Furthermore, it presumably has an effect on what people buy and thus on their activities. Because of this exposure and because of its role as a persuasive vehicle, it is argued that it has an impact on the values and life styles of society and that this impact has its negative as well as positive side. The key issues are what values and life styles are to be encouraged as healthy, which are to be avoided, and what relative impact or influence advertising has on them. Clearly, there are many sources of social influences that have a casual impact on the nature of a culture such as literature, plays and other entertainment forms, the church, the home, and the school. Both

[18] J. Blatt, L. Spencer, and S. Ward, "A Cognitive Developmental Study of Children's Reactions to Television Advertising," *Effects of Television on Children and Adolescents,* unpublished paper (Cambridge, Mass.: Marketing Science Institute, 1971).

TABLE 15-1. RESPONSES TO TV ADVERTISING AMONG 5-12-YEAR-OLDS

I.	Category:	Awareness of what commercials are. Discrimination of commercials and judgments about "how real they are" compared to cartoon (fantasy) and news or documentary (reality) programs.
	Finding:	Children in all age groups could identify the term "commercials," but kindergarten children exhibited confusion, their judgment of the relationship between commercials and reality being based on coincidental reasoning or affect.
II.	Category:	Understanding the *purpose* of commercials. Ability to perceive the intent or "message" of commercials, and the reasoning used in making this judgment.
	Finding:	Kindergartners showed no understanding of the purpose of the commercial; 2nd graders understood that the purpose was to sell goods; 4th and 6th graders commented on techniques employed in constructing commercials.
III.	Category:	Degree of discrimination between advertisement and product advertised. Ability to differentiate the product being advertised from the advertising message itself.
	Finding:	Kindergartners could not discriminate between commercials and products, but older children could; discriminations became sharper with age.
IV.	Category:	Classes of products recalled. Kinds of products and/or advertisements spontaneously recalled.
	Finding:	Kindergartners recalled food product advertising, 2nd graders recalled products with which they could identify (toys), and 4th and 6th graders showed no consistent pattern of recall.
V.	Category:	Complexity of recall. Ability to perceive and recall details of commercials.
	Finding:	Recall becomes more multidimensional and complex with age.
VI.	Category:	Significant other. The individuals spontaneously recalled or associated in children's reactions to or evaluations of advertisements.
	Finding:	Children saw parents and celebrities as significant references, and 6th graders viewed themselves as significant references.
VII.	Category:	Perceived credibility of commercials. Extent to which television commercials are perceived as "true" and/or "trustworthy."
	Finding:	Distrust of commercials increases with age.
VIII.	Category:	Affective responses. Emotional reactions, likes and dislikes, expressed about commercials.
	Finding:	Young children enjoy commercials; children become increasingly contemptuous of commercials as they get older, but they continue to enjoy humor.

Source: Scott Ward, "Children's Reactions to Commercials," *Journal of Advertising Research,* 12, April 1972, p. 38. Reprinted from the *Journal of Advertising Research* © Copyright (1972) by the Advertising Research Foundation.

issues are most difficult to resolve. The first involves highly subjective and individualistic judgments and the second an almost impossible problem of causal inference. Despite their difficulty and their relationship to deep philosophical questions, they are well worth addressing to illuminate judgments and assumptions about our market system and society that are too often glossed over.[19]

There are many concerns that are raised in this context. Some observers feel, for example, that advertising raises the expectations of economically deprived segments of our society to their disadvantage. Others think that advertising tends to create an oppressive conformity of thought and action. Two items in this category that have attracted particular attention are the relationship of advertising to materialism and the role that advertising has played in creating harmful stereotypes of women and ethnic minorities.

Materialism

Materialism is defined as the tendency to give undue importance to material interests. Presumably there is a corresponding lessening of importance to nonmaterial interests such as love, freedom, and intellectual pursuits. In 1949, Bishop wrote:

> It is common ground among the writers that the crisis of today is largely a moral crisis; and not a few of them find its essence in the loss of a sense of social purpose, and the replacement of such a sense of purpose by an acquisitive ideology in which the satisfaction of material desires is held up as the sole or principal end for the individual and the group. They point to the advertiser as the high priest of this false religion and to the all-pervading influence of modern advertising as the main obstacle in the way of those who would guide humanity into a better way of life.[20]

Bauer and Greyser argue, however, that although people do spend their resources on material things, they do so in the pursuit of nonmaterial goals.[21] They buy camping equipment to achieve a communion with nature, music systems to understand the classic composers, and an automobile for social status. The distinctive aspect of our society is not the possession of material goods, but the extent to which material goods are used to attain nonmaterial goals. Bauer and Greyser thus raise the issue of whether material goods are a means to an end rather than an end in themselves. In making such an evaluation it is useful to consider how people in other cultures fulfill nonmaterial goals. The leader in a primitive culture may satisfy a need for status in a different way from someone in our culture, but is the means used really that relevant?

---

[19] J. G. Myers, *Social Issues in Advertising,* New York, American Association of Advertising Agencies Educational Foundation.

[20] F. P. Bishop, *The Ethics of Advertising* (London: Robert Hale, 1949), p. 17.

[21] Bauer and Greyser, "The Dialogue That Never Happens."

Assuming that materialism does exist as an undesirable phenomenon, there still remains the issue of whether advertising creates or fosters it or merely reflects values and attitudes that are created by more significant sociological forces.

. . .

Promoting Stereotypes

Minority groups have been stereotyped by such various sociological forces as movies, literature, and advertising. During the past decade, and before such observations had been forcefully made by spokesmen for the black community, Pettigrew described how blacks were portrayed by a magazine in the 1930s:

> While occasionally portraying Negroes neutrally or as "credits to their race," *Life* in the 1930's overwhelmingly presented Negroes as either musical, primitive, amusing, or religious, or as violent and criminal; occupationally they were pictured as either servants, athletes, or entertainers, or as unemployed.[22]

How much has advertising contributed to this stereotype and how is it changing in this respect? Blacks are of particular interest because they were the first minority group that attracted attention and attempted to apply pressure to decision makers. As a result, action in this area could foretell what might happen in others.

Kassarijian, a UCLA psychologist, examined advertising in 1946, 1956, and 1965.[23] His study, involving 150,000 magazine pages, showed that only 1/3 of 1 percent of the advertisements contained blacks, with the frequency of use of black models the lowest in 1956. The hypothesis was that neither the low-status role that predominated in 1946 nor the higher-status role more apparent in 1965 were appropriate in 1956. The role assigned to blacks did seem to change over time, with blacks appearing in higher-status roles in more recent years. The use of integrated advertising increased over time, but it usually involved black entertainers or black models in a mixed group; the appearance of blacks as true peers was sparse. Cox provided a slightly more recent observation.[24] He

---

[22] Thomas F. Pettigrew, "Complexity and Change in American Racial Patterns: A Social Psychological View," *Daedalus,* Fall 1965, p. 974.

[23] Harold H. Kassarijian, "The Negro and American Advertising, 1946–65," *Journal of Marketing Research,* 6, February 1969, pp. 29–39.

[24] Keith K. Cox, "Social Effects of Integrated Advertising," *Journal of Advertising Research,* 10, April 1970, pp. 41–44.

studied five magazines and determined that the percentage of integrated advertising went from 1/2 percent in the 1949–1950 period to 2 percent in 1967–1968. He observed a major shift in the occupational role of blacks; the stereotype of maids, cooks, and butlers that existed in 1949–1950 had nearly disappeared by 1967–1968. More recent studies would probably suggest that the trend toward the use of blacks in positive roles is still increasing.

The issue of minority stereotypes raises a host of questions. What negative impact does advertising have in creating stereotypes or what positive force in breaking them down? In the absence of a definitive answer to that question, what should the advertisers' positions be? Should efforts be made to introduce minority models into advertisements? In what respect should the criteria of maximizing advertising effectiveness dominate the decision to use black models in roles conventionally dominated by white models? Integrated advertising does seem to have a positive impact on black audiences and a neutral impact on white audiences.[25] Of course, any such generalization would have to be confirmed for a particular product and advertising approach.

More recently, advertising has been accused of stereotyping women. It has been argued that women are usually portrayed as housewives and mothers, only rarely in working roles, and practically never in professional roles. The hypothesis is that such a portrayal has fostered discrimination against women in professional employment and a feeling that it is socially inappropriate for a woman to have a professional career.

Alice Courtney and Sarah Lockeretz attempted to determine how women were portrayed in advertising. They examined 729 advertisements appearing in 7 general-interest magazines published in April 1970. None of the advertisements showed women in a professional capacity, whereas 35 of them so portrayed men. Only 9 percent of the women shown were in working roles and they were clerks, stewardesses, and the like. The authors reported that the advertisements reflected the stereotype that women don't do important things, are dependent on men, are regarded by men primarily as sex objects, and should be in the home.[26]

Questions similar to those posed with respect to blacks arise in this context. Does such a portrayal of women in advertising influence the stereotypes to any meaningful extent? To what extent should advertisers

---

[25] James Stafford, Al Birdwell, and Charles Van Tassel, "Integrated Advertising—White Blacklash?" *Journal of Advertising Research,* 10, April 1970, pp. 15-20.

[26] Alice E. Courtney and Sarah Wernick Lockeretz, "A Woman's Place: An Analysis of the Roles Portrayed by Women in Magazine Advertisements," *Journal of Marketing Research,* 8, February 1971, pp. 92–95.

try to counteract their apparent bias? Finally, what effect will such an effort have on the effectiveness of the advertising? Questions like these are being asked today in modern advertising agencies. Some creative people have been quick to engage in what has been called more "socially responsible" types of advertising, whereas others have not. Like many questions involving social issues, the fundamental question reduces to: What is the most managerially effective advertising, not only in the short run but in the long run, and how can long-term costs and benefits be assessed?

THE ECONOMIC EFFECTS OF ADVERTISING

It is unreasonable to separate the economic and social impact of advertising. The social issues, by themselves, tend to focus on the negative aspects of advertising—its intrusiveness, content that is in bad taste, and the possibly undesirable impact on values and life styles. If advertising were regarded solely on these grounds it would be difficult to defend, despite the fact that much advertising is entertaining, some may even be of real artistic value, and some is directed toward supporting causes that are universally praised.[27] Advertising is basically an economic institution. It performs an economic function for an advertiser, affects economic decisions of the audience, and is an integral part of the whole economic system. Thus, an economic evaluation should accompany other types of appraisal of advertising.

Ideally, an economic balance sheet should be developed in which there are clearly defined dimensions on which advertising could be appraised. If a dollar value could be associated with advertising along each dimension, a net number could be obtained that would represent the economic value of advertising. Such an analysis, if feasible, might be conducted for different industries (or media) to identify subsets of the advertising industry that are not generating a net positive value and to stimulate proposals to alter these subsets. Such an effort is impossible, of course. It is most difficult for a firm to determine the value of its own advertising even to itself. Determining the value of *all* advertising to the *whole* economy is naturally considerably more difficult.

---

[27] In 1970, for example, over $450 million of donated media and agency time was spent on nonprofit public service advertising under the auspices of the Advertising Council. The council estimates that $5 billion have been spent on public service advertising since the council was created in 1941.

Although an economic balance sheet may not be feasible, it is possible to identify several appropriate dimensions of analysis. They include the value of information to buyers, the role of new-product development, the support of media, the impact on distribution costs, the effect on the business cycle, the role in creating brand identification, and the development of brand utility. These dimensions will be examined in turn. Another dimension of analysis is the relationship of advertising to competition. To what extent does advertising create or contribute to oligopolistic market power that, some argue, results in high prices and reduced competition? (This issue is explored in Part V, Section D.)

Providing Informational Utility

Advertising that distributes information to consumers that can help them make better economic decisions than they would in the absence of that information provides a positive economic service. Of course, any advertising that, by deception or any other means, induces consumers to make suboptimal decisions provides a corresponding negative economic service. Some advertising is of more value than others along this dimension. Classified advertising, advertising for retail stores, catalog advertising, and much of industrial advertising are usually sought out because of their informational value. Other types are not so frequently sought out, and their information value is therefore less obvious.

Advertising and Brand Names

Advertising plays an important role in establishing and maintaining brand names. A brand name identifies the source of a product and provides a construct by which a buyer can store information about that source. Such a construct is of little consequence in product lines like screws or shoelaces, wherein the perceived differences among brands are minor, or in products like greeting cards, which can be evaluated relatively competently by the buyer. For products like automobiles, appliances, or men's shirts, however, which have relatively high levels of perceived quality differences among brands and which are difficult to evaluate by inspection, the brand name plays an important role in the buying process. A buyer can reasonably assume that a manufacturer willing to risk large sums of money to tell about his product is not likely to let poor product quality damage his investment. The value of a brand name is evidenced by the fact that they have been introduced into socialistic countries with centrally planned economies, which theoretically have little need for such concepts.

Media Support

Advertising provides more than 60 percent of the cost of periodicals, more than 70 percent of the cost of newspapers, and nearly 100 percent of the cost of radio and television.[28] Television, for example, received $4.1 billion, less the 15 percent agency commission, from advertising revenues in 1972. For this amount, advertisers received approximately 15 percent of the air time.[29] Of course, a pay television system could be developed or public funds could be used, but either alternative would cost the consumer something in direct cash outlays or increased taxes. It might not be a net cost of $4.1 billion (less 15 percent), because consumers probably pay something for television now through higher prices for some products, but it would very probably involve some net cost.

Distribution Costs

Advertising is part of a total marketing program; it does not operate in isolation. Its function is usually to communicate to large audiences, and it often performs this function very efficiently. Without advertising, the communication function would still remain but would probably have to be accomplished in some other way by retailers, salesmen, etc. The alternative in many situations could cost significantly more.

In 1964, cookie companies spent only 2.2 percent of sales on advertising whereas cereal companies spent 14.9 percent.[30] However, the cookie companies spent 22.1 percent of sales on other selling and distribution costs, compared with 12.1 percent of sales for cereal companies. Cookie companies employed routemen to deliver goods and service the shelves. Cereal companies, however, had created sufficient consumer demand so that the retailer found it worthwhile to monitor the stock, and the firms were relieved of this marketing expense. In this instance, then, it can be argued that cookie companies shifted marketing cost from advertising

---

[28] Fritz Machlup, *The Production and Distribution of Knowledge in the United States* (Princeton, N.J.: Princeton University Press, 1962), p. 265.

[29] Julian L. Simon, *Issues in the Economics of Advertising* (Urbana: University of Illinois Press, 1970), p. 276.

[30] "Grocery Manufacturing," Technical Study No. 6, National Commission on Food Marketing, June 1966, p. 147.

to other marketing activities and that an evaluation of their advertising expenses in isolation would be deceptive.

Effect on Business Cycles

Advertising could theoretically be a tool to alleviate the extremes of the business cycle. A knowledgeable businessman, anticipating a booming economy and capacity production, should reduce advertising expenditures. Conversely, when the economy is weak and orders are needed, many firms should increase their advertising. Since the extremes of a business cycle cause inflation or unemployment, any mechanism to stabilize conditions would be an economic benefit. The problem is that many advertisers, especially those who tend to set their advertising budgets at a fixed percentage of sales, actually increase advertising when times are good and decrease it when sales are weak. These firms may thus actually increase the extremes of the business cycle instead of decreasing them. Simon reviewed the literature and concluded that this tendency actually dominates—advertising expenditures generally follow the same course as the business cycle.[31] He also concluded that the potential of advertising to affect the business cycle is small, since decisions such as inventory investment are much stronger determinants of the nature of economic cycles. Advertising may be capable of dampening economic swings for some firms and even for some industries, but the evidence to date, with respect to the whole economy, is that advertising has a negative though small impact in reducing the extremes of the business cycle.

Providing Product Utility

Advertising, by generating associations between products and moods, life styles, and activities, can add to the utility a buyer receives from the product. White pointed out that "the consumer purchases the brand and its cluster of meanings as much as he purchases the literal product."[32] People do not buy cars solely to move from one point to another, but to achieve a feeling of independence, to express a personality, or to establish a certain mood or feeling. Evaluating the amount of utility, if any, that advertising adds returns us to the fundamental issue raised earlier of the definition of such terms as "need" and "product."

---

[31] Simon, *Issues in the Economics of Advertising.*

[32] Irving S. White, "The Functions of Advertising in our Culture," *Journal of Marketing,* 23, July 1959, p. 10.

Encouraging New Products

Advertising encourages product development by providing an economical way to inform potential buyers of the resulting new products or product improvements. In many situations, innovation requires large research and development expenditures and substantial investments in production facilities that might be difficult to justify if advertising could not be efficiently employed to communicate the existence of the innovation. In this respect, advertising encourages product competition.

The development of new products and the improvement of existing ones can mean an expanding economy with more jobs and investment opportunities and a buyer selection that is continually improving in breadth and quality. However, as Borden stated in his classic study of the economic effects of advertising, published in 1942, an expanding set of product options can be disadvantageous for the buyer, especially when they reflect minor differentiation of existing products that add little real utility.[33] In such situations, Borden suggests that the larger number of brands could increase distribution costs and make consumer buying more complex. A central question is whether the value to consumers of the product option expansion exceeds the associated costs. These and related issues will be considered in more detail in Part V, Section D, which examines the relationship of advertising to competition.

[33] Neil H. Borden, *The Economic Effects of Advertising* (Chicago: Richard D. Irwin, 1942), p. 609.

16 THE CULTURAL AND SOCIAL IMPACT OF ADVERTISING ON AMERICAN SOCIETY

Mary Gardiner Jones

Television is said to reach about 80% of the population. The average TV viewer is exposed to some 40,000 commercials a year.[1] HEW's Secretary Robert Finch stated recently that the average human being over his productive life span watches TV commercials for more hours than he ever spends in school. The average pre-school-age child is estimated to have absorbed more hours of unstructured TV input than the hours an average student at a liberal arts college spends for four full years in the class room.[2]

Looking at these facts Secretary Finch then asked: "What is the industry doing with those hours? What are those hours doing to us, as a people? Indeed, do we have ways of measuring the experience of the TV medium or our national life style?"

The question posed by Secretary Finch goes to the basic problem which must be of concern to all of us, government, business and the

[1] Attributed to David Ogilvie, "Advertising's Creative Explosion," *Newsweek,* August 18, 1969, p. 66.

[2] Robert H. Finch, speech to the Television Bureau of Advertisers, Washington, D.C., October 21, 1969.

Excerpted, with permission of the author, from an address before the Trade Regulation Round Table, Association of American Law Schools, San Francisco, California, December 29, 1969.

public. Aware of the dynamism of this media and of its potency as a communications tool, we have to ask ourselves what significance this cultural spillover of American advertising has on the value systems, life styles and attitudes towards society of the many diverse individuals in our nation.

What are the non-commercial messages which come through the advertisement on television. The conscious appeal in the television commercial—understandably enough—is essentially materialistic. Central to the message of the TV commercial is the premise that it is the acquisition of *things* which will gratify our basic and inner needs and aspirations. It is the message of the commercial that all of the major problems confronting an individual can be instantly eliminated by the application of some external force—the use of a product. Externally derived solutions are thus made the prescription for life's difficulties. TV gives no recognition to the individual's essential responsibility for at least a part of his condition or to the importance to the individual of proving his own capacity to deal with life's problems. In the world of the TV commercial all of life's problems and difficulties, all of our yearnings, hopes—and fears—can yield instantly to a *material* solution and one which can work instantly without any effort, skill or trouble on our part.

A second inescapable premise of these ads is that we are all externally motivated, concerned to do and be like our neighbors or to emulate popular successful individuals. Certainly the existence of individuals who are driven by their own inner needs for self-expression and self-fulfillment and more concerned with "being" than with "having" receives no recognition in the TV commercial. Personal success in the TV ad is externally contrived, not the product of years of study and training. In short, advertising's messages tend to convey a single, overly simplistic—and I believe in some instances—distorted answer to the needs and ambitions, fantasy yearnings and fears, the hopes and felt inadequacies of the complex individuals who make up American society.

In addition to the value systems of the TV world, the TV commercial also presents a very special and limited view of American society. Here, according to the TV commercial, are real life people of the real world going about their daily business. Here is what the young and successful are wearing and how they furnish their homes. The cultural setting of the TV world—its people and their surroundings—mirrors a specific aspect of American culture—typically that of the white suburban middle-income, middle class family. Until very recently, blacks and Spanish speaking Americans were unknown to the American society of the TV commercial. Americans living in rural areas or in megalopolis were similarly ignored.

The problems implicit in the world of the TV commercial do not stem from any conception that the picture of American life or of the values conveyed are not found in American society or are inaccurately depicted. Indeed, we must assume that the TV commercial accurately mirrors a part of American life and an integral part of the value systems probably held by many, if not most, Americans. Of course individuals are concerned with interpersonal relations, with status, with success. Ads *do* furnish a vision of a type of life style which many people will desire to emulate or identify with. Material things of course give us pleasure. The white middle class suburban family does typically live in the type of surroundings so exclusively depicted in the TV commercial as American way of life. Thus there is nothing affirmatively misleading about TV's portrayal of this particular aspect of American culture and society. But it is simply one segment of the real world neither better nor worse than any other segment.

Accepting the premise that these advertisements are not false in this sense, we still have to ask ourselves whether the TV world's view of America's life style and value system is representative of all aspects of American society and if not, whether advertising's reflection of selected aspects of America's culture and of America's values to the exclusion of others in fact reinforces and thereby gives undue weight to their credibility and desirability and whether this is in the best interests of society. Do we not have to guard against what is perhaps a natural jump on the part of many—and indeed a jump which is basic to the advertising appeal—that the familiar is good and that the association of things with happiness and other good things does give those things a credibility they might not otherwise have or merit. The advertiser knows this about product association. He has been less aware of this association process with the cultural setting which is also being sold by his commercial.[3]

We have already seen some of the consequences of the cultural blindness found in TV's picture of American society. The Kerner Report said this:

> The communications media . . . , have not communicated to the majority of their audience—which is white—a sense of the degradation, misery, and hopelessness of living in the ghetto . . . They have not shown understanding or appreciation of—and thus have not communicated—a sense of Negro culture, thought, or history . . . Most television programming ignores the fact that an appreciable part of their audience is black. The world that television and newspapers offer to their black audience is almost totally white, in both appearance and attitude.
>
> The absence of Negro faces and activities from the media has an effect on white audiences as well as black. If what the white American reads in the

---

[3] For another highly critical view of the values implicit in today's commercial and its impact on society, see Jules Henry, *Culture Against Man* (Random House, 1963); also Herbert Marcuse, *One Dimensional Man* (Beacon Press, 1969), pp. 57–8 ff.

newspapers or sees on television conditions his expectation of what is ordinary and normal in the larger society, he will neither understand nor accept the black American.[4]

Surely no one doubts today that the almost total absence from advertising's picture of America of blacks and other minority groups in our society, or of any other type of life than that depicted in the typical commercial must have some impact on the countless millions of Americans who live in rural areas or in megalopolis, or whose life style is quite different from that reflected in the advertising message. Certainly the material wealth pouring out of the TV tube in no way reflects the way all or even a majority of Americans are in fact living today—or indeed may want to emulate.

A similar one sidedness characterized the value system implicitly portrayed in the typical TV commercial. To many, this value system represents the typical "American" answer to life's problems. I am not sure—apart from the TV world—that it in fact reflects the complexities and maturity of the responses which many individuals practice in their own lives. Certainly most people in our society, on reflection, would be aware that the purchase and consumption of *things* will not in fact provide answers for most of their inner needs and hopes. Yet the TV commercial tends to hammer away at a notion which many people would like to believe is true—that there *is* an easy simple effortless and instant solution for life's problems. There is a similar distortion in the preoccupation in the TV commercial with externally motivated people concerned with "having" rather than "being." If we tend to believe and give credence to what we see and hear most often, can we be satisfied with the values held by these outer directed individuals. Clearly there are many Americans who attach importance to those individuals who are driven by their own inner sense of self-expression and self-fulfillment regardless of the popular acceptance of their particular value goals. Certainly we as a society find room—and have respect—for all human beings because of their essential humanity and decency, their being rather than their becoming or their having. And if so, should we insist that advertising contribute to an implicit respect for these values, for the diverse expectations of individuals and for their manifold personal wants and needs?[5]

---

[4] While the Kerner Report's discussion of the impact of the media on American outlooks and attitudes was based primarily on its programmatic contents, its observations are even more graphically true of the world of the TV commercial. Report of the National Advisory Commission on Civil Disorders (July 1967), pp. 382–83.

[5] Advertising must resolve the age old question—now far more crucial in today's dynamic society—of whether it continues to respond to the beliefs of the "average" American whoever that may be, whether advertising should in fact cater to that norm or average, as Andrew Kershaw of Ogilvie and Mather urges, or whether this is one of

Since advertising of necessity must replay or reflect some cultural aspects of our society and will inevitably embody selected individual values, we have to come to grips with the question of whether it should consciously reach out to make certain that all aspects of American culture and of individual values are not ignored in the total commercial content of TV so that those not portrayed are not unconsciously rejected as less desirable.

---

advertising's faults which must be corrected as Stephen Dietz urges. Andrew Kershaw, Director, Ogilvie and Mather (Canada) Ltd., "Economic and Social Realities of Advertising,' speech, Toronto, Ontario, Feb. 20, 1967; Dietz, "Are Ad Trends Changing . . . ," *Advertising Age,* May 12, 1969.

17 STATEMENT BEFORE THE FEDERAL TRADE COMMISSION

Donald M. Kendall

As I see it, advertising is an inseparable part of the total marketing function. Essentially, the marketing function is one of identifying consumer wants . . . moving to fill those wants by developing products with appropriate qualities . . . packaging them for attractiveness and convenience . . . pricing them right . . .and ultimately getting them into good distribution.

Advertising's role in this function is to convey the news and the benefits of the products to consumers.

Marketing is a democratic concept and it is not surprising to me that the invention and development of modern marketing practices have taken place in our country, the greatest democratic experiment of all times. I say that marketing is a "democratic concept" because it's based on the principle that underlies our elective system itself: *individual freedom of choice.* Every day the American consumer is free to select or reject any number of products of every type and description. In the food and beverage categories, she returns to select again or reject again in a matter of days. I do not recommend this daily voting procedure for keeping elected officials on their toes, but I think it's the greatest system ever devised for keeping good products on the shelves . . . *and getting bad ones off.*

As I have said, advertising's specific role in the marketing function is

---

Presented at the Federal Trade Commission Hearings 20 October 1971; reprinted by permission of Donald M. Kendall.

to convey the news and the benefits of the product to the consumer. In the simplest phrase of all, this means *selling the product.* As the Commission knows, almost any kind of communication about a product—word-of-mouth, salesman-to-customer, the label itself—might be defined as advertising. Media advertising, which will be the subject of most of the following presentations, is only one way to do the selling job.

It is obvious, of course, that if marketing's first step is to identify a consumer want, advertising's assignment is to communicate *how* the product satisfies that want. A word, therefore, about consumer wants:

It is often said that "advertising sells people things they don't need." The best answer I've heard to that criticism was in a house ad run by the Young & Rubicam agency. It went in part like this:

> Yes, advertising *does* sell people things they *don't need* . . . things like television sets, radios, and automobiles, catsup, mattresses, lipstick, and so on. People don't really *need* these things. They really don't *need* art or music or cathedrals . . . they don't absolutely *need* literature, newspapers or historians. All people really *need* is a cave, a piece of meat, and possibly a fire.

I'm still quoting.

> Certainly, mankind existed on little more for many thousands of years. But the complex thing we call civilization is made up of luxuries. Civilization exists because man has the mind and the ability to *create* his environment instead of *submitting* to it as lesser animals must.

End of quote.

So, when I'm told that people don't really *need* certain kinds of products—I have to agree very quickly. Marketing is a process that satisfies *wants* and *desires,* most of which are not fundamental needs.

Let us pursue this "want" idea a little further.

It's also been said that advertising makes people want things they don't *really* want . . . or which they wouldn't have wanted if the advertiser hadn't somehow *manipulated* them. Indeed, advertising has been depicted as creating or inventing wants that did not, in fact, pre-exist.

I want to be very clear on this point, because I think it's very important.

To the best of *my* knowledge—and that of my business and advertising associates—*advertising has not and cannot invent a human want.* Advertising can and does cultivate or kindle *latent* or *dormant* or *previously unperceived* desires for certain products. But it cannot add *to* or subtract *from* the human senses or the characteristics placed in us by God and nature.

Also in my experience, no amount of advertising can force any large number of people to buy things they *don't want.*

In support of this view, I urge that we look at the evidence . . . evidence which the business community has seldom pointed to for reasons that are embarrassingly obvious. This evidence consists of the myriad *failures* which American business encounters in its new-product ventures every year. You hear from businessmen—as you did from me a while back—mostly about the products that succeed. You don't hear too often that *most* of our new products *fail.*

I cannot give you complete statistics on this, because most product failures occur—as they should—in corporate research and development laboratories where scientists continuously test new products or product improvements that might satisfy consumer wants more effectively.

For my own company, let me admit that if one out of ten of our new-product ideas or product improvements is considered worthy of test marketing, I'd count this a darn good batting average.

However, even after this rigorous pre-screening process within the walls of corporate research centers, the bulk of what gets to the marketplace ends up as a failure. I quote some statistics from a speech given in 1967 by Mr. Graf of the A. C. Nielsen Company:

> Of 103 items on which the Nielsen Company did test-market measurements, 47, or 46%, were withdrawn by the manufacturer after varying test-market intervals, because of poor performance. . . . Taking a separate look at the national picture, of the 1123 items which entered broadscale distribution during late 1965, only 649, or 58% of the total, remained in distribution one year later.

That is, about half failed in test market, and almost half of the products which went national didn't even last a year.

Now, up to this point I've been labeling as a "failure" any new or improved product which didn't meet with broad consumer acceptance. And looked at *individually,* that's accurate—they *are* "failures." But if you step back a bit and look at the whole picture, something different emerges: a story of *success,* the successful functioning of an open, competitive, and *free* economy where consumers relentlessly weed out the products they don't want, and accept only those which serve some useful purpose to them. Right there is the reason for all these so-called "failures": the fact that too few consumers really wanted what the businessman was offering. The products which fail each year do not lack for attractive product qualities, brand names, packaging, and strong advertising pressure, but they fail nonetheless because the consumer simply doesn't *want* them. To anyone who truly believes he can manipulate consumers, I would offer this humble advice: Try it. And after you've had some failures, let's get together and discuss "manipulation" again.

A third criticism sometimes leveled against advertising is that it persuades people to "want" the "wrong things." These critics readily admit that advertising only sells people things which they really want, but they contend that people should not be left to choose by themselves because they'll end up wanting the *wrong* things. I have little to say about this criticism, because it seems to me that either you accept freedom of choice, and a basically democratic procedure, or you don't. If we can't rely on individuals to make good *product* choices based on their own judgment, what, may I ask, is the *next* choice we will deny them?

I mentioned a moment ago that *media* advertising is only one way to do the selling job. Some companies today still sell door-to-door. A greater number rely on dealers or store clerks to *close* the sale which advertising might have initiated. I don't intend here to criticize person-to-person selling. I might, however, remind all of us that the "advertising copy" delivered by the door-to-door salesman or even the salesclerk in the store is neither checked and double-checked by lawyers, scrutinized by Network Continuity Acceptance people, subject to the new 4-A's regulation plan, nor submitted in advance to the Federal Trade Commission. On the other hand, I think that few products in America are inspected as diligently and often as copy prepared for media advertising.

Of course, the basic reasons why companies such as mine prefer media advertising to other, more personal forms of selling are economy and efficiency. There is literally no way to count how many salesmen at the front door it would take to reach the number of people who see and hear a television commercial. But even if such a massive sales force *could* be assembled, the costs of their salaries or commissions would raise product prices astronomically.

The use of media advertising, then, does not spring from some unexamined bias on the part of the manufacturer. Rather, it represents a conscious choice as to the most effective and efficient way to generate consumer demand. Where the product provides a wanted consumer benefit, advertising is a highly efficient way to generate a mass market for this product, lowering the costs of production and distribution.

Let me now move on to some other criticisms of advertising and share my thoughts with you:

1. "Advertising sometimes is deceptive and misleading." *Agreed.* Sometimes it *is* deceptive and misleading, and where that occurs I would encourage businessmen in general, the advertising industry specifically, and the Federal Trade Commission very directly, to attack these problems vigorously. In these hearings, I think you will find that advertisers go to great lengths to ensure that their products are presented honestly and accurately. However, I am sure you also will find that there have been and still are some abuses. We should not tolerate these abuses. And, to the best of my knowledge, adequate legislation and administrative power exist to correct these abuses where they occur.

2. "A lot of advertising is uninformative. Instead of presenting facts and sticking to rational arguments, it plays on the emotions." From my standpoint, if the advertising for one of our products doesn't *inform* consumers as to the pleasure or satisfaction they can derive from the product, then I've got some advertising which needs replacing. Certainly the job of advertising is to *inform*. But to communicate benefits accurately, the informational process often will *have* to recognize *emotional* factors as well as rational arguments. Of *course* there's a lot of emotion in advertising! Our emotional life is vitally connected with what it is we think we "want," and if as marketers we're trying to satisfy consumer "wants," it would be strange indeed if we ruled out emotions. Professor Levitt of the Harvard Business School makes the point this way in a recent article called "The Morality of Advertising":

> The "purpose" of the product is not what the engineer says it is, but what the consumer implicitly demands that it shall be. Thus the consumer consumes not things, but expected benefits—not cosmetics but the satisfactions of the allurements they promise, not quarter-inch drills, but quarter-inch holes; not stock in companies, but capital gains; not numerically controlled milling machines, but trouble-free and accurately smooth metal parts; not low-cal whipped cream, but self-rewarding indulgence combined with sophisticated convenience. The significance of these distinctions is anything but trivial.

I have no axe to grind, as an advertiser, in choosing any one set of advertising appeals instead of another—"factual," "emotional," or what have you. But I *do* feel an obligation to "inform" people about what matters to *them*—that is, the pleasure or enjoyment they can derive from using my product. I simply can't afford to be autocratic. My commitment is to give the consumer what she wants and, if her "wants" have an emotional component to them, it behooves me to recognize that fact.

Recently a new point has been made in regard to "facts" versus "emotion" in advertising. It's been said that in the old days of print and radio advertising, "the product was sold in a simple manner keyed to the rational purchase . . . the rational choice being made by the consumer who knew his need and the cost and range of his alternatives." In contrast to this, today's "television advertising can be, and is, more subtle, more sophisticated, and much more persuasive."

Now, while these views are highly flattering to my many friends in advertising, I find them somewhat hard to square with either my personal memories of those days or some of the actual copy taken from Frank Rowsome's book, *They Laughed When I Sat Down*. Prominent, of course, among magazine ads with an emotional flavor is "Somewhere West of Laramie" for the Jordan car. I think a few lines will demonstrate that emotional copy was an art in those days:

> Somewhere west of Laramie there's a bronco-busting, steer-roping girl who knows what I'm talking about. . . .

> The playboy was built for her. Built for the lass whose face is brown with the sun when the day is done with revel and romp and race.
>
> There's a flavor of links about that car—or laughter and lilt and light—a hint of old loves—and saddle and quirt. It's a brawny thing—yet a graceful thing for the sweep of the Avenue. . . .

Of course, that's a classic and maybe not a fair example.

Pepsodent toothpaste years ago filled its ads with rational promises about ending dingy film on teeth and fighting acid that causes decay. But in an ad headlined "Magic lies in pretty teeth—remove that film," there is the promise that "whole lives may be altered by this better tooth protection."

Cadillac, in its ad "The Penalty of Leadership," took 22 emotional paragraphs to say what it said in the last three:

> Master-poet, master-painter, master-workman, each in his turn is assailed and each holds his laurels through the ages.
>
> That which is good or great makes itself known, no matter how loud the clamor of denial.
>
> That which deserves to live—lives.

Quite possibly the book's best example of emotional ads was a depression ad for Gillette blades. The photograph shows a disconsolate man with his equally unhappy wife. The man has what was later to be called "5 O'Clock Shadow." The headline reads, "I didn't get the job." And copy which was only excerpted says "He'd counted on landing the job—but he missed out. Again he'd have to stall the landlord, the grocer and all the rest."

Very frankly, I recall those radio and print days as full of flamboyant, emotional copy. Lucky Strike Green went to war . . . Halitosis and the B.O. foghorn were scaring just about everyone . . . and even your best friends weren't telling you.

But a lot of copy was as rational as the law allowed. And the law allowed everything.

> Coca-Cola—the ideal brain tonic . . . delightful beverage . . . specific for headaches . . . relieves exhaustion.
>
> Quaker Oats—a mighty factor in contributing to the nation a wholesome sturdiness, a rugged health, a splendid ambition and conquering strength.
>
> Grape Nuts—Diet principally Grape Nuts, no meat, never ill a day.
>
> Bakers's Cocoa—the finest in the world, preserves health, prolongs life.
>
> Pond's Cream—puts insomnia, headache, faceache, neuralgia to flight.

And again a classic:

> Lydia Pinkham's Vegetable Compound is a positive cure for all those painful complaints and weaknesses so common to our best female population. It

will cure entirely the worst forms of female complaints, all ovarian troubles, inflammation, ulceration, falling and displacement of the womb and the consequent spinal weakness, and is particularly adapted to change of life.

I read these not to debate the notion that today's TV advertising is more subtle and more sophisticated. But I believe that today's TV sell is considerably less persuasive.

Two more current complaints about advertising:

1. "Advertising often is in poor taste." *Agreed.* There are many television commercials I find strident, abusive, insulting to my intelligence. I'm sure we all have entries for this category. But all too often, the commercials I find offensive are someone else's favorites. I think taste will always be best left to the marketplace where consumers can, if they choose, demonstrate their own discontent by refusing to buy the offending products. I also suggest—because it is my personal practice—that the chief executive of any advertising company exercise, if need be, the power to eliminate advertising which he or other responsible company officials—or the public itself—identify as dubious in taste.

2. "Advertising inhibits competition by creating 'artificial' differences between products and thus sustaining 'monopolistic' market positions." I do *not* agree. On the contrary, advertising is a constant *spur* to competition, since it provides the means to tell consumers rapidly about my new and improved products, and it gives my competitor the same opportunity to build business, a fact of which I must be ever mindful.

A word on this idea of "artificial differences." Most of the real advances in the quality of human life have been made in pretty small increments. Now, for someone who is not directly involved and responsible, it's possible to belittle this kind of progress, to make fun of it, because we aren't aware of how hard it is to really "improve" on a product or process in a field where we're not expert. But let's not fall prey to this kind of thinking. Let's recognize that the deodorant toilet soap of today *is* indeed a much better product than the brown laundry soap of yesteryear, but we got there in small steps; that the refrigerators and the self-cleaning ovens and the dentrifices and typewriters of today are indeed better products than they ever were before. But we got there in small steps; and so forth. Let's let the *consumer* judge whether the small steps we've taken are worthwhile to *her*. Because if for some strange reason we find ourselves legislating against these "small improvements," then I'm terribly afraid we may find there are no improvements at all. If we only tolerate the "great leap forward," we may fall flat on our faces.

In closing, let me restate a few key points. Advertising is an inseparable part of the marketing function. The effectiveness of advertising is amply witnessed by the growth of our economy and the high level of prosperity which our citizens enjoy. Indeed, advertising now is being criticized for being *too* effective, for "manipulating" people to buy things they don't really want. If that were true, there'd be darn few of you drinking anything other than Pepsi-Cola. However, the facts tell a different story, a story in which consumers choose those products they *want* and ignore those products they *don't* want.

On occasion, advertising appears which is misleading or deceptive. I do not kid myself that this is always accident, the unintentional result of human error or a breakdown in company-agency communications. But I believe that remedies exist for this kind of problem. And I urge that those remedies be used vigorously when they are needed. However, to impose broad new restrictions on all of advertising—based even on the *proven* and *intentional* deceit of a small portion of it—would be, in my opinion, a serious blow to free enterprise and a grave disservice to the very consumers we all hope to serve.

It has been said before by many others, but I think it will bear repeating throughout all the future history of our land: Flawed and imperfect as it might be, the American system of free enterprise has brought the greatest standard of living to the greatest number of people in the recorded history of man. Those who would change this system—who do not believe in it—will be the first to damage a part of it. I believe that advertising is that part.

B *Advertising and Children*

18 RESEARCHERS LOOK AT THE "KID VID" RULE

Scott Ward

CHARLES K. ATKIN

This summary describes the key conclusions drawn from my 70 page statement submitted to the Federal Trade Commission inquiry into children's advertising. The conclusions are based on an extensive review of available research evidence drawn from almost 100 sources, including my own series of investigations conducted over the past six years.

The most important conclusions will be briefly listed. . . .

Children pay attention to about 10,000 commercials per year, including 1,000 Saturday morning ads for toys and food products.

Children under eight years old display little understanding of the persuasive intent of advertising and tend to trust the claims made in commercials.

TV advertising plays a dominant role in shaping children's preferences for toy and food products. Children who heavily view TV ads are far more likely to request and to consume such products.

Children are persuaded to want cereal because a favorite commercial character promotes it or a toy premium is included in the box; nutritional value is not a salient factor.

TV commercials contribute to intra-family conflict when frequent

---

Excerpt from remarks made by Charles K. Atkin of Michigan State University and Marvin E. Goldberg of McGill University at the 1978 Conference of the Association for Consumer Research. Published in William Wilkie (ed.), *Advances in Consumer Research 6* (Ann Arbor, Mich.: Association for Consumer Research, 1979), pp. 7–11. Reprinted with permission.

food and toy requests are rejected by parents. Ads also create some disappointment and irritation for children.

Parents do not play a strong direct role in educating children about TV advertising, and they support additional regulations and reductions in child-oriented TV advertising.

. . . .

The Federal Trade Commission Staff Report offers five possible remedies for the potential unfairness and deceptiveness of children's advertising. These include (a) disclosures of nutritional or health information within ads, (b) nutrition or health messages outside ads, (c) limitations on the amount of advertising, (d) limitations of advertising techniques, and (e) bans on all ads directed to younger children and on those ads directed to older children for products posing dental health risks.

Affirmative disclosures within advertisements may not be comprehended by younger children; most do not comprehend the standard disclaimers presented in contemporary toy commercials. However, there is limited basis for optimism: tests of modified versions of toy disclaimers, featuring simplified or conspicuous statements, show greater effectiveness; and researchers demonstrated that children are capable of learning nutrition information presented with a graphic device in the form of a stylized robot. Nevertheless, it is doubtful that advertisers would produce disclosures of sufficient length, prominence, and clarity to achieve similar effectiveness. Thus, the disclosure remedy does not appear to be highly promising at this time.

Affirmative disclosures outside advertisements would involve PSA [public service announcement]—style messages to counterbalance the generic influence of advertising. There is considerable evidence that current PSA's have an impact on child audiences. Studies show that children pay close attention and learn the content of these messages; behavioral effects have also been demonstrated. Thus, similar types of spot messages promoting nutrition or warning about cavity risks are likely to be an effective remedy.

Limitations on the amount of advertising might involve reductions in advertising time to four or six minutes per hour on Saturday morning. To calculate the possible impact on stimulation of product desires and undesirable outcomes, the responses of current light vs. heavy viewers can be examined. Children who now watch a light diet of advertising have an exposure rate similar to the proposed reduced level. The research shows that these children, compared to heavily exposed viewers, are less likely to accept commercial claims, request products, consume advertised products, argue with parents over purchases, and experience unhappiness and dissatisfaction due to commercials. Thus, some beneficial outcomes might be expected if time limitations were instituted.

Restrictions on advertising techniques is a more ambiguous issue, since proscribed practices have not been specified. There is evidence that many children believe that fantasy characters in commercials are competent to discuss the merits of food products, and that these characters have an influence on product preferences. In addition, premium offers are effective in selling food products and contribute to parent-child conflict. Techniques such as these might be restricted, along with other practices identified in subsequent investigations. The need for centralized regulations is given greater impetus by the findings that parental teaching about advertising techniques isn't widespread.

Banning of advertising directed to children under eight who are too young to understand and evaluate commercials is the final remedy. Evidence supporting the case for a ban includes findings that children's commercials feature sophisticated techniques designed to appeal to the unique vulnerability of young children, the large quantity of ads viewed by young children, their low level of understanding of selling intent and uncritical acceptance of commercials, the strong impact on young children's product desire and requests to parents, their advertising-based inappropriate reasons for food product preferences, the contribution of advertising to parent-child conflict and child unhappiness, and the minimal role played by parents in mediating advertising.

MARVIN E. GOLDBERG

The comments that follow stem first from my own direct experience in observing 1,000 or so children over a series of six or seven studies. Somehow one senses the importance of this type of first hand knowledge, when even researchers tend to refer to "my son" or "my daughter" in substantiating their judgments regarding TV's impact on children. Second and more substantively, of course, the findings suggested by the program of research Gerry Gorn and I have conducted at McGill leads me to a particular perspective regarding the issues we are discussing here today.

Researchers must be careful to balance the immediate policy questions of the day with broader policy alternatives. The particular administration we deal with today may change tomorrow, and the policy options that might now seem unrealistic, may seem quite plausible to a new administration. Thus, while a researcher interested in focusing on questions of social concern should not divorce himself from the real policy options of the day, he ought not constrain himself totally within the parameters of a given administration. To do so would be too much of a "reactive" position.

The opportunity to be considerably more "proactive" is typically available to the researcher when he simulates alternative experiences for individuals through the manipulation of experimental conditions. While some experimental conditions may reflect specific policy options, the researcher can also creatively structure additional conditions, and in so doing he may actually become a change agent himself. While questions of one's own values, biases, etc. may arise, I don't think these are critical and can readily be overcome through standard experimental procedures (keeping experimenters blind, etc.). This is more or less the position we took in developing our "Snack Food" study (Goldberg, Gorn, and Gibson, 1978). The conditions we structured included a TV viewing situation in which children saw a neutral animated cartoon program with either commercials for sugared snacks or PSA's for fruits and vegetables, etc. In these conditions we sought to reflect either current reality or one of a number future realities now sought by the FTC. We went still further, however, asking what would be the impact of TV *programming* that focused on the nutrition issue. Indeed we found this option was most effective in reducing the number of highly sugared foods children selected.

Just as the researcher ought not let government policies totally bound the perspective he uses in framing his research questions, the same caution ought to be a part of his approach to industry. As a case in point, advertisers typically focus on brand-shifting strategies. In their minds advertising to children is largely intended to shift children away from a competitor's candy bar or sugared cereal to the one they are espousing. The researcher must be alert to this limited perspective. The cumulative effect of each advertiser attempting this strategy is an enormous quantity of candy bar and sugared cereal commercials, certainly relative to those available for less sugared or processed foods. If one's perspective relates to the broader question of TV's effects on the child's total diet, the research questions that would follow would likely be quite different from those of the advertising researcher assessing the effectiveness of a given commercial.

. . .

It was suggested that the burden for the FTC is essentially to demonstrate that "grade school children are unaware of long run consequences of eating too much sugar". This seems to me to be an overly narrow and cognitive view of how children are influenced by TV commercials. Our research has shown that while it is true that children may know which foods are, or are not, healthy, this is not really the issue. A more fundamental question is whether children's exposure to TV commercials is such that they are ever motivated to use the healthy-unhealthy dimension in considering what foods to eat. Because the vast majority of foods advertised on children's TV are highly sugared, the child's frame of reference is such that after 2-3 hours of viewing per day, the only alternatives that are likely to be evoked are those he has seen on TV, and by and large these are the highly sugared, processed foods. Joan Gussow (1972) makes this point by analogy to adults; she suggests that just as adults tend to reach for a Budweiser or a Seven-up when thirsty and not the tap for water, so too do kids reach for the products they have been exposed to so exclusively on TV. TV precludes children from active consideration of foods other than those they see on TV. Especially with young children, the notion of "monkey see, monkey do" seems a more appropriate description of their behavior than models which posit intervening cognitive considerations of the nutritional value of these foods.

I would hypothesize that once PSA's espousing a variety of less sugared foods were juxtaposed alongside the current array of TV food commercials, children *would* begin to actively question the relative merits of different kinds of foods. Once provided with a fuller picture of the array of foods available to them, they would become more capable of considering the tradeoffs associated with different food values (nutrition, fun, etc.). Far from leading to some predetermined notion of "what is right for children" this goal of exposing them to a diversity of foods only has balance in the child's diet as an intended outcome. I doubt if many would consider this as an instance of an overly directive or heavy hand of government.

19 CAN AND SHOULD THE FTC RESTRICT ADVERTISING TO CHILDREN?

Michael B. Mazis

This session was organized to present to the consumer research community the views of leading figures in the debate over children's advertising regulation. The Federal Trade Commission's children's advertising proceeding is particularly significant to consumer researchers because after a number of years of limited research utilization at FTC, behavioral science research now occupies a central role in the policy debate. Given the importance of research findings in the proceeding, eight key individuals, who have been associated with the children's advertising controversy over the past decade, agreed to address an ACR audience. The participants shared the common belief that the research community should be apprised of the issues underlying the trade regulation rulemaking proceedings, which were scheduled to commence hearings (and did) in January, 1979.

The Commission's determination to undertake this rulemaking proceeding arises from consideration of two petitions received in April, 1977 from Action for Children's Television and the Center for Science in the Public Interest. While slightly different in approach, these two petitions request promulgation of a trade regulation rule prohibiting the television advertising of sugared products to children.

Excerpt from an FTC sponsored panel discussion on the regulation of children's advertising. Published in William Wilkie (ed.), *Advances in Consumer Research 6* (Ann Arbor, Mich.: Association for Consumer Research, 1979), pp. 3–6. Reprinted with permission.

Following receipt of these petitions, Bureau of Consumer Protection staff undertook an inquiry into the factual and legal issues raised by the petitions. These efforts culminated in a document entitled "Staff Report on Television Advertising to Children." The two petitions and the *Report* suggest that televised advertising of *any* product directed to young children who are too young to understand the selling purpose of, or otherwise comprehend or evaluate, commercials (i.e., under the age of eight) may be unfair and deceptive within the meaning of Section 5 of the Federal Trade Commission Act, requiring appropriate remedy. The *Report* also suggests that current televised advertising of sugared products directed to older children (i.e., between ages of 8 and 12) may be unfair and deceptive, again requiring appropriate remedy.

The staff's recommended approach consisted of a "package" of remedies which included the following three elements:

1. Ban all televised advertising for any product which is directed to, or seen by, audiences composed of a significant proportion of children who are too young to understand the selling purpose of or otherwise comprehend or evaluate the advertising;
2. Ban televised advertising for sugared food products directed to, or seen by, audiences composed of a significant proportion of older children, the consumption of which products poses the most serious dental health risks;
3. Require televised advertising for sugared food products not included in Paragraph (2), which is directed to, or seen by, audiences composed of a significant proportion of older children, to be balanced by nutritional and/or health disclosures funded by advertisers.

In response to the staff's recommendation, the Commission invited comment in an April 28, 1978, *Federal Register* announcement on the advisability and manner of implementation of a rule which would include the preceeding three elements. In addition, the Commission sought comment on the appropriateness and workability of alternative remedial approaches not contained in the staff report.

A distinguished panel of experts, representing the full spectrum of views on these proposals, was assembled to state their positions and to interact with the consumer research audience. [Participants included]

Tracy A. Westen, Federal Trade Commission
Robert B. Choate, Council on Children, Media and Merchandising
John A. Dimling, National Association of Broadcasters
Seymour Banks, Leo Burnett Advertising
Stanley Cohen, *Advertising Age*

Fletcher C. Waller, General Mills, Inc.
William Van Brunt, Hershey Foods Corp.

The panel was organized by Michael B. Mazis, Office of Policy Planning and Evaluation, Federal Trade Commission, who served as chair for the session.

TRACY A. WESTEN

Mr. Westen has been deputy director of the Federal Trade Commission's Bureau of Consumer Protection since August 1977, and has been one of the architects of the proposed children's advertising rule. His remarks were designed to set forth the facts underlying the FTC's children's advertising proposal and to place the proposal in a legal context.

Westen cited a number of "facts" which led staff to consider some action to remedy the children's advertising "problem." Children between the ages of two and eleven see enormous amounts of advertising—about 25 hours per week is spent watching television and approximately 20,000 ads are seen by the average child in a year. In addition, there is considerable research evidence that young children: can't distinguish between programs and commercials; do not understand the selling intent of commercials; cannot distinguish between fantasy and reality.

Mr. Westen also discussed the problems associated with the advertising of sugared products to children. Children see about 7,000 advertisements for highly sugared products each year, but children between ages seven and twelve have difficulty balancing appeals for the immediate gratification afforded by eating highly sugared products with the long-term dental risks. By age two, about one-half of children have diseased gums and decayed teeth.

The unique legal treatment of children was discussed also. Westen suggested that the Supreme Court has ruled that even fundamental civil rights may be withheld from young children who lack the maturity to exercise them. The ability to run for public office and to cast a ballot for candidates of one's choice, for example, are vital Constitutional rights. Yet the Constitution itself withholds these rights from individuals below a certain age. And in the commercial marketplace, the courts have voided contracts made with children and restrained the ability of minors to purchase guns, liquor, and cigarettes—products which are felt to be dangerous in immature hands.

Thus, the notion that children often need special protection from the consequences of their inexperience and immaturity is sanctioned by the Constitution and the decisions of the Supreme Court. The thrust of the FTC's proposals is to withhold advertising from pre-schoolers and other children who do not understand what advertising is, and provide older children with both sides of important nutritional controversies. This approach, Mr. Westen stated, appears consistent with decades of Constitutional precedent.

In the case of children's advertising, Mr. Westen emphasized, there is reason to believe that advertisers are engaging in deception through omission of a material fact. Deception occurs because of the immaturity of the audience (i.e., children may be unable to "fill-in the blanks" in some ads) and the complexity of the product (i.e., children may not understand the consequences of using a potentially dangerous product). While there is sufficient evidence to open the inquiry, Westen stressed the Commission is still actively considering a wide range of possible options.

ROBERT B. CHOATE

Mr. Choate is the President of the Counil on Children, Media and Merchandising—an organization dedicated to studying advertising practices to children and to educating children and their parents about present marketing practices so that they may become more prudent consumers.

The opening portion of Mr. Choate's remarks were devoted to a discussion of Congressional lobbying efforts over proposed children's advertising regulations. He expressed great concern about "overt corporate lobbying against supposed independent agencies." In Choate's view, "corporate lobbyists are trying to emasculate the FTC in its actions vis-a-vis children and advertising."

The proposed children's advertising regulation, Choate asserts, is of far greater significance than the stated issues. Previously, there was insufficient attention to the unequal bargaining power between advertisers and imprudent parties. The proceeding involves a possible alteration of commercial law principles. The real issue is: Should commercial law, dealing with transactions between prudent advertisers and "reasonably imprudent" children, be updated to protect children from television sales pitches?

Mr. Choate also elaborated on Mr. Westen's discussion of television advertising content. He stated that there is an imbalance in the products advertised to children on commercial television. The private enterprise system emphasizes a limited "menu" of highly sugared foods and drinks as opposed to fresh fruits and vegetables or other nutritious foods. The

FTC's inquiry is designed to cope with this advertising "imbalance." For example, public service messages to children or to both children and parents are one important method of partially shifting the advertising "imbalance" in the direction of encouraging the purchase and consumption of nutritious foods.

JOHN A. DIMLING

John A. Dimling, Jr. is Vice-President and Director of Research for the National Association of Broadcasters (NAB). Dimling briefly summarized his perception of the logic of FTC's children's advertising proposals. He stated that the proposed rule rests on the following arguments: (1) per capita sugar consumption has been increasing; (2) sugar (sucrose) causes tooth decay; (3) television advertising to children emphasizes that "sweetness is good" thereby increasing sugar consumption; (4) as a result, we should restrict the number of advertisements directed toward children.

However, the consumption of sucrose, the sugar in candy and pre-sweetened cereals, has remained rather constant. In addition, even if children switched from pre-sweetened cereals to cereals with small amounts of added sugar, they tend to add just as much sugar as exists in pre-sweetened cereals.

In addition, there is very little evidence that eating the most heavily advertised products will cause tooth decay. Pre-sweetened cereal consumed with milk has not been found to have an impact on tooth decay. Also, there is no evidence of a relationship between heavy exposure to television commercials and the incidence of tooth decay. There is some evidence, however, that children are aware that fresh fruits and vegetables are more nutritious than candy bars and other highly sugared foods; as a result the purpose and goal of any FTC action does not appear to be based on a logical foundation.

Finally, Dimling emphasized that the proposed FTC regulations are likely to be counterproductive. The research literature suggests that some children are able to understand the selling intent of commercials earlier than eight years of age, which is the age posited in the FTC staff proposal. Although children below *some* age do not understand selling intent, restricting advertising to this audience will result in denying advertisers the right of free speech to communicate with other audience members. These other members constitute the great majority of the television audience for most children's programs.

As a result of restricting advertising to large numbers of the potential audience, many of the benefits of advertising would be lost. The possible effects of advertising restrictions include: a decline in the quality and quantity of children's programming; a loss of important information communicated to children through advertising; an increase in the price of toys and other children's products; increased costs of marketing new products, raising entry barriers for many firms.

SEYMOUR BANKS

Seymour Banks is Vice-President in charge of Media Research, Leo Burnett Advertising Agency. Dr. Banks discussed two topics during his remarks: the validity of FTC's rulemaking efforts and the need for self-regulation of children's advertising.

Banks confidently predicted defeat of the proposed children's advertising TRR because the FTC staff's conclusions are totally "without merit." There are two main facts leading to this conclusion. First, "the FTC does not have the professional competence to serve as a 'national nanny'." In attempting to present a convincing argument for restricting television advertising to children below the age of eight on the grounds that they cannot understand selling intent, staff engaged in a "highly selective use of research material and an out-of-date oversimplified version of Piaget to the exclusion of social learning theories."

Second, there is little evidence that grade school children are unaware of the long-run consequences of the consumption of heavily sugared products. Banks asserted that the FTC will not be able to defend its position strongly enough to justify First Amendment concerns over the protection of advertisers' rights of free speech.

The second portion of Dr. Banks' remarks was devoted to exploring needed improvements in advertising self-regulation. Advertising agencies and media are "willing to adopt new practices when factual evidence suggests that it would be socially beneficial to do so." What is needed at this point is new research to improve children's advertising. Several areas for additional research were offered: (1) Improvement of children's consumer education skills—such as teaching children to distinguish between programs and commercials; (2) Development of methods to maximize discussion of commercials with children and recommendations about use of these procedures to parents, to maximize incidence of this type of discussion; (3) Development of standards which protect children while allowing for appropriate advertising techniques (e.g., fantasy); (4) Inclusion of pro-social messages in advertising.

STANLEY COHEN

Stanley Cohen is currently Washington Editor of *Advertising Age.* His weekly column and editorials have expressed both concern over the content of children's advertising and the likely success of FTC's efforts to develop a workable solution.

Mr. Cohen's stirring statement focused on the political environment surrounding FTC's inquiry into children's advertising regulation. He is impressed with the "destructive power" of the issue. The inquiry should not be over regulation of children's advertising, however, but what is good for the child?

Mr. Cohen believes that broadcasters and advertisers are losing sight of the threat to their own medium in an attempt to preserve their access to the child. He predicted continued advertising to children will turn parents against advertisers, and turn kids against television.

Mr. Cohen raised the question: What has this done to our political process? He claimed behind the scenes lobbying is a threat to the political process. The FTC has procedures based on statutes and due process, adopted with the participation of the industry. Yet, industry was unwilling to have regulations considered in the proper way—instead went to Congress, behind the scenes, and talked to politicians, who have no real knowledge of the issues and who reached their conclusions without hearings. He called this a "government of men, not of laws."

What is this process doing to the First Amendment? As a journalist, Mr. Cohen regards the First Amendment as sacred. His friends have been hauled before judges who have commanded them to disclose their sources. He does not want the First Amendment degraded to allow corporations to tell five-year-olds to eat chocolate-covered cornflakes.

The basic issue, from Mr. Cohen's perspective is: How does the broadcaster carry out its responsibility toward children? It's broadcasters who plan programs and accept ads. He suggested that the FTC approach might be "counter-productive" because it diverts attention away from broadcasters' obligation to prepare good programming for children.

FLETCHER C. WALLER

Fletcher C. Waller, Jr., was named Vice-President and Director of Marketing Services for General Mills in August, 1976. In this position, he has responsibilities for a group of service departments that execute marketers programs and consult with marketers on problem solving.

Included are The Betty Crocker Food & Nutrition Center, Promotion Services, Advertising Services, Marketing Research, and Marketing Accounting Departments.

Mr. Waller's remarks were addressed primarily to the implicit assumptions underlying the FTC rulemaking efforts. These implicit assumptions as to how we communicate and deal with children in our society must be made explicit to make progress in the policy debate. According to Waller, the FTC assumes that the American family is incapable of healthy interaction between parent and child. He asked whether "irritation of parents" is justification for FTC regulation on what children should and should not see on television. This intra-family conflict should be considered a natural, indeed healthy, part of parenting and should not be used to increase federal regulation.

Waller believes also that the FTC assumes that children under eight years of age do not have adequate nutritional knowledge. However, the concept of "nutritional knowledge" has not been adequately defined.

Finally, the FTC assumes that advertising to children is synonomous with allowing a surrogate salesman into our homes. However, advertising merely communicates the characteristics of products to children so they can express their desires to parents. Children process information in advertising, match their own set of needs, desires, likes and dislikes with the product array, select what they'd like to have and express these interests to parents.

WILLIAN VAN BRUNT

William Van Brunt is Associate Cousel for Hershey Foods Corporation with primary responsibility for regulatory matters. Mr. Van Brunt addressed his remarks to the reasons underlying corporate dissatisfaction with the FTC's children's advertising rulemaking proceeding.

The FTC, in view of the First Amendment protection for Free Speech, and the rule of law that the party seeking to change established customs and practices, has the burden of proof of demonstrating the need and justification for such changes, must prove that the advertising of products to children causes a substantial harm.

On a more specific level, the proposed advertising ban for certain sugared products appears completely unjustified. In fact, no substantial body of data exists: to judge the cariogenicity of food products; to indicate that there is a direct relationship between the percentage of sucrose content and cariogenic potential; to suggest that advertising of sugared products causes harm to children in excess of that which results from the sale of these products without advertising support. The rulemaking effort exhibits a measure of elitism, which assumes that the government knows what is right for people.

The possible effect of these efforts, according to Van Brunt, is the imposition of additional inflationary costs on consumers. This potential waste of millions of taxpayer dollars is a result of the FTC's apparent failure to consider fully all the relevant facts before proceeding. For example, staff has ignored industry's self-regulation efforts and the possibility of working for improvements through the process of voluntary industry cooperation. By ignoring or distorting the findings of the recent NSF-sponsored report on children in the marketplace, staff has similarly failed to consider important research evidence which is pertinent to potential rulemaking.

C *Deceptive Advertising*

20 DECEPTIVE ADVERTISING

David A. Aaker

Advertising has a large responsibility within our economic system for providing information for consumer decision making. If the information provided is misleading or deceptive then that responsibility is not being fulfilled. The result is, in economic terms, a misallocation of resources. In more personal terms, the result is a disappointed buyer, or worse, a real economic or physical injury.

The need to avoid deception in advertising is well recognized by both industry and government leaders. The American Association of Advertising Agencies published a Creative Code in 1962 which affirmed that the members,

> in addition to supporting and obeying the laws and legal regulations pertaining to advertising, undertake to extend and broaden the application of high ethical standards. Specifically, we will not knowingly produce advertising which contains:
> a. False or misleading statements or exaggerations, visual or verbal.
> b. Testimonials which do not reflect the real choice of a competent witness.
> c. Price claims which are misleading.
> d. Comparisons which unfairly disparage a competitive product or service.
> e. Claims insufficiently supported, or which distort the true meaning or practicable application of statements made by professional or scientific authority.
> f. Statements, suggestions or pictures offensive to public decency.[1]

[1] *Creative Code,* American Association of Advertising Agencies, 1962.

Excerpt from David A. Aaker and John G. Myers, *Advertising Management,* © 1975, pp. 567–577. Reprinted by permission of Prentice-Hall, Inc., Englewood Cliffs, New Jersey.

The issue seems rather clear. Advertisers need only follow this code and no problems will arise. It is, however, not that simple. First, all do not agree on the definition of deception. When Blatz claims that it is "Milwaukee's finest beer" some (particularly other Milwaukee brewers) could argue that in fact another beer is superior. Is deception involved? What is meant by finest? One advertisement claimed that a hair dye would color hair permanently. If someone exposed to the advertisement believed that the dye would hold for hair not yet grown and thus a single dye would last for decades, is the claim deceptive? How many need to misunderstand before deception is involved? When there is disagreement as to what is deception who should decide? How can the dishonest and careless advertiser be detected, prosecuted and punished? To what extent can self-regulation be relied upon? What are appropriate remedies? These questions and others make the issue of deception a complex area for the advertiser, the media, and the government.

In the following, the history of regulation will be briefly sketched. The concept of deception will then be considered. Who is it that is being deceived? How does one determine what is promised by the advertisement? Various existing and proposed remedies will then be discussed. Finally, the Truth-in-Advertising legislation will be examined.

HISTORY OF FEDERAL REGULATION OF ADVERTISING

In 1914, the Federal Trade Commission Act was passed which created the federal agency which has had the primary responsibility for the regulation of advertising. Section 5 of the FTC Act contained the prohibition: "Unfair methods of competition in commerce are hereby declared unlawful." The interest was to provide an agency that could deal with restraints of trade. The act was stimulated by a dissatisfaction with the effectiveness of the Sherman Anti-Trust Law. The problem of deceptive advertising was not a target of the FTC Act. Millstein observes: "The most important development in the long history of the FTC's prohibition of false advertising was that the FTC concerned itself with the problem in the first place."[2] In many respects it was a fortuitous accident.

The FTC became concerned with deceptive advertising because of its effect upon competition. In the first test case in 1919 the FTC moved against Sears Roebuck.[3] Sears had advertised that their prices for sugar

---

[2] Ira M. Millstein, "The Federal Trade Commission and False Advertising," *Columbia Law Review,* 64 (March 1964), p. 439.

[3] *Sears, Roebuck & Co.* v. *FTC,* 258 Fed. 307 (7th Cir. 1919).

and tea were lower than competitors' because of their larger buying power. The claim was found to be false but the FTC action was upheld not because of subsequent damage caused the consumer but by the fact that smaller competitors could be injured.

In 1931, in the landmark *FTC* v. *Raladam* case, the Supreme Court specifically held that the FTC could not prohibit false advertising if there is no evidence of injury to a competitor.[4] The ruling struck a decisive blow in that it stopped any movement in the direction of protecting the consuming public directly. However, it was a blessing in disguise as it helped to mobilize support for redefining the powers of the FTC. The ultimate result was the Wheeler Lea Amendment passed in 1938 which amended Section 5 of the FTC Act to read: "Unfair methods of competition in commerce and unfair or deceptive actions or practices in commerce are hereby declared unlawful." Thus, the obligation to demonstrate that injury to competition occurred was removed. The issue then was not a jurisdictional one but rather how to move forward against deceptive advertising.

A basic issue in the enforcement of these laws against deceptive advertising to which we now turn is how to define and identify deception.

WHAT IS DECEPTIVE ADVERTISING?

Conceptually, deception is found when an advertisement is the input into the perceptual process of some audience and the output of that perceptual process (a) differs from the reality of the situation and (b) affects buying behavior to the detriment of the consumer. The input itself may be determined to contain falsehoods. The more difficult and perhaps more common case, however, is when the input, the advertisement, is not obviously false, but the perceptual process generates an impression that is deceptive. A disclaimer may not pass through the attention filter, or the message may be misintepreted. It should be helpful in evaluating the ground rules regarding deception that the Commission and the courts have developed.

. . .

Who Is Deceived?

How extensive must the deception be before deception is determined to exist? If one naive person is misled, is the advertisement deceptive? Or 1 percent, or 10 percent, or 30 percent? Who is it that is to be protected?

---

[4] *FTC* v. *Raladam Co.*, 258 U.S. 643 (1931).

The FTC has determined that essentially all are to be protected, in particular those who are naive, trusting, and of low intelligence, small though the numbers might be. In 1927, the Supreme Court indicated that the FTC was to protect the "trusting as well as the suspicious."[5] In the Charles of the Ritz case in 1944 the FTC found that the trademark "Rejuvenescence" was associated with a foundation makeup cream in a manner which promised the restoration of a youthful complexion. The court noted that:

> The law was not "made for the protection of experts, but for the public—the vast multitude which includes the ignorant, the unthinking and the credulous" . . . and the "fact that a false statement may be obviously false to those who are trained and experienced does not change its character, nor take away its power to deceive others less experienced." . . . And, while the wise and the worldly may well realize the falsity of any representations that the present product can roll back the years, there remains "that vast multitude" of others who, like Ponce de Leon, still seek a perpetual fountain of youth. As the Commission's expert testified, the average woman, conditioned by talk in magazines and over the radio of "vitamins, hormones, and God knows what," might take "rejuvenescence" to mean that this "is one of the modern miracles" and is "something which would actually cause her youth to be restored." It is for this reason that the Commission may "insist upon the most literal truthfulness" in advertisement . . . and should have the descretion, undisturbed by the courts, to insist if it chooses "upon a form of advertising clear enough so that, in the words of the prophet Isaiah, 'wayfaring men, though fools, shall not err therein.' "[6]

In the Gelb v. the FTC case the low intelligence level considered by the court reached an extreme.[7] The FTC had prohibited the claim that a hair coloring product could color hair permanently—that even new hair would have the desired new color. The evidence consisted of one woman who indicated that although she would not be so naive, some may indeed be misled by the use of the word permanent.

The more recent Kirchner case, decided by the courts in 1955, provided some relief to the charge that no deception can exist.[8] It involved a swimming aid and the claim that when the device was worn under a swimming suit it was "thin and invisible." The Commission, who decided that it would be unlikely that a buyer would take this claim literally, noted:

---

[5] *FTC* v. *Standard Educ. Society,* 302 U.S. 112, 116 (1937).

[6] *Charles of the Ritz Dist. Corp.* v. *FTC,* 143 F. 2d 676 (2d Cir. 1944).

[7] *Gelb* v. *FTC,* 144 F. 2d 580 (2d Cir. 1944).

[8] 3 Trade Reg. Rep. 16664 (FTC, Nov. 7, 1963).

> To be sure, "Swim-Ezy" is not invisible or impalpable or dimensionless, and to anyone who so understood the representation, it would be false. It is not likely, however, that many prospective purchasers would take the representation thus in its literal sense. True, as has been reiterated many times, the Commission's responsibility is to prevent deception of the gullible and credulous, as well as the cautious and knowledgeable. . . . This principle loses its validity, however, if it is applied uncritically or pushed to an absurd extreme. An advertiser cannot be charged with liability with respect of every conceivable misconception, however outlandish, to which his representations might be subject among the foolish or feebleminded. Some people, because of ignorance or incomprehension, may be misled by even a scrupulously honest claim. Perhaps a few misguided would believe, for example, that all "Danish pastry" is made in Denmark. Is it, therefore, an actual deception to advertise "Danish pastry" when it is made in this country? Of course not. A representation does not become "false and deceptive" merely because it will be unreasonably misunderstood by an insignificant and unrepresentative segment of the class of persons to whom the representation is addressed.[9]

The Kirchner case also indicated that advertising aimed at particularly susceptible groups will be evaluated with respect to that group. Thus, when children are the target, deception will be evaluated with respect to them. One case was decided on the basis of the advertising impact on a "busy businessman." This refinement is interesting because it recognizes that people may perceive stimuli *differently,* depending on the situational context. Hopefully, the FTC and the courts will continue to become more refined in their perceptions of those who are to be protected.

Despite the Kirchner case, it is still true that deception is defined with respect to relatively small audience segments with above average tendencies to be deceived. Such a posture, when pushed to an extreme as it was in the Gelb case, can mean that there is no defense against an FTC charge of deception. A small segment can always be identified who will misinterpret the clearest communication. In one public opinion survey respondents were asked to indicate which statements from a short list corresponded with their opinion of the Metallic Metals Act.[10] Despite the fact that no such act existed, over 21 percent of the respondents said it would be a good move for the United States and 55 percent agreed that it was a good thing but should be left to the states. Market research studies routinely control for those with tendencies to respond in certain ways and those who are careless and will answer incorrectly. Thus, a demand that

---

[9] *Ibid.* at 21539–40.

[10] Harper W. Boyd, Jr., and Ralph Westfall, *Marketing Research: Text and Cases* (Homewood, Ill.: Richard D. Irwin, Inc., 2nd ed., 1964), p. 285.

the law protect all—even the trusting and the unthinking—is indeed an extreme position.

. . . .

The Entire Advertisement

The advertisement will be judged by its general impression. It may be that all claims made within an advertisement are literally true yet the total impression of the advertisement may still be deceptive. Thus, in a 1950 decision, the courts ruled that Lorillard had developed deceptive advertisements despite the fact that their claims were literally true.[11] *Reader's Digest* had run an article which indicated that all cigarettes were harmful and that the differences between them were minor. To illustrate the point, a list of cigarettes was included with the tar and nicotine content of each noted. A Lorillard brand happened to have the lowest level of tar and nicotine although by an insignificant margin. The Lorillard campaign emphasizing the *Reader's Digest* article was therefore deemed deceptive.

In another example, a television commercial for a car wax used flaming gasoline on an automobile to demonstrate that the wax could withstand intense heat.[12] However, the gasoline was only burning for a few seconds. It was extinguished before any significant heat was generated. Consequently, the advertisement was determined to be deceptive in that the claim was not actually substantiated by the test.

The Ambiguous Statement

If an advertisement can be interpreted in two ways and one of them would be deceptive, the advertisement is regarded as deceptive. Thus, the use of the phrase "government supported" could be interpreted as "government approved" and was therefore challenged.[13] In another case, the FTC held that a toothpaste claim that it "fights decay" could be interpreted as a claim that it provides complete protection and was therefore deceptive.[14]

When a claim is extremely vague the alternative interpretations are not always obvious. An advertisement will claim, for example, that its

---

[11] *P. Lorillard Co.* v. *FTC,* 186 F. 2d 52 (4th Cir. 1950).

[12] Hutchinson Chem. Corp., 55 FTC 1942 (1959).

[13] *FTC* v. *Sterling Drug, Inc.,* 215 F. Supp. 327, 330 (S.D.N.Y.) aff'd. 317 F. 2d 699 (2d Cir. 1963).

[14] Bristol-Meyers Co., 46 FTC 162 (1949) aff'd. 185 F. 2d 58 (4th Cir. 1950).

product tones up muscles, or provides a lifetime guarantee, or is for the treatment of a disease. What do these terms really mean? It may be noted that to an advertising researcher the quantification of the number of interpretations and the extent to which each would emerge would not be an unusually difficult or costly research task. However, the Commission and the courts tend not to rely upon such techniques for reasons that shall be discussed later.

Misleading Silence

The FTC can require that a more complete disclosure be made to correct a misconception. Thus, Geritol was required to indicate that the "tired feeling" it was supposed to help was possibly due to factors that the product could not treat effectively.[15] Similarly, baldness cures have been required to indicate that baldness usually is hereditary and untreatable. Toys usually are assumed to be safe. Therefore, toy manufacturers have a special responsibility to point out possible unsafe aspects of their toys.

It is interesting to consider how far pressure from the FTC for complete disclosure could go. There are a wide variety of advertised brands which differ little in substance from competitors. It is a common practice to associate a brand with an attribute of the product class. Should the brand be required to state in its advertisement that all brands are virtually identical in this respect? For example, an aspirin advertisement may discuss the pain-relieving quality without noting the fact that all aspirin-based brands will have similar effect. It appears that the FTC is moving in this direction. They lodged a complaint against Wonder Bread's claim that their brand builds bodies twelve ways. The complaint charged that the advertisement falsely implied that Wonder Bread differed in respect to the claim from other brands. If this complaint is upheld, it could rather dramatically change the face of advertising. Soon after the Wonder Bread complaint was filed, another manufacturer, Hunt-Wesson Foods, developed a policy of avoiding advertising brands which have little real difference from their competitors.

The argument for such a policy of disclosing that all brands are similar with respect to a certain product attribute is primarily that advertising is a mechanism to communicate information which will be helpful to the consumer in making a purchasing decision and that "image" advertising is not helpful. If advertising content is not informative from this perspective and in fact could lead to nonoptimal brand choice deci-

---

[15] J. B. Williams Co., 3 Trade Reg. Rep. 17, 339 (FTC Dkt. No. 8547, 1965), appeal docketed, No. 16, 969 (6th Cir. Dec. 3, 1965).

sions, it should be curtailed. However, it may be that such a rule could, at least to some extent, reduce the product class information a consumer receives as brands lose their incentive to communicate product class attribute information. If most advertising is brand choice instead of product class choice oriented, this possibility is perhaps a minor consideration. A problem associated with such a proposal is to determine if a brand really has a differential advantage. To a researcher who has the benefit of perceptual maps and sophisticated taste tests, a brand may seem significantly different. To a consumer, and perhaps to the FTC, these differences may seem minor.

Materiality of the Falsehood

For an advertisement to be deceptive, it must contain a material untruth—that is one capable of affecting purchase decisions. It should be likely that the advertisement will result in public injury. Millstein explains:

> "Public injury" does not mean that a consumer must actually suffer damage, or that it must be shown that goods purchased are unequal to the value expended. Rather, "public injury" results if the advertisement has a tendency to induce action (such as the purchase itself) detrimental to the consumer that might not otherwise have been taken. If such action could *not* have been induced by the claim (even though false), there is no "public injury." This requirement comports with the express provision of Section 15 of the FTC Act, as amended, that the advertisement must be misleading in a material respect to be actionable.[16]

The Colgate Palmolive case is one instance in which the Court applied the materiality requirement to modify a Commission decision.[17] The case involved the shaving of simulated sandpaper, sand on plexiglass. The advertisement appeared to demonstrate the moisturizing qualities of Palmolive Rapid Shave. The Commission noted that in fact sandpaper could only be shaved after a lengthy period of soaking and thus the advertisement was deceptive. This type of deception was material in that consumers were likely to rely upon the demonstration in making purchase decisions. However, the Commission went further and noted that the use of a sand on plexiglass mock-up would have been prohibited even if Rapid Shave could shave sandpaper as represented. The Court of Appeals rejected the sweeping language of the complaint arguing that mock-ups are permissible if they do not affect purchase decisions. As a

---

[16] Millstein, "False Advertising," p. 438.

[17] *Colgate-Palmolive Co.* v. *FTC,* 310 F. 2d 89 (1st Cir. 1962).

result, the Commission revised its opinion stating that only mock-ups and props that were intended to demonstrate visually a quality material to the selling of the product would be prohibited. Thus, mashed potatoes could be used in television commercials in scenes depicting ice cream consumption (ice cream would melt too rapidly under lights) if the texture and color of the prop was not emphasized as selling points of the product.

Puffery

A rather well-established rule of law is that "trade puffing" is permissible. Puffing is of two general forms. The first is a subjective statement of opinion as to a product's quality using such terms as "best" or "greatest." Nearly all advertisements contain some measure of puffery. "You can't get any closer" (Norelco). . . . "Try something better" (J&B Scotch). . . . "Gas gives you a better deal" (American Gas Association). . . . "Live better electrically" (Edison Electric Institute). . . . "State Farm is all you need to know about insurance." . . . "Super Shell." None of these statements have been proven to be true but neither have they been proven false. They all involve some measure of exaggeration.

The second form of puffery is an exaggeration extended to the point of outright spoof which is obviously not true. A Green Giant is obviously fictitious and even if he were real, he wouldn't be talking that way. Hi Karate aftershave really isn't so appealing that men must fight off the attacks of aroused females.

Later, in 1946, the court set aside the FTC ruling in the Carlay case that a weight reduction plan involving Ayds candy which claimed to be "easy" to follow was deceptive. The court made the following comments: "What was said clearly justifiable . . . under those cases recognizing that such words as "easy," "perfect," "amazing," "prime," "wonderful," "excellent," are regarded in law as mere puffing or dealer's talk upon which no charge of misrepresentation can be based."[18]

Preston and Johnson examine the puffery issue and note that although it is well established in law, it is at the same time somewhat vulnerable.[19] They note that over the years the puffery defense has been frequently relied upon. Yet the courts have ruled in many of these cases

---

[18] *Carlay* v. *FTC,* 153 F. 2d 493, 496 (1946).

[19] Ivan L. Preston and Ralph H. Johnson, "Puffery: A Vulnerable (?) Feature of Advertising." Paper presented at the annual convention of the Association for Education in Journalism, University of South Carolina, August 1971.

that the claim goes beyond puffery to real deception. The question is, then, what is puffery? One answer is that the definition seems to be changing over time. A claim that would have been regarded as subjective opinion and legitimate puffery years ago might now be viewed in a different light. The consumer movement is forcing a new orientation, which affects when a puffery defense will be regarded as appropriate.

In the Tanners Shoe Company case decided in 1957 the FTC denied the puffery defense, noting that:

> It was stipulated that it is not literally true that respondents' shoes will "assure" comfort or a perfect fit to all individuals. However, respondents contend that such representations constitute legitimate trade puffery and are not false representations within the meaning of the law. . . . The repesentation that the product provides support where it is most needed clearly carries an orthopedic or health connotation, and it is undisputed that respondents' shoes are not orthopedic . . . but are stock shoes. It would appear that such a representation is false in attributing to the product a quality which it does not possess rather than exaggerating a quality which it has.[20]

In the Colgate Palmolive case involving the sandpaper shaving demonstration the respondent claimed that the advertisement was merely fanciful exaggeration. The FTC decision noted that to term the demonstration puffery was "inconsistent with the prevalent judicial and administrative policy of restricting, rather than expanding, so-called puffing."[21]

In the fall of 1970 the FTC published a complaint against Standard Oil of California specifying that their claim that Chevron's F-310 additive was "the most long-awaited gasoline development in history" was false. Although this case has not been decided, it gives further evidence that the puffery defense is much less reliable than it has been in the past. Preston and Johnson note that when the number of exceptions to the puffery defense are few the situation can be compared to the forest which has lost a few trees. It still exists. However, the time can come when the remaining trees no longer make a forest.

> The trees already cut down and those now under attack, have reduced puffery so much in scope that advertising men should no longer rely on it complacently. And further reduction is theoretically possible because the same process which has already made considerable reduction may be applied to the puffery which remains. All it takes is to proclaim that some objective fact underlies the subjective statement, and it is possible to do this for any puffery which ever existed.[22]

---

[20] Tanners Shoe Company, 53 FTC Decisions 1137 (1957).

[21] *Colgate-Palmolive Co.* v. *FTC, op. cit.*, p. 1452.

[22] Preston and Johnson, "Puffery: Feature of Advertising," p. 23.

21 RECENT FTC ACTIONS: IMPLICATIONS FOR THE ADVERTISING STRATEGIST

Robert E. Wilkes & James B. Wilcox

Advertising's function is primarily to inform potential buyers of the problem-solving utility of a firm's market offering, with the objective of developing consumer preference for a particular brand. Consumers, however, are viewing the execution of this function with increasing skepticism and criticism. In a 1972 nationwide survey, approximately 60% of the consumers questioned felt that recent criticisms of advertising were totally justified.[1] Less than half of all advertising was rated as honest and informative, while charges of misrepresentation and exaggeration were prevalent among the complaints encountered.

The Federal Trade Commission (FTC) has responded to this increasingly vocal criticism of advertising by implementing or proposing policies specifically intended to improve the kind and quality of information contained in advertisements. As a result, a new and substantially different environment now faces the marketing strategist. It is important, therefore, for marketers to be familiar with these FTC expectations regarding advertising content and the possible actions which the commission has indicated it may take in cases wherein its expectations are not met.

The primary objectives of this article are: (1) to review and comment

[1] Study by Warwick and Legler, Inc., cited in "The Public Is Wary of Ads, Too," *Business Week,* January 29, 1972, p. 69.

Reprinted with deletions from *Journal of Marketing* 38 (January 1974), pp. 55–61, published by the American Marketing Association.

on the more important policies recently employed or proposed by the FTC, and (2) to suggest a procedure by which the firm may lessen the prospect of FTC intervention. A substantial number of recent cases are discussed to illustrate the development of FTC policy.

THE FTC ADVERTISING SUBSTANTIATION PROGRAM

One of the more far-reaching new undertakings of the FTC is its program for the substantiation of advertised claims. Announced in 1971, this program requires advertisers to submit on demand by the commission data supporting advertised claims relative to product safety, performance, efficacy, quality, or comparative price. Two major goals set for the program were education and deterrence. First, the FTC hoped that public disclosure of the substantiating data provided by the firm would enable consumers to make more rational purchasing decisions. The second goal of the program was to deter advertisers from making unsupported claims by publicly exposing such claims as being unsubstantiated.

What Constitutes Substantiation?

Since the substantiation program began in 1971, supporting data have been requested from manufacturers of color television sets, pet foods, automobiles, automobile tires, hearing aids, cold remedies, and air conditioners on an industry-wide basis, and from numerous firms on an individual basis. A "reasonable basis" criterion has been adopted by the commission in deciding if the advertised claims are supported. Where no "reasonable basis" for a claim exists, making such claims is deemed to be deceptive and unfair.[2] For example, complaints against three air conditioner manufacturers alleged that no reasonable basis exists for claims of quietness and reserve or excess cooling capacity.[3] Two sugar trade associations were charged by the commission as having no reasonable basis for claims that eating sugar before meals is effective in weight reduction.[4] Although early declarations indicated that the FTC

[2] Sugar Association, Inc., et. al., 3 Trade Reg. Rep. ¶20,085 (1972); see also "Legal Developments in Marketing" section, *Journal of Marketing,* Vol. 37 (January 1973), 80, and Vol. 37 (April 1973), 85.

[3] Fedders Corp.; Rheem Manufacturing Co., et. al.; and Whirlpool Corp., 3 Trade Reg. Rep. ¶20,120 (1972); see also "Legal Developments in Marketing" section *Journal of Marketing,* Vol. 37 (April 1973), 34.

[4] Same reference as footnote 2.

substantiation program was intended to provide consumers with whatever information a firm submitted to document specific claims, recent actions suggest that the FTC will also judge the adequacy of the substantiation materials supplied.

Employing a "theory of implied representation of testing," the FTC has argued that consumers may infer from performance claims that supporting tests have been made to back up the claims.[5] The question confronting the marketing manager, therefore, is what type and how much testing is necessary to satisfy the "reasonable basis" standard adopted by the commission. As the following discussion indicates, the answer to this question is difficult to ascertain because of the case-by-case approach of the FTC.

Testing: What Kind and How Much?

In defense of its individual-case approach, the commission has indicated that appropriate testing procedures for claims made are a function of the type of claim involved.[6] With regard to claims made by one tire manufacturer, the commission stated that "a road or user test may be an adequate scientific test to substantiate one performance claim, whereas a laboratory test may be the proper test to substantiate another claim."[7] The appropriateness of the testing procedures, however, is determined by the commission. In a proposed order against General Motors for economy claims for one of its automobiles, the FTC indicated that a reasonable test for such claims "may consist of quantitative data based upon a statistically valid sample or other appropriate substantiating material."[8]

Uniqueness Claims

Under the substantiation program, the FTC seeks not only to require "adequate" support for advertised claims but also to see that uniqueness of a product attribute or characteristic is not implied unless this can also be supported. In a consent order against Procter & Gamble, the commission alleged that, contrary to the implications of certain television adver-

---

[5] National Dynamics, et. al., 3 Trade Reg. Rep. ¶19,653 (1971); see also "Legal Developments in Marketing" section, *Journal of Marketing,* Vol. 36 (January 1972), 81.

[6] The Firestone Tire & Rubber Co., 3 Trade Reg. Rep. ¶20,120 (1972); see also "Legal Developments in Marketing" section, *Journal of Marketing,* Vol. 37 (April 1973), 82–84.

[7] Same reference as footnote 5.

tisements, Crisco Oil does not possess unique properties that produce a less greasy food than other edible oils.[9] Contained in the Crisco Oil case is the following commission statement regarding uniqueness claims:

> A statement as to the qualities or attributes of a product can amount to an implied uniqueness claim *if it is made in a context which conveys an impression of uniqueness for the product.* However, statements as to the qualities or attributes of products covered by the order will not constitute a violation of this order for the sole reason that such statements could also be made with respect to similar products.[10] [Emphasis added.]

Thus, even substantiated claims may not be used if an unsupported uniqueness implication is created by the advertisement. A complaint against ITT Continental Baking Company alleges that claims for Wonder bread ("How big do you want to be?" "Wonder bread helps build strong bodies 12 ways") imply Wonder to be more nutritious than other enriched white breads made with the same ingredients according to United States government standards.[11] A similar case against the Sun Oil Company charges that advertisements for Sunoco gasolines create the false impression that competing gasolines having comparable octane ratings provide less engine power.[12]

POSSIBLE FTC RESPONSES TO UNSATISFACTORY ADVERTISING

Several formal options are open to the FTC when dealing with advertising that does not meet with its expectations in some way, whether related to the substantiation program or another commission policy. Cease and desist orders may be issued, for example, to terminate a questioned advertising practice, with subsequent court action possible if the firm involved fails to comply as ordered. Such orders may also involve monetary fines. The maker of Geritol and FemIron and its advertising

---

[8] General Motors Corp., 3 Trade Reg. Rep. ¶20,120 (1972); see also "Legal Developments in Marketing" section, *Journal of Marketing,* Vol. 37 (April 1973), 84.

[9] Procter & Gamble Co., 3 Trade Reg. Rep. ¶19,889 (1971); see also "Legal Developments in Marketing" section, *Journal of Marketing,* Vol. 36 (July 1972), 78.

[10] Same reference as footnote 9.

[11] ITT Continental Baking Co., et al., 3 Trade Reg. Rep. ¶19,539 (1971); see also "Legal Developments in Marketing" section, *Journal of Marketing,* Vol. 35 (October 1971), 76.

[12] Sun Oil Co., et al., 3 Trade Reg. Rep. ¶19,856 (1971); see also "Legal Developments in Marketing" section, *Journal of Marketing,* Vol. 36 (July 1972), 78.

agency were ordered to pay fines totaling $812,000 for advertised claims challenged by the FTC.[13]

Recent commission decisions and orders have involved two particular techniques or approaches for improving the kind and quality of advertising directed to consumers: affirmative disclosure and corrective advertising. A third and more controversial approach for curtailing deceptive advertising is now emerging in the form of the countercommercial. The impact of these techniques on the firm may be substantial.

Affirmative Disclosure

If, in the FTC's view, an advertisement has provided insufficient information to the consumer to enable an informed decision, an affirmative disclosure order may be issued. Such orders require "clear and conspicuous" disclosure of additional information, frequently relating to certain deficiencies or limitations of a product or service. Affirmative disclosure orders may often relate to matters of health or safety, but they are not restricted to such concerns. Kenrec Sports, Inc., was ordered to disclose certain limitations to its swimming-aid device; for example, that the device is not a life preserver and should always be used in shallow water.[14] Medi-Hair International was required for one year to devote at least 15% of each advertisement or presentation for its baldness concealment system to limitations and drawbacks of the system; specifically, that the system involves surgical implantation of wire sutures in the scalp; that there is a high probability of discomfort and a high risk of infection, skin disease, and scarring; and that the purchaser is advised to consult with his personal physician about the system prior to purchase.[15] The disclosures in this case are significant and far-reaching. And, in a complaint against three computer schools, the commission charged that career opportunities for graduates were misrepresented.[16] The consent

---

[13] "J.B. Williams Appeals Fine, Wants Trial on Geritol Ads," *Advertising Age* (January 29, 1973), p. 1; see also "Legal Developments in Marketing" section, *Journal of Marketing,* Vol. 37 (July 1973), 82–83.

[14] Kenrec Sports, Inc., et. al, 3 Trade Reg. Rep. ¶19,971 (1972); see also "Legal Developments in Marketing" section, *Journal of Marketing,* Vol. 36 (October 1972), 69.

[15] Medi-Hair International, et. al., 3 Trade Reg. Rep. ¶19,982 (1972); see also "Legal Developments in Marketing" section, *Journal of Marketing,* Vol. 36 (October 1972), 69.

[16] Control Data Corp., et. al., Lear Siegler, Inc.,; and Electronic Computer Programming Institute, Inc., et. al., 3 Trade Reg. Rep. ¶19,980 (1972); see also "Legal Developments in Marketing" section, *Journal of Marketing,* Vol. 36 (October 1972), 70.

order requires that future advertisements affirmatively disclose placement percentages, employers who hire graduates, and starting salaries.

Corrective Advertisements

Whereas affirmative disclosure orders seek to augment the information base of consumers by providing information needed but not contained in previous advertisements, corrective advertising orders seek to eliminate the residual effects of inaccurate or misleading information in prior advertising. The first such order under the FTC advertising substantiation program required ITT Continental Baking Company to devote 25% of its media budget for one year, exclusive of production costs, to FTC-*approved* corrective advertisements that Profile bread is not effective for weight reduction as prior advertisements had represented.[17] The makers of Ocean Spray Cranberry Juice were required to incorporate corrective advertisements with FTC-*specified* copy text to eliminate possible misrepresentations of earlier advertisements as to the food energy of its product relative to orange or tomato juice.[18] This order also specified that 25% of the media budget be devoted to the corrective advertisements.

The first *mandatory* corrective advertising order required two sugar trade associations to run advertisements with FTC-*specified* copy text in seven national magazines in which the associations had previously advertised.[19] The order sought to correct certain misconceptions about the weight-reducing qualities of sugar. Unlike the makers of Profile bread and Ocean Spray Cranberry Juice Cocktail (the latter was also required to change the name of its product), the sugar trade associations might have elected not to advertise at all rather than incorporate corrective advertisements; consequently, the order was mandatory. Corrective advertising provisions are also contained in commission actions against Chevron Oil Company (for F-310 gasolines), various analgesics manufacturers, a seller of home swimming pools, and ITT Continental Baking Company (for Wonder and Profile breads).[20]

---

[17] Same reference as footnote 11.

[18] Ocean Spray Cranberries, Inc., et. al., 3 Trade Reg. Rep. ¶19,881 (1972); see also "Legal Developments in Marketing" section, *Journal of Marketing,* Vol. 36 (October 1972), 68–69.

[19] Same reference as footnote 2.

[20] Standard Oil of Calif., et. al., 3 Trade Reg. Rep. ¶19,352 (1970); see also "Legal Developments in Marketing" section, *Journal of Marketing,* Vol. 35 (April 1971), 77. Sanford Levinson, et. al., 3 Trade Reg. Rep. ¶20,080 (1972); see also "Legal Developments in Marketing" section, *Journal of Marketing,* Vol. 37 (January 1973), 80. ITT Continental Baking Co., et. al., 3 Trade Reg. Rep. ¶19,539 (1971); see also "Legal Developments in Marketing" section, *Journal of Marketing,* Vol. 35 (October 1971), 76.

Counter-Commercials

Probably the most controversial stratagem yet proposed for regulating advertising is the counter-commercial. The FTC has proposed that the Federal Communications Commission permit counter-advertising in broadcast media to counteract product claims and advertising themes which raise controversial issues.[21] Under this proposal, those who wished to pay for air time would be allowed the opportunity, and those who could not pay would be afforded free time, subject to limitations. Access to counter-advertisers would be made available for advertisements which (1) assert claims of product performance or stress broad recurrent themes of product performance that explicitly raise controversial issues of current public importance, (2) contain claims that rely upon scientific premises currently subject to controversy within the scientific community, or (3) are silent about negative aspects of the advertised products. Apart from the sizable adverse economic consequences which the broadcast media claim would result from implementation of this policy[22] are the potential pressure and embarrassment which could accrue to advertisers themselves, especially when the firm had made a good-faith attempt to provide accurate and useful information to consumers.

The Stern Community Law Firm has developed at least three counter-advertisements, which the major television networks have so far refused to air.[23] Two of the spots deal with the recall of Chevrolet automobiles for installation of a safety device, and another spot is concerned with the claims of several well-known analgesics.

The procedures now used or proposed by the FTC in its attempts to reduce deceptive advertising may profoundly affect not only the advertising decisions but the entire marketing strategy of a firm. An advertiser may be required to provide additional information to consumers and even retract or mitigate the effects of previously supplied information. The latter may be especially costly. ITT Continental Baking Company estimates that its agreed-to series of corrective advertisements for Profile bread resulted in a sales decline of between 20% and 25%.[24] This figure, of course, is exclusive of any damage to the reputation or credibility of the firm as a result of having to "take back" certain claims already made in

---

[21] "The Fairness Doctrine and the Public Interest Standards of the Federal Communications Act, Part III," *CCH Newsletter,* No. 2 (January 12, 1972).

[22] "Ad Controls: Road to Truth or Invitation to Disaster?" *Broadcasting,* Vol. 82 (May 1, 1972), 20–24.

[23] "Out of the Courts, into the Media with Stern's Public-Interest Campaigning," *Broadcasting,* Vol. 82 (May 1, 1972), 24.

[24] "Wonder Bread Decision Stalls FTC Drive for Corrective Ads," *Advertising Age* (January 1, 1973), p. 26.

previous advertisements. On this point, however, one source suggests corrective advertisements may actually enhance the advertiser's credibility in the consumers' eyes; thus the result would be the opposite of the FTC's intentions.[25]

There are serious questions facing the firm that wishes to compete within the framework of present FTC regulatory policy. For example, what degree of disclosure is required to avoid intervention by the FTC? Should a distiller of alcoholic beverages disclose the potentially addictive and harmful aspects of the consumption of its products? Should a maker of toothpaste intended primarily to brighten teeth disclose that its formula does not contain a proven decay preventive? Or should a manufacturer disclose the contents of his product to the extent that a trade secret is compromised? In summary, substantial uncertainty surrounds the degree of affirmative disclosure which should be required from a firm except in more obvious cases of health or safety.

Regarding corrective advertisements, the commission has reaffirmed in at least two separate cases its authority to issue these orders and its belief that they violate neither the spirit nor the letter of the First Amendment.[26] The 25% level adopted by the commission is essentially abritrary, however, and does not necessarily reflect the degree of misperception of consumers nor the amount of advertising necessary to remedy such misperception.

SUMMARY AND RECOMMENDATIONS

This overview of recent FTC policies and decisions has indicated the framework within which the firm must develop a competitive advertising strategy. The FTC advertising substantiation program requires advertisers to support their claims with tests that are increasingly scientific in nature. Even adequately supported claims may be challenged by the commission, however, if the context of the advertisement implies a degree of uniqueness that cannot also be substantiated. In cases wherein the commission determines that an advertisement contains information that is inaccurate and/or inadequate, the firm may be ordered to provide additional information, to correct the misperceptions from previous advertisements by running corrective advertisements, or both of these. Of course the firm continues to face other FTC action in the form of cease and desist orders, monetary fines, and court action when its advertising

---

[25]James, F. Engel, David T. Kollat, and Roger D. Blackwell, *Consumer Behavior,* 2d ed. (New York: Holt, Rinehart & Winston, 1973), p. 337. See also Robert F. Dyer and Philip G. Kuehl, "The 'Corrective Advertising' Remedy of the FTC: An Experimental Evaluation," *Journal of Marketing,* Vol. 38 (January 1974), 48–54.

[26]Same reference as footnote 5; Campbell Soup, 3 Trade Reg. Rep. ¶20,148 (1972).

practices are challenged. Apart from formal intervention by the FTC, there is also the possibility of counter-commercials from private groups like the Stern Community Law Group.

It is difficult to predict if the FTC will continue its aggressive course on deceptive advertising, although several factors suggest that it will. The new FTC chairman has indicated his approval of recent commission innovations, including the substantiation program and tougher penalties for false advertising.[27] More recently, Chairman Engman directed each of the eleven FTC regional offices to have at least ten cases under investigation by May 30, 1973.[28] The FTC may have enlarged the scope of the substantiation program when it recently announced that future implementation efforts will concentrate upon major themes of the companies whose advertising its involved rather than upon specific attributes or factors as has been the case thus far.[29] Probably the strongest stimulus for continued aggressiveness by the commission will come from consumers themselves. The results of a recent poll indicated that consumers would welcome more restrictions to curb deceptive advertising, including prohibiting firms from advertising for a certain period of time if their advertisements are found to be false or misleading.[30]

The long-term impact of the newer FTC policies and procedures will likely prove beneficial to the firm and to the consumer. Hopefully, the aura of deception and distrust now surrounding much of the advertising presented to consumers will be replaced by a perception of greater honesty and usefulness. For the immediate future, however, more critical attention by the firm to its advertising practices may be required to reduce the likelihood of FTC intervention. A suggested procedure of how the firm might respond to these newer requirements and programs of the FTC is presented in the following guidelines:

1. *Assume a truly consumer-oriented perspective.* Although consumers may not be rational in the strictest sense, they acquire goods and services to solve perceived problems and satisfy felt needs. The advertiser is responsible for determining how his particular market offering fits into this frame of reference and what information the consumer needs to

---

[27] "Engman Says He'll Continue FTC Present Course on Ads," *Advertising Age* (February 12, 1973), p. 3.

[28] "FTC's Engman Tells Directors: Get Moving on Ad Abuse Cases," *Advertising Age* (April 30, 1973), p. 1.

[29] American Motors Corp.; Chrysler Corp.; British-Leyland Motors, Inc.,; Fiat-Roosevelt Motors, Inc.; Ford Motor Co.; General Motors Corp.; Renault, Inc.; Saab-Scania of America, Inc.; Subaru of America, Inc.; Toyota Motor Distributors, Inc.; Volkswagen of America, Inc.; and Volvo, Inc., 3 Trade Reg. Rep. ¶20,168 (1973); see also "Legal Developments in Marketing" section, *Journal of Marketing,* Vol. 37 (July 1973), 83–84.

[30] "Consumers Endorse More Restrictions on Business," *Advertising Age* (October 25, 1971), p. 2.

arrive at a purchasing decision to alleviate the problem involved. Recognition of this problem-solving approach will facilitate the preparation of effective advertising strategies and will simultaneously provide consumers with needed information.

2. *Adopt a reasonable-man perspective.* The fact that consumers are susceptible to persuasive communication should not be interpreted by the firm to mean that "anything goes." Rather, advertised claims should be evaluated by the advertiser in light of the interpretations that consumers in specified target markets could be reasonably expected to make. If, after viewing the firm's advertisements, a significant number of consumers misinterpret the capacity of a market offering to deliver certain benefits, it would seem advisable to recast the advertisement to eliminate the misperception. The advertiser is thus assuming responsibility for a reasonable interpretation of the claims as well as for statements for which the FTC may require substantiation.

3. *Do not imply nonexistent uniqueness.* State claims for parity products in such a way that the context of the advertisement does not imply uniqueness unless adequate support for uniqueness exists. A contemporary version of Ted Bates's "unique selling point" might be "truly unique, substantiated selling point." This guideline follows from the previous discussion of a reasonable interpretation by consumers.

4. *Establish an internal, interdisciplinary advertising screening committee.* Composed of top executives from a cross-section of areas of responsibility within the firm, this committee would screen advertisements to preclude over-promise and under-substantiation. The committee would function in addition to other concepts of effectiveness testing with actual consumers.

5. *Establish better testing procedures.* The firm should consider very carefully the type of testing (e.g., user tests, laboratory tests, consumer preference tests) that would be most appropriate in substantiating the claim being made. In view of recent FTC actions, the tests should be rigorous and methodologically scientific to comply with the commission's concept of "reasonable basis."

6. Support and encourage industry efforts to more comprehensive and effective self-regulation so that government intervention is minimized. Stimulate trade associations to work with the FTC to develop reasonable testing procedures.

A. SOCIAL ISSUES IN ADVERTISING

1. Suppose that a motivation research study found that housewives disliked a certain transparent, clinging, wrapping material because their basic dislike of cooking was unconsciously trans-

ferred to the wrap. As a result, nonkitchen uses were emphasized in the advertising. Is this manipulation? In the research, the housewives were told only that the aim of the study was to determine their attitudes toward housekeeping in general. Was this ethical?

2. Define the terms "need," "product," "information," and "rationality." Does a commercial showing a group of people enjoying a cola drink communicate information? Is the appeal appropriate? Consider other examples. Is manipulation involved?
3. Should certain kinds of appeals be restricted—sex, image, fear? Does it matter if it is the fear of body odor (deodorant), the fear of cancer (antismoking), or the fear of an automobile accident (tires)?
4. People tend to be annoyed more by advertisements for brands they dislike than by ads for brands they like and use. Which do you think comes first—the brand choice or the opinion about the advertisement?
5. Richard Avedon, a photographer and advertising consultant, helped develop for Calvin Klein jeans a controversial set of television commercials. The ads featured the 15-year-old actress/model Brooke Shields in a variety of sultry, sophisticated, suggestive scenes. In one Brooke Shields says in a suggestive manner: "Nothing comes between me and my Calvins." In another controversial TV commercial for a man's fragrance a man wearing a pajama bottom is shown getting out of bed and discussing the previous night by phone with a woman who had slept with him. Do you think such advertising is effective? In what way? If you were an advertiser would you run such commercials on network television if you felt they were effective? If you were an agency whose client insisted on it? If you were a CBS censor, would you allow such commercials on your network?
6. What is materialism? It has been said that our society emphasizes the use of material goods to attain nonmaterial goals. Comment. Is America too materialistic? What is advertising's role in establishing values and lifestyles? How does a nation go about changing its values?
7. Should advertisers be concerned about minority stereotypes developed in advertisements? Why? If you were an agency president, how would you develop a policy and set of procedures in this regard?
8. In an open letter to the makers of Alka-Seltzer, the following questions were posed by Ries, Capiello, Colwell, a New York advertising agency: Why did you spend (in 1969) $23 million to promote a product that everyone knows about? Why did you

spend $23 million to promote a product that is mostly bicarbonate and aspirin? Why not put some of that money into your laboratories? Why not develop new products that are worth advertising? Comment.

9. In your opinion, do TV commercials imply that all of life's problems can yield instantly to material solutions? If so, is this bad and what should be done about it? By whom? It has been said that material things (record players) are sought merely as means to nonmaterial ends (beautiful music or status). Comment. Are advertisements premised on the notion that we emulate others? If so, is this bad and how could it be corrected? Should we eliminate all human beings from advertisements? Does advertising contribute to role stereotyping? If so, how would you remedy this result? Be operational and specific!
10. Distinguish between a want and a need. Can advertising create wants or needs? Illustrate. Does advertising get people to want the wrong things? If so, what should be done? Be specific and think through your proposal. Is advertising uninformative? Is it in poor taste?
11. What would be the economic effect of a ban on all advertising? Of a ban on radio and television advertising?

B. ADVERTISING AND CHILDREN

12. What is your opinion on the advisability and likely result of the three FTC proposals detailed in Chapter 19: ban all television advertising to children unable to understand its purpose; ban the advertising of sugared products to children; and require television advertising of sugared products to be balanced by nutritional disclosures.
13. If children's television advertising of sugared products is to be balanced by a nutritional program, how should the program be developed? By whom? With what objectives?
14. Would you alter or add to the following provisions of a Canadian broadcasting code for children?

    Product characteristics should not be exaggerated.

    Results from a craft or kit that an average child could not obtain should not be shown.

    Undue pressure to buy or to urge parents to buy should be avoided.

    A commercial should not be repeated during a program.

Program personalities will not do commercials on their own programs.
Well-known persons other than actors will not endorse products.
Price information should be clear and complete.
Messages must not reflect disdain for parents or casually portray undesirable family living habits.
Advertising must not imply that product possession makes the owner superior.
The media should contribute directly or indirectly to sound and safe habits.

C. DECEPTIVE ADVERTISING

15. In your judgment are the following deceptive?
    Kirchner case (the Swim-Ezy)
    Wonder Bread (the implied uniqueness issue)
    Colgate-Palmolive case (the use of simulated sandpaper)
    Chocks (the claim was that children using Chocks were thereby grown-up because Chocks, unlike some other vitamins, do not have the shape of an animal or a cartoon character; the issue is whether such an appeal falsely implies that Chocks has higher potency or greater efficacy than does its competition)
16. For the advertisements in Question 15, how would you use advertising research to help determine whether deception is present?
17. All advertisements have the capacity to deceive some audience members. For example, if you just showed a picture of a glass of milk on a billboard some people would believe that the advertisement was falsely implying that everyone must drink at least one glass of milk a day because that belief has been ingrained in them. Comment.
18. Evaluate the following proposals:
    Advertising for brands that are for all practical purposes identical to competitors' products should be eliminated.
    The use of live models or spokespersons should be eliminated.
    Only the product itself, with no background scenes, should be shown in advertisements.
19. The FTC is concerned about commercial endorsements from celebrities and experts (as opposed to spokespersons or actors portraying consumers). What guidelines would you suggest to

help insure that such advertisements not be deceptive? Illustrate how your guidelines would apply in particular examples.

20. If the FTC rules that inadequate substantiation exists for an advertising claim, the commission holds responsible not only the manufacturer but also the agency preparing the ad, the retailer running it, and the celebrity endorsing the product in the advertisement. Comment on this policy.
21. Identify three advertisements that contain claims that should have prior substantiation.
22. Some corrective advertising proposals would limit the corrective ad effort to one year and 25 percent of the company's advertising budget. How should the budget percentage and the time period be determined? Should these vary with products and situations? Give examples.
23. If counteradvertising were allowed, chaos would result because every advertisement has another side. A counter to Smoky the Bear ads might claim that forest fires are ecologically sound. Comment.

PART V

The Purchase Phase

INTRODUCTION

The decisionmaking process that culminates in a purchase transaction is frequently influenced by distortions in the exchange relationship and by external societal factors. These variables are not normally reflected in consumer behavior analyses, which tend to focus on responses to competitively determined prices, features and services provided by various members of the distribution channel.

Yet customer manipulation, fraudulent misrepresentation of the capabilities of the product, and sales pressure do often affect choices. In extreme cases the freedom to choose, an implicit assumption of most analyses of exchange relationships, is effectively nonexistent. In Chapter 22 Magnuson and Carper graphically describe five major deceptive selling schemes and note the difficulty of generating legal procedures to discourage or eliminate them. Although written some years ago this article still stands as one of the best descriptions of the extent of deceit and pressure in direct sales and clearly indicates why so little progress has been made in this critical area of protecting consumers.

As we noted in Part I, there is an increasing overlap between ecological and consumerist perspectives on key issues of environmental quality. This is the theme of Chapters 23 and 24. Henion describes the translation of environmentalist pressures into an ecologically concerned consumer segment whose collective behavior can create marketing threats and opportunities. The packaging case study by Kinnear illustrates what can happen when government takes the initiative away from companies.

Whereas the government and company programs described by Henion and Kinnear were largely reactive, in certain situations proactive measures are needed to deal with consumer problems. Since these approaches usually involve self-regulatory or mandatory efforts to control and change socially undesirable behaviors, they have come to be called negative marketing, or demarketing. In Chapter 26 Molitor describes Swedish efforts to create a climate that, short of prohibiting smoking, is as negative as possible toward smoking. A major implication of this study is that when a government has isolated a serious social problem, in this case a health hazard, the voluntary responses by industry are largely stopgap efforts that serve to buy time. In this context the efforts by the Canadian and U.S. governments to encourage energy conservation, which are described by Hutton in Chapter 25, are not nearly so impressive—perhaps because they are still in an early stage of development.

Finally, Chapters 27 and 28 deal with the use of antitrust legislation to encourage competition and thereby to protect the consumer's right to choose. When competition is weakened, the consumer's voice is muffled and the range of choice is likely to be constrained. Aaker examines some of the hypothesized causes and effects of weakened competition. One major issue is the extent to which heavy advertising expenditures tend to make similar products appear different. According to some critics, this practice can result in an industry with only a few firms—those willing and able to engage in advertising. This interpretation obviously conflicts with widely accepted marketing practices perhaps best known in the cereal industry. In the last selection, Bloom analyzes a major antitrust case that charged that the cereal industry had used a variety of marketing strategies to establish and maintain a shared monopoly.

A *Selling Practices*

22 CAVEAT EMPTOR

Warren G. Magnuson & Jean Carper

One evening, two men in a Cadillac paid a call on an elderly couple in a small town in Arkansas. One of the men, a Mr. G., president of the Superior Improvement Company in Little Rock, presented himself to the couple as an important executive affiliated with Alcoa Aluminum Company. He told the couple that after a careful examination of their house he had chosen it to be a model home as part of a new advertising campaign to sell aluminum siding. Photographs, he said, would be taken of the house "before" and "after" the siding was applied and would be featured in beautiful brochures. Salesmen would bring prospective customers to view the house, and for every sale made as a result, Mr. G. promised to give the couple a commission of $100. When urged to sign an agreement, the couple protested that their house was old and they were thinking of using their savings to rebuild. But the promises of Mr. G were irresistible. He asserted he was giving them the siding at $1,000 below cost, cheaper than they could get it anywhere, and that with the commissions their house would be transformed into a showplace of beauty for virtually nothing. "Well, then, he said one thing that kind of struck me," the homeowner later recalled. "He said to say a little prayer and pray to the Lord and let Him guide us as to whether to sign the contract." Touched by this display of humility, the man and woman signed the contract for $1,480 and gave Mr. G. a down-payment check for $200.

By the next morning, the couple was no longer so spellbound by Mr. G.'s promises. Skeptical, they checked around and discovered they could buy aluminum siding for much less than Mr. G.'s "bargain factory prices." The homeowner, realizing he had been fleeced, tried to

Reprinted with deletions from *The Dark Side of the Marketplace* by Warren G. Magnuson and Jean Carper. © 1968 by Warren G. Magnuson and Jean Carper. Published by Prentice-Hall, Inc., Englewood Cliffs, New Jersey, pp. 3–31.

stop payment on the check, but was told that one of Mr. G.'s representatives had been there that morning as the bank opened and cashed the check. Repeated attempts to reach Mr. G. by phone at his Little Rock office were futile. He was always "out," and, said the homeowner, "His secretary kind of laughed like it was a big joke." Finally, in desperation and worry over his wife's ill health, which had been aggravated by the transaction, the man borrowed money from a bank and paid off the bill in full. He was informed by a lawyer that if he refused to make payments, the finance company Mr. G. had sold the contract to could sue him—and collect. The workmen had already tacked up the siding, such as it was. And the contract he had signed was legally binding, regardless of the verbal misrepresentations.

Hundreds of persons in rural Arkansas, Tennessee and Kentucky, since 1960, have been seduced by Mr. G.'s prayers and phony promises into paying exorbitant prices for shoddy workmanship and poor quality materials. Mr. G. claimed his aluminum was manufactured by Alcoa, Kaiser or Reynolds Aluminum Co.; it was in truth an off-brand, most of it shipped from Illinois. He told customers that it would "never chip, crack, fade or soak up water, would never need paint and had a lifetime guarantee." To many a homeowner's dismay, the siding was not applied by "factory-trained personnel" as promised, but sometimes by local teenagers. It fell off; the caulking was not done properly; the upper layer of finish could be rubbed off with the sweep of a hand. Some homes were left unfinished, aluminum and trash piled high in the yard. One man's house was in such a shambles within a year, pockmarked by the fallen siding, that he needed a completely new siding job. The only thing he had bought from Mr. G. was a $2,400 debt.

Mr. G. and his salesmen preyed shamelessly on the illiterate, the poor, the old and the guileless. One man said Mr. G.'s salesmen kept him up most of the night begging him to sign a note; weary and fatigued, he finally did. An elderly Negro was coerced into putting his X mark on a contract. Many were induced to part with their pensions and Social Security checks. Others said they were tricked into signing mortgages on their homes, and one couple swore their names were forged to a promissory note. In this brutal marketplace, there was no compunction about tacking aluminum siding on a shack in the fork of a dust-covered road and proclaiming it a "showplace."

Many people understood that because of the $100 bonus, they would have to pay little or nothing for the siding. Instead, once their names were on the contract, few homeowners ever saw Mr. G. or any of his salesmen again. No one brought prospective customers to view the renovated house as the salesmen had promised. Some people waited and waited, actually stayed home for days on end, fearing to leave the house, waiting for the customers that never came, until their hope turned to anguish.

Many were left with disastrous debts. A young schoolteacher signed a contract with a total price of $3,650. By the time monthly payments were figured out—84 of them at $73.45 each—he discovered he had agreed to pay $6,132 over a period of seven years. Horrified, he borrowed money from his credit union and managed to persuade the finance company to let him pay off the debt; the company insisted, however, that he pay them more than $1,000 interest for use of the money for "less than a month."

Another couple signed a contract with Mr. G. for what they thought was about $2,000 and a mortgage on their house. Said a government lawyer: "When they sat down that night and in their sober judgment figured out what that was going to cost them over a period of 84 months—84 payments—they were not going to pay $2,000; it would be some $4,000 to $4,400. That fellow attempted to commit suicide." Another pensioned purchaser came home and found his elderly wife unconscious on the bed. She recovered but confessed she had been so worried over the transaction with Mr. G. and the prospect of losing their home that she drank Lysol.

Early in 1964, the Federal Trade Commission issued a complaint against Mr. G. and his company, charging him with a dozen "unfair and deceptive practices." After hearings, he was ordered by the FTC to stop using such sales practices in interstate commerce. Mr. G. chose to take his case through the courts, and finally in early 1967, when the Supreme Court refused to hear his case, he was forced to comply with the FTC ruling. (It is interesting to note that the primary basis for Mr. G.'s defense was not innocence of deceptive selling, for he admitted that he had promised bonuses to prospective buyers. His main contention was that he was not engaging in interstate commerce and that, therefore, the FTC had no jurisdiction over his actions. The FTC can intervene only when it can be proved that a misdoer is operating across state lines.)

It might appear that Mr. G. was forced by the FTC to stop using his lucrative, deceptive sales pitches (his annual volume of business was estimated at $400,000). On the contrary, Mr. G. shows every intention of carrying on. He mapped out for the FTC his blueprint for future business: he will not advertise in interstate newspapers or other media, will not use the mails to send out brochures and will not make sales to residents in other states. In other words, he pledges not to work his deceptive arts on anyone, except, of course, the unlucky prospects he may find within the borders of Arkansas.

At this writing, Mr. G. is still in business, his Superior Improvement Company still in existence. If complaints received by the Better Business Bureau of Little Rock are accurate, his salesmen are still active in Arkansas, using misrepresentations and "questionable advertising and selling practices" to unload shoddy jobs and merchandise at unconscionable prices. Who is to stop him?

Although the Federal Trade Commission may be reluctant to admit it for fear of seeming to condone deceptive practices, the sorry truth in this matter is that as long as Mr. G.'s corporation scrupulously avoids interstate commerce, it can operate with impunity, free from FTC jurisdiction or intervention, no matter how blatantly dishonest the sales practices or how appalling to human sensibilities the amount of human misery left in their wake.

It is certain that the authorities of Arkansas, when informed of this company's intention to hide behind state lines out of the reach of the FTC will *want* to take measures to protect the residents of Arkansas. But the question is: will they be able to? Do they have the authority under existing state law? Although it is impossible to predict the outcome of any legal action—and some states have achieved surprising victories with the imaginative use of seemingly inapplicable laws—legal authorities advise me that Arkansas probably does not have the legal machinery necessary to fight companies like Mr. G.'s. Arkansas does not have a comprehensive law covering deceptive selling. It has only a variety of laws forbidding the use of certain deceptive practices to sell specific products, but aluminum siding is not among them. It is true that Arkansas, like other states, has criminal fraud and false pretenses statutes, resulting in fines or imprisonment for those adjudged guilty. But these statutes are a poor vehicle for preventing deceptive selling. Indictments under the statutes are exceedingly rare and convictions even rarer. As far as we know, neither Federal, nor state, nor any other known authority can under present law take action to protect the citizens of Arkansas against the gouging of companies like Mr. G.'s.

Although the case of Mr. G. is one of the most dramatic on record of how deceptive sellers can operate outside the reach of the law, it would be a mistake to believe that Arkansas is like the old Oklahoma Strip of the 1880's: the only place where robbers could operate without interference from the law. On the contrary, although Arkansas is uncommonly hampered by weak consumer protection laws, it is hardly unique. Consumer deception flourishes nearly everywhere in the country, quite often unimpeded—and sometimes even abetted—by the law. As Helen Nelson, former consumer counsel for the governor of California, has said: "More money is being taken from Americans at penpoint than by gunpoint and the pen often makes it legal."

Deceptive selling by the unscrupulous few in the business underworld is, in fact, our most serious form of theft. It cheats Americans of several billion dollars yearly, more than is lost through robbery, burglary, larceny, auto theft, embezzlement and forgery combined. Unlike the con men of yesterday who were often so heavy-handed that they offended the law, today's modern bandits of the marketplace are the masters of the light touch. With their insidious misrepresentations, silver-tongued lies, half truths and exaggerated promises, these men can reach even deeper into our pockets without producing a rustle to disturb the law, or often the victim himself. From coast to coast we are exposed to their Pandora's box of selling tricks—some old, but handily adapted to modern circumstances, and some new, carefully devised to outwit the law.

Although these schemes are staggering in scope and diverse in their nature (the Better Business Bureau has identified 800 different varieties), they invariably have several things in common: they are lucrative, they are subtle and their purveyors rarely come in conflict with the law. According to a nationwide survey for the President's Commission on Law Enforcement and Administration of Justice in 1966, nine out of every ten victims of consumer fraud do not even bother to report it to the police. Fifty percent of the victimized felt they had no right or duty to complain; 40% believed the authorities could not be effective or would not want to be bothered; 10% were confused about where to report.

It is startling to consider that the vast majority of Americans victimized by consumer fraud feel that the law can or will do nothing to help them; but it is even more startling to realize that in many instances those victims are absolutely correct. Our legal remedies against consumer deception and fraud, some of which were adequate 50, even 20 years ago, are now so outdated as to leave the consumer nearly helpless. Under our present laws, with rare exceptions, we neither give relief to the victimized consumer nor effectively halt the swindlers.

The scheme so successfully used by Mr. G. is but one of five major schemes on which today's pyramid of deceptive selling rests. Although Mr. G. combined several techniques, his primary deception consisted of convincing homeowners that by making their home a "model," he was giving them "a special low price." (The phony "special price" is also used to sell a variety of items, including encyclopedias, automobiles, carpeting, roofing and jewelry.) According to the Federal Trade Commission, the four other schemes that are currently most responsible for fleecing American consumers are *bait and switch advertising,* including "lo-balling," *chain-referral selling,* the *free gimmick* and the *fear-sell.*

BAIT AND SWITCH

Of these, the most troublesome to detect and curtail is bait and switch advertising, in which the merchant advertises goods *which he has no intention of selling* in order to switch the prospective buyer to another item, invariably higher priced and with a greater margin of profit. Not only is bait advertising perfectly legal in most states, but it is so subtle that most victims are never aware that they have been deceived. We all see bait advertising continually, but probably few of us are aware of its insidious calculated nature.

Typically, this is the way the scheme works. A housewife in Alexandria, Virginia, recently noticed this advertisement in the classified section of a newspaper:

> SEW MACH.—1965 Singer
> Touch and Sew***
> Reposs. Balance, $86.40
> New Mach. Guar. Dealer,
> Credit Dept.***

When the salesman arrived at her home, following her telephone call to the company, she was appalled by the machine he carried. He set it down on the table and said: "Well, this is the machine." It was not the new one described in the ad. Rather, as the woman put it, it was "an old beaten-up Singer about 25 or 30 years old. . . . I'd seen machines in better shape at rummage sales." It was battered, scratched, and was a straight-stitch machine with no attachment. "I wouldn't have given more than $5 or $6 for it," she said. Noting her disappointment and admitting his "mistake," the salesman saved the day. He rushed to his car and brought in two sparkling, new, off-brand sewing machines priced at $289 and $365. The housewife chose the one for $289 and was given a discount because it was the "salesman's first day."

There were several glaring misrepresentations, designed to lure prospective customers, in this advertisement. The words "Reposs." (ostensibly standing for repossession) and "Balance" led the readers to believe the machines had been partially paid for by a previous purchaser and thus were being offered for a song. The signature "Credit Dept." created the same impression. In truth, the use of the Singer name was only a lure to support a full-time business of selling off-brand machines. This was proved by the fact that the dealer sold only two or three Singers a month, but spent $400 per month advertising them. Almost the total volume of his business was in the less well-known brand, the more expensive model to which customers were "switched."

Sometimes the salesman actually produced the advertised recent-model Singer, but then actively disparaged the "bait" by finding fault with it: "This machine is delicate and not functioning as it should." "We get a lot of complaints on these Singers." In most other instances, as in the case of the Alexandria housewife, the bait was so offensive that it had "built-in dissuaders," and prospects rejected it on sight. The way was then cleared for the salesman's pitch on the more profitable merchandise. In describing the subtlety of the approach, an FTC lawyer noted: "The prospective purchaser is led on without suspecting the insincerity of the salesman's presentation, and the switch is made to the higher-priced machine of a different make as though the transition were the suggestion of the prospect and not the salesman."

LO-BALLING

A variation of bait advertising is lo-balling, and it is so new that the FTC used the term for the first time in 1967 in a case involving automobile transmissions. In lo-balling, the company advertises or promises a service at an outrageously low price and actually performs the work at the advertised price, but only as an enticement to get possession of the automobile (lo-balling to date has been almost exclusively associated with automobiles) so the company can gouge the owner for additional unneeded repairs.

CHAIN-REFERRAL SELLING

The gist of the swindle is that customers are led to believe that by referring the names of acquaintances as prospective customers, they will have to pay nothing for a piece of merchandise, and very often will make money. For each friend who is sold, or who agrees to participate in the "advertising campaign," as it is invariably called, the victim is promised a commission. Salesmen frequently erase customers' doubts by telling them that 80% of those referred actually "participate" as proved by past experience. In truth, postal inspectors, by painstakingly searching through company records, have discovered that only about 5% of the referred actually sign up. And of course once they have sold the original customer, some companies don't bother to follow up the leads supplied, or to remit the commission if a referred friend does buy. This deceit is all the more cruel for it is being practiced on elderly people who find the lure of making a few pennies to augment their meager income irresistible.

FREE GIMMICK

Another pernicious type of selling which is sweeping the country is the "free gimmick," invariably accompanied by innumerable misrepresentations. It is doubtful that any American of any economic class is untouched by this scheme. A lawyer in New York whose wife was tricked into subscribing to three children's magazines under the impression that it was a "service" from the Board of Education recently wrote: "If wives of persons who are supposedly above average in education, sophistication, etc., and especially the wife of an attorney, can be so easily taken in, you can imagine what this person (a door-to-door saleswoman) must be able to do with less sophisticated persons."

The sales pitches are familiar: "This lovely *x*-cubic-foot freezer is yours absolutely free if you subscribe to our food-freezer plan." The food is usually low quality, overpriced, and the freezer is hardly free. The cost of the food more than covers the retail price of the freezer.

FEAR-SELL

Perhaps no sales pitch has been around longer than the "fear-sell." Even the rulers of ancient countries were intimidated into buying amulets lest their souls be damned or they suffer a dreadful accident. In today's sophisticated marketplace, peddlers still make fortunes preying on people's fears. One woman wrote me she had four perfectly healthy maple trees felled by a wandering "tree surgeon," who told her they were rotten and could come crashing down on her house. Gangs of salesmen, according to the National Fire Protection Association, are scouring the country, displaying gruesome photographs of families burned to death in home fires. Their object is to sell home fire-alarm systems which are invariably outrageously priced and sometimes worthless.

Every spring, as regularly as the rain, reports the BBB, the phony chimney repairmen show up. They knock off a few bricks and claim the chimney is about to topple, or claim it is clogged and that the whole family is in imminent danger of dying from carbon monoxide poisoning. Some termite inspectors carry bugs which they plant in the wood, and then inform an alarmed homeowner that unless the "termites" are exterminated, the house will quickly deteriorate. Often the salesmen pose as government inspectors. That they extort millions of dollars from frightened Americans is well-documented.

A classic case is that of the Holland Furnace Company, which for thirty years conducted what Consumers Union branded "one of the most pernicious sales rackets in the country." Holland Furnace, based in Holland, Michigan, with 500 offices throughout the country and 5,000 employees, was the leading furnace-replacement firm in the nation. Through its "tear down and scare tactics" it victimized hundreds of thousands of Americans. Misrepresenting themselves as "furnace engineers" and "safety inspectors," the salesmen frequently dismantled a furnace, condemned it as hazardous and refused to reassemble it, stating that they didn't want to be "accessories to murder." The salesmen were merciless. In New England, branch salesmen from one office sold an elderly infirm woman nine new furnaces in six years, for a total take of $18,000.

DEFECT IN OUR LAWS

Why are we unable to control such deceptive practices and to prevent consumer exploitation? Primarily because our present laws are outmoded and inadequate to deal with the modern complexities of consumer fraud. Most of our laws on dishonest selling were designed long ago to catch and punish a few "hardened criminals" and not to cope with the vast web of subtle deceits and credit merchandising abuses that characterizes the businesses of today's "soft-sell" swindlers. Generally, our legal remedies have two defects: (1) they are ineffective in halting deceptive selling, and (2) they make virtually no provisions for redressing the wrong, whether by freeing the cheated consumer of a fraudulently induced debt or by reimbursing him.

The Federal Trade Commission, as the Federal agency primarily responsible for stopping deceptive selling on a national scale, has broad powers and has been effective in curtailing unscrupulous sellers in interstate commerce for half a century. Nevertheless, we cannot depend on the FTC alone to halt all deceptive selling nationwide. Even with an addition in personnel it would still be impossible for the FTC to stop all deceptive selling even within its interstate jursidiction. And the FTC also has certain limitations in its powers to protect consumers.

As we have seen, the FTC cannot stop deceptive selling operations that limit their activities to intrastate commerce, staying within a state's borders, which is where most such selling occurs. Nor can the FTC in some cases move fast enough to halt the swindlers before they have victimized a number of consumers and accumulated a small fortune. Nor can the FTC act on behalf of an individual consumer; it can move only when a substantial number of Americans have been injured (enough to make an FTC action "in the public interest").

Then too, the FTC can only compel the offender to stop working his deceptive arts on future customers; it cannot order him to reimburse those whom he has already cheated or to cancel collection of their debts.

The Post Office Department, as the other Federal agency most responsible for halting fraudulent and deceptive schemes, also has been remarkably successful within their jurisdiction. But postal officials, too, are hampered in their efforts to control certain types of deceptive selling by mail. Under present law, they often cannot move fast enough to curtail mail-order schemes and sometimes cannot stop them at all. In testifying to this act before a subcommittee of the House Committee on Post Office and Civil Service in April 1967, Henry B. Montague, chief postal inspector for the Post Office Department, illustrated the difficulty in halting mail-order land-fraud sales:

> The investigation of the Lake Mead Land & Water Company in Arizona began in 1962. Evidence that the desert property was not in fact "an en-

chanted city in the making''; that the ''favorite swimming hole'' pictured in the advertising brochure was in truth a cattle-watering pond not even located on the promoter's property; that various springs and wells depicted in the literature were also not located on the property, was not too difficult to ascertain. Proof of intent or personal knowledge on the part of the principal promoter, of course, required considerably more time.

An indictment was returned in October 1963 and conviction resulted in June 1965. Three thousand home- or investment-seeking persons, many of the elderly class, lost an estimated one million dollars before the enterprise was finally stopped through conviction. The promoter continued to receive payments by mail up to the very end.

Even though a scheme is patently false and postal officials know it, they cannot always stop a perpetrator's inflow of mail containing the lucrative rewards of deceit. Postal authorities must stand helpless, witnessing the bilking of the elderly and the hopeful, until it can be proved that the purveyor of falsity *intended* to defraud, which as Mr. Montague pointed out, takes much longer than just proving untruth by comparing the brochures or advertisements with the lay of the land. Partially as a result of this time lag while investigators try to fathom the state of a man's mind, the 49 land-fraud swindlers finally brought to justice were able to accumulate, through a steady flow of mail payments, more than 50 million dollars from an unsuspecting public before they were convicted and their mail was marked ''fraudulent; return to sender.''

At the state level, officials who attempt to protect consumers are incredibly handicapped by inadequate laws. Although many states have recently passed effective laws and set up machinery to enforce them, the picture of state consumer legislation is, as a whole, dreary indeed. An informal survey by the FTC in June 1967 showed that only 19 states could be said to have ''good'' or ''excellent'' laws prohibiting deceptive selling practices. At least one-third of the states have pitifully weak laws. Effective consumer legislation is especially lacking in Alabama, Arkansas, Indiana, Mississippi, New Hampshire, North Carolina, Ohio, Oklahoma, South Carolina, South Dakota, Tennessee, Texas, Virginia, West Virginia and Wyoming.

In a few states legislation is simply nonexistent. Only a handful of states regulate correspondence schools, fraudulent selling of land or unsolicited merchandise sent through the mails. Only 20 states specifically outlaw bait advertising.

Absence of laws, however, is not the only problem in the states. For as the *Columbia Law Review* has noted, ''The states have adopted a staggering number of statutes noteworthy for their ad hoc and piece-meal approach to the problems of advertising control and for the very slight degree to which they are enforced.'' In truth, all but three states —Arkansas, Delaware and New Mexico—have a ''Printer's Ink'' statute (named for the advertising magazine of the same name) making it a misdemeanor to make an "untrue, deceptive or misleading" statement with the intent to sell a product.

One would think this law so comprehensive that it would virtually wipe out deceptive advertising in the states. Such is not the case, for the law, broad as it is, contains an insurmountable flaw: it is a *criminal* statute, as are many of the other measures adopted by the states to halt deceptive selling. Under the criminal statute, conviction demands proof beyond a reasonable doubt, and carries with it fines, possible jail sentences and the stigma of being branded a criminal.

Since its adoption in 1911, the Printer's Ink statute may have deterred some sellers from deceptive practices, but the number of culprits it has actually brought to justice is infinitesimal. Law enforcement officials overwhelmingly consider the law so unrealistic that they don't attempt to enforce it. A survey by the *Columbia Law Review* in 1956 discovered that during nearly 50 years, only "a handful of prosecutions" had been brought under the Printer's Ink statutes throughout the country. Many attorneys general and county prosecutors freely admitted that they had never tried to enforce it. One reason is that local prosecutors are burdened with trying to halt major felonies such as murder, rape and robbery, and are disinclined to waste their time on such a relatively small "crime" as false advertising or selling. Another reason is that few prosecutors believe they will get a conviction. They have found that juries are hesitant to find a man guilty of a crime for what may merely be "overzealous salesmanship"; consequently, few public officials prosecute.

Two law students at the University of Pennsylvania, investigating the ineffectiveness of consumer legislation, recently found:

> Even when a law enforcement official believes that a particular scheme has been made actionable by statute, he often does not prosecute because of a widely held belief that, except in the most egregious circumstances, fraudulent operators should not be treated like criminals. Lawyers, business leaders and prosecutors have stated that "judges, juries and district attorneys do not like to put businessmen in jail." One district attorney, when asked by the attorney general to prosecute an alleged fraudulent operator, retorted: "I can't even get a conviction when they stick a gun in somebody's back; how can I get one when they just talk him out of his money?"

Trying to completely control consumer fraud by proving criminality is an outmoded concept. But even if the criminal statutes could be enforced (and New York, for example, has achieved rare success in obtaining convictions), it is doubtful that society's purpose is best served by only putting a swindler behind bars. The sentence is usually short (in Pennsylvania one man who made $300,000 selling fake automobile parts was sentenced to a term of one year), after which the wrongdoer is set free to spend his ill-gotten money, and the cheated consumer, who understandably wants no justice so much as his money back, is left to suffer without restitution.

Additionally, the hit-and-miss proposition of locking up criminals who defraud the public is inefficient in halting consumer fraud on a broad scale. Only one operator can be put out of business at a time, after long, costly court proceedings, while thousands of other gypsters—perhaps associated with the same company or swindle—are allowed to flourish. And even after a short prison term, the ex-convict can start up a new racket, using the same fraudulent techniques, and rob Americans of a fortune, while local authorities once again gear up their machinery to start the slow, painful process of gathering evidence against him on the new charge.

The injured consumer can bring suit himself, but few do. They soon discover that lawyer's fees, court costs and time away from employment will cost more than they can possibly recover. A woman in Ohio, who hired an attorney to keep from losing her $15,000-house because of a home-improvement repairs bill of $7,200, had already paid a legal fee of $1,500 and still did not receive her house back. Under strict legal requirements in most states, the complainant must have an exceptionally good case in order to win; many times it is only his word against that of the shady seller.

Invariably, the victim has also unknowingly, by signing the contract, given away a number of rights of defense and agreed that nothing the seller told him, unless specifically stated in the contract, is binding. When a group of lawyers in Pennsylvania were asked in an informal survey what they would do with a client who had been gypped out of several hundred dollars for carpeting in a "bait and switch" scheme, they unanimously agreed: "Send him home."

Clearly, the weak, inappropriate, poorly enforced, hit-and-miss legislation that is the rule throughout the nation is quite undependable in combating the complexities and size of our present-day consumer deception. In this antiquated system of justice, the dishonest steal quitely off to count their loot, while the injured consumer is sacrificed on the altar of legislative short-sightedness.

B *Social Dimensions: Ecology*

23 ECOLOGICAL MARKETING: WILL THE NORMATIVE BECOME DESCRIPTIVE?

Karl E. Henion II

Since 1968, U.S. environmental policy has been characterized by a steady increase in the regulation of business. Governmental regulation has been directed chiefly at industries responsible for causing unacceptable levels of air and water pollution. Associated with these two modes of pollution have been pressing environmental health problems requiring serious attention. Consequently, problems created by the other principal mode of pollution—solid waste—have been given relatively little attention by the U.S. government.

Such neglect has been a mixed blessing. On the plus side, it has probably meant postponement in the government's adoption of a regulatory approach to the problem of solid waste pollution. Hence, the inevitable economic inefficiencies that a regulatory approach almost always creates have been avoided, at least for the time being. On the minus side, mounting post-consumer solid waste continues to overwhelm present urban disposal capabilities. The U.S. literally faces a crisis in solid waste management. A viable policy is needed.

Economists who shrink from the thought of direct product controls as a solution to pollution problems are inclined to favor a policy that makes greater use of free-market mechanisms. They would incorporate appropriate taxes and subsidies into the market's price system. Such a

---

Reprinted, with permission, from George Fisk, Johan Arndt, and Kjell Gronberg (eds.), *Future Directions for Marketing* (Boston: Marketing Science Institute, 1979), pp. 33–41.

policy has clear advantages over regulation, theoretically anyway. These are greater efficiency in the expenditure of pollution control funds, a continuing incentive for product manufacturers and consumers to control pollution, and greater equity.

This approach to pollution abatement would be a step toward making pollution control profitable for producers. Self-interest would be put to work in favor of pollution reduction. Yet, there is another approach to the problem of managing the social externalities created by product marketing, especially those related to solid waste pollution. Called *ecological marketing,* this approach amounts to a policy that is more free, flexible, and viable than policies based on either taxes and subsidies or increased regulation of business.

ECOLOGICAL MARKETING

Although now emerging as a new field of study under the subdisciplinary heading of social marketing (Henion, 1976, p. 26), ecological marketing can be considered a marketing strategy for the environmental crisis. It is based principally on engaging the profit motive of producers of *environmentally beneficial products.* These producers then are seen as marketing such products to target markets, which initially would consist of a subset of the population called the *ecologically concerned consumer.*

Under this strategy the government plays a leading role as a more active environmental educator of concerned and unconcerned consumers. Its role as regulator is played down. Instead of focusing on the supply side of the economy—through the imposition of more governmental restrictions on product manufacturers—ecological marketing is demand-oriented. Based on this concept, marketing programs are designed to decrease consumer demand for products that are relatively incompatible with a cleaner environment and to increase demand for substitute products that are more compatible.

The consumer, after all, is at the heart of the problem of solid waste pollution. His consumption behavior directly contributes to air pollution through the purchase of automobiles and to water pollution through the purchase of detergents. But his most important direct contribution, by far, is to solid waste pollution through the purchase and eventual discard of a host of consumer products, including the automobile.

Most discarded consumer products end up as municipal solid waste. The waste management problem in the U.S. is most acute in the urban areas. In 1973, post-consumer solid waste—namely, waste generated from products discarded by consumers and by commercial firms, e.g., at retail stores and in offices—totaled 144 million tons (U.S. Environmental Protection Agency, 1975, pp. 7-10).[1] The municipal waste stream is growing at such a rate that the nation's mayors warned in 1973 that a majority of U.S. cities will have no disposal sites left by 1978 (U.S. Conference of Mayors, 1973).

The Ecologically Concerned Consumer

Standing at the center of the problem of solid waste, the consumer also holds the key to its solution. For, in the consumer population at large, a growing number of consumers are concerned about the ecological damage caused by product consumption. Recent research suggests that this number may represent 20 to 33 percent of the total consumer population (Henion, 1976; Kinnear and Taylor, 1973; Kinnear, Taylor, and Ahmed, 1973; Nelson, 1974). This concerned type of consumer may be defined as follows:

> The *ecologically concerned consumer* is a person whose values, attitudes, intentions or behaviors exhibit and reflect a relatively consistent and conscious concern for the environmental consequences related to the purchase, ownership, use or disposal of particular products or services (Henion, 1976, p. 8).

There is little doubt that such a person exists. The evidence is not hard to find. There are persons who patronize recycling centers as a matter of course. There are persons willing to shop and buy in an ecologically constructive way. For example, in one of the earliest marketing research papers on this subject, the results of an experiment were reported in which supermarkets had prominently posted on their shelves the percentage of phosphate contained in the detergents they were carrying. Their customers responded positively to this ecologically relevant information and bought significantly more of the lower phosphate brands than before (Henion, 1972).

This type of consumer constitutes a market segment. The segment is, research suggests (Henion, 1976, p. 65), substantial, measurable, and—to some extent—accessible, the three conditions Kotler has prescribed for practical segmentation (1972a, p. 167). Based on recent research, this segment can be characterized according to demographic and psychographic variables (Henion, 1976, Ch. 3).

---

[1] The amount of waste represented by discarded automobiles (about 11 million tons in 1970) is excluded from data reported for post-consumer solid waste. Automobiles rarely enter the municipal waste stream. Also of minor importance to that particular stream of solid waste arising from industrial processing and from demolition and construction, since little of this type of waste enters that stream either (U.S. Environmental Protection Agency, 1974, p. 65).

Environmentally Beneficial Products

Yet, for the most part, such a segment is still waiting to be tapped—to be appealed to—by producers of environmentally beneficial products (or EN-products, for short). This type of product has been defined as follows:

> An *environmentally beneficial product* is a product containing a set of environmentally related attributes which, on balance, either already contribute, because of the materials the product is made of, or eventually will contribute, significantly more to the reduction in pollution than do those of another product with which it is compared (Henion, 1976, p. 12).

Examples of EN-products are carbonated beverages in returnable bottles instead of in throwaway bottles; small vs. large cars; roll-on deodorants vs. those that come in an aerosol with a fluorocarbon propellant; and milk containers made from paper instead of polyvinyl chloride plastic. Products such as these tend to be classified as EN-products because they possess one or more waste-reducing attributes. These product attributes may result in products having one or more of the following ecologically desirable properties:

- long lifetime
- reusable
- non-resource-intensive
- repairable
- low disposal cost
- recyclable
- made of non-scarce materials
- made of renewable materials
- made by non-pollution-intensive process

Examples of Ecological Marketing

Two products—beer in returnable bottles and beer in recyclable aluminum cans—whose waste-reducing attributes qualify them as EN-products, are featured in the following example, which illustrates ecological marketing at work. The example is based on the marketing activities of three regional beer competitors whose principal markets are in Texas.

> In September 1973, one of these companies, Pearl Brewing Co., decided to enter the business of recycling aluminum cans. This was done not only to cut materials cost but also to increase revenues through the aggressive promotion of its recycling centers. In conjunction with its distributors and local radio stations, Pearl sponsored clean-up and collection campaigns throughout Texas. The promotions were highly successful and citizen response was enthusiastic. To encourage even greater citizen participation, Pearl raised its initial offer of ten cents per pound of returned aluminum cans to fifteen cents in May 1974.

> To counter this merchandising effort, a competitor, Lone Star Brewing Co., launched its own successful mass advertising campaign. Its theme, ''Long Live Longnecks,'' helped create demand for its beer packaged in a tall 12-ounce returnable glass bottle. This theme got across in part because Austin, the capital of Texas, and home of the state's major university, had come to be identified in recent years as the birthplace and center of ''Progressive Country'' music. As this type of music flourished and grew into a cultural movement, the ''longneck'' beer grew as a symbol of the movement. It was this association on which Lone Star capitalized in its advertising theme. Bumper stickers bearing the theme were believed to be especially popular with university students. Students often seem to be ecologically minded, and, of course, they are also an excellent market for beer.
>
> . . . Retailers prefer selling beer in the nonrefillable instead of in the refillable container. Notwithstanding the increased handling costs that carrying ''longnecks'' would mean, one major chain of convenience stores anticipated the demand for ''longnecks'' that the Lone Star advertising eventually created. The chain introduced ''longnecks'' in the Austin area before its major competitors did and thus got a jump on its competition. Eventually, the chain's major competitors were forced to carry beer in returnable bottles, which became top sellers by mid-1975. It is remarkable that sales of regional beer in any market are able to pull even with those of national brands at a time when these brands generally are dominating beer markets everywhere. It is noteworthy that ecological marketing was an important factor in the sales success of regional beer at both producer and retail levels.
>
> Still another beer competitor in the Texas market, Falstaff Brewing Corporation, adopted the ecological marketing approach. In the summer of 1975, Falstaff announced in newspaper advertisements across the state a reduction in the price of its premium beer packaged in returnable bottles. In this way, it pointed out, a premium product was being brought within reach of every Texas beer drinker. Several reasons were stated for repositioning this quality product at a lower price. Falstaff wanted to provide the inflation-battered consumer with an economic benefit, to protect the environment by encouraging the use of an ecologically sound package, and to offset the rising packaging costs of its one-trip containers. These costs had risen 51 percent since 1973 and by 1975 represented one-third the cost of a six-pack of 12 oz. cans. The repositioned price was in part justified on the grounds that one of its breweries was so located with respect to Falstaff's market that long-range freight expense could be avoided. Furthermore, rapid turnover was expected on its returnable bottles. Here again we see another situation in which economic and ecological interests converge (Henion, 1976, pp. 166–167).

Other examples of ecological marketing could be cited. For instance, at the beginning of the decade, Sears successfully introduced its phosphate-free detergent, ECOLO-G, making the most intimate connection possible between the brand name and the environmental quality of the product. This EN-product is still being successfully marketed today long after the public's outcry over a deteriorating environment reached its peak in the early 1970s. The success of this product over a considerable period of time is indicative of how effective a policy of ecological marketing can be.

EN-Product Positioning

Granted, the marketing strategy adopted for ECOLO-G is an unusual case of EN-product positioning and brand naming. Usually, the ecologically beneficial features of an EN-product, when they are mentioned, appear in subordinate fashion in the advertising for the product or somewhere on its package. An example where such features have been actually highlighted, though, is provided by the prominent label on Johnson Wax's line of 1975 aerosol-packaged products. The label reads: "Use with confidence, contains no fluorocarbons, claimed to harm the Ozone layer."

Profitable opportunities for the ecological marketing of certain products may exist for producers who have overlooked and neglected to promote, say, the solid-waste-reducing attributes of those products. For example, a product manager may see a chance to breathe new profit life into a product that has reached the mature stage in its product life cycle. During this stage, the prices of most products typically come under great pressure. Most sales represent repurchase by a stable set of customers. Under these conditions a typical marketing response is to increase market segmentation. The ecological marketing of a maturing product by appeal to the ecologically concerned segment is one possibility.

If a maturing product has no striking waste-reducing attributes, then one or more such attributes might be incorporated as new features of the product. This is a common practice in marketing. New features represent relatively minor changes in the manufacture of a product. Even a very minor change, such as reducing the amount of material used in packaging it, might help, to a certain extent, position a product as an EN-product. In this connection, there appears to be developing a backlash among consumers against overpackaging. In 1975, 90 percent of a nationwide cross section of adults indicated they would be willing to "cut down sharply on the plastic bags and packaging that most products are sold in" (Harris, 1975a, 1975b).

Yet, throwaway packaging characterizes the growing convenience orientation of consumers in advanced industrial countries. And the demand for convenience appears well-entrenched. There are encouraging signs, however, that some consumers are willing to forfeit a portion of their convenience in exchange for an improvement in environmental quality. Still other consumers, unmindful of environmental considerations but concerned over rising prices, also seem ready to forego some measure of convenience.

Other Factors

Rising prices and other factors could result in wider adoption by product managers of a policy of ecological marketing—consciously or unconsciously. For it is quite likely that, in the last quarter of this century, management will be making product decisions in an economic climate drastically changed from the one that existed during mid-century. In addition to the usual issues of product policy that product managers ordinarily deal with, they will have to consider an entirely new set of factors. These include severe, periodic shortages in natural resources—be they raw materials, food, or energy. Another is the probable decline in the relative purchasing power of the consumer in the West. Such erosion will almost surely occur, whether fueled by an inflation politically difficult to control or brought on by geopolitically-inspired economic initiatives capable of producing a marked redistribution in world income in favor of developing countries.

Should these trends materialize, they would hasten the day when there is a much wider representation in the American marketplace of consumer products with waste-reducing attributes. These would include products that last longer, can be reused, are less resource intensive, are repairable, easily recycled, or made of plentiful—not scarce—materials. These products are EN-products and they could be credibly promoted as such by product managers under a policy of ecological marketing.

POLICY APPROACHES OF U.S. GOVERNMENT

If product managements are reluctant to undertake some kind of marketing strategy such as ecological marketing, then the government stands ready eventually to step in with its own prescription—and proscription—for achieving solid waste reduction. The prescription is called *product control,* which has been defined as "any public policy measure directed at regulating either the volume of sales (quantity) or the physical design characteristics (quality) of specific products or groups of products. . ." (U.S. Environmental Protection Agency, 1974, p. 59). One example of product controls would be regulations requiring refrigerators to be made with replaceable doors, an illustration of product redesign. Another example would be banning, taxing, or imposing a mandatory deposit on throwaway containers, thereby encouraging the use of refillable containers, and hence an example of product reuse.

The U.S. Environmental Protection Agency (EPA) has argued that intervention in the private market system may be needed, since the social costs of product production, consumption, and waste disposal are not internalized in the product prices of many products. The agency has stated: "Product control policy draws its theoretical justification from the failure of private market decisions to achieve maximum social welfare" (1974, p. 59).

That the government is actually considering a policy alternative such as product controls is evidence of the seriousness of the waste reduction problem. However, the EPA also admitted in 1974 that "little or no theoretical or empirical economic analysis exists on the subject of the social efficiency of product design" (p. 60). And, moreover, despite its support in behalf of a national deposit law, the EPA's overall position in 1975 in respect to waste reduction was readily apparent in the following statement that appeared in the Agency's report of that year to the U.S. Congress: "Voluntary programs seem to hold more promise (than mandatory programs) . . . EPA is now actively urging voluntary waste reduction and has established a program designed to focus industry efforts on product redesign for decreased material use" (1975, p. 31).

A policy alternative of voluntary efforts by industry and consumers is compatible with the concept of ecological marketing. A broadened interpretation of this concept would have government—and conservation and consumerist groups, as well—direct at consumers and industry a great deal of educational and persuasive communication aimed at increasing the preference for and consumption of EN-products. By broadening the ecological marketing concept—as Kotler has broadened marketing itself under his generic concept of marketing (Kotler, 1972b)—the government is cast in the role of a more active environmental educator of consumers. Its role as regulator is played down. Whether implementation is done through recourse to product controls or voluntary programs, U.S. policy for reducing solid waste pollution is based on two concepts. These are source reduction and recycling.

Source Reduction

Except for recycling properties, most waste-reducing attributes that are used to characterize an EN-product can bring about an actual reduction in solid waste. This is so because products with such attributes are capable of replacing other products that generate more solid waste. That is, replacement can occur at a lower level of output. Thus, consider two products serving the same use function. Suppose the first is an EN-product lasting four times as long as the second product. Successful marketing of the EN-product might drive down demand for the other product sufficiently to reduce the overall contribution to solid waste generated by the two products.

Product attributes that result in increased product lifetime, product reuse, and reduced resource intensivity of a product—plus the aim of actually decreasing product consumption itself—together form the concept EPA has called *source reduction.* In other words, source reduction cuts down on the amount of waste produced by reducing demand for certain goods at the "source," i.e., the consumer (U.S. Environmental Protection Agency, 1974). The concept strikes at the very heart of the businessman's interest: less of a product sold means less profit.

There is a noticeable lack of support by business for the source reduction concept. This was evident during the 1975 Waste Reduction Conference sponsored by the EPA. While consumerists and a number of legislative aides to congressmen at the conference appeared to back source reduction, business leaders were hostile to the approach. Nor did this approach receive the support of representatives of organized labor at the conference. They were concerned over the threat to jobs implicit in the concept (Henion, 1976, p. 117).

Furthermore, the idea of the government's achieving source reduction by means of product controls would be quite unacceptable to the business community. On this point, there is little doubt. Under ecological marketing, however, an attempt would be made to accomplish source reduction voluntarily. But the government would help. A major educational role would be assigned to it, and this would amount, in effect, to the creation of a substantial advertising subsidy for producers of EN-products. Hence, the result would tend to contribute to the profits of such producers, an important stipulation in the concept of ecological marketing.

Recycling

Complementary to source reduction and much more acceptable to the business community—because it does not threaten to reduce the rate of increase in actual consumption levels for products—is the other concept on which the U.S. bases its policy for solid waste pollution. And that is recycling or, more technically speaking, resource recovery. Recycling does not reduce the actual level of solid waste generated, but it is an ecologically desirable way to handle the waste.

Of the 144 million tons of post-consumer solid waste generated in the U.S. in 1973, only 9.4 million tons—mostly paper—were recycled.

Recycling is beginning to receive wider support throughout the U.S. Recognition is growing that many of the U.S.'s raw materials and energy sources are being seriously depleted by the continually increasing demands of its industrial economy. Almost half of the country's dozen or so key raw materials will soon be in short supply, and the supply of as much as three-quarters of these materials will depend significantly on imports (National Commission on Materials Policy, 1973). Recycling could become a partial solution to the important long-term problem of acute shortages in national resources.

Yet there are many serious obstacles to recycling. These include the nascent state of recovery technology, the suitability of virgin materials to modern product technology, and tax breaks and freight rates that favor virgin materials. Consequently, the American economy and the economies of other developed nations have a considerable distance to go before their cities become, in the words of Jane Jacobs, "huge, rich, and diverse mines of raw materials" exploited through recycling and not subject to the law of diminishing returns as are other mining operations (Jacobs, 1969, pp. 110–111). But the possibility is there. And resource recovery could become a future growth industry of great consequence. This will occur, however, only if profit opportunities are attractive, a condition that underpins the formal definition of ecological marketing, with which this paper now concludes.

ECOLOGICAL MARKETING: A FORMAL DEFINITION

Ecological marketing can be visualized as a point of view on how better to advance environmental quality. Normative in character, the viewpoint advocates a national policy for the environmental crisis which facilitates profit-making by the private sector through the marketing of environmentally beneficial products. The profitable marketing of such products is considered to be viable policy because self-interest is put to work. This policy is the one recommended for the marketing profession and government to adopt, and it encourages the soft-pedaling of increased governmental regulation.

These ideas are embodied in the following formal definition:

Ecological marketing is:

(a) The marketing effort of a profit-making entity or

(b) the marketing effort, typically a communications effort, either educational or promotional, of a nonprofit entity, whether organization or individual, expended directly or indirectly in behalf of selling or

> marketing goods, services, or ideas whose positive ecological attributes or content constitute a minor or major appeal for the buyer, user, or adopter for the purpose of making, or which tends to result in, a short-term or long-term profit for a profit-making entity (Henion, 1976, pp. 1-2).

The initial target market is seen as the ecologically concerned consumer to whom EN-products are marketed in the sense of the marketing concept of our discipline. Future target markets will consist of persons now indifferent to the ecological appeals made today by producers on behalf of EN-products. To such persons the ecological benefits of EN-products—and the products themselves—must be *sold.* Thus, part of the ecological marketing strategy tends to compromise the marketing concept.

But an important selling job needs to be done. First, present favorable attitudes that many consumers have toward the environmentally harmful product need to be changed. Next, such attitudes need to be replaced with ones favorable toward EN-products. Finally, these attitudes need to be strengthened to the point that the consumer will be led to substitute the EN-product for the harmful one.

Changing basic attitudes and preferences of consumers by means of governmental education or business advertising has never been easy. Most economists say it cannot be done. And the marketer does not usually claim any ability to do more than canalize an already existing attitude for a class of products in a direction that builds a preference for his brand (Kotler and Zaltman, 1971; Lazarsfeld and Merton, 1949). Yet, today many consumers in Western countries are undergoing major changes in values, life styles, and cultural orientations. In the process traditionally held views about consumption are changing. Therefore, an attempt to change consumption preferences and tastes in a direction more favorable to improving environmental quality is now more likely to succeed. So is ecological marketing.

REFERENCES

HARRIS, LOUIS, "Public Convinced Its Lifestyle Must Change," *Chicago Tribune* (December 1, 1975a), sec. 2, p. 4.

HARRIS, LOUIS, "Many See Sacrifices as Solution," *Chicago Tribune* (December 4, 1975b), sec. 2, p. 5.

HENION, KARL E., "The Effect of Ecologically Relevant Information on Detergent Sales," *Journal of Marketing Research,* 9 (February 1972), pp. 10-14.

HENION, KARL E., *Ecological Marketing* (Columbus, Ohio: Grid, Inc., 1976).

JACOBS, JANE, *The Economy of Cities* (New York: Random House, 1969).

KINNEAR, THOMAS C. AND JAMES R. TAYLOR, "The Effect of Ecological Concern on Brand Perceptions," *Journal of Marketing Research,* 10 (May 1973), pp. 191–197.

KINNEAR, THOMAS C., JAMES R. TAYLOR, AND SADRUDIN A. AHMED, "Ecologically Concerned Consumers: Who Are They?" *Journal of Marketing,* 38 (April 1974), pp. 20–24.

KOTLER, PHILIP, *Marketing Management* (Englewood Cliffs, N.J.: Prentice-Hall, 1972a).

KOTLER, PHILIP, "A Generic Concept of Marketing," *Journal of Marketing* 36 (April 1972b), pp. 46–54.

KOTLER, PHILIP AND GERALD ZALTMAN, "Social Marketing: An Approach to Planned Social Change," *Journal of Marketing,* 35 (July 1971), pp. 3–12.

LAZARSFELD, PAUL F. AND ROBERT K. MERTON, "Mass Communication, Popular Taste, and Organized Social Action," in William Schramm (ed.), *Mass Communications* (Urbana, Illinois: University of Illinois Press, 1949) pp. 459–480.

National Commission on Materials Policy, *Materials Needs and the Environment Today and Tomorrow* (Washington, D.C.: U.S. Government Printing Office, 1973).

NELSON, JAMES E., "An Empirical Investigation of the Nature and Incidence of Ecologically Responsible Consumption of Housewives," Unpublished doctoral dissertation, University of Minnesota (1974).

U.S. Conference of Mayors, *Cities and Nation's Disposal Crisis* (Washington, D.C.: National League of Cities, 1973).

U.S. Environmental Protection Agency, *Second Report to Congress: Resource Recovery and Source Reduction* (Washington, D.C.: U.S. Government Printing Office, 1974).

U.S. Environmental Protection Agency, *Third Report to Congress: Resource Recovery and Waste Reduction* (Washington, D.C.: U.S. Government Printing Office, 1975).

24 A NEW MILK JUG

Thomas C. Kinnear

The story takes place in the faraway Province of Ontario in 1972. The industry of interest is the retail milk industry and the primary company of concern is Dominion Dairies, a subsidiary of Sealtest. Dominion was the largest dairy in Ontario. There were also four other dairies of significant size in the market.

Before 1972, retail milk was sold in three types of containers: a three quart returnable polyethylene jug, a three quart plastic milk bag and a plastic coated paper carton. The jug accounted for the majority of sales and carried a $.40 deposit. In 1972, Dominion Dairies introduced into test market a three quart disposable polyethylene jug.

The new jug overcame some health problems associated with returnables. Specifically, polyethylene would maintain in its structure some toxic materials that consumers could store in these containers. These materials could then seep out into the refilled milk jug. Also, foreign objects were quite often returned in the jugs, including bottle caps, insects etc. Both of these types of contamination were difficult to detect. A number of years before, a significant number of medical people asked the Ontario government to ban returnable milk jugs. Also the new jug would avoid the problem of volume shrinkage in jugs when cleaned before refilling. From an ecological point of view the new jug was completely biodegradable.

In early 1972, Dominion put their new jug in test market and also approached the federal and provincial governments with the story of the

---

Reprinted with deletions from Thomas C. Kinnear, "Some Perspectives on Business-Government Relations with Respect to the Environment," *Ecological Marketing,* edited by Karl E. Henion II and Thomas C. Kinnear, pp. 107–112, published by the American Marketing Association.

jug. On all fronts everything seemed fine. The test market was a resounding success. It looked as if Dominion could substantially improve their market position with the jug. It would take their competition over a year to have a supply of these jugs. Also, two departments of the federal government and one of the provincial gave their "approval" to the jug. Everything seemed fine but the opposition had not yet come to bat.

THE OPPOSITION

The following groups made a case against the new jug to the provincial government and the public:

1. Pollution Probe: This group was founded in 1968. Its aim is "to alert Canadians to the price we pay for uncontrolled exploitation of our water, forest, mineral and energy resources. Probe attempts to translate sound environmental principles into action toward concrete changes in legislation, economic priorities and consumer habits."[1]

In 1972 Pollution Probe was a powerful force. It had launched a major attack on the new jug claiming that the old jug was not a health hazard, cost less (it did by $.05) and that the new jug added to pollution. They described Dominion claims as "at best ignorant; they are more accurately labeled 'deceptive'. . . . Neither landfill nor incineration is environmentally desirable. Prevention of waste through re-use and recycling is the only answer."[2]

Adding support to Pollution Probe's attack were the other opponents:

2. Consumer's Association of Canada,
3. Conservation Council of Ontario,
4. Office of the Mayor of Toronto,
5. Certain Parts of Organized Labor,
6. Major parts of the media—the attack by Pollution Probe was receiving major coverage.

These groups together could exert extreme pressure on the provincial government. Also some of the other large dairies were rumored to have solicited the government to stop the new jug. Indeed, they did have a lot to lose. During this period Dominion did little to counter the charges.

---

[1] *Keep it Clean—A Manual for the Preservation of the Cottage Environment,* Pollution Probe, 1968, p. 1.

[2] *Throwaway Milk Containers—The Facts,* Pollution Probe, 1972, p. 1.

THE MINISTER

Into this scene, we introduce the Provincial Minister of the Environment. He was new to his position and Dominion had not discussed the jug with him. He came to this situation armed with *The Environmental Protection Act of 1971*. Under this act the minister has the power to issue "control-and-stop-orders" which limit or stop the amount of pollution from its source. In other words, he could do whatever he wished to the new jug. His power seemed only one step short of King Edward I, who in the 1300's decreed the death penalty for the burning of coal.

And act the minister did. On July 5, 1972, he announced plans to ban the new jug on the basis of the added cost to consumers and the questions related to disposal. The ban was to take effect about thirty days hence, hardly enough time to clear the channel of the new jugs.

In response, Dominion Dairies put a $.05 deposit on the jugs, in effect making them a returnable, plus started a system to recycle the containers. To this a very angry minister added a provision to his earlier ruling that a returnable must be returned for the purpose it was previously used for. He had in effect eliminated the new jug from the market. He was most intemperate in his description of Dominion at that time.

THE MORALS OF THE STORY

Obviously, Dominion Dairies was the big loser in this situation. How is it that the development of a container that was sound both from a health and ecological point of view resulted in such a major disaster? The following list of morals attempts to help explain this, plus at a more general level, is designed to guide the businessperson in these types of matters:

1. The skills of marketing management, so long relied on are no longer enough; i.e., identifying consumer needs and satisfying these needs through the mobilization of company resources is now only half the art of decision making in what can only be called the era of public influence on marketing. The marketing manager now must have outward oriented skills as well. He must be able to deal with all the "publics" who claim to have a stake in his decisions. Clearly, the management of Dominion demonstrated little skill in this regard. In the milk business, they were extremely skillful, but in the public arena they were rookies.

2. Expect your competitors to try and use government or other action groups against you. This is true even though they may claim to support a "free market." Anticipate this and be prepared to counter it. Dominion did not.

3. Understand that the publics you are dealing with have different sets of concerns than you do. For example, to you the concern is profit but to the politician it is his continued survival in office. You should be prepared to talk to each group in its own terms. You should anticipate the reaction of each group. Dominion did not.

4. Understand that government is complex in much the same way that some types of industrial selling are. There are multiple influences on decisions. You must find the right people in the right departments. Dominion did not.

5. Understand that certain government people may have veto power over the decision of interest. You absolutely must find them.

6. To weave your way through the maze of influencers and vetoers you should have a champion within government. Perhaps, the provincial minister of health could have provided this support to Dominion. He was never approached.

7. Understand that a verbal-nonpublic commitment from government can evaporate quickly under pressure from others. Keep in continuous touch with developments and be prepared to present counter arguments. Dominion did not.

8. Expect the press and certain regulatory bodies to paint you as the villain no matter how factual your case or how truthful your presentation. You start one down in every "public" debate. Be prepared to fight hard. Dominion was not.

EPILOGUE

The environmental example presented here illustrates the need for new skills in marketing decision making. The marketing manager of the future will need these skills to navigate the complexities of the marketing environment.

C *Social Dimensions: Demarketing*

25 THE ENERGY CRISIS AND CONSUMER CONSERVATION: CURRENT RESEARCH AND ACTION PROGRAMS

R. Bruce Hutton

Since the Arab oil embargo, efforts in public policy . . . reflect an urgent need to find solutions to energy problems. While early efforts focused on hardware development, it has become increasingly evident that the consumer is equally important in achieving viable solutions to the "energy crisis." Support for this contention is gained when it is realized that 50% of the population do not know the U.S. has to import oil and another 30% do not know how much. These facts coupled with the current beliefs of a substantial part of the consumer population that there really is *no* energy problem provides an interesting and challenging arena for consumer researchers.

Consequently, the purpose of the workshop was threefold: (1) to inform ACR members about the magnitude of the energy problem, (2) describe pioneering programs from two countries (Canada and U.S.) designed to inform and motivate consumers to conserve energy, and (3) provide background and stimulate interest in consumer research focused on providing input to policymakers facing important and increasingly serious energy problems. To help accomplish these objectives three individuals representing Canadian and U.S. energy departments de-

---

Excerpt from a workshop convened by the Association for Consumer Research (ACR) to discuss energy problems and solutions. Published in William Wilkie (ed.), *Advances in Consumer Research 6* (Ann Arbor, Mich.: Association for Consumer Research, 1979), pp. 12–14. Reprinted with permission.

scribed current programs and research: Brian Kelly, Canadian Department of Energy, Mines, and Resources; Jeffrey Millstein, U.S. Department of Energy (DOE); and Bruce Hutton, U.S. DOE/University of Denver.

CURRENT RESEARCH ON PUBLIC ATTITUDES AND BEHAVIOR

Jeffrey Millstein provided an overview of consumer attitudes and behavior regarding energy conservation and how they have changed over the last five years. This span represents the time since the Arab oil embargo and subsequently when much of the current conservation effort in the U.S. begin.

Mechanisms for gathering this descriptive data included 25 national sample surveys and various metropolitan surveys, focus group interviews, and sales data. Purposes for the research were to:

1. Monitor consumers' awareness of the need to save;
2. Monitor attitudes toward proposed or actual conservation policies, actors in the energy situation, and means to save energy;
3. Monitor knowledge of how to save energy and where to get information;
4. Monitor energy saving behaviors, both continuing and one time only kinds;
5. Help design more effective communications.

In evaluating the results of the research, Millstein reports that energy conservation is basically a two-fold concept involving *efficiency* and *cutbacks*. Most Americans appear to be practicing the former. For example, more than 80% of U.S. homes now have some insulation, 50% of the homeowners have added insulation since purchasing their house, and people are buying more efficient cars. Some cutbacks are also being practiced (e.g., 50% cut back lighting, 60% do not cool below 78% in summer). However, many more are not being demonstrated: only 20% of the population carpools, 12% use public transit to and from work, actual highway speeds are increasing, and vacation travel is rising.

Why people have been reluctant to adopt many of these viable alternatives is not fully known. However, research data suggest several possibilities. First, policy proposals least preferred by a majority of consumers are those that hit closest to home. People do not want to pay more in prices or taxes for energy or related comforts, conveniences, and life styles. They certainly do not want to sacrifice them unless they get something of equal or greater value in return.

Second, people do not want to pay higher prices for energy because, for most, the higher prices are perceived to *be the* energy problem. Consequently, consumers are baffled by proposals to solve the energy problem through the price mechanism (How can you solve high prices by making them even higher?)

Third, most Americans are poorly informed about important dimensions of the energy problem. The lack of information on factors mentioned earlier such as flagging domestic production and dependence on foreign oil has led to a general lack of concern along a number of fronts. For example, only about one-half the population think energy poses a serious problem, 40% are concerned that foreign oil producers will stop shipments again, only 20% are worried about natural gas shortages, and one-third of the people do not like paying higher prices because they believe the whole issue has been fabricated by oil companies and politicians.

Finally, aside from information and education, people need to feel that measures taken to deal with the energy problem should result in equitable sacrifices. This is one important way to help remove doubts and skepticism about the reality of the energy problem.

CANADIAN ENERGY CONSERVATION INFORMATION PROGRAM

Much of the suspected causes for current levels of consumer attitudes, knowledge, and behavior are being addressed in a variety of programs directed by Brian Kelly in Canada. Kelly reported that since February 1975, the Office of Energy Conservation, Department of Energy, Mines, and Resources has operated an active and diverse information program.

Program Review: 1975–1978

The introductory phase of the program began February 1975 and ran for one month. Objectives focused on awareness of the importance of energy efficiencies among all Canadian publics and changing attitudes toward energy use. To accomplish objectives, the plan incorporated four major elements: (1) advertising through newspaper, radio, and television drawing attention to the need for conservation presented in a positive environment; (2) publications designed to transmit "how to" information; (3) promotional activities aimed at specific market segments: (4) public relations programs to precede the advertising campaign utilizing a special "Speaker's Bureau." Overall, this phase focused on the benefits of energy conservation using credible, straight forward, and positive messages. Both a "crisis atmosphere" and "trivial approaches" were avoided.

Phase Two ran for one year, April 1975 to March 1976. The objectives of this phase were a natural outgrowth of the introductory phase including encouragement to adopt less energy consumptive life styles. Goals, however, became more specific (e.g., to effect a reduction in the rate of growth by 2% or a dollar saving of $400 million). Target groups also became more specific, ranging from single unit households to specific industries to various ethnic groups. The same major elements were used to meet objectives but with some new features. Special emphasis in advertising was given to the rationale for conservation. A slogan was developed: "If you're not part of the solution, you're part of the problem." In addition, advertising focused on a variety of themes including one designed to capitalize on concerns over inflation: "When we save energy, we fight inflation. One solution to two problems." In addition, Fernand Seguin, a well known French popularizer of science, was chosen as spokesperson for French Canada.

Following Phase Two, Phase Three ran from April 1976 to March 1977. Objectives of the program were extended slightly to encompass an understanding of how energy is linked to other problems, to include other agencies and organizations, and to become more action oriented. Three more target groups were added to the list—agriculture, clergy, and citizen's groups. In addition to the same major elements, this phase marked the beginning of a number of "vertical programs" employing a wide range of communication vehicles focused on a specific area. The first such program dealt with reinsulation, and a new slogan evolved reflecting a more solution oriented direction: "Energy conservation—be part of the solution." The major emphasis in this phase was on practical steps and self-help (especially through dollar savings). In order to emphasize potential savings, comparison ads were run showing before/after results of reinsulation.

The most recent phase ran between April 1977 and March 1978. Objectives for this phase encompassed those of Phase Three with additional emphasis on implementation. Increased attention was paid to car drivers, industry, children, and the commercial sector as target groups. The same basic elements for meeting objectives was employed with a variety of updates. The addition of special job creation programs and energy conservation was personified in the form of individuals actively working in community programs for the benefit of everyone. This phase also marked the introduction of "The Hottest Show on Earth," a half-hour television program on insulation. This unique film is a mixture of animation, comedy, drama, and popular science designed to appeal to prime time T.V. audiences. The program has proved extremely popular among several audiences.

The plan for Phase Five (1978–79) is to concentrate on four important areas with the same basic elements. One is automobile transportation which represents the most immediate opportunities for conservation. Second is the industrial sector, the largest energy consumer in the economy, accounting for about 30% of Canada's energy consumption. Third is the residential/farm sector which consumes 20% of the energy budget. Fourth is the commercial sector which consumes only 14% but is the fastest growing sector in terms of energy use.

Program Evaluation

Over the course of the Canadian program, Kelly reports various measures have been used for evaluation including wave data, readership studies, coupon responses, demand for publications, press coverage, and opinion polls. As a result, several conclusions were drawn by Kelly summarizing the Canadian experience to date:

1. The program must be credible, and scare tactics or frivolous approaches do not produce credibility. Straight-forward, factual and interesting approaches have proven most successful.
2. Saving money has the greatest appeal both to the public and business. However, a number of rationales should be developed (e.g., energy supply, balance of payments, national security, enhanced life styles, future generations, etc.) in order to provide a broad basis for conservation.
3. Present energy conservation as a positive alternative. Energy shortages and suffering do not represent conservation but rather the inevitable result of not conserving.
4. Conservation comes in several types or stages, and an incremental approach to addressing them is advised. In the immediate term concern is with reducing outright energy waste and increasing efficiency. Beyond that are a number of more fundamental issues involving value changes, life styles, urban development, etc. leading to what has been termed "The Conserver Society."
5. The execution of an information program should be broad but integrated. It should involve media advertising, publications, promotion, public relations, etc. Media vehicles should be mixed. Publications should be in the form of books wherever possible. Cooperative programs are important. Paid advertising is advised. These vehicles, strategies, and activities should evolve over the life of the program from general to increasingly specific messages.

CONSUMER RESEARCH AND PROGRAMS IN THE DOE

Bruce Hutton noted that the U.S. has a number of programs comparable to Canada's in the area of information dissemination, but they are less well integrated. Hutton concentrated on one area in Conservation where program strategy and objectives are well defined and consumer research is an integral part of both program formulation and evaluation—the Consumer Motivation Branch (CMB).

The overall objective of the CMB is to encourage private sector groups (e.g., financial institutions, retailers, etc.) to voluntarily work with the DOE to test and evaluate approaches which the private sector can later implement to motivate consumers to become most efficient users of energy. While the ultimate target of CMB activities is the consumer, it is the private sector which is the focus of CMB actions and the mechanism through which objectives will be achieved.

Feedback: A Motivation and Information Program

One example where the above strategy has been implemented is the area of feedback. A great deal of research has shown that giving people immediate and understandable feedback on the effects of their actions enables them to better control those actions much as a dieter is assisted by a scale. In research funded by the CMB and conducted by Princeton University, the conservation achieved by providing homeowners with daily weather-corrected feedback was 10%. The problem involved in this initial study was that procedures for information dissemination were not practical on a large scale.

Subsequently, two research programs were developed and implemented. The first was a pilot test with a local Washington, D.C. utility using the only commercially available feedback device (Fitch Energy Monitor) on the market at the time. The Fitch monitor provides a display in cents-per-hour of the total household electricity use. It also serves as a conventional digital clock, alternating the two types of information. Analysis of data from all all-electric homes outfitted with the monitor (prior to the pilot test) indicated energy savings of 12%. A representative sample of utility customers were taken and assigned at random to treatment and control conditions (70 subjects in each group). This pretest-posttest control group design will run one year concluding December 1978.

This first test was not designed to answer the question of the most effective type of feedback (DOE does not, for example, endorse the Fitch monitor), but is being used as a preliminary study advancing knowledge, especially as it relates to technical and legal dimensions, utility role, and customer acceptance. A concurrent test, involving focus groups and a controlled experiment, was designed to address issues of information effectiveness (e.g., information types, amount of information utilized, cumulative versus instantaneous, etc.)

The output from these studies will be used to develop specifications for a feedback device to be used in a major demonstration starting in the Fall of 1979. The device plus educational information will be tested in a series of experiments across geographic regions, fuel types, and fuel prices. Dependent measures will include consumption, attitudes, knowledge, and awareness of energy related factors in the environment.

Energy Cost of Ownership: A Communications Program

The premise for the Energy Cost of Ownership Program (ECO) is that most consumers are not yet considering energy costs in the purchase of many products. This has resulted in a major barrier to acceptance of new energy efficient technologies since many of these products have higher first costs or replacement costs.

In making a decision about which product to purchase, it is generally true that the energy saving product (e.g., insulation) or energy efficient appliance (e.g., refrigerator with power switch) will be a good investment for the consumer over the life of the product, even though it may cost more initially. Consequently, the *objective* of ECO is to accelerate the acceptance of energy efficient products by testing methods of increasing consumer awareness, attitudes toward, and use of the concept of energy cost of ownership in the marketplace.

The ECO Program is designed to include three major steps with consumer research in integral part in developing each step as well as evaluating the feasibility of going on to each successive step. First, an integrated marketing/communications program was developed as a pilot study in Denver, Colorado. The two major components were: (1) a communications project including paid multi-media advertising, a home energy retrofit contest, and a shopping center display of a home energy use simulator; and (2) a research phase involving measurement of the overall program and concept and evaluation of the various strategies. Advertising was done on radio and T.V. emphasizing specific products (automatic set-back thermostats, electric ignition pilot lights, storm windows). The campaign theme was "Products That Save Energy Pay For Themselves." This was displayed in all advertising and promotions and on color in-store materials.

Utilizing a nonequivalent control group design, results were encouraging. There was a favorable impact on consumer knowledge and attitudes toward energy conservation dimensions, energy efficient products, and about costs and savings resulting from various energy measures. In addition, over 100 retailers participated in the program.

The results of the pilot test have served as input into ECO II, a major demonstration designed to create a similar positive selling environment. In this phase, even greater emphasis will be placed on the concept of energy costs and specific dollar savings. The focus, through T.V. and print ads, will be on applying the concepts across a package of products instead of a few specific ones. This demonstration will take place with heavy private sector participation in five test markets coinciding with the market territories of the major retailers. This will allow for close evaluation of the program across varied geographic regions, fuel types and prices, and climatic conditions in order to determine the feasibility of ECO III national program the following year.

26 SWEDISH TOBACCO CONTROLS—PRECEDENT SETTING "NEGATIVE MARKETING" APPROACH

Graham T. T. Molitor

The Swedish Committee on Smoking and Health was not the first such national government committee to respond to health problems connected with smoking. Among the first reports were those emanating from the Royal College of Physicians in London in 1962, and an advisory committee to the U.S. Surgeon General in 1964. The significance of these two early reports was the official government stance and the strident stand taken. They provided a note of finality to long term controversies surrounding smoking and health.

What was precedent setting about the Swedish report was its boldly innovative approach and massive scope. Sweden was the first country to propose a long term, all out coordinated program for combatting smoking, using nearly every technique imaginable.

The remarkable character of these sweeping arrangements merits careful examination. The step by step program aims at all segments of society. It employs all media and information channels.

"Negative marketing" is a newly coined term devised to characterize this massive consumer control effort. The overall objectives are to eliminate, or discourage smoking, to provide as many environments as possible that are free from smoking, and to create a marketing climate as negative towards smoking as can be achieved—short of prohibition.

Reprinted with permission from Marilyn Chon and David P. Harmon, Jr. (eds.), *Critical Food Issues of the Eighties* (Elmsford, N.Y.: Pergamon Press, 1979), pp. 80–90.

Many of the concepts, if proven effective, almost certainly will be applied to a considerable range of consumer control policies in other nations. Principles involved are likely to be adopted to control hazardous, harmful or deleterious products (and services). Already under debate for similar treatment are proprietary drugs, sugar, and alcoholic beverages.

Tobacco use is characterized by official Swedish government documents as a "major hazard to public health." Annual per capita consumption of tobacco products in Sweden is almost one third that of the United States. Tobacco use, nonetheless, is considered to be a major health problem. Per capita annual consumption for all tobacco products during 1970 stood at 9.63 pounds in America (for persons 18 years and older). In Sweden, consumption for all tobacco products stood at 3.59 pounds (for persons 15 years and older). Per capita annual consumption of cigarettes during 1970 stood at 3,971 in America (for persons 18 years and older). In Sweden, cigarette consumption stood at 1,620 (for persons 15 years and older) (see Figure 26-1).

SELF-REGULATION PROGRAMS

Self-regulation efforts often are voluntarily undertaken by industries facing the prospect of public controversy and impending government regulation. Such responses are a part of a familiar pattern of accomoda-

Figure 26-1. Cigarette Annual Consumption per Capita (15 Years & Older).

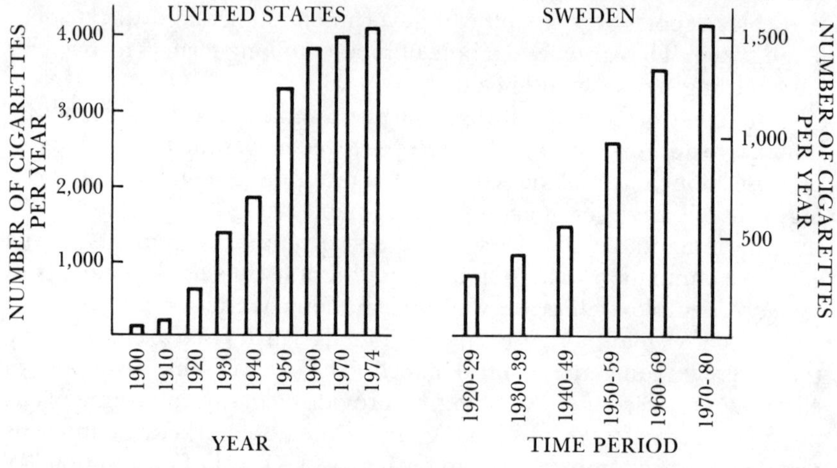

Source: Public Policy Forecasting, Inc. (1900–1960 data based on USDA-ERS data; 1970 & 1974 data based on USDA data and reflects per capita usage for persons 18 years & older), and National Smoking and Health Association data, Sweden, 1973.

FIGURE 26-2. TIME SEQUENCES: TYPICAL CONVERGENCE OF EVOLUTIONARY WAVES OF CHANGE.

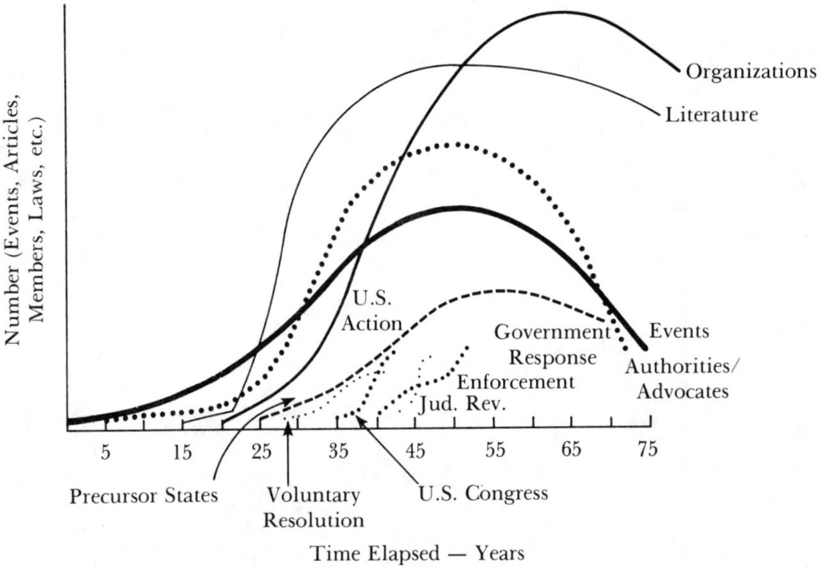

Source: Public Policy Forecasting, Inc. (based on National Smoking and Health Association data, Sweden, 1973).

tion in public policy processes (see Figure 26–2). In the United States there often is a sequence of events to voluntary industry regulation efforts (see Figure 26–3).

Various self imposed restrictions have been undertaken incrementally by the tobacco industry. Recently established agreements restraining promotion of all tobacco products in Sweden go to some extraordinary lengths. Major details provide insight as to the trend and direction of possible future limitations on tobacco products in other countries.

The voluntary regulation agreement between the Swedish Tobacco Branch Association and the Consumer Ombudsman became effective in 1975. Voluntary self-regulation of tobacco product advertising includes the following principles:

1. Media Limitations
   ban on direct mail advertising addressed to consumers' homes
   ban on cinema advertisements
   prohibition of outdoor (billboard) advertising, except in relation to places of sale
   proscription of ads in magazines directed to persons less than 21 years of age (a listing of affected publications is prepared yearly)
   ban on ads on newspaper sport pages
   ban on ads in sports magazines

FIGURE 26-3. VOLUNTARISM: THEORETICAL MODEL.

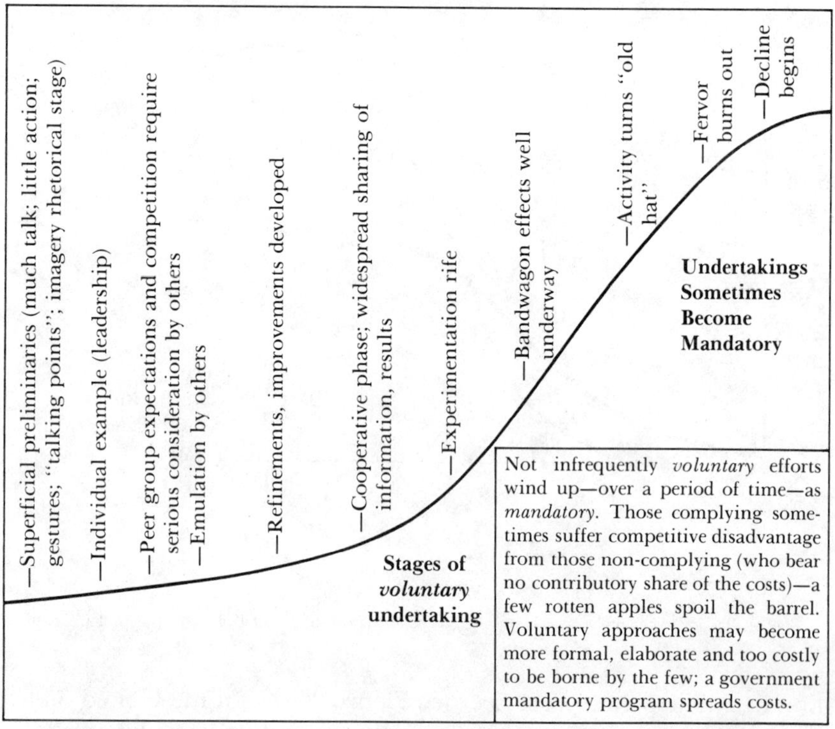

Note: Voluntary efforts at self-regulation can be looked upon as a stop gap, as a natural adjustment mechanism —voluntarism often "buys time" for laggards, smaller units to begin preparing themselves to phase-in to new and usually higher levels of performance.

Source: Public Policy Forecasting, Inc.

limitation of newspaper ads to a size not exceeding 1520 column millimeters

restriction of ads in other publications to a size not exceeding one full page.

2. Advertising Content Restraints

balance and moderation

disallowance of pictures of humans or nature scenery unless the picture is part of the trademark

limitation of pictorial displays to a reproduction on the product, its package, trademark or brand name, or usage (e.g., smoking a pipe)—such pictures are to be neutral and not imply messages with persuasive overtones

insistence on informative headline copy and test results limited to: type of product; contents; method of manufacturing; taste, strength, and other characteristics; usage of the product; raw material origin; disclosure of manufacturer name of location; price; and sales outlets.

3. Additional Promotional Restrictions
   ban on ads in a variety of institutional settings, including schools, health facilities, and places mainly frequented by youth
   limitation of consumer testing (and testimonials) of tobacco products
   ban on distributing any tobacco products to youth.

LABELING DISCLOSURES AND WARNINGS

Stern warning declarations recently were mandated for tobacco packages offered for sale in Sweden. Disclosure was directed by the Swedish Parliament (Riksdag) in 1975. Label designs were completed in May 1976. Implementation commenced January 1, 1977.

Most novel is the requirement for constantly changing the message. This concept has potential application to other consumer products for which cautionary warnings of hazards may be appropriate. (Similar warnings have been suggested or implemented in Western European countries for products other than tobacco—alcohol, sweets, pharmaceuticals.)

Cautionary health warnings and messages for tobacco products are drawn from a repertoire of different texts. There are 16 of them for cigarette packs alone, and special sets of declarations pertain for other tobacco products (see Table 26–1). The current set of declarations is intended to be discarded after two years at which time an entirely different set of declarations will be approved for use. The continual variation in text is intended to draw renewed and maximum attention to the various health hazards posed.

Disclosure of certain "harmful" components of tobacco smoke—not only tar and nicotine, but also carbon monoxide—also is required. Not only must the declaration state tar, nicotine, and carbon monoxide for the brand concerned, but the *mean contents of all the brands marketed in Sweden must also be indicated,* (a "comparative yardstick" approach), according to a recent report from the Swedish Institute.

Usual format requirements also are imposed for declarations to assure prominence and help put across the intended message. Packaging declarations must appear on the largest surface of the package. In addition, they must be in clear and contrasting color to ensure maximum visibility and impact.

TABLE 26.1. TOBACCO PRODUCTS: REPERTOIRE OF CAUTIONARY LABELING DECLARATIONS, SWEDEN 1977.

THE PERSON WHO STOPS SMOKING WILL SOON BE MORE FIT *NATIONAL BOARD OF HEALTH AND WELFARE*	SMOKER'S COUGH IN THE MORNING? *Smoker's cough is a sign of* *early ill-health. The cough* *will cease if you stop smoking.* *NATIONAL BOARD OF HEALTH AND WELFARE*
THE MORE YOU SMOKE THE GREATER HEALTH RISKS WILL THERE BE *NATIONAL BOARD OF HEALTH AND WELFARE*	SMOKING DAMAGES THE LUNGS! *It begins with a smoker's cough and* *it may end up with lung cancer* *or other lung diseases.* *NATIONAL BOARD OF HEALTH AND WELFARE*
ASBESTOS *is especially dangerous to smokers.* *If you work in an environment with* *such pollution you should stop smoking.* *NATIONAL BOARD OF HEALTH AND WELFARE*	THE PERSON WHO STOPS SMOKING INCREASES HIS CHANCES OF REMAINING HEALTHY. *NATIONAL BOARD OF HEALTH AND WELFARE*
YOU WHO HAVE BEEN SMOKING FOR A LONG TIME! *It has been proved that* *those who stop smoking* *will decrease the health risks* *NATIONAL BOARD OF HEALTH AND WELFARE*	SMOKERS HAVE MORE SICKNESS THAN NON-SMOKERS *NATIONAL BOARD OF HEALTH AND WELFARE*

WHICH CIGARETTES ARE MOST DANGEROUS?
those yielding most carbon monoxide, tar and nicotine. But it also depends How you smoke.
NATIONAL BOARD OF HEALTH AND WELFARE

DISEASES OF THE HEART AND ARTERIES
Smokers run an increased risk of heart attacks and certain diseases of the arteries.
NATIONAL BOARD OF HEALTH AND WELFARE

NON-SMOKERS HAVE LONGER AVERAGE LIFE THAN SMOKERS
NATIONAL BOARD OF HEALTH AND WELFARE

SMOKING DURING PREGNANCY MAY HARM THE CHILD
NATIONAL BOARD OF HEALTH AND WELFARE

YOU WHO HAVE BEEN SMOKING FOR A LONG TIME!
Stopping smoking is useful— the risk for disease will decrease and your fitness will improve.
NATIONAL BOARD OF HEALTH AND WELFARE

IF YOU STILL MUST SMOKE
Avoid inhaling and leave long butts and you will absorb less of dangerous substances.
NATIONAL BOARD OF HEALTH AND WELFARE

SMOKING AND AIR POLLUTION
is a bad combination. Smokers are more sensitive to air pollution.
NATIONAL BOARD OF HEALTH AND WELFARE

YOU WHO ARE YOUNG!
The earlier you begin smoking the more seriously your health will be affected.
NATIONAL BOARD OF HEALTH AND WELFARE

CIGARETTES: 16 ALTERNATIVES TO BE CONTINUOUSLY ROTATED AND REPLACED (SUPPLANTED) EVERY TWO YEARS.

Source: Public Policy Forecasting, Inc. Based on data from National Smoking and Health Association, Stockhom, Sweden.

LONG TERM TOBACCO CONTROL PROGRAMS AND PROPOSALS

Sweden's Parliament (Riksdag) passed legislation in 1968 urging appointment of a smoking and health committee to develop plans for reducing tobacco consumption. The Minister of Finance refused to create such a committee in January, 1971.

Subsequently, the Ministry of Health and Social Affairs was petitioned by the National Smoking and Health Association. The petition resulted in the National Board of Health and Welfare appointing a Smoking and Health Advisory Committee in December, 1971. The Committee's report was submitted in June 1973. Some five years had elapsed from the time of the initial legislative behest.

The Swedish formula starts with the basic premise that society increasingly should undertake programs that are preventative in character. This admonition is part of a general trend toward preventative public policy making. The objective is to eradicate root causes. Such efforts are calculated to eliminate or at least control problems before they pose too great a hazard or burden upon society.

Comprehensive proposals have been developed to ameliorate health hazards associated with tobacco use. Many proposals are still in the discussion stage. More government controls are in the offing.

PRODUCT AVAILABILITY AND PRICING PROGRAMS AND PROPOSALS

Pricing, a traditional regulatory gambit, is heavily relied upon by Swedish government officials to discourage consumption. Comparative prices for a pack of popular cigarettes, in 1976, were almost four times more costly in Stockholm as compared to major cities in the United States.

Yearly price increases were proposed by Sweden's Smoking and Health Committee. Under the proposal, prices would be increased annually by 10% "in relation to the general price and income level."

In an effort to make tobacco products less available the following proposals were put forward: a ban on coin-operated (vended) sales by 1979, the outlawing of sales or distribution of tobacco to persons under 16 years of age, the termination of tobacco sales in food and other shops not expressly established for the purpose of selling tobacco and the restriction of the maximum amount of tobacco brought into the country by travelers (to the low level now allowed for persons outside the country less than 24 hours).

Reducing cigarette consumption to the low level of the 1920's was an overall goal set by the Committee. Programs also would aim at preventing increased consumption of other alternative tobacco products. However, snuff was recognized for use as a last resort cure.

Not unexpected for any nation with socialized industry segments, government take over of the tobacco industry also was put forward by the Committee. Among the proposals was one reestablishing the state tobacco monopoly. It was contemplated that this would facilitate implementing "negative marketing." Until 1961 all importing and manufacturing of tobacco was handled by a monopoly corporation. Since 1961 there has been a free market. However, the former monopoly corporation, now a state owned company (operating as the Swedish Tobacco Company, Ltd.), dominates tobacco trade with an 85% market share.

ADVERTISING PROGRAMS AND PROPOSALS

Tobacco advertising already is severely restricted in Sweden. Sweden's Consumer Ombudsman and the Market Court, two principal and powerful adjuncts of Swedish consumer policy, exercise substantial powers over advertising of tobacco products. Between them they are empowered to intervene and regulate the content and design of advertising. In a 1973 case referred to the Market Court by the Consumer Ombudsman, a Prince cigarette advertisement showing signatures and photographs of well known persons whose attributes were associated with their occupations and an endorsement, "I have gone over to Prince," was deemed improper. Objection was taken to its suggestive design as well as the health risks involved in tobacco smoking.

Outright and total prohibition of all tobacco product advertising has been suggested time and again in Sweden. Freedom of the press and avoidance of censorship have been impelling reasons for the reluctance to impose such additional advertising bans. Most recently a Royal Commission studying advertising policy rejected any such ban. Advertising over state owned radio or television broadcasting channels already is prohibited. Because there is no commercial radio or TV in Sweden, printed advertising is the most widely used medium. Current controversy is pretty much limited to printed advertising.

The Smoking and Health Committee prosposals would virtually do away with marketing and promotion of tobacco products. Among their recommendations were the prohibition of all advertising and promotion unless contributing toward developing negative marketing attitudes, a ban on advertising that is "intrusive, outgoing, *persuasive* (emphasis added) or otherwise more active," a mandate on health warnings in all advertising, the prohibition of scenes in films or television programs that encourage cigarette consumption, the proscription of "obtrusive" marketing and the termination of all commercial marketing promotion.

RESTRICTING TOBACCO USAGE IN PUBLIC SPACES PROGRAMS AND PROPOSALS

Wide ranging attention was given by the Smoking and Health Committee to suggestions for barring tobacco usage in a variety of different confined public spaces. Objection to smoking in such closed spaces is prompted by "passive smoking"—inhalation of "smoking pollutants" by non smokers. Prominent among the recommendations were the restriction of employers' rights to engage smokers in certain tasks posing adverse synergistic reactions (for example, lung cancer among asbestos workers who smoke is eight times greater than that of non smokers), the investigation and identification of occupations and environments where other such restrictions should be imposed, the phasing out of smoking privileges in other than working space locations which workers frequent (e.g., recreation areas), the elimination, by steps, of smoking on public premises, the establishment of a non smoking environment status in schools and the creation for children born after 1975 of environments frequented during their formative years that are as free from smoking, and as negative toward smoking as possible.

ANTI SMOKING INFORMATION PROGRAMS AND PROPOSALS

Experimental anti smoking information programs have been undertaken in preschools, schools, mother care and child care centers, and various places of employment. The Smoking and Health Committee recommendations included expanding information campaigns stage by stage. Anti smoking campaigns, after tried and proven, would be extended to the following areas: maternal and child health centers (by 1975), kindergartens (by 1979), elementary schools (by 1981), and secondary schools (by 1985).

Further dissemination of anti smoking information by the Committee included the following recommendations:

educate children continually as to harmful effects of tobacco use;
conduct public information anti smoking campaigns in the mass media;

- promote anti smoking informational programs at courses and conferences held by the National Board of Health and Welfare;
- direct informational programs to the popular movements, youth organizations and other public spirited groups;
- encourage study circle organizers to include smoking health issues in their programming;
- provide government financial support to organizations willing to conduct anti smoking activities;
- distribute anti smoking government publications through chemists' shops (state owned), post offices (also state owned), and tobacconists' shops (Swedish government tobacco companies dominate all trade and command an 85% share of market, consequently, the pressure on tobacconists to distribute such literature probably is quite strong);
- compel smoking and health education component during compulsory military service.

HEALTH CARE RELATED PROGRAMS AND PROPOSALS

Emphasizing preventative health measures, the Smoking and Health Committee preferred a number of suggestions aimed at improving health:

- designate the medical care delivery system as an anti smoking channel;
- start with at risk groups (advise all chronic bronchitis patients they ought to stop smoking, etc.);
- provide similar information to all relatives of patients suffering from or susceptible to tobacco smoke;
- provide at smoking withdrawal clinics (established at each of the five regional hospital centers) therapy for high priority persons (e.g., parents of small children, school teachers, etc.);
- provide voluntary access to antidotal clinics;
- rename chronic bronchitis "Cigarettossis" (this is in line with other maladies where the causative agent lends its name to describing the disease, e.g., asbestosis, silicosis);
- discourage smoking which may bring harm to persons other than the smokers themselves, for example: unborn children (women smoking during pregnancy may experience unsuccessful outcome); unborn children/youngsters (mothers-to-be and other mothers may contribute to retardation of physical and/or mental development for children up to seven years of age);

encourage diagnosis, information and treatment in company health services;

encourage life insurance companies to increase premium rates for smokers;

extend air pollution standards to include regulation over tobacco generated pollutants (for example, carbon monoxide concentrations in small, poorly ventilated rooms under some circumstances exceed those permitted in working spaces);

reduce maximum allowable concentration of all constituent substances of tobacco smoke (whenever another country adopts a standard lower than the one pertaining in Sweden, revise the standard to an even lower level);

commit research to the following areas: antidotal treatment, commencement of smoking habits, recidivism, and influence of smoking.

SIGNIFICANCE OF SWEDISH TOBACCO CONTROLS

The vast and varied nature of innovative efforts either proposed or actually undertaken in Sweden to control tobacco use are being carefully watched by other governments and the tobacco industry. Positive results, once demonstrated, can unleash a domino-like sequence of similar actions being taken elsewhere in the world.

D *Constraints on Choice: Antitrust Issues*

27 ADVERTISING AND COMPETITION

David A. Aaker

The existence of vigorous competition is important to a market economy. Competitive forces lead to real product innovation, the efficient distribution of goods, and the absence of inflated prices. The question is: What impact does advertising have on competition? There have been hypotheses put forth indicating that advertising can actually decrease the level of competition. For example, it is argued that heavy advertising expenditures in many industries generates strong brand loyalty that tends to create barriers to potential competitors. The hypothesized result is fewer competitors, less competition, and higher prices. Fortunately, these hypotheses have been examined theoretically and empirically by economists and, although few definitive conclusions are yet available, it is now possible to structure the argument, identify some key issues, and marshal some empirical studies that bear on these issues.

A MEASURE OF COMPETITION

A widely used measure of competition within an industry is the degree to which the sales of the industry are concentrated in the hands of a few firms. The specific construct is the concentration ratio—the share of the industry sales held by the four largest firms.

. . .

Excerpt from David A. Aaker and John G. Myers, *Advertising Management* © 1975, pp. 554–563. Reprinted by permission of Prentice-Hall, Inc., Englewood Cliffs, New Jersey.

The concentration ratio as an indicator of market concentration and competition has intuitive appeal and is convenient, but conceptual and theoretical problems are associated with it. The main problem is in defining the industry meaningfully. Theoretically, an industry should include all brands from which buyer choice is made. Such a judgment is not easy to make. Does the cereal industry include instant breakfast, breakfast squares, and pop tarts? Do aluminum companies compete only with one another or do they also compete with copper and steel companies? Should import competition be included? What about industries in which regional brands are important? Consider the cement industry; the four leading firms accounted for only 29 percent of national sales in 1963, but 90 percent of all cement produced is shipped 160 miles or less. When the nation was divided into fifty-one regions, in only three of the regions did the production of the four leading firms account for less than 50 percent of all sales. The definitional problem is compounded by the fact that most empirical studies are based on the Standard Industry Classification (SIC) of the United States Census Bureau whose categories are somewhat arbitrary. Despite the definitional problem, the concentration ratio provides a central construct in the exploration of advertising and competition.

A CAUSAL MODEL

Figure 27–1 provides a simplified causal model that summarizes various hypotheses suggesting that advertising contributes to a reduction of competition in the marketplace. The model introduces several crucial constructs such as market concentration, barriers to entry, and product differentiation. The arrows represent hypothesized causal relationships among these constructs. After presenting these hypotheses, some counter-argument will be raised and several relevant empirical studies will be examined.

The central construct in the model is market concentration. The basic argument is that when concentration exists, there is little incentive to engage in vigorous price competition since any price decrease would be immediately neutralized by a similar price change by the other major competitors. A direct result, therefore, is higher prices and profits.

With price competition inhibited, there is a hypothesized incentive to advertise heavily, since a competitor will not be likely to duplicate an advertising campaign. An advertising campaign that duplicates a competitor's is rarely successful. Thus, one result of concentration is thought to be heavy, noninformative advertising, the cost of which is passed on to the buyer in the form of higher prices. The reduced price of private label brands is cited as evidence of such higher prices.

Another hypothesized effect of concentration is the attempt, by

FIGURE 27-1. MARKET CONCENTRATION: SOME HYPOTHESIZED CAUSES AND EFFECTS.

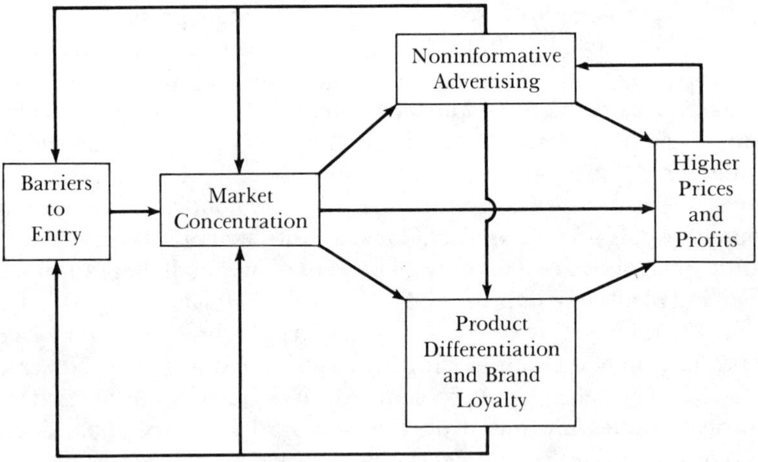

advertising and minor product changes, to differentiate products that are essentially identical with respect to their primary function. Differentiated products can generate brand loyalty and thus escape vigorous price competition. The result is another link to higher prices and profits. Product differentiation can be a highly desirable response to diverse market needs and wants and is not bad per se. As Scherer points out:

> The relevant question for economic analysis is not . . . whether product differentiation is a good thing but rather, how much product differentiation there should be, and whether certain market conditions might lead to excessive or inadequate differentiation. . . . Product differentiation activities most often singled out for a vote of public disapproval include image differentiation and those aspects of physical differentiation which entail the most superficial, transitory variations in product style or design. Was the American economy better off for having spent $17 billion on advertising in 1968, or was an appreciable fraction of this sum wasteful or even counterproductive? Were the users of deodorants, pain remedies, hair bleach, and similar products benefited because Bristol-Myers devoted 28 percent of its 1966 sales revenues to advertising? What are the consequences of the American automobile industry's annual model change cycle, which rapidly renders aging vehicles stylistically obsolete?[1]

The higher profits are not considered earned rewards of product innovation but the result of market power. The issue of the definition of a

[1] Frederic M. Scherer, *Industrial Market Structure and Economic Performance* (Chicago: Rand McNally, 1971), p. 325.

product is, of course, central—recall discussion on the definition of product and related terms in Chapter 1.

Concentration is said to be perpetuated and increased by the existence of barriers to entry that prevent or at least discourage potential competitors from entering the market. Advertising is thought by some to generate entry barriers directly and through the product differentiation it generates. The purpose of product differentiation is presumably to develop a reason for a buyer to buy one brand over another, to generate brand loyalty. This brand loyalty is hypothesized to be a barrier to entry. It is argued that a potential new competitor finds it difficult to compete against established products. He must attract the attention of habitual and satisfied consumers and motivate them to change loyalties. He must also convince retailers to remove from their shelves established products to make room for the new entries.

Advertising is also hypothesized to generate entry barriers by providing the large advertiser in some industries with two kinds of advantages over his smaller competitor. First, the large advertiser is thought to receive preferential treatment by the media with respect to the cost and selection of advertising space. Second, a threshold level of advertising is hypothesized to exist, below which advertising would be ineffective simply because the exposure frequency would be too low to communicate. When this threshold level is high, the cost of entering a market—and thus the risk—becomes excessive.

. . .

Notice that, to the extent that advertising and product differentiation places the small competitor at a disadvantage, it not only represents a barrier to entry of new competitors, but could also impede the growth of existing ones, thereby increasing the level of concentration. If existing competitors weaken and perhaps disappear, the concentration, and thus the market power, of those remaining could be increased.

One additional feature of Figure 27-1 should be emphasized. The existence of higher prices and margins tends to generate advertising since it "pays" to advertise high-margin products. Thus, the feedback from higher prices to advertising. The result is that an ever-increasing cycle of concentration-profitability-advertising-concentration, etc., is created.

Advertising, then, is not only considered an effect of concentration generating economic waste, it is also an important cause. The argument is that it helps create "artificial" product differentiation that, in turn, creates brand loyalty—a major entry barrier. Furthermore, it has the potential of discouraging a small competitor by increasing the market risk and by placing him at a cost disadvantage.

CONCENTRATION AND PRICES

A viable level of competition and relatively low prices might exist with high levels of concentration in at least two situations. The first is when it is feasible to enter the market on a local or regional scale. Brands that dominate the market nationally may be vulnerable in a local market where buyer tastes and needs may be somewhat unique. Furthermore, while the cost of a national entry may be large, the cost of reaching a small geographic segment may be more modest.

The second type of situation is where there exists what Galbraith termed countervailing power on the buyer side.[2] If concentration exists on the buyer side, it can counter the market power of a few sellers. Thus, Sears Roebuck, Montgomery Ward, and the major automobile companies can extract price concessions from the tire companies. A & P, Safeway, and the other large grocery chains are in a position to gain price reductions from grocery manufacturers. Galbraith has also suggested that there exists a systematic tendency for power on the buyer side to develop when power exists on the seller side. He noted that "retailers are required by their situation to develop countervailing power on the consumer's behalf."[3] Of course, there is no guarantee that price reductions obtained by the strong buyer will be passed on to the ultimate consumer. They could result in increased profits instead for the buying organization.

EMPIRICAL STUDIES

Several of the hypotheses imbedded in the model represented in Figure 27-1 have been explored empirically. Several of the relevant studies will be examined. The intent is to suggest generalizations where they emerge and to illuminate the issues further.

Advertising and Concentration

If advertising indeed causes concentration, there should be an association between advertising levels and concentration. Those industries with heavy advertising expenditures should have a greater

---

[2] John K. Galbraith, *American Capitalism: The Concept of Countervailing Power* (Boston: Houghton Mifflin, 1956).

[3] *Ibid.*, p. 117.

tendency toward concentration than other industries. In a well-known study, Lester Telser, a University of Chicago economist, explored this hypothesized tendency, using as an indicator of advertising intensity the advertising to sales ratio (A/S), which reflects the percentage of an industry's expenditures devoted to advertising.[4] He found that in a sample of 42 industries there was no significant correlation between the A/S ratio and concentration in 1948, 1954, and 1958. Neither did he find significant correlation between changes in the A/S ratio and changes in concentration during these periods. A similar study, however, involving fourteen industries did find a significant relationship.[5] Furthermore, Blair found that out of 36 product classes that used television extensively, 25 of them increased their concentration from 1947 or 1954 to 1963.[6] Other studies provide conflicting conclusions, some indicating no significant relationship[7] and others finding positive evidence.[8] In general, it might be concluded that there is evidence of positive association but that it is somewhat weaker than might be expected given the nature of the argument reflected in Figure 27-1.

The problem of industry definition on which the concentration ratio is based has already been examined. But there are other methodological problems that these and related studies must face. First, industries with very low advertising, like meat and sugar, will be less likely to demonstrate an advertising relationship yet they are often included in the analysis. Second, it is brands, not companies, that really compete and yet the analysis is with respect to industries and firms. Third, large advertising expenditures or large A/S ratios may reflect industry size or the number of products involved, yet few studies attempt to control for such factors.[9] Finally, association does not mean causation. As Figure 27-1 shows, advertising can be viewed as an effect as well as a cause of concentration.

---

[4] Lester G. Telser, "Advertising and Competition," *The Journal of Political Economy,* December 1964, pp. 537-562.

[5] H. M. Mann, J. A. Henning, and J. W. Meehan, Jr., "Advertising and Concentration: An Empirical Investigation," *Journal of Industrial Economics,* November 1967, pp. 34-45.

[6] John M. Blair, statement before the Hearings of the Subcommittee on Antitrust and Monopoly, Committee on the Judiciary, in *Concentration and Divisional Reporting,* part 5, U.S. Senate, 89th Cong., 2d sess. (Washington D.C.: U.S. Government Printing Office 1966), pp. 1888-1910.

[7] Jules Backman, *Advertising and Competition* (New York: New York University Press, 1967), pp. 90-94.

[8] Lee E. Preston, "Advertising Effects and Public Policy," *Proceedings of the AMA 1968 Fall Conference* (Chicago: American Marketing Association, 1968), pp. 563-564.

[9] P. K. Else, "The Incidence of Advertising in Manufacturing Industries," *Oxford Economic Papers,* March 1966, pp. 88-110.

Advertising and Profitability

The evidence of an association between advertising and profitability is stronger. Economists Comanor and Wilson, in an influential study, attempted to explain interindustry differences in profit rates.[10] They examined the return on equity after taxes of forty-one consumer-goods industries, using both the A/S ratio and the average advertising expenditures of the major firms as indicators of advertising intensity. Although they did not find high correlation (only 0.10) between four-firm concentration ratios and the A/S ratio, they did determine, using a regression model, that both advertising measures were significantly related to profitability. Thcy concluded that industries with high advertising outlays earned approximately 50 percent more than other industries. They further attributed much of the profitability differential to entry barriers created by advertising expenditures, arguing that such a cross-sectional study (as contrasted with a time-series study) tends to emphasize the long-run difference among industries and thus should reflect basic structural characteristics like concentration. However, such speculation on causal explanations for the association is naturally less than definitive. Other explanations might be just as convincing. It may be, for example, that there are industry characteristics that could jointly cause profits and a tendency to rely on advertising. Or it may be that advertising in some industries is often a more economically efficient means of marketing than any other marketing alternative. From this perspective, the finding that firms in an industry who use advertising compared with those that do not (or use it less), are more profitable is not surprising. In such instances, the nature of the causal link might be quite different from what is implied by Comanor and Wilson.

Media Discounts

Substantial discounts for volume purchasers exist in the published media rate schedules, a fact used to claim that large advertisers have an advantage over smaller competition. David M. Blank studied this hypothesis in the context of the television industry and found that the actual prices paid do not reflect any consistent structure of discriminatory pricing.[11] Many time slots are not sold in advance and become available at

[10] William S. Comanor and Thomas A. Wilson, "Advertising, Market Structure and Performance," *Review of Economics and Statistics,* 49, November 1967, pp. 423–440.

[11] David M. Blank, "Television Advertising: The Great Discount Illusion, or Tonypanda Revisited," *Journal of Business,* January 1968, pp. 10–38.

substantial discounts regardless of total commitments by an advertiser. Furthermore, the tendency to share a program with other firms and variations in audience sizes over time and over programs also tend to neutralize the power of a large firm. It may be that a firm that can make large early commitments may have an advantage with respect to obtaining time slots, but it does appear that media discounts, at least in television, provide a large advertiser with only a relatively small differential advantage.

Advertising and Brand Stability

Brand loyalty, created in part by advertising, is hypothesized to be a barrier to entry and thus to competition. If such a hypothesis holds, relatively stable brand shares might be expected in industries with extensive advertising. Telser, however, examined the leading brands of various product categories in 1948 and 1959 and found an inverse relationship between product class advertising intensity and the stability of the market share of the leading brands.[12] He suggested that the advertising helped to encourage new brand introductions, which, in turn, contributed to the lack of brand stability.[13] Backman showed that, from 1952 to 1965, the sales rankings of the top eight brands in the beer industry (characterized by a high A/S ratio) exhibited extreme fluctuations.[14] He also pointed to major shifts in the market shares of cigarette firms (the tobacco industry is also characterized by high A/S ratios) from 1955 to 1966.[15] Preston, however, observed that the striking fact about these two industries was not the turnover of the middle group of firms but the apparently impregnable position of the top firms—Anheuser-Busch and Schlitz in the beer industry and Reynolds in the tobacco industry.[16] He concludes that the association between concentration and industry performance measures such as profitability "appears to arise from the effect of advertising on the size and stability of market shares and on brand loyalties, particularly for advertised vs. unadvertised brands—rather than from advertising cost structures."[17] Clearly the data are open to different interpretations.

[12] Telser, "Advertising and Competition."

[13] New brand introductions, of course, are far different from the entry of new competitors.

[14] Backman, *Advertising and Competition,* pp. 102–104.

[15] *Ibid.,* pp. 104–107.

[16] Preston, "Advertising Effects and Public Policy," 563.

[17] *Ibid.*

REMEDIES

The problem of the relation of advertising to concentration and competition has been studied in some detail. Yet, it is still far from clear whether advertising has any independent causal effect on concentration. However, even if it is assumed to have an effect, the question remains of what remedy might be useful in altering the effect. The issue, in part, is if the argument represented by Figure 27-1 is accepted, what should be done about it? In particular, are additional restrictions on advertising appropriate?

Assume, for example, that some advertising actually does encourage concentration and results in anticompetitive effects and that therefore some restraints could be justified. The problem is, as Preston observes, "which part of whose advertising results in anticompetitive effects?"[18] Should restrictions be placed on the cereal industry or only on its largest firms? Or should any restraints apply to the entire food industry? What kinds of restraints? Should advertising actually be banned in some industries? What impact would that have on new-product development?

There are restraints on some advertising now. Certain services like legal and medical services are restricted in the way they can be advertised. In most states, the prices of prescription drugs cannot be advertised. There are restraints with respect to certain media. Liquor and cigarettes cannot be advertised on television. It is instructive to review these situations and to consider whether the reasons for the restrictions are defensible and whether they have had undesirable, unanticipated consequences. To what extent, for example, will television advertising expenditures for cigarettes simply be directed into other media? Furthermore what impact will the ban on television advertising and the threat of a total ban on all cigarette advertising have on industry efforts to produce safer cigarettes? Proposals to restrict advertising selectively because of a concern with industry competition should be similarly evaluated both in terms of rationale in a specific context and the likely consequences.

It might be possible for the government to restrict advertising levels in certain industries. This restriction could take the form of mandatory controls on the rates at which firms could increase their advertising budgets. It could even include a provision for firms to decrease their level of advertising. A problem with any such proposal is that it would work to the disadvantage of the small, vigorous firm that is trying to compete with larger organizations and of the innovative firm that must announce new-product developments. If the absolute level of advertising were controlled, the smaller firms would not be inhibited, but the large firms

[18] *Ibid.*, p. 564.

would be penalized simply because of their size. Furthermore, there is the sticky issue of determining the exact level of advertising expenditures that would be desirable in any given context. There is precedent for such a move, however. In 1966, the Monopolies Commission in Great Britain recommended a 40 percent cut in advertising expenditures of the leading detergent companies and a 20 percent reduction in wholesale prices. However, partly because of threats to move some of their operations to the European continent, an alternate proposal was adopted. The two involved companies agreed to introduce new, less promoted detergents, priced 20 percent below existing brands.[19]

There have been proposals made to place a tax on advertising or to reduce the tax deduction allowed for advertising over a certain amount. It presumably would not affect the small competitor who would not be advertising at the affected level. Of course, the determination of the amount of reduction and the level at which the reduction would be applicable would be difficult to fix. Furthermore, companies could alter their marketing mix in ways to shift the advertising dollar to other forms of promotion that might have an impact similar to that of advertising. Also, any such plan would discriminate against those companies that tend to rely on advertising in favor of companies like Avon, for example, that rely mainly on direct selling.

The practical question of the nature of the remedy and how it should be implemented needs to be more formally introduced into the analysis.[20] It is tempting to propose a remedy that will seem to rectify obvious problems. However, in many cases, the remedy can be worse than the original problem.[21]

---

[19] Scherer, *Industrial Market Structure and Economic Performance,* pp. 344–345.

[20] Philip Kotler, Fred C. Allvine, and Paul N. Bloom, "Public Policy Alternatives for Regulating Advertising: An Evaluation," in *Public Policy and Marketing Practices,* edited by Fred C. Allvine (Chicago: American Marketing Association, 1973), pp. 355–375.

[21] Many judge the Robinson-Patman Act to be in that category. Instead of a simple tool to protect competition, it has become, in the eyes of some, a bureaucratic nightmare that has, in fact, greatly inhibited price competition.

28 THE CEREAL COMPANIES: MONOPOLISTS OR SUPER MARKETERS?

Paul N. Bloom

Marketing is on trial in a courtroom in Washington, D.C. Three of the most prominent and successful marketing organizations in the world—Kellogg, General Mills, and General Foods—are being accused by the Federal Trade Commission of using a wide range of common marketing practices to help them establish and maintain a shared monopoly of the ready-to-eat breakfast cereal industry. Instead of seeing the cereal industry as providing numerous textbook examples (as it has, in fact, provided) of how marketing should be done by large-scale consumer products manufacturers, the Federal Trade Commission sees the industry as "a textbook example of the dangers of concentration and the evils of monopoly."[1] If the courts eventually rule in favor of the position taken by the FTC, then substantial portions of many of today's marketing texts and guidebooks may have to be rewritten.

This article contains a description of the FTC's antitrust case against the three largest cereal companies. The purpose is to spotlight the conflicts which exist between the interpretations given to certain marketing practices by the FTC attorneys and the interpretations given to these practices by most marketing scholars and practitioners. An attempt is made to show how a large number of marketers could find themselves in Catch-22 situations if the thinking of the FTC is upheld. These market-

Excerpt from Michigan State University's *Business Topics,* Summer 1978, pp. 41–49. Reprinted by permission of the publisher.

[1] FTC Complaint Counsel, *Trial Brief—In the Matter of Kellogg Company et al.*, Docket No. 8883, Federal Trade Commission, 1976, vol. 1, p. 1.

ers could face the prospect of being damned if they used certain marketing practices and damned if they did not, as the FTC could attack them for choosing one course of action, and their competitors could attack them for choosing the other.

One warning must be offered. This article is *not* meant to contain an evaluation of the charges being made; it is primarily designed to give the reader a better understanding of the significance these charges have for marketing practitioners. A comprehensive evaluation of the case would require much more space than is available here and would require access to information submitted in the trial that has not yet been released to the public. Without doubt, a variety of complicated legal and economic issues must be resolved in this case.[2]

The trial of the cereal case before an FTC administrative law judge in Washington began in April 1976, four years after the FTC originally filed a formal complaint against the three respondents and Quaker Oats. This initial trial is expected to last into the 1980s. The FTC staff attorneys took until January 1978 to present their case (at which time the charges against Quaker Oats were dropped). The defense arguments of the three respondents should take several years to complete. A final determination may not occur until the late 1980s, since the law judge's decision could be appealed to the five FTC commissioners, and their decision could be appealed to a U. S. circuit court of appeals and to the Supreme Court.

The charges leveled against Kellogg, General Mills, and General Foods have evolved as the case has proceeded. The complaint filed in 1972 did not accuse the four original respondents of collusion or conspiracy, but instead placed considerable emphasis on how the respondents had used intensive advertising to help them establish a shared monopoly of the ready-to-eat cereal market. In fact, observers speculated that the case was being used to test certain economic theories about the anticompetitive effects of advertising.[3] These theories—which claim that advertising produces entry barriers by creating brand loyalties or by allowing large advertisers to achieve economies of scale—have received widespread attention in the economics and business literature.[4]

---

[2] For an in-depth evaluation of a portion of the FTC staff's charges, see the author's monograph. "The Cereal Antitrust Case: An Analysis of Selected Issues," in *Research in Marketing: An Annual Compilation of Research, Volume 2,* edited by Jagdish N. Sheth (Greenwich, Conn.: JAI Press, forthcoming).

[3] See Yale Brozen, "New FTC Policy from Obsolete Economic Doctrine," *Antitrust Law Journal* 41 (Issue 3, 1973): 477–87; and William E. Huth, "The Advertising Industry—An Unlikely Monopolizer," *Antitrust Bulletin* 14 (Winter 1974): 653–79.

[4] See James M. Ferguson, *Advertising and Competition: Theory, Measurement, Fact* (Cambridge, Mass.: Ballinger Publishing Co., 1974; and Jean Jacques Lambin, "What Is the Real Impact of Advertising?" *Harvard Business Review* 53 (May–June 1975): 139–47.

However, the pre-trial brief submitted by the FTC attorneys in 1976 gave only secondary emphasis to the argument that intensive advertising had produced anticompetitive effects. Instead, emphasis was given to the notion that an intricate tacit conspiracy has developed among the respondents which violates Section 5 of the Federal Trade Commission Act. The following paragraphs are devoted to discussing what the FTC staff sees as the dimensions of this alleged tacit conspiracy, based on what is said in the 524 pages of the pre-trial brief. Apparently, the FTC staff has not changed its arguments substantially since publication of the brief.

The FTC staff seems to be saying that a tacit conspiracy consisting of four major components has been maintained in the ready-to-eat breakfast cereal industry. These components are:

1. the use of competitive monitoring procedures;
2. the use of noncompetitive pricing policies;
3. the *non*use of certain promotional techniques and other policies that could stimulate price competition; and
4. the use of exclusionary practices of shelf-space allocation, brand proliferation, product differentiation, and intensive advertising.

The arguments of the FTC staff concerning each of these components of the alleged tacit conspiracy are presented in separate sections below. In each section, the interpretations given to certain marketing practices by the FTC staff are contrasted with the interpretations a marketing textbook might provide. A summary of these contrasting interpretations can be seen in Table 28–1. The discussion and table should clearly point out that the FTC staff has mounted a fundamental challenge to marketing thought and practice.

COMPETITIVE MONITORING CHARGES

The FTC staff views the first component of the tacit conspiracy as being essential for holding the conspiracy together. Without a formal or written agreement, the respondents allegedly keep their conspiracy healthy by closely watching one another's activities. Firms supposedly will be afraid to do anything that would draw quick, retaliatory actions from observant competitors. They will, instead, restrict their actions to those that fall within the industry's permissible code of conduct—something which has been learned over the years with the help of competitive monitoring. Thus, competitive monitoring allegedly can permit a tacit conspiracy to develop and thrive without the benefit of any formal communications or agreements among the conspirators.

TABLE 28.1. A COMPARISON OF INTERPRETATIONS OF THE CEREAL COMPANIES' BEHAVIOR

BEHAVIORS	FTC STAFF'S INTERPRETATION	MARKETING TEXTBOOK INTERPRETATION
1. Monitoring of competitors' activities through: a. Salespersons' reports b. Subscriptions to Nielsen, SAMI, etc. c. Participation in a trade association	1a,b,c, Policing actions designed to ensure compliance with a code of conduct.	1a,b,c. Marketing intelligence gathering
2. Use of pricing policies such as: a. Prior announcement of increases	2. Avoiding price competition by: a. Reducing uncertainty	2a,b,c,d. Helping a manufacturer establish better relationships with retailers.
b. Delivered pricing	b. Keeping wholesale prices uniform geographically (reduces uncertainty)	
c. Offering "price protection	c. Allowing instant retaliation to a price cut	
d. Suggesting retail price	d. Keeping retail prices uniform (reduces uncertainty)	
e. Making price changes at different times than cost changes	e. Reducing uncertainty by cutting frequency of changes	e. Demand-oriented pricing
f. Keeping high prices for failing brands	f. Avoiding price cuts	f. A milking strategy

(continued)

Table 28.1. *Continued*

Behaviors	FTC Staff's Interpretation	Marketing Textbook Interpretation
3. Nonuse of: a. Trade allowances and discounts b. Cents-off deals c. Private labels d. Vitamin fortification (until pressured) e. In-pack premiums (for 10 years)	3a,b,c,d,e: Avoiding actions that could stimulate price competition.	3a,b,c,d,e. Avoiding destructive, costly forms of competition. Also avoiding government accusations of using predatory or discriminatory practices.
4. Use of: a. Promotion of shelf-space plans	4. Excluding entry by: a. Allowing new firms only poor shelf locations	4a. Helping retailers
b. Brand proliferation c. Product differentiation	b,c. Leaving no profitable positions for new firms	b,c. Serving diverse consumer tastes
d. Intensive advertising	d. Building brand loyalty and setting scale-economy barriers	d. Stimulating primary demand, creating brand awareness, and reinforcing purchase decisions.

The competitive monitoring activities that have drawn criticism from the FTC staff include the following:

1. using salespersons to collect information on the prices, shelf locations, new product introductions, and promotions of rivals by observing shelf displays, consulting with buyers, or conversing with salespersons from competing firms;
2. using standard reports on industry marketing activities obtained from Nielsen, SAMI, and other widely used data reporting services;
3. using the A. C. Nielsen Company for several years as a clearinghouse for advertising data. (The respondents allegedly submitted data on advertising expenditures in each media for each brand to Nielsen and then received from Nielsen, as a supplement to the firm's regular reports, detailed information on the advertising expenditures of all the cooperating firms.):
4. using the results of studies on competitors conducted by advertising agencies and marketing research firms: and
5. participating in the activities of The Cereal Institute, a trade association.

As indicated, the FTC staff sees these activities as policing actions used by the respondents to ensure that no firm deviates from the accepted industry code of conduct. Of course, these activities (perhaps with the exception of the clearinghouse operation) could also be viewed as attempts to gather timely, useful marketing intelligence data. Business firms always have a need to know about their competitors and the rest of their environment, and the procedures cited by the FTC staff are commonly used to gather intelligence. Without this information, a firm could find itself unprepared for an initiative by a competitor or unable to make a timely response to a rapid change in the feelings of consumers or public policy makers. By keeping on top of things through the use of salespersons, reporting services, research firms, and trade associations, a firm can avoid a host of difficulties and probably keep itself *more* competitive than it might be otherwise.

Thus, the FTC staff is labeling as anticompetitive a group of activities which conventional marketing wisdom would tend to label as competitive. If the viewpoint of the FTC staff is eventually upheld in the courts, then firms in oligopolistic industries such as cereals will be confronted with the problem of determining how much marketing intelligence they are permitted to and should collect. Collecting too much intelligence could get a firm in trouble with the FTC, while collecting too little could get a firm in trouble with its competitors and customers. Under these circumstances, the amount of intelligence a firm could collect would probably depend on how closely its behavior corresponded to that of its competitors. A firm that did things differently from its competitors could collect as much intelligence as it wanted, while a firm that followed industry marketing norms would have to limit its intelligence gathering or risk being labeled as a tacit conspirator.

NONCOMPETITIVE PRICING CHARGES

The second component of the alleged tacit conspiracy is an understanding among the respondents as to what constitutes permissible pricing behavior. The FTC staff seems to feel that the industry code of conduct limits the respondents to using pricing policies which encourage interdependence and leader-follower pricing, with Kellogg generally serving as the price leader. The pricing policies they allegedly have used to help them avoid competing with one another on a price basis include the following.

1. The announcement of price increases to the public well before they are to take effect. This supposedly helps the companies reduce uncertainty about one another's actions and thereby keeps the leader-follower pattern intact.

2. The use of delivered pricing systems which charge all customers the same price for a given shipment, regardless of location. This supposedly reduces the chances that price competition will emerge since price differentials between brands will always be the same nationwide, and price skirmishes will therefore not occur as a result of attempts by some firms to keep differentials the same across locations.

3. The offering of price protection to retailers. This protects retailers by giving them an immediate credit if a price reduction occurs on goods that are in transit to them or are sitting in their warehouses. This supposedly discourages price cutting by a manufacturer because it allows immediate retaliation by competitors. A firm that wants to meet a price cut by a rival would not have to wait until the next shipment eventually appears on retailers' shelves to have its response noticed by consumers, but could use price protection to get a lower price on goods already in the retailers' possession.

4. The suggesting of retail prices to retailers, accompanied by considerable sales efforts to get the retailers to follow these prices. This supposedly reduces uncertainty and reduces the chances of price skirmishes resulting from inconsistent price differentials.

5. The changing of prices in a timing pattern inconsistent with (and more spaced out than) the incidence of cost changes. This supposedly reduces the frequency of price changes and thereby reduces the chances that price competition will emerge.

6. The charging of high prices for failing brands (a milking strategy), rather than price cuts to stimulate sales. This supposedly conveys a message that price cutting is not acceptable in the industry.

In sum, the FTC staff believes that firms interested in competing on a price basis would not use pricing policies such as these.

Clearly, there are logical alternative explanations for using these policies. For example, early announcements of price increases, delivered pricing systems, price protection, and suggested retail prices could be used as part of an effort by manufacturers to establish good relations with retailers. These policies could help reduce uncertainty for retailers, simplify their record keeping, and eliminate any concerns they might have about being victimized by price discrimination. The use of alternative pricing policies could put the cereal manufacturers in troublesome conflict with many of their retailers.

The failure of price changes to follow cost changes could be viewed as an attempt by the manufacturers to avoid the relatively unsound practice of cost-oriented pricing and to substitute demand-oriented or competition-oriented pricing. Similarly, the use of milking strategies for failing brands could be seen as an attempt to make the best of a situation in which even a lower price might not help the sales situation.

Marketers will face a serious dilemma if the thinking of the FTC staff about these pricing policies is upheld. Abandonment of these policies could seriously damage manufacturer-retailer relations and could complicate the price-setting task for manufacturers in innumerable ways. Nevertheless, a manufacturer in an oligopolistic industry with a history of parallel pricing behavior would probably find it wise to abandon these policies in order to avoid difficulties with the FTC. The firm would have to find other and potentially less efficient ways of pleasing retailers and setting prices. A manufacturer who was not part of a parallel pricing pattern, however, would probably be able to continue using these policies.

PASSIVE BEHAVIOR CHARGES

The FTC staff sees the third component of the tacit conspiracy as an understanding to avoid or limit the use of certain marketing strategies that might stimulate price competition among the respondents. The industry code of conduct allegedly forbids or discourages the use of promotional strategies or product modifications that might lead firms to use lower prices as a means of drawing customers away from competitors.

The FTC staff believes the respondents have behaved passively in the sales promotion and product modification areas, and have avoided taking aggressive actions that might stimulate price skirmishes or even price wars.

Several examples of passive behavior are cited by the FTC staff. First, it is claimed that trade allowances and discounts are relatively nonexistent in the cereal industry, as are cents-off offers to consumers. The FTC staff indicates that if more of these dealer-directed and consumer-directed promotional techniques were used, more variability in retail prices would exist, and more price competition would result (since parallel pricing would be more difficult to maintain). Second, it is claimed that the respondents have refused to produce or sell private labels, even when asked to do so by major supermarket chains. This is viewed by the FTC staff as an attempt to stifle price competition. Finally, it is claimed that the respondents held back on the vitamin fortification of their products until they were pressured by the government to do so in the early 1970s, and that they maintained an understanding for more than ten years (1957 to 1968) to limit the use of in-pack premiums. The failure to act aggressively in fortifying brands and in using premiums is seen by the FTC staff as indicating a desire to avoid all competition that could eventually lead to price competition.

An alternative interpretation can be given for the reluctance of the respondents to use the cited practices. These practices could be seen as costly, inefficient ways of attracting customers when compared to the practices the respondents have tended to use—heavy advertising, brand proliferation, and product differentiation (discussed later in this article). It may not be wise for these firms to use *push* strategies (for example, deals, promotions) to get their brands on the shelves and favored by consumers, when *pull* strategies (for example, advertising, differentiation) might work more effectively. These widely known firms might not need to give retailers and consumers incentives to try their products. In addition, it might not be wise for these firms to manufacture private label cereals for retailers when a better return on investment could be obtained by manufacturing their own brands or by taking advantage of other investment opportunities. Furthermore, vitamin fortification and the inclusion of premiums may not have been of much concern to consumers during the time they were not offered.

If the FTC staff's arguments are accepted by the courts and marketers can get into trouble for *not* engaging in certain practices, numerous problems will emerge for top executives and legal staffs. These people will have to learn not only what their firms *cannot do* under the FTC Act, but also what they *cannot not do* under this law.

Moreover, the problems of business executives could become even more acute if the FTC staff is successful in two other antitrust cases it is pursuing. In cases involving ITT Continental Baking (for its marketing of Wonder Bread) and General Foods (for its marketing of coffees), the FTC staff is, among other things, questioning whether the *selective* use of trade allowances and discounts where competition is more severe constitutes predatory conduct designed to injure competitors. Thus, a situation could arise in which large-scale marketers of consumer products could not choose to refrain from offering trade deals, but could also not choose to offer them on a selective basis. Trade deals would, therefore, have to be offered to everyone.

EXCLUSIONARY CONDUCT CHARGES

The last component of the tacit conspiracy view is the one that allegedly allows the respondents to keep any new firms from obtaining a significant market share. The FTC staff indicates that the respondents have informally agreed to engage in the practices of *shelf-space allocation, brand proliferation, product differentiation,* and *intensive advertising* to exclude entry to the industry and to retain their more than 90 percent share of the market. In other words, the industry's code of conduct allegedly permits these forms of competitive behavior because they hurt industry outsiders more than insiders.

By labeling practices such as product differentiation and intensive advertising as exclusionary, the FTC staff is questioning the essence of modern marketing. Therefore, the reasoning of the FTC staff deserves careful examination.

Shelf-Space Allocation

The FTC staff claims that the three respondents have promoted an exclusionary shelf-space allocation plan that has received widespread acceptance by retailers. The plan, promoted by Kellogg, gives each brand a share of the available shelf space in proportion to its share of the market. Although the other respondents offer shelf-space plans to retailers, the FTC staff says these plans have been promoted lightly and that there generally has been acquiescence to the Kellogg plan. The other respondents allegedly have seen no need to challenge the Kellogg plan as long as they have gotten their share of the space, especially since Kellogg has a larger and more experienced sales force.

The Kellogg plan has, according to the FTC staff, managed to exclude entrants and discourage competition in several ways. First, the plan gives the brands of the three respondents better locations at the center of the aisles while relegating other brands to poorer locations at the ends of the aisles. Second, the plan has the brands of each manufacturer displayed in a separate grouping, making it difficult for consumers to compare similar items (for example, branded and private label corn flakes), and making it more likely that consumers will select second brands made by the company that manufactures their first selection. Third, the plan displays the respondents' brands in a billboard fashion (several facings are put next to one another), getting them more attention and impulse purchases. Last, the plan's fair-share concept of allocating space based on market share tends to stabilize market shares, since a brand's share depends to some extent on the amount of shelf space it receives.

Brand Proliferation

The respondents' practice of continually bringing out new cereal brands is the second major activity that has been labeled exclusionary by the FTC staff. Brand proliferation allegedly excludes entrants in the following way:

1. Virtually every profitable position in the product space of the ready-to-eat cereal industry is occupied by several brands belonging to the respondents.

2. With so many brands competing to let consumers know where they stand in the space, the costs of getting the attention of consumers and establishing just one new brand in a profitable position in the space are high.

3. With so many brands already established in each profitable position in the space, it is extremely difficult for one brand (such as a private label) to create enough preference for itself to obtain a share of the total cereal market large enough to take advantage of economics of scale in production (approximately a 4 to 6 percent share).

4. Even if a new firm manages to establish a brand in some unoccupied, profitable position, it will not be able to maintain a high share for this brand for long. The respondents can be expected to bring out new brands immediately to compete in this location—as they did with natural cereals.

5. Thus, in order for a new firm to attain competitive production costs, it will need to establish several successful brands (industry experts consider a one percent brand share to be good) in multiple positions across the product space. The promotional costs needed to establish several brands in profitable positions, and to obtain adequate market shares for each, serve to deter entry.

In addition to the above argument, the FTC staff is also claiming that brand proliferation discourages entry by making less shelf space available to new firms.

Product Differentiation

The FTC staff's criticism of the respondents' product differentiation practices is tied closely to its argument about brand proliferation. The staff essentially sees product differentiation, supported by intensive advertising, as the means by which the respondents are able to place brands in profitable positions all across the product space. As discussed above, this positioning allegedly helps insulate the respondents from new competition—especially from private labels. In addition, the FTC staff argues that this positioning helps insulate the respondents from competition from one another—since a brand only has to compete with the few other brands that are positioned near it.

The FTC staff defines *product differentiation* as "conduct which draws the consumer's attention to minor variations between products, thereby diverting his attention from a comparison of the basic similarities between them."[5] Practices identified in the pre-trial brief as constituting this form of conduct include the use of product symbols (for example, Cap'n Crunch and Tony the Tiger), unique package designs, trademarks, nutritional claims, premiums, and changes in the shapes, colors, textures, flavors, additives, or sugar content of old brands in order to create new brands. In essence, the FTC staff is arguing that these practices make it more difficult and time-consuming for consumers (particularly children) to make value comparisons between brands to discover their true similarities, and that, therefore, consumers start to prefer brands that are perceived to exist all across the product space.

Intensive Advertising

The FTC staff is charging that the respondents use intensive advertising not only to support brand proliferation and product differentiation, but also to discourage entrants in other ways. Intensive advertising is allegedly used to create consumer brand loyalties for the respondents' products, making it more difficult for new firms to acquire customers. The staff also claims that intensive advertising gives the respondents an advantage with retailers in getting shelf locations. In addition, it is argued that intensive advertising allows the respondents to obtain quantity discounts from the media, putting small firms that cannot obtain

[5] FTC, *Trial Brief* p. 325.

such discounts at a cost disadvantage. Finally, intensive advertising has allegedly allowed the respondents to obtain product protection from the television networks—isolating their advertisements in time (for a substantial period both before and after) from ads for other cereal brands. In sum, the FTC staff believes that newcomers to the cereal industry simply could not afford the advertising campaigns needed to overcome the advantages the respondents have obtained through intensive advertising.

Alternative Viewpoints

A marketing professional might offer several explanations for use of the allegedly exclusionary practices.

1. Shelf-space plans are promoted to provide a service to retailers which can help them lower their costs and increase their revenues.
2. Brand proliferation and product differentiation are used to cater to diverse and rapidly changing consumer tastes.
3. Intensive advertising is used to stimulate primary demand for ready-to-eat cereals, to create awareness of individual brands, and to reinforce recently made brand choices of consumers.

If the courts fail to accept explanations such as these and find the practices to be exclusionary, then organizations in the detergent, paper product, automobile, cosmetic, and many other industries may have to redesign their marketing programs to avoid difficulties with the FTC. They may have to start marketing a smaller number of less heavily advertised brands with reasonably uniform characteristics. Needless to say, developing a profitable marketing program under these constraints would be a severe challenge.

ADDITIONAL CASE DETAILS

The FTC staff is also offering a variety of backup arguments, just in case the tacit conspiracy argument is rejected. These arguments basically say that the respondents should be found in violation of Section 5 because the *results* produced by the industry's concentrated structure and distinctive conduct (whether or not a conspiracy exists) have been poor for society. High profits, high selling costs, and infrequent innovations are cited as some of the signs which suggest that industry performance has been lacking. The FTC staff seems to believe there is legal precedent for this backup argument in the decisions in several other antitrust cases.

The remedies sought by the FTC staff in the cereal case are designed to restructure the industry so as to prevent the re-emergence of the current situation. This means that in addition to prohibiting the respondents from engaging in certain practices such as allocating shelf space or exchanging advertising data the FTC staff would like to create eight cereal firms out of the three respondents and require the three to license most of their trademarks on a royalty-free basis to any firm (except Quaker Oats) that is willing to maintain the necessary quality control standards.

The divestiture plan of the FTC staff would break three new firms away from Kellogg and one each from General Mills and General Foods. Each new firm would be given the exclusive rights to the trademark of at least one major brand (for example, Special K, Rice Krispies, Wheaties) in order to give it a sound basis on which to expand its operations. Royalty-free licensing of trademarks would be required for a twenty-year period for all the remaining brands of Kellogg, General Mills, and General Foods. In addition, during the same period, these three firms (1) would have to license the trademarks of any new brands they develop on a royalty-free basis after five years, (2) would have to provide licensees with formulas and methods of production, including quality control standards, (3) would have to license package design as part of the trademark licenses, and (4) would have to avoid acquiring any cereal firms. The FTC staff believes these remedies will restore workable competition to the cereal industry by discouraging brand proliferation, product differentiation, and intensive advertising and by encouraging new firms to enter the industry with low-price strategies.

CONCLUSION

Marketers will want to pay close attention to how the courts answer the question posed in the title of this article. If they decide that the three major cereal companies are monopolists, then many large-scale organizations may have to make substantial revisions in marketing policies and programs. Giant organizations such as General Motors, Procter and Gamble, Revlon, and Kodak may no longer be able to do a host of things textbooks have called good marketing practice, and they may be forced to use marketing strategies they avoided in the past. They may even have to *demarket* certain brands or employ other strategies that could reduce their risk of government antitrust action.[6]

[6] For further discussion of the strategies firms could be forced to use to avoid antitrust difficulties, see Paul N. Bloom and Philip Kotler, "Strategies for High Market Share Companies," *Harvard Business Review* 53 (November-December 1975): 63–72.

On the other hand, if the courts decide that the major cereal companies are super marketers with sound competitive reasons for using the practices they use, then modern marketing will have won a victory. Product differentiation, intensive advertising, market intelligence gathering, and other common marketing procedures will be cleared of the charge that they are anticompetitive forces.[7]

A. SELLING PRACTICES

1. What are the basic problems that arise in person-to-person selling situations? If you were an executive for Avon, how might you address these problems? If you were with Electrolux or New York Life Insurance, how would your approach differ? What about requiring salesmen to initiate the visit with the following statement: "My name is ____________. I'm with ____________ and I'm here to try to sell you my product. May I come in?"
2. Comment on the view that salesmanship is inherently unethical.
3. Cooling-off legislation, intended to curb abuses by door-to-door salesmen selling installment contracts, allows the buyer to cancel an agreement within four business days. Will such laws be helpful? Should the number of days vary with the situation? Should the law apply only to sales in the home? Only to installment sales? Should it apply if the customer has used the product?
4. It is argued that cooling-off legislation will not affect the unscrupulous but only put the honest merchant at a disadvantage. What effect would the legislation have upon the situations described by Magnuson and Carper?

B. SOCIAL DIMENSIONS: ECOLOGY

5. What factors should Lone Star consider before introducing longnecks? How should the product be positioned—as an ecology product or as a country product? Will such an effort by Lone Star

[7] The author would like to thank William Nickels and Robert Spekman for their helpful comments. Financial support for this research was provided in part by the Bureau of Business and Economic Research of the University of Maryland.

replace the need for a state bottle bill that would require a deposit on all soft drink and beer containers?

6. A law firm permits its lawyers to spend office time on socially useful projects like defending the poor. An advertising firm sets out to devote 20 percent of its work effort to good causes. A firm develops an ecological product despite the fact that its profit potential is less than that usually sought. Another firm avoids an attractive package, despite indications that it would sell well, because it would contribute to pollution. What is the social responsibility of the firm in each case? Can a social budget be justified? How should it be allocated to specific projects?
7. Hunt-Wesson Foods developed a program to plant a tree in a burned out national forest in the name of each consumer who purchased one of nine Hunt-Wesson products. What are the benefits of such a program to Hunt-Wesson? How could they be quantified?
8. The social responsibility of business is to make profits. Comment.
9. What does the nonreturnable bottle appeal to the consumer? Could the consumer be "sold" returnable bottles on the basis of the ecological advantages?
10. Is it the consumer who is at fault for littering? How might you get people to stop littering parks?
11. What should Dominion Dairies have done differently? Be specific. Outline a complete plan of action and indicate who in the organization would be involved.

C. SOCIAL DIMENSIONS: DEMARKETING

12. What are the strengths and weaknesses of the Canadian energy conservation program?
13. Why don't people conserve more energy at home? In commuting to work?
14. Assume that the U.S. government were to sponsor an information program on evergy saving in the home with a $200 million budget. How would you administer such a program? What would be its objectives? Would you design special programs for different segments or a single program for all? What elements would you feature? What appeals would work best? How would you measure results? Should the United States have such a program? Comment on the view that the only way to get Americans to conserve is to ration energy.

15. Analyze Sweden's program to demarket tobacco. Which elements seem most effective? Least effective? Which elements are offensive in the sense of restricting freedom of choice or imposing unwanted "noise"?

D. CONSTRAINTS ON CHOICE: ANTITRUST ISSUES

16. What is the economic impact of advertising? When does it generate lower prices? Under what conditions does it increase prices?
17. Nader proposed that a 100 percent tax be applied to all advertising expenditures in excess of a percentage specified for different industries by the FTC. Evaluate this proposal. How else might large advertising expenditures be reduced? What would be the effect on the cigarette industry of a law outlawing advertising? On the detergent industry (where 11 percent of sales is spent on advertising)?
18. Concentration in the beer industry increased from 21 percent in 1947 to 34 percent in 1963, yet the fact that Pabst was third in 1952, ninth in 1957, and third again in 1962 indicates that the industry was far from stable. Furthermore, regional brands like Lone Star and Pearl, two Texas beers that forced a national brand out of their market, compete very effectively with national brands and require only a regional advertising budget. Comment.
19. What is the definition of a market? What is the distinction between the compact car market and the automobile market? Campbell had 8 percent of the dry soup market in 1962 versus 57 percent for Lipton and 16 percent for Wyler's. Should an analyst discuss the soup market or the dry soup market?
20. Do you think that the business practices relating to pricing in the cereal industry described by Bloom are sound marketing tactics or anticompetitive behavior that should be changed?
21. Is the introduction of new cereal brands evidence of vigorous competition or of brand proliferation, which makes it difficult for smaller companies to get shelf space?
22. Comment on the FTC divestiture plan that would create eight firms out of the current big three: Kellogs's, General Mills, and General Foods. Do you think that competition would increase? How would you measure competition before and after?

PART VI

The Postpurchase Phase

INTRODUCTION

Negative postpurchase feelings, or cognitive dissonance, frequently surround a major purchase. In part this is a consequence of the difficult process of making a choice among many attractive alternatives. In chapters 29–33 we are concerned with the particular dissatisfactions and dissonance associated with the following circumstances:

- Usage results in unexpected failure; recourse to the manufacturer for service or replacement is unsatisfactory.
- A personal injury occurs with the proper use of a product or warnings of foreseeable hazards were not provided and injury results.
- Performance does not match expectations or promises.

Chapter 29 deals with the necessity for expanded and clarified warranties to establish the manufacturer's performance responsibilities. Feldman examines the 1975 Magnuson-Moss Act, which responded to this necessity by making it easier for consumers to obtain redress for their warranty claims. A review of the provisions of this act makes it clear that there is no certainty of real reform in this area without much better understanding of the role of warranties in the consumer decisionmaking process.

Few aspects of consumerism have had greater impact than the pursuit of the right to safety. Since 1970 we have seen regulatory agencies granted broad discretionary powers to recall defective products and to prevent the introduction of unsafe foods and drugs. At the same time, the courts have substantially broadened their interpretation of the liability of manufacturers in the event of a product related injury. According to recent rulings, manufacturers can be held fully liable and subject to enormous damages for products that are not safe for expected use or for a reasonably foreseeable misuse and for which adequate warning was not provided. In Chapter 30 Guzzardi examines present trends, with particular attention to the extent and consequences of the broad recall powers that have been conferred on regulatory agencies. Two key points in the chapter are that the trends can ultimately be traced to the sense of rising entitlements—rather than declining safety performance—and that government action and private litigation tend to reinforce each other. While readily granting that the result will be safer products, Guzzardi raises a number of provocative questions about both the direct costs and the side effects of recalls. The fundamental issue is whether or not the balance of power has shifted too far in the consumer's favor.

The legal affairs commentary in Chapter 31 carries Guzzardi's theme further, examining the reactions to liberalized interpretations of product liability. These responses have frequently taken the form of laws that specifically curb recent court decisions. In general the legislature has not rejected the doctrine of strict liability but has limited the circumstances that can lead to legal suits, thereby widening the range of defenses that a company can employ in court. Clearly, it would be better for companies to take marketing actions that minimize hazards. Indeed, as Trombetta shows in Chapter 32, many preventive actions could and should be taken—especially if the courts expand the foreseeability concept, which holds that product designers should be able to anticipate misuse by the consumer.

Chapter 33 looks at postpurchase dissatisfaction. The available measures, although apparently flawed and incomplete, suggest substantial and justified dissatisfaction. However, the source and extent of these feelings is unclear. Is dissatisfaction due to excessive expectations or to poor product performance? Are the problems severe or minor? How many complaints are not registered by any of the reporting systems? Perhaps the most perplexing question concerns the acceptable level of dissatisfaction—an issue that pervades most discussions of consumerism.

A *Warranties and Service*

29 NEW LEGISLATION AND THE PROSPECTS FOR REAL WARRANTY REFORM

Laurence P. Feldman

For many years, consumer interest groups sought reforms in consumer product warranty practices through either legislation or regulation. Early efforts in these directions were largely without success, although the new consumer protection climate that evolved over the last decade saw some changes in warrantor practices on a voluntary basis. Warranties of such appliance makers as Whirlpool and General Electric were simplified, and these and other firms took steps to see that consumers seeking redress for their complaints were more fairly dealt with.[1]

However, these efforts relied solely on the goodwill of the warrantor; they provided little in the way of practical recourse to consumers who believed that they had been treated inequitably. Furthermore, the voluntary warranty reform movement was not broad enough to offer major benefits across a wide range of products.

It was largely because of these shortcomings that in 1975 Congress passed the Magnuson-Moss Warranty–Federal Trade Commission Improvement Act, a major purpose of which is the reform of consumer product warranty practices. This article examines the question of just how effective the act will be in achieving real warranty reform. Specifically, the purpose here is to (1) describe the problems that the Magnuson-Moss Act is designed to solve or ameliorate, (2) review the

[1] U.S., Congress, Senate, Committee on Commerce, *Initiatives in Corporate Responsibility,* 92nd Cong., 2d sess., 1972.

Reprinted from *Journal of Marketing* 40 (July 1976), pp. 41–47, published by the American Marketing Association.

provisions of the act as they apply to these problems, and (3) examine the prospects for their solution given the provisions of the new law. In this regard, fundamental procedural, structural, and other difficulties involved in instituting warranty reform are also discussed.

CONSUMER PROBLEMS WITH WARRANTIES

Differing Perceptions of the Warranty Function

A basic cause of warranty problems is that consumers and warrantors have quite different perceptions of the role that a warranty plays in the marketplace. For the consumer, the mere existence of a warranty is a positive influence in the purchasing process. Offered the choice between two similar products, one of which is warranted, a consumer will prefer the one that is warranted, even in the face of some extra cost. The warranty is taken as an added assurance of product quality and value, even though this may not be the case.

In part, this misperception arises from consumer ignorance of warranty law. The consumer's assumption is that the warranty grants rights of redress in the event of a product malfunction that do not exist in the absence of the warranty. But under the Uniform Commercial Code, which is in effect in all states except Louisiana, most sales of tangible goods are covered by implied warranties of merchantability and fitness even in the absence of an explicit (express) warranty. An implied warranty of merchantability warrants that a product is fit for the ordinary purpose for which it is sold, is properly packaged and labeled, and conforms to any promises or affirmations made on the label. An implied warranty of fitness applies in the special situation where a buyer relies on the warrantor's judgment that the product will be fit to use for a particular purpose.

Warrantors, however, have regarded their warranties in a different light. Often warranties are perceived as promotional devices in a market characterized by physically similar competing products, rather than as instruments offering real consumer benefit. There is another, more fundamental, difference between consumer and warrantor perceptions. While consumers have regarded warranty provisions as a grant of rights of redress that might otherwise not exist, to warrantors a warranty was a legal instrument that limited their obligations to the purchaser. It did this principally by disclaiming all rights of recourse arising under the implied warranties of merchantability and fitness.

In principal, a warrantor has every right to limit his obligations on the premise that a warranty is part of the bargain between warrantor and consumer, that a consumer is free to modify or reject it if he finds its terms unacceptable. But the fact is that the two parties to the transaction are not in an equal bargaining position. As warrantors became more remote from consumers, as products became more complex and difficult to evaluate, and as mass merchandising and packaging became commonplace, the assumption of equality of bargaining power that underlies the Uniform Commercial Code became increasingly unrealistic. The effect of these factors was to make it difficult for consumers both to determine and understand the terms of warranties prior to purchase and to ensure that warrantors lived up to their obligations in the event of product malfunction.

Lack of Consumer Comprehension of Warranty Terms

Consumer comprehension of warrany terms has been clouded by several factors, including misleading representations of warranty terms, lack of access to written warranties prior to purchase, and the obscurity of terms in which warranties are couched.

Misleading Representations

Although the FTC has guidelines to prevent the use of deceptive language in the advertising of warranties, promotional stakes have been sufficiently high to encourage warrantors to use advertising that creates a misleading impression with respect to warranty coverage. The automobile company that stressed the availability of free loaner cars as part of its warranty program placed consideraby less emphasis on the fact that the dealer must have your car for at least eight hours before the loaner would be made available.

A less widespread problem of misrepresentation arose in the case of irresponsible statements by salespeople. Intent on making the sale, a salesperson might assure the customer that the product was "fully guaranteed," without concern for the correctness of such assurances.

Lack of Access

Another complaint voiced by critics of consumer warranty practices was that it was difficult, and sometimes impossible, for consumers to determine the precise terms of the warranty prior to purchase due to lack of access. The warranty document itself was usually sealed in a package designed to provide security against damage and pilferage. One effect of this emphasis on package security was that salesclerks were unwilling to open a package to procure the warranty unless the consumer committed himself to the purchase. Two researchers, who spent a month shopping in an attempt to compare written warranties for various products, were frequently told by salesclerks that they could not see the warranty in advance of purchase because the opened package would suggest to subsequent buyers that the item had been purchased and returned.[2]

OBSCURITY OF TERMS

Even if the warranty was available for inspection prior to the consummation of the sale, often it was couched in obscure terms that served to impede, rather than promote, consumer understanding. In part, this was due to the warrantor's greater concern with the legal precision of the language used than with the extent to which the document communicated to the buyer. Few consumers could be expected to understand the relatively commonplace disclaimer that "this warranty is in lieu of all others, express or implied." A lawyer commenting on the language used described the documents as " 'boiler plate,' prepackaged warranties presented on a take it or leave it basis."[3]

Unreasonable Warranty Provisions

In combination, misleading representation, lack of access, and obscurity of terms permitted warrantors to use written warranties that imposed unreasonable burdens on the unwary buyer. An example is the stove manufacturer's warranty that stated: "Our obligation under this warranty will be to *repair or replace at our option F. O. B. our factory* without charge by us any part or parts that prove defective within the terms of warranty—*said defect being confirmed by our inspection*"[4] Not only did this warranty leave it entirely up to the warrantor to determine both whether the defect would be corrected and the form that correction would take, but it also contained the unreasonable requirement that this bulky product be shipped back to the factory at the consumer's expense. Similarly, it was commonplace for mobile home warranties to require that a purchaser seeking satisfaction under the warranty return the mobile home to the factory for repairs, by appointment, with transportation charges in both directions prepaid.[5]

Industry representatives argued that reputable manufacturers did not enforce provisions requiring that bulky products be returned to the

---

[2] U.S., Congress, House, Committee on Interstate and Foreign Commerce, *Hearings, Consumer Warranty Protection, 1973,* 93rd Cong., 2nd sess., 1973, p. 101.

[3] U.S., Congress, House, Committee on Interstate and Foreign Commerce, *Hearings, Consumer Warranty Protection, 1971,* 92nd Cong., 1st sess., 1971, p. 234.

[4] U.S., Congress, Senate, Committee on Commerce, *Hearings, Consumer Product Guaranty Act, S. 3074,* 91st Cong., 2nd sess., 1970, p. 246. [Emphasis added.]

[5] Same reference as footnote 2.

factory for service, but rather made arrangements to have their products serviced in the field. Nonetheless, such provisions gave the warrantor complete discretion over the circumstances under which the warranty would be honored and were regarded by many consumer advocates as unconscionable.

Lack of Performance

It was not until he experienced trouble with the product that the consumer became aware of the deficiencies in warranty protection. Such product malfunctions became more frequent in recent years, in part because of the growing complexity of consumer products and in part, according to some critics, because warrantors failed to provide adequate quality control. The effect of this practice, the critics alleged, was to shift the burden of defective products out of the factory and onto the shoulders of the consumer.[6]

Regardless of the cause of the malfunction, consumers experienced difficulty in obtaining satisfaction of their warranty claims for several reasons. In some instances, it was not clear who was responsible for the provision of warranty service. For example, a product might be accompanied by a written warranty that failed to give the name and address of the warrantor, leaving it to the consumer to determine for himself the source from which satisfaction was to be obtained.

The determination of responsibility for warranty obligations was particularly difficult where the satisfactory operation of the product depended on expert installation by a third party, as in the case of air conditioners and plumbing fixtures. In such instances, manufacturers would frame their warranties so as to protect themselves from liability in the event of improper installation. When the product malfunctioned, the warrantor could claim that it was the installer who was at fault, regardless of the true cause. The installer, for his part, would counter that the defect lay in the product and not the installation. Often, the hapless consumer was caught in the middle of these conflicting claims. Even more complex problems arose when the warrantor's product was sold by a retailer who contracted the installation to a fourth party.

Once such problems were overcome, consumers still had the difficulty of obtaining satisfactory warranty service. This was particularly true, for example, in the case of new cars, as was attested to by a long parade of witnesses at FTC hearings on automobile warranties. In the automobile industry, the practice of "fobbing off" customers with non-performed warranty work was so prevalent that the trade had developed

[6] Same reference as footnote 4 and footnote 3.

its own terms to describe the treatment: *wall jobs* or *sunbaths,* where a car received for warranty repairs was parked by a wall or left out in the sun, remaining unrepaired in both instances.[7]

Apart from this pseudo performance of warranty service, consumers frequently encountered situations where the quality of the warranty repairs that were done was substandard. In some cases, multiple warranty repairs were dragged out until the warranty period expired, with consumers being forced to assume the full cost of now out-of-warranty repairs.[8]

REFORMS EMBODIED IN THE MAGNUSON-MOSS ACT

The result of numerous congressional hearings at which consumer problems with warranties were aired was the passage of the Magnuson-Moss Act. The act contains specific provisions with respect to warranties, and gives the Federal Trade Commission the power to promulgate rules affecting warranty practices for any product warranted in writing with an actual cost to the consumer exceeding five dollars. Following are selected provisions of the act that pertain to the warranty problems just discussed.

Measures to Improve Awareness and Comprehension of Warranty Terms

Several provisions of the act are designed to overcome the problem of misleading representation of warranty terms prior to purchase. The FTC is directed to institute a rule that requires a warrantor to make the terms of the written warranty "available to the consumer (or prospective consumer) prior to the sale of the product to him." In addition, the act empowers the FTC to promulgate rules that specify the manner and form in which warranties may be used in advertising and other promotional material.

Other measures are designed to see that the warranty provides consumers with necessary and meaningful information. The FTC has the power to require that warranties contain specific information, including such items as the identity and location of the warrantor, exceptions or exclusions from warranty coverage, and the procedure to be followed for a

---

[7] Federal Trade Commission Report on Auto Warranties, p. 36.

[8] Same reference as footnote 3.

consumer to obtain satisfaction under the warranty. Unless specifically exempted by the FTC, warrantors of products that cost consumers more than ten dollars are required to designate their written warranties as either "full" or "limited" to indicate the type of coverage.

A seller giving a "full" warranty is required to remedy the defective product within "a reasonable time" without charge. In fact, he may be required to compensate a consumer for incidental expenses arising from the warrantor's failure to remedy a defect within a reasonable time. After the warrantor has made "a reasonable number" of unsuccessful attempts at remedy, the consumer may elect either replacement or refund without charge. A full warranty must also state conspicuously any limitation of damages under the written or implied warranties. A "limited" warranty is one that falls short of these and other stipulations necessary for a full warranty.

The FTC has the power to specify in detail the obligations of sellers offering a full warranty and their applicability to different classes of products. This flexibility permits the FTC to establish differential standards, by product class, as to what, for example, constitutes "a reasonable number" of attempts at remedy before replacement or refund must be offered.

An important provision, long sought after by consumer advocates, is an outright prohibition on disclaiming implied warranties; although, for limited warranties only, they may be restricted as to duration. The intent here is to prevent a warrantor from escaping his obligations under the Uniform Commercial Code with respect to the implied warranties of "merchantability" and "fitness."

Strengthening Consumer Recourse

Consumer recourse in the event of a defective product is strengthened under the Magnuson-Moss Act in two ways: (1) by spelling out the obligations of warrantors in the event of a malfunctioning product, and (2) by indicating the type of recourse available to both consumers and the FTC when satisfaction of consumers' claims is not forthcoming.

As has already been discussed, the act explicitly defines the obligations of warrantors offering a full warranty. In addition, in the case of both full and limited warranties, the FTC is empowered to make rules with respect to the extension of the warranty period in those instances where consumers are deprived of the use of a product because of its failure while under warranty. Another measure, intended to clarify the responsibility of third parties, makes warrantors directly responsible for the actions of their designated service representatives.

The act also spells out the means by which recourse can be sought. Warrantors are encouraged, but not required, to establish informal dispute settlement procedures that meet FTC standards. Where they choose to do so, the procedure must be incorporated into the written warranty. An incentive to warrantors for the establishment of such procedures is that consumers are required to resort to the informal settlement procedure before taking civil action in the courts.

Where informal procedures are not available, or fail to provide remedy, the act helps both consumers and regulators by providing avenues of recource in addition to the normal channels available under civil law. One of these permits the filing of a federal class action suit in cases where several consumers have been similarly damaged by a warrantor's failure to perform, subject to the following conditions: the amount of any individual claim must be $25 or more, the total claims of the class must amount to at least $50,000, and the number of named plaintiffs must be equal to or greater than one hundred. The first condition represents a considerable relaxation of the normal jurisdictional requirement for such suits of a minimum individual claim of $10,000; it is intended to make class action a viable means of obtaining redress in warranty disputes. The other two limitations serve to restrict its use only to instances where significant issues affecting many consumers are involved.

The act also provides for the exercise of regulatory sanctions by making a warrantor's failure to comply with any of its provisions a violation of Section 5(a) of the Federal Trade Commission Act, which declares "unfair or deceptive acts or practices . . . unlawful," and therefore subject to FTC sanction. In addition, the FTC and the U.S. attorney general are empowered to obtain a temporary restraining order or preliminary injunction if they can make a proper showing that a violation of the act makes it in the public interest to do so.

PROSPECTS FOR IMPROVED WARRANTY PROTECTION

A basic objective of the Magnuson-Moss Act is to reform questionable warranty practices while maintaining equity in the marketplace. In light of the great diversity of products for which express warranties are given, the task of attaining this objective is a formidable one. These products have differing servicing requirements and are sold under widely varying circumstances. In many instances, the only common motivation of the consumers who purchase them is the desire to receive good value.

The Regulatory Challenge

It is not surprising, therefore, that the framers of this legislation found it necessary to give the Federal Trade Commission a great deal of discretion in formulating rules necessary for its successful implementation. An examination of some of the problems inherent in this task, and the initial efforts by the FTC to resolve them, sheds light on the prospects for substantive warranty reform.

The FTC's job of devising effective trade regulation rules covering warranties is complicated by the wide variety of product and market situations to which they must apply, including differences in product type, packaging, and the method and control of distribution. In the area of prior warranty disclosure, the commission has promulgated a rule applicable to all warranted products that cost the consumer more than $15. Under this rule (with the exception of catalog, mail-order, and door-to-door sales, where special provisions apply), sellers may elect to use one or more of the following means of prior warranty disclosure: (1) displaying the text of the warranty "in close conjunction" to each product, (2) maintaining a binder of written warranties close to the point of sale, (3) displaying the warranty on the package, and (4) placing a notice disclosing the text of the warranty "in close proximity" to displays of the product to which it applies.[9]

While this rule embodies considerably more flexibility than the original FTC proposal, which was restricted to the use of binders only, its enforcement will present numerous problems. Where the warrantor and seller are different parties, it will be difficult in some instances to determine the responsibility for noncompliance. In many cases effective compliance will hinge on the willingness of indifferent store personnel to keep warranty binders intact and up-to-date or to stack merchandise so that the warranty on the package is displayed. An additional problem that will ultimately have to be resolved in the courts is the determination of what constitutes "close conjunction" or "close proximity."

Product diversity, in particular, will also influence the effectiveness of FTC rule making with respect to the requirement that warranties be designated as full or limited. For example, should the requirements for a full warranty on a refrigerator be the same as those for a full warranty on a can of paint? The act allows the FTC to formulate requirements for full warranties that differ by product class. In addition, the commission has the discretionary power to determine which warranties may be excused from the designation requirements. But these provisions for adminis-

---

[9] *Federal Register,* December 31, 1975, pp. 60189–60190.

trative flexibility do not solve the designation problem. They merely place the responsibility for decion making in this area in the hands of a regulatory agency that is not well known for either its discrimination or its decisiveness.

In one area covered by the act, regulatory problems stem from the difficulty of determining the point of diminishing returns with respect to the provision of consumer information. The act empowers the FTC to require up to thirteen specific items of information in a written warranty with the objective of providing consumers with more and better warranty information. Accordingly, the FTC has promulgated a rule requiring nine separate items of information in consumer product warranties. Some of these, including the name and address of the warrantor and the part or parts that are covered, are clear-cut and undoubtedly beneficial. But three of the items may include such statements as the following:[10]

> Some states do not allow limitations on how long an implied warranty lasts, so the above limitation may not apply to you.
>
> Some states do not allow the exclusion or limitation of incidental or consequential damages, so the above limitation or exclusion may not apply to you.
>
> This warranty gives you specific legal rights, and you may also have other rights which vary from state to state.

From the viewpoint of effective regulation, it is valid to ask first whether consumers will understand these legalistic statements, and second whether a written warranty that includes all the required information will deter consumers rather than encourage them to read warranties and to obtain the redress to which they are entitled.

Effect on Consumers

Another way to evaluate the effect of the Warranty Act is to consider it in terms of its probable impact on consumers.

Let us look first at the impact of one of the most fundamental provisions of the act: the restriction on warrantors' freedom to disclaim implied warranties. While the intent is to preserve consumers' rights with respect to implied warranties, its effect may be minimal because it does not remove burdens on the consumer that may make the exercise of these rights impractical.

---

[10] Same reference as footnote 9.

The fact is that a consumer who wants to invoke his rights under an implied warranty must take the initiative. This may involve relatively little effort where an informal dispute settlement mechanism exists. However, where that is not the case, or when satisfaction is not forthcoming, the consumer will have to resort to other measures such as a civil suit or regulatory action. In most cases, the cost in time and money to an individual consumer is not likely to justify the prospective benefits. An exception occurs when a large number of consumers are similarly damaged and the situation meets the requirements for class action. These requirements, while not as restrictive as formerly, still do not overcome the procedural obstacles that have been placed in the way of such suits.[11]

Another problem may arise if a large number of warrantors find the requirements for a full warranty to be too onerous and opt for a limited warranty or none at all. The effect would be to make the value of the protection afforded consumers by full warranties almost irrelevant. If that is not the case, and full warranties are offered, consumers who buy fully warranted products should experience real benefits arising from such provisions as those imposing a time limit on the repair period and those allowing consumers to opt for replacement or refund if the repair is unsatisfactory.

Even these benefits, however, may be more apparent than real. Underlying the Magnuson-Moss Act is the idea that the unsatisfactory warranty service experienced by consumers has been the result of a deliberate warrantor policy. An intent of the act is to change such policy. In many cases, however, the frustration encountered by consumers seeking redress on their warranty claims has been experienced not as a result of deliberate warrantor intent, but because of structural factors in the marketplace. These structural problems are less amenable to correction through legislation of the type embodied in the act.

The nature of this problem is exemplified by the case of a major source of warranty dissatisfaction: automobiles. Undoubtedly, some of this dissatisfaction has arisen because of sharp practices of the type already described. But in many cases, consumer problems with automobile warranty service are symptomatic of a more fundamental problem: the shortage of mechanics. A 1969 study of Ford Motor Company dealerships showed that Ford dealers could have effectively used an additional 18,000 mechanics.[12] Similar situations exist in other industries where the technical complexities of the product has outpaced the available supply

[11] Laurence P. Feldman, "Expanding the Potential of Federal Consumer Class Action," in *1975 Combined Proceedings,* Edward M. Mazze, ed. (Chicago: American Marketing Assn., 1976), pp. 597–600.

[12] Same reference as footnote 4.

of trained servicepeople. The best solution to poor warranty service arising from an inadequate pool of knowledgeable repairmen is not regulation of the terms of the warranty, but increased provision for the recruitment and training of service personnel.

Unanswered Questions

There is reason to believe that the beneficial effect of the Magnuson-Moss Act on consumer warranty problems will not be as great as its proponents have suggested. Although the testimony supporting the consumer position on the legislation suggested that there was some basis for warranty complaints, it failed to outline either the scope of the problem or how the new act would solve them. It was, in many ways, reminiscent of the consumer testimony that preceded the passage of the Fair Packaging and Labeling Act, which has not been noteworthy for its real furtherance of the consumer interest.

For example, many of the Warranty Act's provisions were intended to make consumers more aware of warranty terms prior to purchase and to increase their understanding of warranty coverage. Yet little evidence was presented at the congressional hearings to show how the measures now embodied in the act would achieve these objectives. In fact, little is known about the role of the warranty in a sales transaction or about the extent to which this role varies by product and by the circumstances surrounding the sale.

Passage of the act should have been *preceded* by systematic and controlled research on warranty issues. For example, with respect to the prior disclosure of warranties, what proportion of consumers wanted to see the terms of the warranty before buying but were unable to do so? Would those who wished to read the warranty be more likely to do so if it were posted in the store as part of the sales display, or would it be more beneficial to have it printed on the carton? To what extent will the inclusion of all the terms the FTC may require in a written warranty actually deter consumers from reading it? Will consumers really understand the significance of a "full" warranty as opposed to one that is "limited"? What will their reaction be to warranties of each type? How will the answers to each of these questions differ by product class and circumstances of sale? Last, but not least, assuming the answers to these questions are known, it is necessary to answer the crucial question of whether the costs for consumers that the warranty reform measures are likely to entail are worth the benefits that consumers will receive from them.

Now that the Magnuson-Moss Act has become law, it is the responsibility of the FTC to obtain the answers to such questions prior to engaging in rule-making activity in the field of warranties. Past performance on other consumer issues casts a shadow on that agency's ability either to obtain this type of behavioral information itself or to require it from others who testify at its proceedings. For these reasons, despite the intentions of the act, the prospects for real consumer benefit arising from its implementation are clouded at best. At worst, the warranty provisions of the Magnuson-Moss Act will constitute one more piece of consumer legislation where the form far out-shadows the substance.

B *Safety and Liability*

30 THE MINDLESS PURSUIT OF SAFETY

Walter Guzzardi, Jr.

Out of this nettle, danger, we pluck this flower, safety.

Henry IV, Part I

Now ascending among the many blessings that the citizenry expects of government in our society is that flower, safety. Popular demand for this latest entitlement has become practically a national frenzy, and the rush is on to give us full protection from those former-friends-turned-enemies, the myriad products and conveniences and adornments of the industrial age. The presumption is that safety can be wrung in ever-larger increments from manufacturers, who are thought to be exposing us all to needless hazards in return for the equally needless addition of a few pennies of profit. Only make them forgo this petty gain, only force them to build more safety into new products and to fix what they have already put out there on the market, and there you have it—behold the bargain-rate splendors of the riskless world.

Right now, we are pursuing this chimera in two different but related ways, both of which can safely be called dangerous. Carrying out with religious zealotry the sweeping mandates of Congress, regulatory agencies engaged in social governance are forcing the recall of millions of products in the name of consumer protection. And instead of supplying sanity, the courts are regularly interpreting the law to hold manufacturers liable for huge sums when their products can in some way be

---

Reprinted from *Fortune,* April 9, 1979, pp. 54–64, by special permission.

blamed for injuries. Both agencies and courts frequently ignore or misrepresent true cost and evade the question of who is going to pay it; both accept the appearance of social benefit in place of its reality; and both bring about an uneconomic allocation of risk shifting too much away from the consumer and back upon the manufacturer. Cost/benefit ratios are admittedly complicated in this field, especially when they concern, as they sometimes must, suffering or death. But it remains inexcusable for our society to be so deceived by the desire for yet another gift by government that we refuse to consider how today's policies will run up tomorrow's bills. Relatively speaking, Faust was a long-range planner.

The primary enforcement tool being used to bring us more safety is the product recall, and the most convincing display of its power can be seen in the confrontation between the government and the auto industry. The protagonist there is Joan Claybrook, the intelligent, formidable, Nader-trained, bred-in-the-bones adversary of the industry who is now head of the National Highway Traffic Safety Administration. Cars were being recalled long before Claybrook came to her present eminence. But NHTSA's policy then gave greater weight to working out standards beforehand with manufacturers, and ordering recalls when the standards were not met; although the manufacturers groaned about the standards, at least they knew what they had to do. But today, while NHTSA is still writing standards, the agency seems to have lost its interest in them as a means of effecting recalls. "NHTSA's standards have to be so minimal that they would be self-defeating," says Lynn Bradford, director of the office of defects investigation. Besides, NHTSA took one of its few beatings in court after trying to impose complicated standards for air brakes on trucks.

So NHTSA has been moving its legal base to higher ground. It is now making extensive use of its power to order recalls whenever *substantial numbers of a safety-related defect* show up, and present an *unreasonable risk* of accident or injury. From those wide-branching concepts, which derive from the Congress, the bodies of the auto companies as we know them today may presently swing. For by its rulings and the generous interpretations of the courts, NHTSA has made those italicized words mean almost anything it has wanted them to mean. Any number can be substantial; any failure of any part even after years of good performance can be a defect; any defect may be safety-related; and any defect related to safety can present an unreasonable risk—not literally, but very nearly, that is the legal case today. As one embittered official at Ford Motor says, "There are no standards. Whatever we do, NHTSA and the courts just say we should have done it better."

For a while, Ford and General Motors fought to keep from ensnarement in that particular web. But the courts, which like Congress have felt

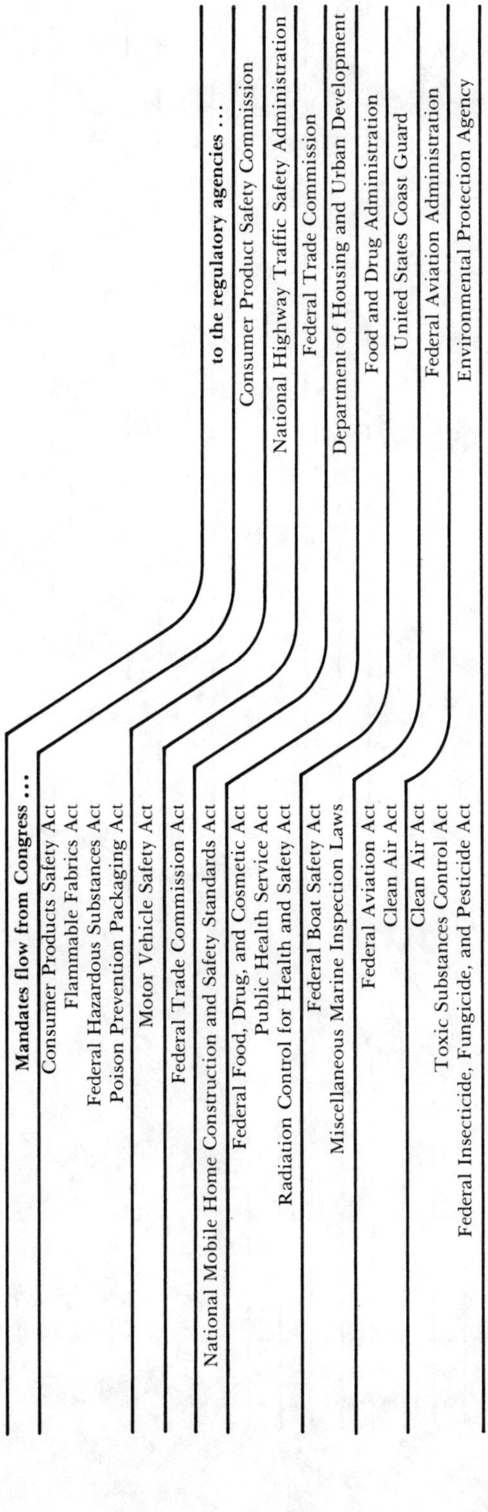

Mandates flow from Congress ...
Consumer Products Safety Act
Flammable Fabrics Act
Federal Hazardous Substances Act
Poison Prevention Packaging Act
Motor Vehicle Safety Act
Federal Trade Commission Act
National Mobile Home Construction and Safety Standards Act
Federal Food, Drug, and Cosmetic Act
Public Health Service Act
Radiation Control for Health and Safety Act
Federal Boat Safety Act
Miscellaneous Marine Inspection Laws
Federal Aviation Act
Clean Air Act
Clean Air Act
Toxic Substances Control Act
Federal Insecticide, Fungicide, and Pesticide Act
to the regulatory agencies ...
Consumer Product Safety Commission
National Highway Traffic Safety Administration
Federal Trade Commission
Department of Housing and Urban Development
Food and Drug Administration
United States Coast Guard
Federal Aviation Administration
Environmental Protection Agency

conferring these recall powers ...	involving millions of products ...	and leading to these recalls
★ ● ■	Most consumer products	75 Chance Manufacturing amusement-park rides
★ ● ■	Hazardous substances	5 million Mattel Battlestar Galactica toy missiles
◆	Medical devices	
★ ■	Motor vehicles and tires	1.4 million Ford Pintos and Bobcats 14.5 million Firestone "500" radials
★ ● ■	Advertising	Corrective ads for Listerine
★ ■ ▲	Mobile homes	2,000 Tappan gas stoves
■ ▲	Food, drugs, and cosmetics Medical devices Radiation-emitting devices Biologic products	Ralston Purina animal feed Pepperidge Farm pretzels
★ ● ■ ▲	Ships Pleasure boats	4,000 Johnson and Evinrude outboard engines
	Aircraft and components	335 wide-bodied aircraft
	Motor vehicles and engines Hazardous chemical substances Pesticides	310,000 American Motors cars and trucks

★ Can order recalls

● Can effect recalls by threat of seizure, injunction, etc.

■ Can make rules that bring about recalls

▲ Can suspend certification

◆ Can force recall of misleading advertising

the heat of the consumer movement, have found NHTSA to be very, very right. For instance:

A stop at the Pitman Arms. "Pitman arms," part of the steering mechanisms, were failing in some 1959–60 Cadillacs when NHTSA began its investigation in 1974. The failure was coming only with very sharp turns made at very slow speeds—most often when a car was being parked. Since no one could prove injuries as a result of the failures, and since the 43,400 cars of that model still left on the road had gone through 96 percent of their lives, G.M. could not see the "unreasonable risk." But the court held that whenever steering or other vital components fail without warning, that's an unreasonable risk. In the end, G.M. had to notify the owners of the remaining cars (by then eighteen years old) that they had a defect. G.M. made the repairs without charge.

Breaking point. Seat pins were breaking off one side of the driver's seat in some 1968–69 Mustangs and Cougars. NHTSA cited a failure in fifty-seven out of some 500,000 cars. Ford pointed out that the defect had never led to a serious injury. The company lost, and recalled the cars.

Reinventing the wheel. A number of wheels on some 1960–65 G.M. trucks were collapsing when the load limits of the trucks were exceeded by overweight campers. G.M. argued that the overloading, against which it warned in its instruction manuals, constituted owner abuse. The court held that there was abuse, all right, but it was "reasonably foreseeable"; everybody knows trucks are going to be overloaded. Only "unforeseeable abuse" might have excused G.M.

Supporting a G.M. petition to the Supreme Court, Volkswagenwerk AG made the point that "nearly every accident situation involving an automobile, no matter how bizarre, is foreseeable, if only because in the last fifty years drivers have discovered just about every conceivable way of wrecking an automobile." But the Supreme Court declined to hear the case. Since then, the auto industry has been reluctant to fight NHTSA in the federal courts.

Recalls also dump truckloads of unfavorable publicity on the car companies because of the tone of the letters that the companies have to send out to begin the recall. Millions of copies of the letter may go to owners of the cars being recalled, even when only a small percentage of the cars have that particular defect. The letters, which are practically dictated by NHTSA, recount the horrors that *might* happen: a typical one might say that the owner's car may have this defect, that if it does the part might fail, and if that happens the driver may lose control of the car and there may be an accident. All that is true. But it is also a doomsday scenario.

Just what would happen if the angry Claybrook became angrier still nobody knows, but the scene might do for a movie by Irwin Allen, the master of disaster. In 1975, about 1.5 million vehicles were recalled. In 1976, still pre-Claybrook, the number went to three million. In 1977, however, a record number of 10.7 million vehicles were recalled; that number included about as many cars as were manufactured that year. Last year recalls came down to 7.9 million. But if that made the year a numerical disappointment for NHTSA, there were compensations: victories were won over Firestone (14.5 million tires recalled) and over Ford with the Pinto recall.

As for 1979, it could be a wonderful year for NHTSA. The agency has issued two "consumer advisories," and has got out other kinds of publicity as well, warning that transmissions in some Ford vehicles have been jumping from park into reverse; included in the advisories are allegations that twenty-three deaths occurred as a result. (NHTSA's advice to drivers includes the suggestion that they turn off their engines when they get out of their cars, which would certainly be a cheap fix.) Ford has done enormous amounts of testing, but says it has found no evidence of any defect; it thinks that the information coming in about the number of accidents has been skewed by NHTSA's publicity. But the shadow of a recall, amounting to nine million cars and trucks made from 1970 to 1978, still hangs over Dearborn. Whether NHTSA would ever recognize any limits to recalling is anybody's guess: Frank Berndt, associated administrator for enforcement, muses that "if we were faced with a massive recall, say 15 million cars, we might try something else, rather than destroy the industry."

The crucial questions about all those recalls, of course, are how much they cost, and how much safety they are buying. None of the car companies breaks out figures about recall costs, which consist of payments at retail labor rates to the dealers who do the work, and the cost of the replacement parts plus some profit to the dealers for handling them. Neither will any of them estimate the value of the executive time spent on recalls—Henry Ford II himself worked hard on the Pinto case—or the public-relations damage. Still, there's not much doubt that the auto companies have had to lay out hundreds of millions of dolllars for recalls, and that amount is being repaid by new-car buyers. When it passed the law obliging manufacturers to pay for recalls, the Senate Commerce Committee thought it was ensuring that "the consumer never again will be forced to pay for the repair of safety related defects," but its rhetoric was better than its economics. Chester V. Barion, general manager of the parts and service division at Ford, remarks, "These recall costs are substantial, and they will be reflected in future pricing." To whatever the total cost is to the industry must be added, of course, the social cost of operating NHTSA: it has spent $1 billion in its twelve-year life.

As for safety, a very strong inference can be drawn that society could be getting much more of it by spending the money in a different way. Lots of research goes to show that unsafe vehicles cause a very small proportion of highway accidents and deaths. The definitive study on accident causation by a special research group at Indiana University found that some 75 percent of auto accidents are caused by "human factors," generally meaning speeding, inattention on the part of the driver, and bad decision-making in a crisis—all worsened by drinking. "Environmental factors," such as icy roads, obstructed view, and poor highway design are the next most frequent cause. "Vehicle factors" cause only about 5 percent of accidents. Brake failures and bald or underinflated tires take a big chunk of that percentage.

So instead of pressing on with recalls, it would be more rewarding to urge better driver education, regular vehicle inspection, and tougher laws about drinking. But those are unpopular causes to promote. NHTSA has found it politically much more rewarding to wheel up the cannons and open fire on those centers of power around Detroit.

The terrain there is also pocked with shells fired by another body, the Environmental Protection Agency, which has the power to order recalls of cars that do not meet emission standards. Since the advent of the Carter Administration, the EPA, like NHTSA, has been shooting from the high ground. The shift in emphasis has come with the methods of testing for emissions, which have moved from inspection and certification of new cars in the plants to what is called "end-use enforcement"—testing cars chosen at random from models suspected of being in violation after they have been driven for a while by their owners. EPA says this is the way to find out what is happening in the real world. But a Ford executive points out, "In new-car testing, the average is what governs. Now EPA is looking not at averages but at individual cars. We're petrified."

What worries Detroit most is that this shift may oblige the companies to pay for fixes on cars whose antipollution devices have been abused or tampered with by their owners. There's some reason for this fear, because while pollution controls can upgrade the quality of the air, they can also downgrade the performance of the car. Lots of owners make adjustments to get smoother rides and better mileage—and don't worry much if they increase emissions.

Consequently, there's a big battle coming between the industry and EPA over what constitutes proper maintenance, with Chrysler as the point company. EPA wants Chrysler to recall 208,000 of its 1975 cars that the agency insists are exceeding emission standards. Chrysler says the owners have tampered with the carburetion. EPA replies that the fault lies with Chrysler's carburetor designs and adjustment procedures. Millions of dollars in fixing costs for all the auto companies hang on the case, now before the courts.

Although EPA's new policies toward emissions may greatly increase the costs to the industry and the number of recalled cars, the agency is far from satisfied. Ben Jackson, a deputy assistant administrator at EPA, says, "We could go on ordering recalls and logging numbers and looking good. But it's fool's play to make a numbers game out of this. We want the standards met." Jackson claims that after the manufacturers have been advised that some of their cars aren't qualifying, they present plans for the cheapest possible fixes—"a tweak of the carburetion mixture when a carburetor replacement might be best." Negotiations over what constitutes a proper fix can go on for months, Jackson says, while the companies benefit from the delay: the more time that goes by, the fewer the cars they have to adjust. To end this Ping-Pong game, Jackson wants the EPA to be given more punitive powers, so that the costs of the dilatory tactics to the companies would become too high. Ford denies using such tactics, and shudders at the prospect of still higher costs for emissions control.

By way of its authority over marketing practices, including advertising and warranties, the Federal Trade Commission is also prancing around on the recall stage. Its most interesting role so far began in 1976, when Ford discovered that some of its small cars had pistons that were scuffing cylinder walls. Although the warranties on some of the cars had expired, Ford was making what it calls "goodwill adjustments"—repairs free to those customers who complained. The FTC took the view that the repairs should be offered to all customers, not just complaining ones: what Ford called "goodwill adjustments" the agency looked on as "secret warranties." Ford notified about two million customers that it would make a free fix.

The FTC, though, had got the wind up, and it has gone on to develop a very expansive case against Ford, going far beyond piston scuffing. The commission is charging that Ford is offering "seriously defective cars" for sale, and is misrepresenting them in its advertising as "durable and reliable." In a proposal lunatic even in the religion of regulation, the FTC is suggesting that to protect itself from charges of false advertising, Ford must conspicuously display in every showroom a poster enumerating the twenty principal flaws, both potential and known, to be found in its cars, and must also plaster a defect notice to the windshields of new cars that are "subject to a substantial defect."

Swallowing hard, Ford has responded by saying that its cars are indeed reliable and durable, that it can't find out about defects (which the FTC can't define anyway) until they show up, and besides, in effect, the FTC should drop dead—the case is way beyond its purview. Ford has not got around to suggesting that the FTC should post in its corridors a list of the agency's twenty greatest failings, including its recent questionnaire about practices in the legal profession that the American Bar Association calls "unreasonable, of questionable legality and doubtful usefulness." Still, if the FTC has its way, the auto industry may end up with yet another overseer with de facto power to effect recalls—assuming, that is, that when NHTSA and the EPA get through, there are still some cars left out there.

The FTC has also just worked out with Fedders a consent agreement for the repair of some 40,000 heat pumps. There, the commission contended that selling a product is an implicit assertion that the product is free of defects. That broad theory could serve as the basis for many other FTC-influenced recalls in lots of other industries. Formerly, the FTC confined its recall actions to making manufacturers eat their words. The most famous example involved Warner-Lambert, which was forced to include in its next $10 million of advertising an assertion that "Listerine will not help prevent colds or sore throats."

For all of the deficiencies of those belligerent agencies, they do have generally understandable recall policies, if costly ones, and they never have to wonder what to do. But the Consumer Product Safety Commission, which has played a role in over 1,200 recalls of millions of products during its six-year life, lacks both surety and a proper occupation. The fault lies not with the people but with the purpose. The Consumer Product Safety Act, and the four other acts that Congress has charged the commission with carrying out, add up to the loosest and most indistinct mandate ever conferred on a regulatory body. Without too much exaggeration, the mandate might be summed up as a collective command to make almost everything safer.

Despite the commission's Herculean efforts, there is no way to accomplish that task by regulatory authority. Here and there, the commission may keep or get a perniciously shoddy product off the market. But basically, the CPSC, like NHTSA, has a fatal defect. Its primary thrust has to be directed against product defects and design. But the overwhelming number of product-connected injuries probably come not from faulty products, but from errors or recklessness of the consumer. As E. Patrick McGuire of the Conference Board puts it, "The most dangerous component is the consumer, and there's no way to recall him." By government standards, the CPSC may be a modest spender, but it will cost about $40 million this year, and it requires lots of paperwork from many different companies. On balance, the CPSC just doesn't pass the cost/benefit test.

The troubles and issues go deeper and are far more important at the Food and Drug Administration, but they do not for the most part center on arguments over recall power. The FDA technically has such power only in its oversight over medical devices, such as pacemakers, and over products that emit ratiation, such as TV sets and microwave ovens. It has had some disputes over standards with companies like General Electric, Zenith Radio, and RCA in those fields. Besides, while medical devices are usually simple to track down, they can be hard to fix: it's not easy to put a screwdriver to an implanted pacemaker. TV sets, on the other hand, can be fixed readily enough, but they are hard to track after they have been sold to the consumer. Generally, though, industry and agency manage to coexist without too much acerbity and waste in this field.

With food, the FDA has the authority to ban or seize what it regards as a menace to health. It cannot order recalls, but the threat of those other measures is usually enough to motivate a company to run its own recall. Although the FDA sometimes leans too hard on publicity as a weapon against food producers, it manages pretty well in the traditional fields, getting adulterated tuna, lye-sprinkled pretzels, poisonous mushrooms, and botulin-infested soup off the shelves about as well as possible, given the long chain of distribution. The more profound difficulties come with the waves of scientific and technological change that have brought food additives, such as nitrites, and products like saccharin. That area is now swirling with conflict and confusion.

The danger is that the FDA, always being carped at for inaction by some pressure group, will end by opting for safety over all other considerations. It may be moving that way with cosmetics, where it wants authority to certify ingredients as safe before they get to market. The FDA for many years has had that kind of authority over ethical drugs, keeping them off the market until they are certified "safe and efficacious"; the results range from dubious to bad. In a study that stands as a landmark in the field, Sam Peltzman of the University of Chicago has shown that the proof-of-efficacy requirement has kept some useless drugs from going on sale. But it has also deprived us of lots of beneficial new drugs, and has kept the prices of existing drugs higher by shielding them from competition. On balance, Peltzman computed a huge net loss.

The growth of the recall phenomenon in the past decade has roughly coincided with an explosion in the number of lawsuits brought against companies, large and small, for injuries associated with the use of their products. The two developments have the same provenance: the sense of rising entitlements, and the efforts of the courts and the Congress to institutionalize it.

In the field of product liability, the change comes close to a doctrinal revolution. Until a few years ago, anyone claiming damages for a product-related injury usually had to prove that the product was defective, in the sense that it failed to meet the manufacturer's own standards. One important case held the Coca Cola Bottling Co. of Fresno liable when a waitress was injured by a bottle of Coke that exploded when she was putting it into a refrigerator. She did not have to prove that there had been negligence somewhere in the long skein of Coke production. Obviously, the company didn't intend its bottles to explode; it was liable when they did.

Now that sensible doctrine is being taken to extremes, and strict liability, like Calvinism, holds the maker responsible for everything. We may be coming to the point where all the fault lies with the product, none with the conduct of its owner. Lawsuits have been entertained claiming that cars are defective (that is, not "crashworthy") when they are demolished by railroad trains, and that a car is unsafe when it hits a pedestrian. If football players sustain head injuries, the maker of helmets didn't design in enough shock resistance. The manufacturer has not yet been held liable when some swinger mashes his thumb with a hammer, but that day may come. And the link of causation has been weakened, too: courts have expanded liability to include defects that enhance or aggravate the injury, rather than directly cause it. And some awards have surpassed even the hopes of the plaintiffs, running up beyond all reason.

Recalls have fed this liability monster in several ways. "The number of recalls has surely disabused the public of the notion that we make perfect cars," dryly remarks one company lawyer. "Twenty years ago, people thought Detroit made a pretty good automobile. Now people—and jurors—are saying, 'Can't you do anything right?'" Corporate lawyers also say that after a big recall, the number of private lawsuits increases. And one of them adds, "We often notice that the legal complaints paraphrase the recall letter"—the doomsday scenario.

Government actions and private litigation also have a way of feeding on each other. When the government starts an investigation, the target company has to produce piles of documents, which later can provide the basis for private suits. The reverse is also true: government agencies monitor civil litigation looking for clues. Warnings issued by regulatory bodies also stir up suits: "Say the FDA starts to talk about side effects from a drug that has been on the market for twenty years," says Michael Hoenig, a lawyer with Herzfeld & Rubin in New York and an authority on products liability. "Shortly thereafter, you might see 200 women claiming to suffer from that complaint." Violations of FDA or CPSC or NHTSA standards can lead to private charges of negligence against a company, but the knife doesn't cut the other way: compliance doesn't immunize a company from strict liability.

In a broad sense, the process at work here is serving a moral imperative. Judges and juries are setting out not to right wrongs, but to compensate the injured. As Reynold M. Sachs, a professor of economics at American University, has explained, the emphasis is not on who is responsible but on who is best able to pay—on who, in other words, has the "deep pocket." So the laws of liability may be turning into a subterranean means for redistributing wealth.

As the trends toward more recalls and more liability go on, manufacturers will indeed make safer products. They will do more testing in their plants and, since absolute safety will remain unattainable, they will take out plenty of liability insurance. But intramural procedures can never be as efficient as the tests of actual use that the consumer carries out, and the premiums for liability insurance have gone up rapidly with the size of the awards being made for damages. So the total costs for putting so much of the incentive for safety on the manufacturer will be very high.

All this will have social effects that Congress, the agencies, and the courts would do well to ponder. To begin with, prices of products will go up to cover these new, forever-escalating components of cost—the added charges for safety. Every consumer, whether he wants or needs the new layer of protection, is going to have to pay the charge: as Reynold Sachs says, "It's a tie-in sale." What is made safe for the village idiot will cost the man of common sense more. Many people would choose to be careful, or to buy their insurance in some other form. Nonsmokers don't want to pay extra for fireproof bedsheets; people who fasten seat belts don't need the costly air bag. But everybody will have to buy such refinements anyway.

Like so many other losses of freedom, this loss will hurt more people than it helps. The beneficiaries will be those who are reckless, for we shall all be guaranteeing them compensation for the injuries they sustain, the cost of which they ought to bear themselves. Further, their ranks may increase as the penalty for recklessness diminishes. To the well off, the cost of subsidizing the reckless won't matter very much; the rich are liable to buy the most expensive products anyway. Most disadvantaged will be the poor, who will find less on the market that they can afford. The low-income man who know how to handle a chain saw or maintain a truck or take his own fire precautions in a cheap house may find those items beyond his means when they are inseparable from fancy and costly safety devices.

In order to be both free and efficient, it seems better to strive for policies that distribute incentives to avoid accidents more sensibly between consumer and manufacturer. Sometimes manufacturers make sleazy and dangerous products, and the consumer feels powerless to change that. But the corrective action transferring more incentive to the manufacturer to make products safe is now going too far.

Buyers and sellers should share more equitably the total costs of accidents—the costs to the consumer of property damage, medical expenses, and forgone income, and the costs to the manufacturer of making a safer product. One way of doing this, which follows a rule by Learned

Hand, starts with the assumption that the cost of an accident is $100,000 and the chance that it will happen is one in a hundred. The expected accident cost is thus $1,000. If the manufacturer could have avoided that accident by an expenditure of, say, $300, he ought to have done so, and should be held liable. If it would have cost him $2,000, it would be uneconomic for him to bear the whole burden; the consumer must share it by taking some risk. Such equations can get complicated and tenuous, but they can help point the way to efficiency.

That kind of analysis is often attacked on the ground that, if pushed far enough, it requires that we assign a value to human life, which is too heartless for a humanitarian society. On one level, that is true: life is priceless, death is final. But all that is beyond the reach of law and government. On a different level, we have to affix a value to life, and we do, all the time: for an additional given number of millions of dollars we could build every bridge, or mine every ton of coal, without losing a life, and we could make every railroad crossing accident-proof. But, in a difficult balance, we have decided that we cannot afford those things. Some of that same contour of thought should enter now as the government strives, from our present nettle of danger, to bring us that flower, safety.

31 THE DEVILS IN THE PRODUCT LIABILITY LAWS

Business Week

The costs of product liability are becoming a horrendous problem for U.S. industry. Last year alone manufacturers and retailers paid an estimated $2.75 billion for product liability insurance, compared with an estimated $1.13 billion in 1975—and with rising deductibles they are self-insuring still more, though nobody knows by how much. Some even speculate that the U.S. is on the way to becoming a "no-fault" economy, in which producers and sellers will be held responsible for all product injuries.

"We're getting closer and closer to making the manufacturer into the full insurer," says Robert J. Steinmeyer, legal vice-president at Beckman Instruments Inc. Paul Nelson, senior counsel for product litigation at International Harvester Co., agrees: "There's an increasing disinclination of the public to accept responsibility for its acts."

In what some insurance executives concede was a "moment of panic" three years ago, insurance companies posted overnight liability premium increases of 1,000% for some manufacturers. What prompted the dramatic rise was the fear that a major, but little understood, transformation of U.S. product liability law would open all companies to potentially limitless financial risk. Although the insurance panic is over now—indeed, some companies' premiums are dropping—the law continues to change sharply.

Spearheading this legal revolution are state supreme court judges. Beginning in California, they have announced in state after state a new rule of law in cases where users of products sue for injuries caused when something goes wrong. The judges have tossed out the old rule—that manufacturers or sellers are liable only when they are negligent, or unreasonably careless, in what they made or how they made it. In its place the courts borrowed a much tougher standard—"strict liability"—from earlier cases involving products such as dynamite. In effect, strict liability puts the product itself, including its packaging and promotion, on trial.

By easing the plaintiff's burden in proving a case, injured persons are winning—or settling on favorable terms—suits that might never have even been filed before. At the same time, the courts have been liberalizing procedures to make it easier for plaintiffs to get to court and have been casting a colder eye on traditional defenses. The result has been cases like these:

To scent a candle, a teenager poured perfume made by Faberge Inc. over a lit wick. The perfume ignited, burning a friend's neck. Claiming that Faberge had failed to warn consumers of the perfume's flammability, the friend won a $27,000 judgment. Despite its argument that there was no way to foresee that someone would pour perfume onto an open flame, Faberge lost its appeal.

A construction worker was riding a forklift truck, which was not equipped with a roll bar, on steep terrain when the truck capsized and injured him. In a unanimous decision, the California Supreme Court last year ruled that the burden is on the manufacturer to demonstrate that the forklift's benefits outweighed its risks. Otherwise, said the court, the operator's injuries show that it was defectively designed.

In 1975 a paralyzed high school football player won a $5.3 million judgment against Riddell Inc., a maker of football helmets. A Miami jury came in with the verdict even though the helmet was never introduced at trial. Today, 14% of a Riddell helmet's cost is due to insurance, litigation, and settlements; before the Florida case, these factors cost 1%.

As a result of these and scores of other cases, a counterrevolution is just beginning. Legislation in several states are trying to close off the more extreme outgrowths of the law, which threaten to leave industry exposed to completely open-ended risk. Nevertheless, there is no doubt that a time-honored legal concept is vanishing—that a defendant is responsible for injuries only when his wrongful conduct has caused them.

Some courts have moved so far that in a 1972 case, the California Supreme Court rejected the law that it pioneered in earlier decisions and which now applies in about half the states. That law says that an injured person can win a suit only if the product is

> "unreasonably dangerous" and if injuries resulted from its "intended use." But even in states where this rule is still valid, it is becoming increasingly difficult for corporate defendants to prevail—even against plaintiffs who use products stupidly. Says Richard A. Epstein, a University of Chicago law professor: "It is possible to argue that any product which can be made safer, regardless of cost, is a product which the jury can find unsafe."

Continuing liberalization of the laws could lead to a ruinously high price tag and significantly slower product innovation. "The pendulum is swinging so that the consumer is the all-important thing," argues Robert H. Rines, president of the Franklin Pierce Law Center in Concord, N.H. But, he adds, the consumer "will wake up one day with nothing to consume."

How realistic these fears are remains an open question. Misinformation is far easier to come by than reliable statistics. One set of numbers cited often—that 1 million product liability suits were filed in 1976—has proved to be grossly inaccurate. The actual number is closer to 84,000, according to Victor E. Schwartz, chairman of the U.S. Commerce Dept's Task Force on Product Liability & Accident Compensation. And large jury verdicts are usually headlined more prominently than later reductions. A Los Angeles jury's rare award of $122 million punitive damages, in addition to $3 million general damages, to a 13-year-old boy for injuries suffered in the explosion of a Ford Pinto gas tank was reduced before appeals to $3.5 million one month later.

Moreover, despite the insurance industry's claim that premium boosts were economically necessary, no sound actuarial data exist to prove it. Even so seemingly simple a figure as the total U.S. product liability premium is not known, mainly because product liability has been an unsegregated part of comprehensive liability policies. Only now, under prodding from several state insurance commissioners and criticism from a federal interagency task force on product liability, is a separate line of coverage being established for product claims. Nor, despite a massive study by the major insurance rate-setting organization, the Insurance Services Office (ISO), of 24,000 claims closed in 1976 by 23 major insurance companies, has there been any showing of the increased dollar exposure of companies resulting from the liberalization of liability law.

Nevertheless, the interagency task force conducted a major study in 1976 and concluded that the current legal system is one of three main causes of the product liability "crisis." (The other two are manufacturing practices and insurance rate-setting procedures.) Although the task force could not rank the three, it noted that "the law of product liability has become filled with uncertainties creating a lottery for both insurance

THE LANDMARK CASES IN PRODUCT LIABILITY

MacPherson vs. Buick Motor Co., New York, 1916: A manufacturer is liable for negligently built products that are "reasonably certain to place life and limb in peril," even though consumers do not buy directly from the manufacturer

Greenman vs. Yuba Power Products Inc., California, 1963: A manufacturer is strictly liable when he sells a product that proves to have a defect that causes injury

Larson vs. General Motors Corp., U.S. Court of Appeals, 8th Circuit, 1968: When faulty design of a product worsens an injury, a plaintiff may recover damages for the worsened part of the injury, even if the design defect did not cause the injury in the first place

Cunningham vs. MacNeal Memorial Hospital, Illinois, 1970: It is not a defense to claim that a product (in this case blood infected by hepatitis) could not be made safer by any known technology. This ruling of the Illinois Supreme Court, the only case in which judges squarely refused to consider "state of the art," was reversed by a state statute defining the selling of blood as a service

Cronis vs. J. B. E. Olson Corp., California, 1972: A product need not be "unreasonably dangerous" to make its manufacturer strictly liable for defective design

Bexiga vs. Havir Mfg. Co., New Jersey, 1972: If an injury is attributable to the lack of any safety device on a product, the manufacturer cannot base a defense on the contributory negligence of the plaintiff

Berkebile vs. Brantly Helicopter Corp., Pennsylvania, 1975: Whether the seller could have foreseen a particular injury is irrelevant in a case of strict liability for design defect

Ault vs. International Harvester Co., California, 1975: Evidence that a manufacturer changed or improved its product line after the manufacture and sale of the particular product that caused an injury may be used to prove design defect

Micallet vs. Miehie Co., New York, 1976: Evidence that an injured plaintiff obviously knew of a danger inherent in using a product will not defeat his claim if the manufacturer could reasonably have guarded against the danger in designing the product

Barker vs. Lull Engineering Co., California, 1978: A manufacturer must show that the usefulness of a product involved in an accident outweighs the risks inherent in its design. In this radical ruling, the court shifted the burden of proof in design defect cases from plaintiff to defendant

ratemakers and injured parties.'' And it is an expensive lottery to operate: Data that ISO collected in its closed-claim survey showed that $40.5 million worth of settlements of 10,469 bodily injury claims cost an extra $14 million in expenses, nearly $12 million of which was attributable to attorneys' fees.

Intense lobbying by industry and insurance groups in state capitals during the past 18 months gives some reason to believe that the drive toward a no-fault economy may be halted. Starting with Utah in May, 1977, 16 states, mostly less-populated ones but including Illinois and Michigan, have enacted laws that curb many recent court decisions. These laws do not reject strict liability, but they do place limits on liberalized procedures and open up a range of defenses that companies may raise in court when hit with a product liability claim. Hundreds of similar bills have been debated in most other states, and some will probably pass this year.

REFORM POSSIBILITIES

These enactments are unprecedented in American history. Until now, state legislatures have deferred to state courts, which have developed the law on a case-by-case basis. But as a result of the legislation, says Harvard Law School Professor Robert E. Keeton, coauthor of the original proposal for no-fault automobile insurance, it is ''very much in dispute'' whether corporate defendants will face a constantly growing risk of being sued for liability. ''I don't think [the trend] is likely to be reversed, but it could be held in check,'' says Keeton.

In 1979 a new political element has been added to the legislative picture. On Jan. 15, in a move as unprecedented as the wave of new state laws, the Commerce Dept. unveiled a ''model'' uniform product liability law that would, if adopted, change the ground rules for product litigation throughout the U.S. This is the first time that a federal agency has proposed a thorough revision of tort law. Though Commerce mildly suggests that the model bill is for ''use by the states,'' already Representative John J. LaFalce, chairman of a House subcommittee that in 1977 probed the insurance crisis, has introduced it in Congress, along with three other related bills. Whether or not Congress ultimately enacts some version of the model bill, it is certain to influence state legislatures this year, because it is comprehensive and fairly evenly balanced between producers and consumers. ''The federal model code is a neutral law: that's what the state legislatures want and that's what they've got,'' says Schwartz, who headed the drafting effort.

By providing a focal point for debate, it may also draw out for the first time opposition other than bar groups. Consumer groups, for example, have been a weak voice in the legislative debate so far, "because they have difficulty in spending resources" on abstract issues, says Anita Johnson, a Washington attorney and consumer spokeswoman. But with a federal bill to engage their attention that may change.

Critics and students of product liability have identified more than 30 reform possibilities. Of these, six loom largest in the state and federal bills.

Statutes of Repose

One of the most frequently voiced concerns is the length of time a product may circulate before a suit is filed. In 14 of the 16 states to act so far, so-called statutes of repose, ranging from 6 years in South Dakota to 10 to 12 years elsewhere, eliminate this "long tail." Many products with long lives, especially capital goods such as presses used in manufacturing, may cause injuries decades after they are first sold. By then they may have been altered or badly maintained by subsequent owners. Data from the ISO closed-claims survey show that "some 4% of bodily injury claims, involving 10% of ultimate payment dollars, still have not occurred eight years after the date of manufacture" of the maching involved.

The insurers' fear, says Hofstra Law School Professor Aaron D. Twerski, that they "cannot close their books because there is no finite limit to claimsmanship." And even if most suits are lost, defense expenses can be considerable.

Commerce's model bill would impose liability on the product seller beyond the "useful safe life" of the product and defines this period as "the time during which the product reasonably can be expected to perform in a safe manner," with five factors for the judge or jury to consider. After 10 years, a court must presume the product to have outlived its useful safe life, and an injured plaintiff could rebut the presumption only by "clear and convincing evidence," a more difficult burden than usual. For workplace injuries, the model bill would prohibit a worker from suing the manufacturer 10 years after the product was first sold, but it would permit a suit against the employer if the worker could show "by the preponderance of evidence" that the product was unsafe.

State of the Art

Because engineers are constantly developing safer designs and methods of production, a product introduced on the market today may be unsafe by tomorrow's standards. Many manufacturers fear that they will be held liable for failing to adhere to an advance "state of the art," because court rules in many states permit plaintiffs to introduce evidence of design changes not technologically feasible when the original product was made.

Some years ago, for example, Black & Decker Mfg. Co. realized that metal housings on power tools sold to consumers could present a shock hazard. The company "changed to plastic as soon as the state of the art got to the point where plastics could take the abuse," says Eugene Allen, vice-president for legal affairs. But in a suit after the changeover for an injury caused by a tool housed in metal, the company could have been in a difficult legal position.

Many of the new state laws prohibit technological advances to be held against a manufacturer, if it was truly impossible to use the new technology earlier. According to Keeton, however, these new provisions change little if anything, because a "careful reading of the cases" shows that the courts have never adopted the view that the defendant should have done better than the known "state of the art."

But some of the new laws go further, by defining "state of the art" to mean industry custom as well as technical knowledge. Twerski says that those pushing this view come close to outright lying" about the direction of the law. "It has never been the law that custom is binding," he says. Nor should it be, adds New York University Law School Professor Sheila L. Birnbaum, a product liability expert and counsel to the New York law firm of Skadden, Arps, Slate, Meagher & Flom. "A whole industry can be wrong," she notes.

The Commerce model bill distinguishes between state of the art and industry custom. To overcome manufacturer fears that modernizing will be used against them, the bill would permit custom to be introduced at trial, but not evidence of changes in the state of technical knowledge after manufacture.

Private and Public Standards

Before the recent legislation, failure to comply with private industry or government-set standards has virtually guaranteed a manufacturer's liability, but strict adherence to such standards has not necessarily been a defense. Some of the state statutes now allow such a defense. For example, the Michigan provision enacted last December says that the defendant is off the hook if it can demonstrate that all aspects of the product, from design through marketing, conform to the tougher of either generally recognized nongovernmental standards or state and federal regulations in effect at the time the product was sold or first delivered.

Such immunities make plaintiffs' trial lawyers apoplectic. Says

Melvin Block, former president of the New York Trial Lawyers Assn., "It is ironic that industry, which is the last group in the world to want government regulation, is the first to want regulations telling how to make products."

Under the federal model bill, compliance with certain standards would create a presumption that the product was free from defect. But not many current standards would likely pass muster under Commerce's strict guidelines.

Alteration

Many injuries occur because customers alter a product's original design. Producers of industrial machinery are particularly open to suits because injured factory workers, barred by workers' compensation laws from suing employers, claim damages from the original manufacturer, even if the employer was largely at fault for modifying or failing to maintain the machine. Farrel Co., now a division of USM Corp., was recently sued when a rubber mill it manufactured chopped off seven of the operator's fingers in 1970. He could not sue his employer, so he sued the manufacturer and all subsequent owners. Farrel built the machine in 1911. The mill had changed owners six times, and the only original piece of equipment left on it was the frame, with the maker's nameplate stamped on it. Because the company could prove that the mill had never been under contract for maintenance, repair, or service and that it had been totally altered, Farrel won its case—but at legal costs of $20,000.

Many of the new state laws bar suits when substantial modifications beyond the seller's control have been made to the product. So does the model federal bill, although it would permit a suit when the seller should have anticipated that modifications might be made.

Failure to Warn

Increasing numbers of product liability suits turn on whether the seller provided the user with adequate warnings of potential risks. Proper warnings, though often strenuously resisted by industry because they clash with marketing strategies, can reduce legal exposure. For example, since 1964, when by law the Surgeon General's warning was put on every cigarette pack, no tobacco company has lost a cigarette cancer case.

Lawyers are increasingly bringing cases based on a company's failure to post proper warnings of potential hazards in using products, because it is much easier to show an ineffective warning than a defect in design. But critics argue that corporate defendants are being judged by hindsight in cases where the plaintiff misused the product. Several of the new state statutes permit a company to defend a case by showing that it could not have foreseen how a plaintiff would misuse the product.

The federal model code is more rigorous. It would require juries to assess the likelihood that customers will misuse a product and the seriousness of harm. The more serious the potential injury and the greater the probability that it will occur, the greater the legal duty to warn.

Consumer Misuse

Closely related to product alteration is the user's own negligence. Consumers expect too much from new products and make unreasonable demands on them, says Spencer J. Traver, assistant treasurer in charge of risk management at B. F. Goodrich Co. He cites the example of drivers who underinflate tires and sue when the tires blow out. David R. Williams, an Akron lawyer, cites the case of a man who was awarded $6,000 after losing part of a foot in a lawn mower. The user manual warned not to cut wet grass, but he did it anyway and his foot slipped.

But strict liability often allows consumers who act foolishly to win. Indeed, one of the reasons that strict liability was adopted was to get around a common law rule that threw a plaintiff's suit out of court if he was in the least bit negligent himself. The theory behind strict liability is that manufacturers can better absorb the cost of safety than can the injured plaintiff. But it has come to the point, says Chicago's Epstein, that "the plaintiff who neglects a warning or disregards a safety precaution may still be able to recover full tort damages." Reacting against this, a number of states and the model federal code are adopting "comparative fault" laws, which reduce the plaintiff's award by the percentage of his culpability for causing the injury.

Twerski concedes that comparative fault will probably carry the day, although he is uncomfortable with the doctrine because it undercuts the very premise of strict liability. "We shouldn't cut a plaintiff's recovery by X-percent because he's a *schlemiel,* when the reason for saying there's a design defect in the first place is that it didn't protect the *schlemiel,*" he says.

Provisions in many state bills would also limit the seller's liability to injuries that occur when the consumer uses the product as the manufacturer "intended" it to be used, rather than when the use was "forseeable." Paul D. Rheingold, a New York City product liability lawyer, complains that such provisions are "reactionary." Under these bills, he says, "you couldn't win a case if a screwdriver shattered while you were opening a can of paint with it."

Beyond these major areas of reform are a host of other issues with vociferous advocates on both sides. Jury reform is one. Many critics charge that jurors, believing that well-known, large companies are capable of paying any amount, give the injured plaintiff the benefit of every doubt. The statistics are inconclusive. ISO figures show that only 21% of claims that go through trial result in awards to plaintiffs, but they do not show how many large companies are included in those verdicts. But the jury tradition is so deep that major change is not probable.

On the federal level, what has perhaps the best chance for passage is a set of tax incentives to alleviate the pressure of rising insurance premiums. Last year, Congress extended from 3 years to 10 the period for deduction from previous taxable income operating losses that result from product liability suits and payments. Resulting tax refunds, Commerce Secretary Juanita Kreps noted last July, should enable companies to buy insurance. But Charles Stewart, president of the Machinery & Allied Products Institute, thinks the tax carryback provision is "pitifully inadequate." He and others are pressing for a tax change that would permit companies to finance a self-insurance program by putting money, which would be deductible, into a trust to be used for product liability suits. One of Representative LaFalce's four bills would permit this.

If companies set up such self-insurance trusts, the result could be a major change in the incentive to investigate accidents and claims. Companies generally rely on their insurers to look into the facts of most claims, because the usual policy covers defense and settlement costs as well as judgments. But much of the preliminary work is perfunctory. "Accident investigation is in the Neanderthal stage in America," says Twerski. Texas-based Johnson Ladder Co. used to have great difficulty getting its insurance company to show it exact figures of settlement payouts. Finally it gave up and formed an insurance company with other ladder manufacturers. "The straw that broke the camel's back," says President Jack Dunlop, "was a case in which our insurance company settled for $200,000 a $3 million claim against us for a defective ladder we never manufactured."

The bane of many executives—the contingent fee system that allows lawyers to pay all costs of a suit and to be compensated only if they win—will almost certainly not be changed significantly. Without this system, few injured plaintiffs could afford litigation costs. Philip H. Corboy, a well-known Chicago product liability lawyer who has sued GM, Ford, Sears, Hertz, Searle, and Standard Oil, among others, says that an average well-documented case can easily cost $25,000 to bring to trial.

At bottom, the legislative reforms now pending may alter the character or outcome of some suits, but they will not deter most Americans who have been seriously injured from seeking out someone to sue. When the daughter of Seymour W. Croft, senior attorney for International Harvester, lost her leg in an accident in October, 1971, on a Yamaha motorcycle, Croft hired Corboy to represent her. Corboy says that his best evidence in that case was presented by Yamaha's chief designer, who testified that the motorcycle was originally built with a safety guard for sale to the Tokyo police, but it was sold in the U.S. without the guard. The jury bought Corboy's demonstration at the trial last May that a safety guard would have lessened the injuries or even prevented them.

Croft says his attitudes in dealing with product liability for the manufacturers' side have not changed. But, retorts Corboy, speaking generally, "All these corporation lawyers and executives complain and cry about strict liability, but when a tragedy occurs to them, they're the first to use it so they can be compensated for their losses."

32 A MARKETING MANAGER'S PRIMER ON PRODUCTS LIABILITY

William L. Trombetta

Although products liability is receiving more attention from marketing managers, its relationship to the variables within the marketing manager's control has not yet been synthesized or integrated in a fashion lending itself to useful analysis. From a table of contents analogy, there is virtually no area within the province of marketing that has gone untouched as a consequence of the intrusion of products liability upon the domain of the marketing manager. Indeed, one might not be far off the mark if he were to substitute *marketing* liability for *products* liability to underscore the significance of the transformation of a legal concept that was barely relevant a few years ago to a consideration that is ever-present today, and which introduces both problems and opportunities for marketers. The purpose of this paper is to examine the products liability nexus in order to determine and clarify its relationship to marketing management. The insights afforded by such an examination are intended to provide a working perspective from which marketers can more effectively make decisions on strategy and tactics when confronted with a potential products liability situation.

Reprinted with permission from Cynthia J. Frey, Thomas C. Kinnear, and Bonnie B. Reece (eds.), *Public Policy Issues in Marketing* (Ann Arbor: University of Michigan, Division of Research), pp. 98–113.

USEFUL DEFINITIONS

At this point, a clarification of legal concepts and terminology on the subject of products liability is in order. An overview of legal definitions and concepts will be helpful in attempting to understand the relationship between products liability and marketing, both for purposes of the present article and for future reference.

Products liability refers to the legal responsibility that a manufacturer or supplier incurs to compensate a user who has been harmed by his product [1]. Since the term *defect* is so important in a products liability action, a number of interpretations are presented: (1) the product is not safe for expected use or a reasonable unintended use; (2) the product is unmerchantable; (3) the product fails to match average quality of like products; (4) the product has the potential of resulting in a condition not contemplated by the ultimate consumer which would be unreasonably dangerous to him; (5) sufficient warning has not been given; and (6) the product is not reasonably fit for the ordinary purpose for which such articles are used.

Negligence is basically the failure to exercise reasonable care. The producer is negligent if he fails to exercise reasonable care in the manufacture of his product. The seller should recognize that, if the product is carelessly made, he also is creating an unreasonable risk of causing substantial bodily harm to those who lawfully use it if for a purpose for which it is intended. An *implied warranty of merchantability* means that the product is reasonably fit for its intended purpose. *Strict liability in tort* confers liability upon one who sells any product with a defect which makes it unreasonably dangerous to a user. This is true even though the seller has exercised all possible due care in the preparation and sale of his product [8]. The term *tort* is explained through a definition of tort law: ". . . a body of law concerned with the claims of individuals against each other for damages. . . . The law of torts [deals] with suits by individuals seeking redress for interference with their person, property, or intangible interests" [5]. From a consumer's perspective, the basic difference between negligence and strict liability in tort is that the latter might be more advantageous to the consumer in those situations where proving negligence could be very difficult. In such a situation the possibility of a favorable decision may be somewhat enhanced when the consumer is required to show only that (1) a defect existed (2) when the product left the hands of the defendant and (3) the defect proximately caused the injury.

Privity allows a suit only between those who purchased a product and those who sold it directly to the buyer, and thus refers to a direct contractual relationship. The concept of *foreseeability* suggests that the seller is expected to anticipate reasonable uses of his product and the environment in which the product is used [12]. Two defenses to a products liability suit should be noted. *Contributory negligence* exists where the user carelessly or indifferently handles the product. In contrast, one *assumes the risk* when he goes out of his way to virtually disregard all reason and common sense—for example, when the user purposely and knowingly ignores a direct warning instructing him on the perilous consequences of misusing the product.

THE MARKETING/PRODUCTS LIABILITY INTERFACE

Market Segmentation

The marketing strategy of segmentation can play an important role in minimizing the firm's vulnerability to products liability, particularly with respect to negligence. Since negligence reflects a failure to adhere to a reasonable standard of care, marketing management can take steps to protect itself by practicing what it preaches when it attempts to carve up a heterogeneous market into a number of homogeneous markets characterized by some degree of commonality among users, as ultimately manifested in terms of buyer behavior or purchase patterns. In addition to developing a package of unique benefits designed to fit the wants and needs of various market segments, management can also differentiate among consumer groups on the basis of product usage patterns, "normal vs. abnormal users," differences between purchasers and users, socio-economics and demographics, and consumer perception and understanding of advertisements, warnings, and labels.

For example, firms that manufacture and market drain solvents designed for use by final consumers as well as industrial users would be well advised to segment the two groups on the bases of ingredients and effective strength of the product for each end user group, as well as effectiveness and understanding of warnings. A highly technical, complex label with warnings and instructions suitable for a licensed plumber may not be appropriate for a nonprofessional consumer. Certain segments may not appreciate or understand a warning which is adequate for the population as a whole. Suppose, for example, that a powerful drain cleaning solvent with a relatively technical warning label were to be distributed in low-income, disadvantaged neighborhoods. The likelihood that a warning manifesting technical chemical terminology, antidotes, and numerical measurements would not be appreciated or understood by a disadvantaged consumer behooves management to take reasonable steps to deal with this situation. Such reasonable steps could take the form of redesigning and market testing the warning label, using control and experimental groups to statistically determine the consumer's sensitivity to and appreciation of inherent dangers associated with a product. Courts, particularly at the federal level, are increasingly inclined to admit statistical analysis as evidence under the new Federal Rules of Evidence Act.

Another way in which segmentation can assist in reducing products liability exposure is by differentiating between purchaser and user in industrial markets. A marketing package that emphasizes financial attractiveness, productive efficiency, and cost-benefit analysis, while ignoring how the industrial user actually handles the product, can result in increased products liability exposure. While discounted cash flow and payback are music to the purchaser's ears, the indirect party to the sale must be considered in terms of how he might reasonably misuse the product, whether he removes safety guard devices, whether foremen pass on warnings adequately, and whether service manuals that accompany the sale of complex industrial equipment are as readily understood by the average machine operator as they are by the repair technician in regard to dangers inherent in using the machinery.

Consumer Behavior

In addition to buyer behavior and usage patterns, what happens after the transaction is also related to products liability. Reassurance by a sales intermediary after a sales transaction for the purpose of reducing cognitive dissonance can result in liability to the marketer. Postpurchase statements consisting of material facts which the consumer is likely to rely upon can result in an express warranty under section 2–313(1)(a) of the Uniform Commercial Code. For example, if a hair dye preparation is marketed with a warning restricting its use to certain market segments only under certain conditions, and if after the sale the sales intermediary makes a statement that has the effect of warranting that the consumer can ignore the warning, liability could be established on the basis of breach-of-express warranty.

Postpurchase activity, in attempting to minimize products liability exposure, affects consumer transactions as well as industrial marketing. How the consumer can misuse the product after sale, what the consumer does with warnings and manuals, and who might be affected by misuse of or a defect in the product are all considerations that are in the realm of reasonable foreseeability of the marketing manager. The fact that many durable and industrial goods have long lives and are likely to pass through a succession of owners would seem to call for a de-emphasis of primary reliance on service manuals and an increased reliance upon attachment of warnings to the product itself, along with oral reinforcement of warnings by appropriate middlemen.

Consumer behavior methodology can assist in analyzing varying degrees of perception and understanding of warnings. For example, when the phrase "for professional use only" is observed on the label of an inherently dangerous product such as a drain cleaning solvent, does the consumer interpret this to mean that the product is too dangerous to be used by the average person or that the product is more effective than a competitive alternative on the market? Careful research at the product and concept testing stages, as well as testing of the design and appearance of the warning, can be used to refute a claim that the marketer did not conduct himself reasonably in placing a product into the stream of commerce.

Every consumer behavior model traces the consumer decision-making process from arousal to the postpurchase stage. At various points throughout this process, the consumer turns to a number of sources of information for purposes of education and evaluation. Increasingly, courts are looking at methods of delivering warnings. . . . It would appear that those sources of information which prove to be the most effective in informing consumers of product availability and desirability of purchase would also be the safest means for warning them adequately of latent defects that are not discovered until after the sale.

The Product Component

The product component of the marketing mix presents marketing management with perhaps the most obvious prospect of a products liability dilemma, since it involves so many diverse aspects, both physical and nonphysical: design and manufacture, packaging, foreseeability of use and environment, and warranty, to name but a few. The nature of the relationship between product and products liability can be illustrated by examining the direction the courts are taking in the so-called car crash-worthiness cases. These cases, sometimes referred to as "second collision" cases, are concerned not with the initial impact of the collision but rather with injuries that result from a defect in the design of the car which enhances the likelihood of injury in case of collision. These cases also illustrate the concept of forseeability: reasonably foreseeable risks of harm to the user of a product are to be take into consideration ideally at the product-planning stage by all those involved in the process. The seller's sole concern with the functional, intended use of the product may be misguided if the consumer handles the product in an unintended but reasonably foreseeable manner.

Again, using automobiles as an example, if the product planner foresees the possibility of injury as a result of internal design, he may take steps, through advertising, brochures, and salesmen, to deal with the more subtle design conditions which are not likely to be appreciated by the average consumer. A reasonable consumer would not require great amplification of the risks inherent in driving a small car rather than a heavy car or the failure to wear seat belts or in such internal design characteristics as an unpadded dash; on the other hand, such characteristics as the placement of the fuel tank or the steering column, or the design of the car frame, may not be obvious to a reasonable consumer and should be scrutinized to foresee the ways consumers can misuse the product unintentionally. This is true even in regard to relatively obvious dangerous product attributes. Seat belts provide a case in point. Notwithstanding all the public pronouncements encouraging car users to buckle up, it is clear that such suggestions are often disregarded. Does this flagrant, active, reckless disregard on the part of the consumer insulate the manufacturer from liability, or is it a case of carelessness on the part of the consumer which is reasonably foreseeable by the product planner? The safer position is the latter view. The auto could be designed in such a fashion that it will not function without the use of the seat belt, or, at least, that the seat belt signal will create such a notice that to disregard it the driver must take some active, voluntary measure such as disconnecting it.

Mickle v. Blackmon, a "second collision" case with far-reaching implications for the product planner, involved a defective gearshift knob [7]. Upon collision, the gearshift knob shattered and pierced a passenger's spine, causing permanent paralysis below the point of injury. One of the issues in the case was whether Ford Motor Company, in the design of and selection of materials for the gearshift knob, negligently created an unreasonable risk of enhanced injury to passengers upon collision. While claiming that the gearshift knob was not defective at the time of production and sale, Ford also disclaimed any responsibility for minimizing injury potential through the design of the interior of the car (the second collision issue). It is foreseeable that such injuries will accompany the normal and expected use of an automobile.

Complicating the *Mickle* case was the passage of thirteen years between the production of the car and the mishap. While the decision reinforces the longstanding principle that normal wear and tear in itself will not make a seller liable for injuries associated with the use of a product, it also underscores the magnitude of the product planner's task. Ford should have used materials which would remain strong and durable throughout the life of the product, even though that life could be relatively long. The defect was in the material used for the gearshift knob; the passage of time was coincidental.

The foreseeability concept expands the duty of the product planner to reasonably anticipate those contingencies which have a probability of occurring, but should not result in a heavy addition to the planner's responsibility to foresee what is done by the consumer. The foreseeability doctrine is replacing the intended use doctrine. Until recently, the seller in many cases could rely on the intended use argument; that is, the marketer never intended his product to be used for a certain purpose or in a particular manner. Clearly, in a proconsumer climate this kind of product orientation is not as forward-thinking as the marketing concept orientation which attempts to place the planner in the consumer's shoes in anticipating unintended but reasonably foreseeable misuse of the product.

Pricing

When one speaks of the impact of products liability upon the managerial decision-making process, the repercussions for the product itself, as well as for distribution, promotion, and research and development, come quickly to mind. Foreseeability affects pricing indirectly, by raising prices to consumers as the burden of injury to the consumers from a defective product is shifted back through the channel of distribution to those best able to bear the burden as a matter of public policy. Foreseeability also affects pricing directly, however. The automobile industry provides an example of the direct relationship between foreseeability and pricing. One of the pricing mechanisms employed by the industry combines various pricing techniques with the overall goal of arriving at a suggested retail price that is targeted for a particular market segment. For example, if a company has delineated a market segment based on key socioeconomic and demographic variables that reflect a capacity to purchase a car in the price range of $3,500 to $4,000, the total cost of all components—assemblage, distribution costs, and overhead—cannot exceed the targeted price bracket. All profit margins and material inputs to the car, particularly physical components, will have to meet set cost specifications that will result in bringing the product in at the targeted price. In the case of General Motors' Corvair, for example, a swing axle design allowed GM to bring the Corvair in at the bracketed price. Link-type independent suspensions, which are found on front and better rear suspensions and provide the best system in terms of ride, noise and handling, and safety, are costlier and therefore would not be used in such a case because of their potential for exceeding the programmed price.

The crucial point related to foreseeability is that the court is no longer likely to rule as a matter of law that the manufacturer was not obligated to go beyond the industry design standards. More likely, this question will be an issue for the trier of facts—the jury. In other words, knowing that there existed the possibility of improving the margin of safety for the driver and his passengers (all of which fits neatly into the concept of foreseeability), was it reasonable for the manufacturer to forego the extra effort to make the car, to some degree, safer? Before, the manufacturer was not obligated to go beyond the technological state of the art in the industry. Now, the fact that more could have been done by the manufacturer to make the car safer (at a cost to both society and the company in the form of higher prices) can be put to a jury in a products liability suit on the basis of reasonableness. This is certain to have a significant effect on traditional pricing mechanisms and formats for evaluating new product decisions.

The Channel of Distribution

In products liability cases, the burden of injury to the consumer may attach not only to the manufacturer of the product but to any intermediary in the channel of distribution—assemblers, component suppliers, selling agents and representatives, wholesalers, retailers, franchisees, lessors, and service outlets. Suppliers must be concerned with knowing what goes on in the channel of distribution with respect to the handling of their products. It follows that great care in selection of channel intermediaries is necessary to minimize possible negligence that is foreseeable by the manufacturer.

Van dermark v. Ford Motor Co. [13] illustrates some of the products liability problems inherent in the channel of distribution. In *Vandermark,* the plaintiff bought a new Ford car from an authorized Ford dealer. About six weeks later, the plaintiff lost control of his car, which went off the highway and collided with a light post. He and his sister, both severely injured, brought an action against the dealer and Ford Motor Company. Ford claimed that it could not be held liable in negligence or strict liability since the car had passed through two other authorized Ford dealers before it was sold to the dealer in question and that the third dealer was responsible for the defect in the car. Apparently, Ford does not deliver cars to its dealers ready to be driven by the final purchaser but relies on its dealers to make the final inspection, corrections, and adjustments.

The court made much of the entire distribution process. It likened retailers to manufacturers in that both are engaged in the business of distributing goods to the public. This view means that any entity involved in providing a package of benefits to the consumer as an integral part of the overall producing and marketing enterprise could be considered responsible for bearing the cost of injuries to the consumer.

Specifically, since Ford, as the manufacturer of the completed product, did not fulfill its duty to have its cars delivered to the final consumer free from dangerous defects, it could not escape liability on the ground that the defect in Vandermark's car may have been caused by an error on the part of the dealer.

The net result of this nondelegable duty approach is a diminution of the likelihood that a manufacturer or supplier can insulate himself from the ultimate consumer. A mere contractual statement to the effect that the middleman is not an agent of the manufacturer or supplier will no longer be sufficient, if it ever was. *Vandermark* portends that a supplier cannot escape liability for a defect in his product by authorizing someone between himself and the final consumer to complete the product.

Promotion and Advertising

The promotion component of the marketing mix is the variable that exhibits the nonfunctional, nonphysical aspects of products liability, particularly with regard to the duty to warn. An argument might even be made that the advertising agency is itself one of those marketing entities integral to the effective placing of a product into the stream of commerce.

The special world of drugs and medicine provides particularly insightful examples of the kinds of difficulty a marketer can encounter, either by overpromoting a product or by failing to warn adequately of dangers inherent in its manufacture and sale. Although drug/medicine cases are viewed as a separate and distinct area within the topic of products liability, courts dealing with issues of promotion and duty to warn frequently cite such cases for support even though the product involved is not a drug or medicine [2,4]. The drug/medicine cases are a valuable source of much of the law on promotion, advertising, warnings, directions, and labeling because drug companies, from a products liability perspective, are most susceptible to charges of failing to warn adequately.

In *Toole v. Richardson-Merrell, Inc.* [11], it was brought out that the toxicologist for Merrell had presented a paper on the drug MER/29 which included a falsification of test results on MER/29 and other false statements. The president of the company was aware of this and later referred to the presentation as the most terrific selling tool that Merrell had ever had! Merrell also eliminated certain data detrimental to MER/29 from its reports to the Food and Drug Administration. MER/29 had been introduced by the greatest promotion and advertising campaign ever conducted by Merrell in support of a product. An advertising brochure stated that MER/29 was virtually nontoxic and remarkably free from side effects even with prolonged use.

At the trial, expert testimony revealed that a number of negative reports and studies conducted by other researchers on MER/29 indicated that Merrell should have withdrawn the drug from the market. Nevertheless, Merrell's advertisements for MER/29 continued unabated. The marketing powers at Merrell instructed drug detailers that MER/29 was a proven drug and that there was no longer any valid question as to its safety or lack of significant side effects. But the ultimate outrage was yet to come. An article in *McCall's* magazine written by a doctor had been particularly critical of MER/29. Merrell's vice-president in charge of sales promotion advised his salesmen: "I suggest twisting this query into a positive sales aid when brought up, rather than agreeing with Dr. (Fishbein's) negativism" [11].

Amidst this background, the plaintiff sued on theories of negligence and breach of express and implied warranties of merchantability. Essentially, the plaintiff claimed that after Merrell knew of the toxic effect of MER/29, it continued to press its sale without warning of the dangers associated with the drug.

Merrell was nothing if not imaginative in its defense. It characterized such statements as "free from side effects," "a proven drug," "no question as to its safety," and "lack of significant side effects" as mere expressions of opinion addressed to doctors and claimed that there was no evidence that the deceased had ever relied on such statements. Granted that many times there is a thin line between sales puffing and the creation of an express warranty, this was not one of them. The statements had been widely disseminated to the medical profession through presumably reliable sources of information such as drug detail men and medical periodicals and journals, and the drug company clearly had superior knowledge. In other words, the overwhelming strength of the assertions made through effective sources resulted in an overpromotion of the drug that literally cancelled out a perfunctory warning on the label to the effect that the long-term effects of MER/29 were unknown. This activity was especially reprehensible in light of the severity and gravity of the side effect.

Incollingo v. Ewing [3] was another drug case involving the issue of overpromotion. A minor died as a result of using Parke, Davis's drug, Chloromycetin. Chloromycetin was a popular and widely used drug. The warning appearing on the immediate container and outer carton was as follows:

> WARNING—Blood disorders may be associated with intermittent or prolonged use. It is essential that adequate blood studies be made.
> CAUTION—Federal Law prohibits dispensing without prescription.

In addition, Parke, Davis distributed the following literature on the drug:

> Chloromycetin is a potent therapeutic agent and, because certain drug disorders have been associated with its administration, it should not be used indiscriminately or for minor infections. Furthermore, as with certain other drugs, adequate blood studies should be made when the patient requires prolonged or intermittent therapy.

Although these warnings complied with federal Food and Drug Administration requirements, it was questionable whether they were specific enough, whether they went far enough in warning effectively of the drug's potential toxicity, whether they were displayed prominently enough on the package, and whether the effectiveness of the warning was diminished by the alleged overpromotion of the detail men.

The interesting thing in this case, as in *Toole,* is that even if the warning and the method of transmitting it were proper and adequate, they would have been rendered ineffectual by the marketing efforts of Parke, Davis. In other words, a warning may be sufficient, explicit, prominent, and so on, but all this goes for naught if the product is overpromoted. Even if the warning is timely, accurate, and delivered properly, the product has not been properly marketed if the promotion is so powerful that it outweighs the effectiveness of the warning.

Sterling Drug, Inc., v. Yarrow [10], a case with most interesting implications for marketing, dealt with the method of promotion and mode of delivering the warning. The injured consumer suffered damage to his vision as a result of using the drug Aralen. The basis of the claim was the drug company's negligence in failing to warn of known dangers inherent in the use of Aralen.

Drug companies usually promote their products by the following methods: (1) by sending detail men (field representatives) to make calls in which oral presentations are made and literature and samples are delivered; (2) by listing drugs in an annually published advertising vehicle known as the *Physician's Desk Reference;* (3) by mailing product cards to doctors and distributing them at conventions; and (4) by mailing to doctors special letters known as "Dear Doctor" letters. Curiously, when Sterling discovered the adverse facts about Aralen, it confined its methods of warning to the last three with no use of detail men. In court, it was brought out that physicians receive so much literature on drugs that it is virtually impossible to read all of it; however, they do rely on detail men. The drug company countered by saying that letters to doctors constituted a reasonable means of warning; indeed, this was the custom in the profession. The court ruled that what is usually done is not necessarily the criterion for what ought to be done. Admittedly, reasonable efforts to warn were to be made; under the circumstances, however, given the severity and gravity of the harm incurred, failure to use detail men was unreasonable and negligence was established against the drug manufacturer. Interestingly, Sterling might have met its responsibility to warn adequately by certifying or registering the warning letters in order to reasonably assure that they would reach the addressees.

The main marketing management principle to abstract from the drug cases is that it is not necessary either in negligence or strict liability that the product be defective in manufacture or contain a physical malfunction; proving that the product is unreasonably dangerous is sufficient. A product may be perfectly manufactured and meet ever requirement for its intended purpose and still be unreasonably dangerous because of the manufacturer's failure to warn adequately of dangers associated with the product. That the entire marketing scheme can constitute defect is made clear in *Reyes v. Wyeth Laboratories, Inc.* [*9*]: "By rephrasing the defectiveness requirement in terms of 'unreasonable danger,' it becomes clear that the circumstances of marketing themselves can amount to a defect; the defect can be extrinsic to the product."

Marketing Research

The scope of marketing research and marketing information systems should be extended to enable marketers to become aware of circumstances and precedents involving products liability actions which are relevant to their own situation. Product usage complaints should be catalogued and carefully scrutinized in order to develop a defense to the effect that management is on notice and aware of its responsibilities and duties to the product user and is taking action to minimize the possibility of harm to the consumer.

Recall the Incollingo case where the overpromotion of Chloromycetin by Parke, Davis was held to be a proximate cause of the minor's death, keeping in mind that Chloromycetin was a popular and widely used drug. Parke, Davis had a duty to unsell the drug. Marketing research and internal sales data analysis would have disclosed that Parke, Davis's warnings were not being heeded and that the company consequently had a duty to develop a warning that would not be disregarded—either by redesigning the appearance and attention-getting qualities of the warning or by oral reinforcement through its detail men.

From the injured consumer's side, it is necessary to prove that a drug company (or any firm) knew its warning was not being heeded. In the case of Chloromycetin, heavy sales volume should have put Parke, Davis on notice that its warnings were ineffective. In fact, two California decisions have gone as far as to hold that profit data from the sale of a drug are admissible to show motive for overpromotion that may have diminished the effectiveness of any warnings [2,6].

As discussed earlier, the manufacture and sale of an inherently dangerous product such as an industrial-strength drain solvent may require market segmentation. Suppose a manufacturer of such a product intended that it never be sold at retail. Suppose further that the warning on the label says "for professional use only" and that the independent sales representatives who distribute the product understand generally that the product is to be sold only to industrial and commercial users. But the product has somehow found its way into inner-city hardware stores where it is questionable that the average disadvantaged consumer can understand the ordinarily strong but complex warning. Suppose such a consumer is injured in the use of this product. The manufacturer will of course deny liability, on the basis that the product was not intended for this particular consumer and that he had no knowledge of its sale in such areas. Marketing research and sales analysis can be used to establish notice, foreseeability, and failure to warn.

Sales receipts can be used to pinpoint where sales are occurring by census tract. Census tract data will supply the socioeconomic demographics of the various trade areas. Abundant research exists in the marketing literature to inform the manufacturer that the disadvantaged market segment tends to behave differently in terms of key variables such as understanding, perception, and sources of information. Having established that the product is being purchased by a consumer relatively more susceptible to harm through use of such a product, the final step would be to redesign the warning for two groups of consumers representative of the market area where the product has been found to be distributed and to test for any significant differences in appreciation and understanding of the warning's message between the control group and the experimental group.

CONCLUSIONS

The relationship between marketing and products liability is summarized in Table 32-1.

The current trend in court decisions might lead one to refer to products liability as marketing liability. Inherent in the application of marketing strategy and the marketing mix are products liability problems and opportunities such as the differentiation of products users by certain characteristics that make them more or less vulnerable to misuse of the products; marketing information systems analysis that can be broadened to include industry experiences and complaints with respect to products liability actions; consumer behavior patterns that reflect what management warrants about the product after it is sold and the ways, abnormal and normal, in which a consumer uses a product; product planning and development that foresees unintended but reasonable

TABLE 32.1. OVERVIEW OF THE MARKETING/PRODUCTS LIABILITY NEXUS

LEGAL CONCEPTS	MARKETING IMPLICATIONS
Appreciation and understanding of danger (knowledge, experience, and ability to recognize harmful consequences may vary greatly among users)	Segmentation: Definition of target group Development of profiles of "normal users" and "abnormal users" by socio-economic and demographic variables
Foreseeability: anticipation of unintentional but reasonable use of the product in user's environment Duty to warn and mode of delivery of the warning	Consumer behavior: Use of postpurchase analysis to determine how consumers are likely to use or misuse product after purchase. Determination of sources of information relied upon for warnings and directions
Doctrine of what is reasonably foreseeable (tending to replace functional intended use philosophy) Defectiveness (in design and/or manufacture)	Product planning: Research and development directed to design and manufacture of product with consequences of unintended but reasonable misuse in mind. Design of more protective packaging Manufacture of product which cannot function without safety devices
State of the art: what others in the industry are doing Feasibility of alternative design	Price: Changes in typical pricing procedures and formats for new product evaluation as a result of substitution of better, safer materials
Implied warranty of merchantability Notice Foreseeability (foundation of liability for negligence is knowledge or [what is deemed in law to be the same thing] opportunity by the exercise of reasonable diligence to acquire knowledge	Place: Shifting of burden of injury to consumer back through channel of distribution Anticipation that manufacturer may be responsible for knowledge of operations and practices of entities in the channel Manufacturer's foreseeability of negligence on part of middlemen
Duty to warn Overpromotion Misrepresentation Defectiveness (defect can be intangible and extrinsic to physical product itself) Adequacy of warning (a function of gravity, severity, and extent of danger)	Promotion: Emphasis on dangerous consequences of product misuse Development of different messages for differentiated market segments Avoidance of overpromotion and misrepresentation which may cancel out effectiveness of warning Care in instructing sales force Attention to method of delivering warning
State of the art Prior complaints Record of product's safe history Precedents Notice	Marketing research and marketing information systems: Analysis of complaints Acquisition of feedback from legal decisions to assess implication for decision making Attention to industry and government standards and regulations

misuse of the product; pricing analysis that takes into consideration the trade-off between controlling costs and making a product reasonably safe; channel of distribution systems that recognize the implied warranty of merchantability accompanying a product as it moves from raw material stage, through assembly and component supplier, and finally through manufacturer, middlemen, and consumer; and promotion decisions that recognize the advantage of the advertising message as a warranting mechanism and a possible tactic for defusing a potential products liability action. The evidence points to an extensive reciprocal relationship between marketing and products liability.

The same methodologies and techniques useful in analyzing what product attributes result in a more positive marketing experience can be used in analyzing what product attributes and consumer behavior patterns expose management to products liability. Indeed, there may well be a legal counterpart to benefits segmentation—"hazards segmentation."

REFERENCES

1. BERENSON, CONRAD. "The Product Liability Revolution: Let the Manufacturer and Seller Be Sued." *Business Horizons,* Oct. 1972, p. 71.
2. *Davis v. Wyeth Laboratories, Inc.*, 399 F. 2d 121 (9th Cir. 1968).
3. *Incollingo v. Ewing,* 444 Pa. 264, 282 A. 2d 206 (Pa. Sup. Ct. 1971).
4. *Jackson v. Coast Paint and Lacquer Co.*, 499 F. 2d 809, 811 (1974).
5. KEETON, PAGE, AND KEETON, ROBERT E. *Cases and Materials on the Law of Torts.* St. Paul, Minn.: West Publishing, 1971.
6. *Love v. Wolf,* 226 Cal. App. 2d 378, 38 Cal. Rptr. 183 (1964).
7. *Mickle v. Blackmon,* 252 S.C. 202, 166 S.E. 2d 173 (1969).
8. Restatement (second) of Torts, Section 402A (1965).
9. *Reyes v. Wyeth Laboratories, Inc.*, 498 F. 2d 1264, 1273 (1974).
10. *Sterling Drug, Inc., v. Yarrow,* 408 F. 2d 978 (8th Cir. 1969).
11. *Toole v. Richardson-Merrell, Inc.*, 251 Cal. App. 2d 689, 60 Cal. Rptr. 398 (Ca. 1967).
12. Trombetta, William L., and Wilson, Timothy L. "Foreseeability of Misuse and Abnormal Use of Products by the Consumer." *Journal of Marketing,* July 1975, p. 49.
13. *Vandermark v. Ford Motor Co.*, 37 Cal. Rptr. 896, 391 P. 2d 168 (Cal. Sup. Ct. 1964).

C Consumer Satisfaction

33 ARE CONSUMERS SATISFIED?

George S. Day

Adverse public opinion, the antecedent of government regulation, has been shaped to a large degree by the failure of business to satisfy the customer. Other factors are involved, but much of the public's antipathy toward big business is rooted in the American consumer's own bad experience in the marketplace. To the extent that it is rooted there, it can be remedied only there.[1]

How disenchanted and dissatisfied is the public with the everyday performance of business in providing goods and services? Surprisingly, there is very little data that is pertinent to this question. Despite the centrality of consumer satisfaction in the marketing concept, it is invariably subordinated to objective measures of sales, repeat purchase rates, market shares, and profitability when marketing programs are evaluated. The closest most marketers get to explicitly considering consumer satisfaction is a review of consumer complaints. Unfortunately, it is increasingly apparent that complaints present only a distorted and incomplete picture.

Some firms have been routinely measuring satisfaction with specific products, using surveys of overall satisfaction, intentions to repurchase, or willingness to recommend to a friend. Only recently have these methods been employed in surveys of large numbers of products and services to determine the frequency and seriousness of consumers' problems with their specific purchases and their level of ensuing dissatisfaction. Such data are essential to help us understand whether the evident disenchantment with business is a cumulative consequence of unhappy

---

[1] Thomas A. Murphy, Chairman, General Motors Corp., in *Newsweek,* December 20, 1976, p. 11.

Adapted from an article written for *The Wharton Magazine* and published in its Fall 1977 issue. Printed here by agreement with *The Wharton Magazine* under separate copyright.

day-to-day experiences or a reflection of a more fundamental disillusionment with all institutions. As we will see, the evidence concerning consumer satisfaction with specific goods and services is very mixed, maddeningly difficult to interpret, and only partially supports the concerns voiced by Murphy.

WHAT DO THE SURVEYS SHOW?

Surveys can be broadly classified according to whether the underlying orientation is one of maximizing consumer satisfaction or minimizing dissatisfaction and problems. These are not incompatible orientations, but one may be preferred over another on philosophical or practical grounds. For example, government agencies tend to view their role as one of minimizing abuses in the marketplace and to focus on the large *numbers* of consumers who are aggrieved. Business, on the other hand, emphasizes the large *proportions* of consumers who are typically satisfied. The two orientations do yield different perceptions of the state of consumer satisfaction and consequently introduce further distortion into the dialogue between business and its critics.

Satisfaction-Oriented Approaches

The best example comes from a continuous survey program conducted by General Electric. As of 1972 they had asked 48,000 respondents to describe their "overall satisfaction or dissatisfaction" with some 665,000 individual appliance products on a five-point scale ranging from "extremely satisfied" to "extremely dissatisfied." They found high average levels of satisfaction—94 percent were extremely or somewhat satisfied *at the time of the survey.* This proportion varied considerably by product category, age of appliance, time since a recent repair experience, and so on. The most useful diagnostic information came from an open-ended question asked of those who were dissatisfied. Little was learned by asking the others why they were satisfied; they expected to be satisfied and therefore did not find the question meaningful.

Similar results were obtained during a 1974 mail survey by Sears, Roebuck of 52 general merchandise categories.[2] Using a three-point

---

[2] Donald A. Hughes, "Considerations in the Measurement and Use of Consumer Satisfaction Ratings," in William Locander, editor, *Marketing Looks Outward* (Chicago: American Marketing Association, 1977).

scale, they found that 80.6 percent were "completely satisfied," 16.3 percent were "fairly satisfied," and 3.1 percent were "not too satisfied" with their most recent purchases. The proportions of completely satisfied customers ranged from 94.9 percent for men's dress slacks and 90.4 percent for automatic dryers to 71.9 percent for pantyhose and 72.5 percent for stoves.

Two problems of interpretation that bedevil this type of survey are: (1) variability among respondents in defining terms such as "somewhat" or "fairly" satisfied and (2) uncertainty as to whether the respondents are referring to their initial reactions to the products, or to their residue of unsatisfied complaints and repair efforts. A further problem is whether respondents can accurately recall instances of dissatisfaction that took place more than a few months previously.

Problem-Oriented Approaches

This approach was employed by A. C. Neilsen and Co. in a 1975 survey of problems with packaged food products and health and beauty aids.[3] The survey was initiated with a pre-mailing to a national probability sample. This was done to give the principal grocery shopper in each household an opportunity to think about past experience with product defects. After the respondent had read the material, a telephone interview was conducted to determine how many could recall encountering a product defect in the past year. Out of the 1,000 respondents, 330 could not recall a single defect and 130 others reported only package defects. However, the remaining 540 households encountered a total of 1,307 product defects. The meaning of these results is somewhat compromised by the reliance on recall over a long period of time and the difficulty of translating the results into problems with specific purchases. Since the survey deals with low-cost, repeat-purchased items, the results are probably best interpreted as relating to problems with relatively recent purchases. Even in this light, the incidence of defects is not high; it ranges from 18 percent for refrigerated foods and 16 percent for packaged dry grocery products to 7 percent for health and beauty aids—each of which is a broad product category in itself.

Combined Approach

Neither of the above approaches has revealed a serious incidence of dissatisfaction. This is somewhat illusory, partly because of ambiguities in the methods, but mostly because the products are among the least

[3] "Caveat Venditor," *Nielsen Researcher* (1975), 2–13.

troublesome in the marketplace. A 1975 survey sponsored by two consumer action groups, using a combination of methods over a much broader array of products as well as services, has uncovered more discouraging results.[4] A total of 2,419 households were interviewed by phone in the spring of 1975. Respondents were asked to answer (on a four-point scale) two questions about their most recent purchase in each of 34 product categories:

Question 1: Was the purchase "satisfactory" or "unsatisfactory"? (In response to this question, about 11 percent of all products and 13 percent of all service purchases were rated "unsatisfactory" or "somewhat unsatisfactory.")

Question 2: (A) What was the problem? (asked of those who were dissatisfied) and (B) Could the purchase have been better in any way? (asked of those who were satisfied or somewhat satisfied).

Using this sequence of questions, about 28 percent of all purchases were found to be unsatisfactory in some respect. However, because the survey was conducted during a period of high inflation, 25 percent of all reported problems were price-related. About half of the remaining product problems were mentioned before the probe.

Unfortunately, while the probe does clarify the reasons for the dissatisfaction, it also introduces an upward bias. A further difficulty is that the problems perceived by consumers may not be valid; i.e., they could stem from misuse, or misapplication. Also, it is not possible to determine the seriousness of the problems from this data. Finally, one

TABLE 33–1. PERCEIVED NON-PRICE PROBLEMS (Proportions of Recent Purchases)

	BEFORE PROBE	AFTER PROBE	TOTAL
Car repair	21.5	13.5	35.0
Mail order	19.4	11.7	31.1
Home repair	18.6	9.8	28.4
Car	13.8	18.5	32.3
Grocery items	10.6	15.2	25.8
TV set	9.7	11.1	20.8
Appliance repair	9.6	19.9	29.5
Cosmetics	3.5	5.7	9.2
Credit	6.0	4.6	10.6
Lamps	2.6	5.9	8.5
AVERAGE—ALL PRODUCTS	9.5	10.5	20.0
AVERAGE—ALL SERVICES	12.0	8.9	20.9

[4] Arthur Best and Alan R. Andreasen, "Talking Back to Business: Voiced and Unvoiced Consumer Complaints," Center for Study of Responsive Law, 1976.

could question the ability of respondents to recall problems with purchases made in the distant past, as would be the case with many major appliances. Nonetheless, it remains that consumers are unhappy with some aspect of 20 percent of their recent purchases. Lending some credence to the results is the fact that there is a great deal of variability between products—and those with high levels of dissatisfaction are known trouble spots. Table 33–1 is a sampling of the results of this study. A conservative interpretation of the data, looking only at dissatisfaction registered before the probe, still gives a bleak picture in certain high visibility product areas. Laudatory performance in other categories may not offset this poor performance, for consumers do take acceptable performance for granted.

COMPLAINTS: ONLY THE TIP OF THE ICEBERG

Given the deficiencies and difficulties of surveys, it is not surprising that many companies and government agencies use complaints as their primary source of evidence about consumer dissatisfaction. Complaint letters have an immediacy and a directness that cannot be ignored. Someone has taken the time to single out one among the many aggravations and frustrations of daily life and to express his feelings, albeit often in the hopes of redress. A further virtue of complaint letters is the insight they sometimes provide into the problems of small groups with unusual requirements or problems. Such people are unlikely to be represented in small-scale tests of responses to product reformulations. For example, a premarket skin abrasion test of a new talc base in a bath powder uncovered no problems, but the complaint letters that poured in shortly after the reformulated product was marketed revealed serious problems.

Analyses of changes in the content of letters can also reveal emerging consumer attitudes. A manufacturer of aspirin for babies found that product safety had become the primary concern of letter writers. This appreciation of consumer concern was used to justify investment in a new safety cap, which was developed in advance of consumer and government pressures.

Interpreting Complaint Letters

It would be very misleading for most companies to rely solely on complaint letters as an indicator of their products' performance. First, people who write complaint letters are not typical buyers or consumers. They are most likely to be poeple who have time on their hands and/or who may be highly educated and articulate. People who do not fit into these two categories are less likely to complain. Instead, they take other actions, such as switching brands or retailers. Low-income buyers are especially unlikely to complain, even though they may have strong grounds for complaint.

A more serious limitation is the size of the submerged "iceberg" of problems, dissatisfaction, and consumer initiative beneath the visible complaints. For example, a majority of the defects in grocery and health care products reported in the A. C. Neilsen survey did not trigger a complaint to either a manufacturer or retailer. In 40 percent of the defect situations a complaint was made to the retailer, which almost always resulted in a merchandise exchange. Only 3 percent of the defects led to a letter of complaint to the manufacturer. Much less complaining behavior was found in a 1974 telephone survey of consumers' problems with personal care products—5 percent went to the manufacturer, 15 percent to the retailer, and the remainder took no direct action, although 34 percent said they had complained to their friends.[5] Even the study by the two consumer action groups, which dealt with a wide array of more expensive products, found that only 31 percent actually voiced a complaint to a manufacturer or retailer. However, a further 1.2 percent did complain to some other source, including the Better Business Bureau, government agencies, media, or the courts.

The picture that emerges from the three studies suggests a series of filters between a felt complaint or dissatisfaction and direct consumer actions (see Figure 33–1). The manufacturer is especially isolated by these filters. After all, what motivation is there for the retailer, or the company salesman calling on the retailer, to report systematically on complaints and dissatisfaction to the head office? Informal studies by the author indicate that the head offices of chain retailers are almost as isolated. Many complaints are dealt with at the store clerk or department manager level and never come to the attention of the store manager, much less the head office.

Of course, the size of the filter will depend on the seriousness of the problem. While disastrous failures demand and deserve everyone's attention, one could argue that the smaller problems can be just as destructive of buyer-seller relationships. These problems are the ones that seldom get voiced, perhaps because the consumer (1) is pessimistic about a favorable outcome, (2) perceives that the time could better be used doing something else, (3) does not know how to proceed to make a complaint, or (4) feels intimidated by the prospect. Their voices are not muted, for they do have one eloquent method of telling the manufacturer

---

[5] Betty J. Diener, "Information and Redress: Consumer Needs and Company Responses," *Marketing Science Institute,* June 1975.

FIGURE 33-1. HOW COMPLAINTS ARE FILTERED

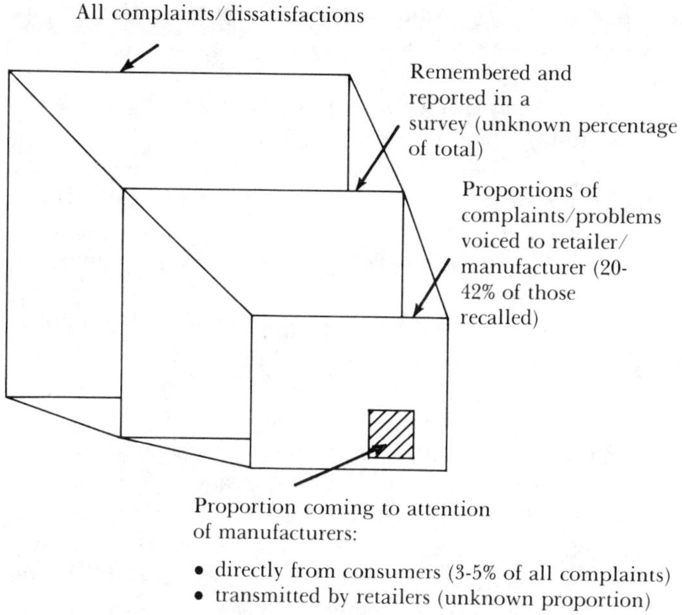

that his product was unsatisfactory—they simply stop buying it. Among those reporting defects in the A. C. Neilsen study, 19 percent stopped buying the product type, 25 percent switched brands and 13 percent inspected the products in the store. If sufficiently aggrieved, no doubt they will also complain to friends and neighbors. Thus, it is in the post-purchase behavior that the negative consequences of product dissatisfaction are felt by the manufacturer.

CONSUMER SATISFACTION IN PERSPECTIVE

Studies of complaints or levels of satisfaction usually pertain to specific shopping or using experiences. But consumers can be satisfied or dissatisfied with almost any aspect of the market environment. For example, as marketing programs are increasingly tailored to specific target markets, those people not in the intended audience become annoyed and frustrated by appeals for products they do not want or cannot afford to have. The difficulty in taking a broader perspective is that dissatisfaction with overall marketing practices is to a large extent a reflection of disillusionment with all institutions of society. Hence, a more realistic picture comes from the specific experiences of consumers.

Even when dealing with satisfaction at the level of a specific shopping or using experience, there is ambiguity of meaning. For example, dissatisfaction with a product could stem from:

poor performance of the primary function (nutrition and transportation, for example);
poor performance of secondary functions (characteristics such as taste and texture that are usually the basis for brand differentiation);
disparities between prior expectations and perceived performances; and
deficiencies compared to alternatives, whether or not the alternatives were affordable or available at the time of purchase.

Certainly dissatisfaction is most intense when the product does not perform the basic functions. Freezers that do not freeze, detergents that cannot lift stains, and lawnmowers unable to cut grass are undeniably serious, but probably rather rare, failures. Deficiencies of this magnitude are also quite obvious. This is not so with secondary functions, where the standards of acceptable performance are more variable and subjective. For this reason, it is more meaningful—both theoretically and empirically—to consider dissatisfactions as resulting from perceived discrepancies between prior expectations and perceived performances. Whether the expectations are realistic or not, they are the standards that the buyer/consumer uses to assess the acceptability of performance.

There are a number of situations where the product may meet or even exceed expectations but the consumer is still dissatisfied. The person might have preferred not to use the service; this was found in a study of nursing home patients who were forced into that situation because of illness. More often, a shopper may be forced for budget reasons to settle for what is affordable rather than what is preferred. This may mean forgoing some desirable but nonessential features. A buyer may also be dissatisfied if a more desirable alternative is found immediately after the purchase decision. Finally, the passage of time also contributes to dissatisfaction with products such as appliances, due to both declining performance and "psychological obsolescence." The older the appliance the more likely it lacks features or performance characteristics that are desirable.

All these possibilities make interpretation difficult. For example, someone could respond "I'm dissatisfied with my refrigerator because it is not frost-free," for many reasons, including (1) a decision not to buy this feature when the refrigerator was first bought, (2) the realization that new refrigerators have features that obsolete the present model, or (3) a disparity between the prior expectation that defrosting would not be difficult and the actual problems encountered in defrosting—which may loom larger as time passes.

Some of the reasons that underlie *manifest* consumer dissatisfaction clearly do not represent valid consumer problems. However, this distortion is at least partially offset by the inability of consumers to report sources of *latent* discontent. For example, there are situations where the consumer does not know that he is being abused—for example, when unnecessary repairs are made. Often there is no basis for evaluation of performance, as in the case of the toxic side effects of food additives. Second, it is difficult for the consumer to determine what constitutes relevant purchase information and to know whether the claims being made are deceptive and without substantiation. Yet, a corporation cannot evade responsibilities in these types of situation on the grounds that these dissatisfactions cannot be articulated.

The Elusive Question of Standards

Businessmen and consumerists are clearly at odds on this question.[6] Not only do the two groups appear to have different standards of what is an acceptable level of dissatisfaction, they also come to different conclusions as to whether the ability of business to satisfy consumers is improving or deteriorating. The position of consumerists seems to be that the quality of products is deteriorating and that this development is accurately perceived by consumers. Furthermore, consumerists believe that consumer performance expectations are reasonably constant, although probably inflated by the hyperbole and exaggeration endemic to consumer advertising. The widening gap between performance expectations and perceived quality means that expectations are more frequently not confirmed and, hence, the magnitude of consumer dissatisfactions is large and increasing (see Figure 33-2).

Businessmen have a different perspective, which emphasizes the problems stemming from increasing and perhaps unrealistically high performance expectations. Some responsibility for the situation is placed on advertising, which proclaims a flow of continuously improved products. At the same time, the performance and quality of the products is seen to be improving, although not at the same rate as consumer expectations. Thus, businessmen also see a growing potential for consumer dissatisfaction. A representation of the businessmen's perspective appears in Figure 33-3.

[6]Raymond C. Stokes, ''Consumerism and the Measurement of Consumer Dissatisfactions,'' a speech delivered before *Attitude Research Bridges the Atlantic,* Madrid, Spain, February 1973.

FIGURE 33–2. CONSUMERISTS' VIEW OF PRODUCT DISSATISFACTION

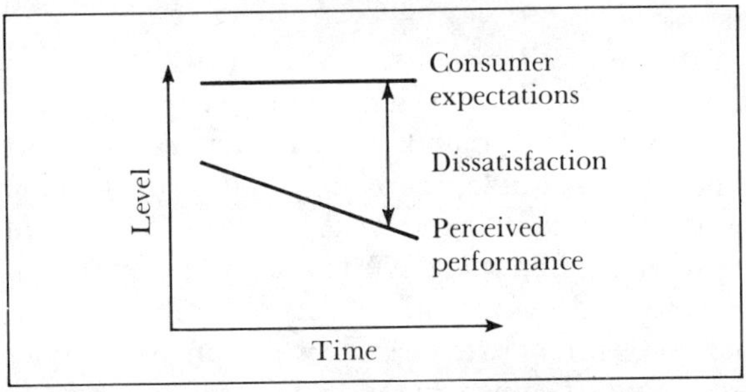

FIGURE 33–3. BUSINESSMEN'S VIEW OF PRODUCT DISSATISFACTION

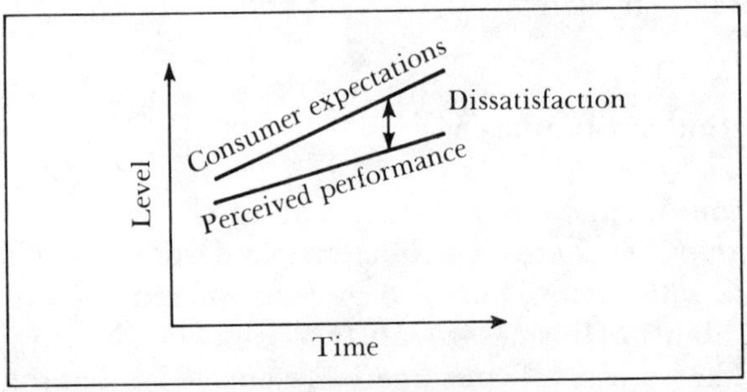

There is also a third perspective, which suggests that although the basic product may be more reliable and perform better (and there is good evidence that this is the case), the performance of the improved product is perceived as deteriorating. This problem is particularly acute in the appliance and automotive industries, where improvements generally make products more complex and provide new possibilities for malfunctions. Thus, even though the failure rate of the basic product may have declined, the overall rate of product failure has probably increased. (Another interpretation related to perceived product performance concerns the decline of caveat emptor—"let the buyer beware"—as the creed of the marketplace. Under these circumstances, consumers are perhaps more willing to return defective or unsatisfactory merchandise, which, in earlier days, would have been discarded.)

What Is Acceptable Performance?

There is no obvious way to establish a consensus standard on the acceptable level of satisfaction or dissatisfaction at any point in time. Businessmen would prefer to emphasize the proportion who are satisfied, for this puts them in the best light. Consumerists will dwell on the large numbers who are dissatisfied. Both, however, would probably agree that continuing improvement in performance from either baseline would constitute a minimum standard.

Both points of view regarding standards must be sensitive to the findings of the Sears, Roebuck study: that 73 percent of all complaints were registered by only 34 percent of the respondents. By contrast, in another group, 32 percent of the respondents reported no complaints with any of their recent purchases in the 52 product categories. The "dissatisfaction-prone" group may (1) be more critical, i.e. have higher standards, (2) have less tolerance for shortcomings because of problems in the past, or (3) court dissatisfaction in their purchasing habits by paying lower prices and buying more of their goods at discount outlets. This group would provide a source of dissatisfaction for any reasonable level of performance. Accordingly, Hughes, of Sears, Roebuck, proposes a level of 85 to 90 percent complete satisfaction, as measured in consumer surveys, as a realistic goal.

IMPLICATIONS

The available evidence on consumer satisfaction suffers from numerous inadequacies and problems of interpretation and comparability. Nonetheless, several clear conclusions emerge from the welter of results. First, there is a high level of satisfaction with the majority of products. Unfortunately, there are highly visible exceptions, notably all types of repair services, direct mail, toys, automobiles, and some clothing articles, in which performance is poor by any measure. They are these products that contribute disproportionately to consumer antipathy toward marketing practices and institutions.

The fact that a minority of products accounts for most of the problems does not absolve all manufacturers from continually improving their performance. This requires attention to both objective product performance and expectations of the product formed by advertising and selling methods. For example, salesmen are seldom penalized for over-promising product or service performance, yet this is a significant source of complaints.

The second significant conclusion is that most dissatisfactions and problems are not voiced to either retailers or to manufacturers. The latter are especially isolated, with between 3 and 5 percent of the total complaints coming to their attention from various sources. Those companies that rely on complaint data are likely to be getting very biased and limited insights into consumer satisfaction. Further, if only a small proportion of all complaints are voiced, the company loses many opportunities to satisfy unhappy customers. For these reasons, there are benefits to encouraging more complaints by the use of hotlines, product inserts, and improved communications. Regardless of the effect of such encouragement, it is clear that complaints cannot serve as the sole source of information on consumer dissatisfaction.

In the absence of continuous survey information, it is not possible to say whether performance is improving or deteriorating. Yet, in the absence of absolute standards of acceptable performance, evidence of continuing improvement may have to serve as the minimum standard. This suggests that surveys measuring consumer satisfaction should be part of a continuous market monitoring system. To make it even more useful, the survey results should also give detailed insights into consumer problems as a guide to new product research.

A. WARRANTIES AND SERVICE

1. Obtain several warranty statements. Do you understand them? How could they be improved? Would they influence your purchasing decisions?
2. Do you think that the 1975 Magnuson-Moss Warranty Act will be effective? What changes would you suggest in the law?
3. How would you go about designing a warranty program for a small appliance manufacturer? Consumer complaints made to the FTC about warranty programs have involved delays in repairs, faultily designed products, lack of convenient service, excessive labor charges, failure of the retailer or service organization to honor the guarantee, and lack of a form for redress. How would your system handle these problems? Would you use retailers, a service organization, or your own company to perform the function?

B. SAFETY AND LIABILITY

4. Why don't manufacturers of items such as appliances, cars, and toys try to differentiate their products from those of competitors on the basis of safety?
5. What criteria should be used to demonstrate, for the purpose of establishing product liability, that a product is unreasonably

dangerous? According to these criteria, would a ladder or a kitchen knife be unreasonably dangerous or reasonably safe?

6. A regulation has been considered that would ban all toys intended for children under five that have parts small enough to fit within a 1¼-inch sphere. What are the arguments in favor of and against such a proposal?
7. What social, legal, and economic factors have contributed to the decline of the legal defense based on lack of privity of contract (a direct contractual relationship between a manufacturer and an aggrieved user)?
8. Are the proposed changes in products liability litigation described in Chapter 31 fair to consumers? Rank each of the proposals according to their probable acceptability to the consumer movement and to the lawyers prosecuting product liability suits.
9. Recently the major drug manufacturers were rated according to the number of product recalls they had initiated. Is a large number of recalls (relative to the number of products and sales activity) an indication of good or poor performance?
10. The first debate proposition of the 1980–1981 National Debate for High Schools was "Resolved that the Federal Government should initiate and enforce safety guarantees on consumer goods." What are the major opposing arguments on this topic?

C. CONSUMER SATISFACTION

11. Respondents in surveys frequently voice high levels of dissatisfaction with products in general but appear to be satisfied when asked about specific purchases and products. How would you account for this disparity?
12. Are there any characteristics shared by products or services associated with high levels of complaint?
13. Should government agencies such as the FTC or the FDA use the incidence of complaints received by their Washington offices to determine which consumer problems deserve high priority in the allocation of scarce agency resources?

PART VII

Responding to Consumerism

INTRODUCTION

There are two major sources of programs responsive to consumer problems. One is business and the other is government. Examples of programs from both sources and associated difficulties appear throughout the book; however, it is useful to consider in a more focused way these two very different types of response.

In Chapter 34 Day and Aaker discuss industrywide efforts, particularly self-regulation, an apparently logical and efficient but imperfect strategy. Chapter 35, by Dornoff and Tankersley, is a thought-provoking portrayal of the opinions of retailers toward practical consumer problems. In the third selection, two award-winning consumer programs, instituted by Stop & Shop and Penney's, are described. Finally, in Chapter 37 Sitter, an Exxon executive, suggests that business and consumers have a commonality of interest that does not surface as often as it should.

One of the central issues of the eighties is the role of government regulation. Under what circumstances is regulation appropriate and when should it be avoided? What are the costs and benefits and how can they be measured? Chapters 38–41 provide an in-depth look at government regulation. Schuck attempts to identify the conditions under which regulation is appropriate and potentially effective. Ross provides a structure from which to measure both the costs and the benefits of regulation. Brummet suggests another way to measure the costs of regulation and describes an effort by Dow Chemical to assess their costs of complying with regulations. In the last chapter of the book, Claybrook, former administrator of the National Highway Traffic Safety Administration, defends regulation and criticizes the reaction of business to it.

A *Business Responses*

34 INDUSTRYWIDE RESPONSES TO CONSUMERISM PRESSURE

George S. Day & David A. Aker

Until very recently, most trade associations were viewed by their members as defense mechanisms or negative lobbyists. This has changed with various pressures on them to be more responsive and with the increasing threat of government regulation. Individual companies are now turning to their trade associations for leadership in the four basic areas of (1) coordinating and disseminating research, (2) consumer and dealer education, (3) development of standards, and (4) complaint handling.

The first responsibility of trade associations is to keep their members properly informed by coordinating and disseminating research.

This activity may either supplement or be a substitute for the efforts of individual companies to become sensitive to consumerism problems and government initiatives. Without such information the members may pressure the association to take unrealistic and unattainable positions that work against the long-run interests of the industry.

Furthermore, if the information is objective, and not subject to restrictions because of confidentiality, it can be very useful in presenting industry arguments to governmental bodies. There is no question that research findings would be welcomed in both sectors, in preference to the "relatively unstructured and unscientifically assembled information

Reprinted by permission from *Harvard Business Review,* Vol. 50, No. 6 (Nov.-Dec. 1972), pp. 120–124.

which comes to us either out of our own experience or the experience of friends or in individual letters of complaint, in testimony of individual consumers and out of the experience of those who deal with and work with consumer problems."[1]

These considerations have led to the formation of the Consumer Research Institute by the Grocery Manufacturers of America, and the support of basic research on advertising by the American Association of Advertising Agencies and the Canadian Advertising Advisory Board.

The second responsibility of trade associations is to provide leadership in consumer and dealer education.

An industry association has an enormous comparative advantage over individual members in the educational function. This is most obvious in broad-scale controversies such as nutrition, where education can play a big role but no individual company can undertake the responsibility.

Associations are also in a good position to work through dealers, where the education function frequently fails. This was the experience of the Outdoor Power Equipment Institute in its efforts to acquaint users with the hazards and proper use of power mowers. The dealers should have been the most influential channel of information about safety, but they needed stimulation and education before their potential was achieved.

The third responsibility of trade associations is leadership in the development of standards.

The most common form of self-regulation is the product standardization and certification program in the areas of quality, reliability, safety, and/or healthfulness. Standards may also apply to size, shape, and style variations, where necessary to facilitate consumer comparisons, reduce product proliferation, or ensure interchangeability of parts. Certification is the mechanism for identifying whether the product conforms to the standard. This judgment is made by one of approximately a thousand laboratories that test products.

There are various explanations for the motives behind the development of standards. One view is that the subscribers to a standard do so out of a sense of public responsibility and professional ethics combined with a desire to prevent similar standards from being imposed from the outside.

The Federal Trade Commission has recently argued that the character of the market on the buying side is the major determinant of the extent and quality of standards. The FTC observed that most of the estimated 20,000 sets of industry standards in effect in the United States exist in in-

---

[1] Mary Gardiner Jones, "Enough Talking—Let's Get on With the Job," address to Illinois Federation of Consumers, Chicago, Illinois, April 3, 1970, p. 12.

dustrial markets where the buyers are large and expert and can force the development of this kind of information. One outcome of this analysis is a proposal that the law itself must provide the incentive for the development of standards for consumer products.

In many ways, the standards for advertising and promotion practices are the most difficult to set because of the problems in deciding what is inappropriate, deceptive, tasteless, or not in the public interest. Such standards are frequently only recommendations or suggestions (e.g., those of the Proprietary Association for the advertising of medications).

The fourth responsibility of trade associations is to provide leadership in the area of complaint handling.

In an effort to forestall the aggrieved consumer from turning first to the government, many industries are considering or implementing their own hearing boards for processing complaints. These are similar to the efforts of individual companies to provide an independent ombudsmen-like function.

As an illustration, the appliance industry, in conjunction with major retailers, has set up a major appliance consumer action panel which will act as a "court of last resort," should retailer and manufacturer contact fail to resolve a complaint problem.

A similar principle is followed by the National Advertising Review Board. This organization utilizes the resources of 140 local Better Business Bureaus to monitor national advertisements, evaluate complaints, and advise advertisers on planned campaigns. If a complaint cannot be resolved at the local bureau level, it is referred to a review board of five people (one of whom represents a consumer group). If the advertiser is found to be in violation of review board standards and refuses to change or withdraw his ad, the disagreement is publicized and the case is turned over to the Federal Trade Commission.

PROBLEMS WITH SELF-REGULATION

Experience indicates that purely voluntary efforts at self-regulation are not likely to be successful. There must be some enforcement mechanism by which violations of regulatory norms can be punished through collective action against the violator.

Unfortunately, such private power can also be used to enforce product standards rigged in favor of one or two producers or to dictate a safety certification program that is too costly for small manufacturers. Such actions are clearly anticompetitive and therefore forbidden by antitrust legislation.

The courts have used the potential for such abuses as reason to declare many enforcement techniques illegal—including the circulation of blacklists, withholding of a seal of approval, and the use of indirect boycotts. Many of these judgments against self-regulation are made without reference to the social merit of restraint.

This presents a real dilemma. An industrywide agreement on standards is unlikely to be effective without inducements for compliance that are beyond the scope of a voluntary agreement. Yet the stronger the enforcement procedure, the greater the degree of potential coercion and danger of an antitrust violation.

This threat can be substantially diminished (a) by industry-government teamwork (in which industry proposes and implements the rules and standards by which the government regulates the industry), and (b) by the public and other interested parties playing a significant role both in developing and administering the rules and standards and in avoiding any discrimination against specific manufacturers.

Presuming that enforcement problems can be overcome, there remain four other barriers to the effectiveness of self-regulation (insofar as effectiveness means forestalling other forms of regulation):

1. The industry members may simply fail to see that there is an injustice in a practice and hence not take any regulatory action. Consequently, "such abuses as the advertisement in poor taste, unsolicited merchandise, the engineered contest, shrinkage of package weight, the unsubstantiated claim, and the negative option sales plan are all defended by sellers who perceive no wrong in them."[2] Their insensitivity leaves room for government investigation if not regulation.

2. The quality of the decision making and leadership of the association is frequently weakened by the need for consensus among a majority of members. This has particularly weakened safety standards for many products to the point that they represent nothing more than an affirmation of the status quo. The antitrust question also complicates the search for consensus.

3. Virtually every industry or trade association is accused of, and complains of, having inadequate resources to carry out its responsibilities (with the probable exception of lobbying efforts). Inadequate resources mean outdated and inadequate standards, poor research and communications efforts, and complaint mechanisms that are inaccessible or unknown to the consumer.

One measure of the seriousness of the resource problem in the United States is found in the product-safety area. Although there are more than 1,000 standards covering 350 product categories, the National Commission on Product Safety found that industrywide voluntary safety stan-

---

[2] Louis L. Stern, "Consumer Protection via Self-Regulation," *Journal of Marketing*, July 1971, p. 49.

dards applied to only 18 of the 44 categories that are highest in the number of estimated annual injuries.[3]

Efforts to provide complaint-handling mechanisms are particularly vulnerable. For example, the experience of Great Britain with "consultative machinery" in four major nationalized industries—gas, electricity, coal, and transportation—is sobering. After 22 years of publicizing these channels for complaints, a consumer study found that unaided recall awareness by industry varied from 4% to 12% of the population.[4]

The reason is that a complaint about the performance of a specific industry is a rare event for most consumers. Herein lies the strength of the Better Business Bureaus, for they are readily accessible and well-known to consumers as a place to register all kinds of complaints. The long-run prospects for specific industries to reach out and find aggrieved consumers (without an intermediary) appear slim.

4. Some problems may be beyond the scope of the responsibility that the industry is willing or able to accept. This seems to characterize many pollution-related issues, including nonreturnable bottles, auto emissions, and other currently intractable problems such as advertising clutter in all media.

The effectiveness of self-regulation ultimately depends on the public's willingness to accept industry regulations and standards in lieu of government intervention. This, in turn, requires that the public trusts the intention and effectiveness of business in solving consumer problems. Here, the climate is distinctly unfriendly.

A recent national probability sample of 1,613 adults, age 18 or over, found substantial support for new government restrictions and regulations. For example, 75% of the sample supported a regulation that would "require major companies to set strict standards of quality which would be enforced by government inspection."[5]

The context was certainly not one of complete mistrust of business; there was evidence of a "readiness to give the private sector credit for what it can do for itself" (it is interesting to note here that the much-maligned Better Business Bureau was given the highest proportion of positive ratings of any consumer protection group or individual), as well as distinct ambivalence about the effectiveness of government.

However, this standing is vulnerable to rising criticism, especially over the conflict of interest implications of financial dependence on the

[3] *Final Report of the National Commission on Product Safety* (Washington, Government Printing Office, June 1970), p. 48.

[4] *Consumer Consultative Machinery in the Nationalized Industries,* A Consumer Council Study (London, Her Majesty's Stationery Office, 1968).

[5] John Revett, "Consumers Endorse More Restrictions on Business," *Advertising Age,* October 25, 1971, p. 98.

business being regulated. The big question is whether recent efforts at reform, including regional rather than local control, can offset this criticism.

Overall, the loss of confidence in the ability of business to adequately respond to the pressures of consumerism is the greatest threat to industry self-regulation as it is currently conceived. This does not preclude such efforts; it simply means that industry associations are going to have to demonstrate greater leadership and extend their efforts further than they appear to be doing.

This will almost certainly mean broadening the participation of the public in both the setting and enforcing of standards. Such a move, with all its threatening ramifications, is likely, on balance, to be superior to government regulation for most consumerism problems.

35 PERCEPTUAL DIFFERENCES IN MARKET TRANSACTIONS: A SOURCE OF CONSUMER FRUSTRATION

Ronald J. Dornoff & Clint B. Tankersley

A major interface between consumers and retailers occurs during pre- and post-market transactions, through a market transaction and the corresponding use of products and satisfaction. The attainment of this satisfaction is often hindered by the cumulative frustrations associated with transactions that do not conform to expectations.

Although presumably most retailers are interested in guarding against transactions causing consumer frustrations, an equally important interest is short-term profit maximization, and though the two appear to be harmonious there exists a tendency to believe that the realization of one is inconsistent with the actualization of the other. This possible inconsistency, which may lead to differing opinions between consumers and retailers of actions taken in market transactions, could act as a catalyst for consumer frustration.

The purpose of this study is to compare consumers' and retailers' perceptions of actions taken in particular types of market transactions. Specifically, this study was designed to test the following hypothesis: Differences exist between the perceptions of retailers and consumers of actions taken in market transactions.

From *Journal of Consumer Affairs* (Summer 1975), pp. 97–103. Reprinted by permission of the American Council on Consumer Interests.

METHODOLOGY

A consumer sample was selected using a systematic random sample from the Cincinnati Metropolitan Area Telephone Directory.[1] A total of 300 consumers were selected and a questionnaire was mailed to each. The questionnaires were self-administered and returned by mail. A total of 187 usable questionnaires were returned.

Three types of retail establishments were chosen to be sampled: discount houses, specialty stores and department stores. The sample was selected using a systematic random sample from the Cincinnati Metropolitan Area yellow pages. Those stores selected which could not be classified into one of the three types sampled were excluded. Each retailer was contacted in person by the interviewer, and either the store manager or assistant store manager was asked to complete the same questionnaire sent to the consumers. A total of forty retail establishments participated in the study.

To compare consumers' and retailers' perceptions of actions taken in market transactions, a questionnaire involving fourteen scenarios depicting interactions between retailers and consumers was developed. These were obtained in interviews with retailers' consumer complaint departments, consumers and retailing authorities. Those most frequently mentioned as prominent causes of consumer frustration were summarized and included in the questionnaire.[2] In each scenario, a market transaction revealing a possible source of consumer frustration was presented and then a corresponding resultant action was stated. Respondents were requested to indicate their agreement with the actions taken by checking the following Likert type scale:

Strongly Agree	Agree	No Opinion	Disagree	Strongly Disagree

The questionnaire was used to measure both consumers' and retailers' perceptions. The differences between consumers' and retailers' perceptions were tested for significance by a chi-square analysis.

RESULTS AND DISCUSSION

A comparison of consumers' and retailers' responses to the actions depicted in the scenarios is presented in Table 35-1 where the responses

[1] After a random start, every one-thousandth person was selected.

[2] The questionnaire was validated by asking a convenience sample of thirty consumers to rate each of the scenarios listed on a scale of frustration from 1 (low) to 5 (high). The same scale was presented to a convenience sample of ten retailers. From the sample of consumers 83 percent rated each of the fourteen scenarios as 4 or 5. Seven of the ten retailers rated each of the scenarios as 3 or more.

TABLE 35.1. CONSUMER AND RETAILER PERCEPTION OF ACTIONS BY RETAILERS IN SITUATIONS INVOLVING PURCHASE CONFLICT

SITUATION	DESCRIPTION, ACTION, AND JUDGMENT	SIGNIFICANCE

1 A young man, recently hired as a salesman for a local retail store, has been working very hard to favorably impress his boss with his selling ability. At times, this young man, anxious for an order, has been a little over-eager. To get the order, he exaggerates the value of the item or withholds relevant information concerning the product he is trying to sell. No fraud or deceit is intended by his actions, he is simply over-eager.

Action: His boss, the owner of the retail store, is aware of this salesman's actions, but he has done nothing to stop such practice.

	Perception			
	Agree	No Opinion	Disagree	
Consumer	17	3	80	
Retailer	32	26	42	.001

2 A local retailer has a coat with a fur collar that he wants to get rid of. He has tried unsuccessfully for months to sell it for $89.95. He then decides to put it on sale at his approximate cost, $63.95. He still is unable to sell the coat, so he makes a new price tag listing an original price of $129.95.

Action: The retailer marks down this price ($129.95) to the sale price ($63.95).

	Perception			
	Agree	No Opinion	Disagree	
Consumer	10	1	89	
Retailer	52	20	28	.001

3 A person bought a new car from a franchised automobile dealership in the local area. Eight months after the car was purchased, he began having problems with the transmission. He took the car back to the dealer, and some minor adjustments were made. During the next few months he continually had a similar problem with the transmission slipping. Each time the dealer made only minor adjustments on the car. Again, during the 13th month after the car had been bought the man returned to the dealer because the transmission still was not functioning properly. At this time, the transmission was completely overhauled.

Action: Since the warranty was for only one year (12 months from date of purchase), the retailer charged full price for parts and labor.

SITUATION	DESCRIPTION, ACTION, AND JUDGMENT			SIGNIFICANCE
	Perception			
	Agree	No Opinion	Disagree	
Consumer	21	8	71	
Retailer	60	14	26	.001

4 A woman purchased a dress from a local retail store. Instructions for washing the dress were attached to the garment by the manufacturer. These instructions were still attached to the dress at the time of the sale and the customer was fully aware of them. After wearing the dress one time she washed it, carefully following the manufacturer's instruction. Much to her dismay, the colors in the dress faded with the washing. Also, the colors ran and made colored streaks in the white collar and cuffs of the dress. She returned to the retail store within three days after the purchase date with the merchandise.

Action: The retailer refused to refund her money since the dress had been worn and washed.

	Perception			
	Agree	No Opinion	Disagree	
Consumer	6	3	91	
Retailer	54	13	33	.001

5 A local retail store ran an ad in the Sunday newspaper announcing a sale on a well-known brand of high-quality men's slacks. The ad read that a large quantity of these slacks were available in all sizes, colors, fabrics, and styles. Response to this ad was very enthusiastic. After the second day of the sale, only ¼ of the advertised merchandise was still available.

Action: The retailer continued to run the same ad each day for an entire week up to and including the following Saturday.

	Perception			
	Agree	No Opinion	Disagree	
Consumer	36	7	57	
Retailer	77	10	23	.001

6 Sets of a well-known brand of "good" china dinnerware are advertised on sale at a considerable discount by a local retailer. Several patterns of a typical 45-piece service for eight are listed. The customer may also buy any "odd" pieces which are available in stock (for instance, a butter dish, a gravy bowl, etc.). The ad does not indicate, however, that these patterns have been discontinued by the manufacturer.

Action: The retailer offers this information only if the customer directly asks if the merchandise is discontinued.

TABLE 35.1. *(Continued)*

SITUATION	DESCRIPTION, ACTION, AND JUDGMENT			SIGNIFICANCE
		Perception		
	Agree	No Opinion	Disagree	
Consumer	15	5	80	
Retailer	80	6	14	.001

7 A retail grocery chain operates several stores throughout the local area including one in the city's ghetto area. Independent studies have shown that prices do tend to be higher and there is less of a selection of products in this particular store than in the other locations.

Action: On the day welfare checks are received in the area of the city the retailer increases prices on all his merchandise.

	Perception			
	Agree	No Opinion	Disagree	
Consumer	0	1	99	
Retailer	57	20	23	.001

8 Some recent research has shown that many consumers are misusing Product X, a product distributed and sold through local retailers. There is no danger involved in this misuse; the consumers are simply wasting their money by using too much of it at a time. Displays, which actually seem to encourage this misuse are provided by the manufacturer to each retailer. A certain retailer is aware that consumers are misusing Product X. He is also aware that the manufacturer's display encourages this misuse.

Action:The retailer continues to use this display in his store.[a]

	Perception			
	Agree	No Opinion	Disagree	
Consumer	7	2	91	
Retailer	57	17	26	.001

9 According to a local retail store's credit policy, any purchase made before the 10th of the month is included on that billing. Full payment is required on an account within 25 days of this day (usually this is the 5th of the following month). If not paid in full, interest charges are then added to the balance. A person ordered a piece of furniture from this store on May 9 and charged the purchase to his credit account. The particular piece of furniture was not available for immediate delivery. By June 5, the furniture still had not been delivered, so the bill was not paid. The furniture finally arrived on June 7, and a check was then sent to the store for payment in full. The June 10 billing was received the following week.

SITUATION	DESCRIPTION, ACTION, AND JUDGMENT	SIGNIFICANCE

Action: On the bill sent by the retailer interest charges were included since the bill had not been paid by the due date, June 5.

	Perception			
	Agree	No Opinion	Disagree	
Consumer	16	4	80	
Retailer	86	6	8	.001

10 A customer brings a coffee pot into the store which he explains was a wedding gift. He indicates that he already has a fine coffee pot and would like a cash refund. The pot is carried by the store, but since it was a gift the man has no sales slip. The pot retails at $12.00.

Action: The man should receive a full cash refund.

	Perception			
	Agree	No Opinion	Disagree	
Consumer	95	1	4	
Retailer	44	11	45	.001

11 A customer purchased a bicycle from a store at a cost of $59.95. A week later the same bicycle is put on sale by that store for $49.00.

Action: The store should refund the customer the difference.

	Perception			
	Agree	No Opinion	Disagree	
Consumer	90	3	7	
Retailer	20	9	71	.001

12 A customer purchased a foundation garment. A year later the garment was returned with no sales slip. Since that time, styles had changed and the garment had been reduced to half price. The customer requested a full cash refund.

Action: The customer should not receive the full refund but should receive the current selling price.

	Perception			
	Agree	No Opinion	Disagree	
Consumer	41	1	58	not
Retailer	52	6	42	significant

13 A customer calls the retailer to report that her refrigerator purchased two weeks ago is not cooling properly and that all the food has spoiled.

TABLE 35.1. (*Continued*)

SITUATION	DESCRIPTION, ACTION, AND JUDGMENT			SIGNIFICANCE
	Action: The retailer should repair the refrigerator at no cost.			
	Perception			
	Agree	No Opinion	Disagree	
Consumer	96	2	2	not
Retailer	88	9	3	significant
14	A customer calls the retailer to report that her refrigerator purchased two weeks ago is not cooling properly and that all the food has spoiled.			
	Action: The customer should be reimbursed for the value of the spoiled food.			
	Perception			
	Agree	No Opinion	Disagree	
Consumer	89	8	3	
Retailer	37	9	54	.001

[a]This summarized version of situation 8 is adopted from the work of C. Merle Crawford, "Attitudes of Marketing Executives Toward Ethics in Marketing Research," *Journal of Marketing*, Vol. 34, No. 2, April, 1970, pp. 46–52.

are dichotomized into agree versus disagree. Responses of consumers and retailers were significantly different ($\alpha = .001$) in twelve of the fourteen transactional situations. The results do support the hypothesis that the perceptions of retailers and consumers toward actions taken in frustrating situations are different. The only exceptions were situations 12 and 13. In situation 12 there was no consensus among either retailers or consumers on the acceptability of the action taken. The action depicted in situation 13 is usually covered by the manufacturer under the warranty agreement and does not directly effect the profitability of the retailer. In all other situations the retailers' objectives of consumer satisfaction and profitability were obviously not harmonious. Each time the retailer opted for the more profitable course of action while the consumer favored the reverse.

Given this significant difference in perception between consumers and retailers, it was felt that these perceptions may not be the same for each type of retailer. Thus, the differences in perceptions of consumers and each type of retailer were tested. The results were the same as for retailers in general. It seems evident that the perceptions of retailers, both collectively and individually, toward actions causing frustration are in contrast to the perceptions of consumers. This implies that in the future consumer frustrations will remain as an outcome of many, if not all, market transactions.

SUMMARY

This study has demonstrated that differences do exist between what consumers and retailers feel are appropriate actions to be taken in market transactions. Perhaps it is time for retailers to re-examine their objectives and seriously attempt to create a better balance between the apparently inconsistent goals of consumer satisfaction and profitability if they want to continue to enjoy the valuable franchise afforded them by the environment.

36 *BUSINESS AND SOCIETY REVIEW* CORPORATE RESPONSIBILITY AWARDS

Business and Society Review

J.C. PENNEY COMPANY

Award: Consumer Protection Programs

At J.C. Penney, the nation's second largest general merchandise retailer, "consumerism" is not a dirty word. It is, in fact, a concept that has long guided the company, which now boasts annual sales of $6.2 billion.

Because of its enormous purchasing clout—all of that $6.2 billion in goods is bought from outside suppliers—Penney can demand adherence by those suppliers to strict specification standards. Several plants may be supplying Penney with work clothes, but each will be turning out garments with the same number of stitches per inch. A Quality Assurance Department monitors product quality at Penney, it is an outgrowth of a merchandise testing laboratory established in 1925.

Penney is not afraid of consumer protection legislation. In 1972, it testified before the U.S. Senate, expressing its "wholehearted endorsement of effective product safety legislation, including the promulgation and enforcement of mandatory federal product safety standards."

[Editors Note: The Business and Society Review recognized eleven companies in 1974 and thirteen in 1975 for outstanding contributions in the field of social responsibility. J.C. Penney was a 1974 winner and Stop & Shop was one of the 1975 winners.]

Nor is the company afraid of scrutiny by outsiders. Early in 1974 the Council on Economic Priorities published "Buyer, Beware!" a study of product safety and credit policies in effect at Sears, Penney, Montgomery Ward, W. T. Grant, and Kresge's K-Mart. Penney was the only one of these giant retailers to extend full cooperation to the CEP. The study also found Penney to be "the most cognizant of its responsibility." It led all the other retailers in offering flame-retardant children's sleepwear, safe toys, and power lawnmowers with the greatest number of safety features.

Penney has a simple production guarantee. Here's how it reads, for blenders, in its entirety: "Within one year of purchase we will replace this blender if defective with a new one of equal or superior value. Just return it to Penney's."

Every large Penney store now has a Customer Service Manager. His function is to serve as the local ombudsman for customers.

Penney issues a mountain of consumer information materials. Its Home Laundry Reference Chart, for example, is a model of clarity in explaining how different garments should be washed and dried.

The company's latest move was to create a Consumer Affairs Department, headed by Mrs. Satenig St. Marie, a Penney vice-president. Reporting to her are educational relations and a new department, consumer relations, managed by David Schoenfeld, who was formerly educational director for Consumers Union.

Addressing a company meeting four years ago, Penney's chairman, William M. Batten, stated: "If there was no such movement as Consumerism, we would do well to invent it. For it provides unprecedented opportunity for our company."

STOP & SHOP COMPANIES

Award: Consumerism

Concern for customers is alive and well at this Boston-based retailer, operator of the Stop & Shop supermarkets, Bradlees discount houses, Medi Mart drugstores, and Perkins tobacco shops. The company maintains a unique consumer information program that enables management to reach customers, and customers to "talk back" to management.

Since 1967, Stop & Shop has maintained consumer boards in the seven-state area it serves. The first one was set up in South Plainfield, N.J. Today, there are forty-seven local consumer boards. Each board consists of about twenty consumer members and several neighborhood store managers. A board meets about once every six weeks, with the agenda open to any aspect of the shopping experience: poor service at a Stop & Shop, inferior merchandise, high prices, misleading advertising, suggestions for improved service.

Minutes are kept of each meeting, and store managers are expected to follow up on complaints.

To insure that the consumer voice reaches top management, Stop & Shop has also established a corporate consumer board composed of company executives and representatives from the forty-seven local boards. Stop & Shop has used the corporate board as a forum to explore pressing issues. In 1974, for example, when sugar prices soared out of sight, the board heard directly from representatives of Coca-Cola, General Mills, and Amstar.

In May 1974, Stop & Shop began reaching out to its customers in another way with the launching of a weekly newsletter, *Consumerism,* which is distributed at all its supermarkets. This letter has tips on shopping and cooking, discusses nutrition and grocery industry problems, and includes cents-off coupons. It also invites letters from readers. During the first nine months of publication, the Stop & Shop consumer affairs department received more than 4,000 letters. Every one was answered. Stop & Shop has a four-member consumer affairs department.

Stop & Shop has acted on many of the suggestions that have come from its consumer boards. It adopted unit pricing long before this was legislated. It adopted a "no-repricing" policy for products already marked on the shelves. It reevaluated its "rain-check" policies. It put into effect a "Playsafer" toy safety program at Bradlees. In March 1975 it became one of the few major companies in the nation to endorse formally the legislation before Congress to establish an Agency for Consumer Advocacy.

37 THE COURAGE TO WORK TOGETHER

C. R. Sitter

. . . There are two fundamental routes for resolving differences between consumers and producers. One is the direct method, i.e., the consumers and the producers concerned with an issue work together to find an acceptable solution.

The second method is indirect. In this case the issue is taken to a third party for resolution. The third party is usually government. In recent years this seems to be the more popular route for consumer groups. That is unfortunate, in my opinion, both because it signals a breakdown in the direct relationship and because in the long run "government solutions" oftentimes end up costing consumers at least as much as they gain from them.

The direct approach provides the quickest and most effective route for consumers and businesses to resolve their differences. A continuing, open dialogue between consumers and business is more likely to lead to improved understanding, growing cooperation, constructive solutions, and long-term benefits for both.

The indirect approach, however, produces the opposite effect. When government is interposed as a third party, direct personal communication is lost and the process becomes adversarial. The principal parties (consumers and producers) address themselves primarily to the intermediary instead of to each other.

Government then passes laws to address the perceived problem, issues regulations to implement the laws, builds a bureaucracy to adminis-

---

Excerpt from a presentation to the American Council on Consumer Interests, San Antonio, Texas, April 27, 1979. Reprinted with permission.

ter the regulations, raises taxes to pay for the bureaucracy, and sits in pontifical magnificence in Washington, making decisions that end up raising costs for producers and prices for consumers.

A recent study estimates that the nation's 48 largest companies are spending $2.6 billion this year complying with the rules of just six federal regulatory bodies. We as consumers are paying this cost—some as increased taxes, but most of it in higher prices of the things we buy.

The cases of governmental mismanagement of consumer issues are growing—be it interlocking seat belt systems, air bags or a ban on saccharin. I am not arguing that there is no role for government; obviously there is. But whenever a direct solution or reasonable compromise can be found by direct communication between producers and consumers, I submit that *both* will be far better off if they solve the problem themselves rather than handing it to government to resolve.

Producers and consumers have on occasion worked together—without help from government—to solve some important consumer issues.

Unit pricing in the food industry was prompted by a consumer suggestion to help shoppers compare prices. The food industry agreed to label items so that the price per quantity was readily apparent to the shopper. Now unit pricing is commonplace in supermarkets from coast to coast.

Food producers and retailers also agreed to replace coded dating with open dating, so that shoppers can tell how long a perishable item has been on the shelf. Voluntarism *can* work if it is given a chance.

IS BUSINESS SERIOUS?

I recognize that many of you may have reservations about whether large corporations, including large oil companies, are truly receptive to consumer proposals and interests.

Let's discuss a few specific consumer-oriented things Exxon is doing. Perhaps in the discussion period you will add some more constructive suggestions. I would welcome any ideas you might care to offer.

We have established a consumer affairs group in Exxon USA whose function is to maintain an effective dialogue between Exxon and consumers, to ensure that the voices of our customers in particular and consumers in general are heard by Exxon management, and that our customers' problems are properly handled.

That is organization; now let's talk action.

1. With the aid of experts in the field, we have revamped our customer complaint handling system, written a new complaint philosophy, and trained almost 1,000 personnel in how to handle customer grievances and questions. We are following up on *all* registered consumers' complaints to find out whether customers are satisfied with the actions taken.

2. In response to expressed consumer interest, we have developed and tested a program under which customers wishing to pay cash for gasoline could receive a discount. We are prepared to offer this opportunity more broadly to consumers but for reasons I'll discuss in a minute, archaic federal regulations still prohibit our doing so.

3. In all states in which we market, our district managers have established a working dialogue with state consumer protection agencies and offered to cooperate with them in solving consumer grievances.

4. We have established a consumer panel in Boston. It is chaired by a leading local consumerist, and is composed of about a dozen state and local consumer representatives and leaders.

We provide information to this group on a wide range of topics chosen by them. Company executives regularly visit with this group to answer candidly their questions.

5. I am a member of the Consumer Affairs Committee organized about two years ago by the American Petroleum Institute. This committee is working very actively to increase awareness in the petroleum industry of consumer issues and to develop improved responses by all portions of the industry to legitimate consumer expectations.

6. An offshoot of this committee is an Automobile Repair Task Force, which I presently chair. This group has been formed to address specifically this major area of consumer dissatisfaction. Among other things it is working to upgrade mechanic proficiency in conjunction with the National Institute of Automobile Service Excellence (NIASE)—a successful non-governmental testing and certification organization. It is also trying to develop a suggested code of conduct for service stations offering auto repair service.

7. In conjunction with the National Association of Women Highway Safety Leaders and NIASE, Exxon has prepared audio visual presentations and written material for group meetings on driving skills, car maintenance, and gasoline saving. By the end of the year, we expect approximately one million women to attend free instructional meetings using this material.

8. In cooperation with the Walt Disney organization, we have produced two comic books for young readers. One deals with the fundamentals of energy production, supply and use and the other with energy conservation. We have distributed about 10 million of these free books to the consumers of the future—primarily through local schools.

These are but a few of the consumer activities we have under way, but perhaps they are enough to make the point—business *is* serious. We are trying to be alert to what consumers want, and what consumers need or don't like. Most businesses want to respond to those stimuli wherever possible—not for public relations reasons, but because it makes good economic sense.

No business will ever satisfy all the expectations of all customers. No individual here today will ever satisfy all the expectations of the others with whom he or she associates.

That is simply not a reasonable expectation. What is reasonable to expect, however, is a genuine effort to work out difficult problems in good faith. That can only be done if we talk to each other, try to understand each other, work out reasonable compromises, and above all have the *courage* to work together when our interests are similar.

Now, why should it take "courage" to work together? Obviously, it should not. But it does. That is because the instinctive "we/they syndrome" or the "good guy/bad guy complex" still governs so many consumer/producer relationships.

SOME COMMON INTERESTS

You probably have on the tip of your tongue a list of issues where business and consumer associations have lined up on the opposite side of the fence. There have been and will continue to be such cases. It is also true that business has joined with consumer groups on several questions of public policy. Business and consumer groups have joined together in the fight against costly and unproductive government regulations and paperwork.

We have joined in striving for reasonable protection of the natural environment, for example in the reclamation of land used for mining.

Along with consumer groups, many oil companies have endorsed the 55-miles-an-hour national speed limit and encourage its enforcement. This, along with other energy conservation measures, will reduce upward pressure on energy prices.

Last year, a bill was introduced in Congress to provide federal funding for small claims courts in which consumers seek redress of their grievances. The bill was stongly supported by consumer organizations. The visceral "we/they" syndrome suggests that business would automatically oppose such legislation. But that was not the case. The bill was in fact endorsed by the Chamber of Commerce of the United States, the Business Roundtable, and the National Association of Manufacturers.

Let me offer some examples of oil industry issues where I believe that the interests of Exxon and consumers are very similar, if not identical. Yet on few of them has there been any effective consumer/producer cooperation.

Earlier I mentioned our testing of a Discount for Cash program at service stations. Clearly, this is as pro-consumer a program as can be imagined. A federal law was passed about two years ago removing old legal obstacles to this consumer option. We have tested the idea and are ready to try it on a large scale. However, we cannot do so because of archaic Department of Energy gasoline regulations. Yet not one consumer group has joined in an effort to remove these regulations. Perhaps the reasoning is that "if Exxon wants it, it must be bad." If so, this is an excellent example of where an anti-big business attitude is also an anti-consumer attitude.

The assurance of a dependable supply of gasoline, home heating oil and other petroleum products obviously is in the best interests of consumers. That is what deregulation of domestic oil prices is intended to advance. Although deregulation will raise the price of petroleum products in the near future, over the long haul the revenues produced by those increases can finance expanded exploration and production of domestic energy supplies and thus reduce U.S. dependence on uncertain foreign supplies that are rapidly rising in cost. Although almost 60 percent of this increased revenue will flow to government under existing tax laws, a so-called "windfall profits tax" is being proposed. Whether or not a "windfall profits tax" is imposed, consumer cost of petroleum products will go up the same amount. The effect of such added taxation will be to reduce the revenues available to producers to find and produce more U.S. oil. Thus, consumers will pay the higher prices for oil, but will be deprived of the full supply benefits that could accompany and justify this higher consumer expense. Yet I wonder how many consumer groups will see it in their interest to oppose such a new tax.

Retail Divorcement legislation is another potential ground for producer-consumer cooperation. These laws in some states prohibit one of the three typical forms of gasoline marketing, that is, direct retailing by refiners. Divorcement laws are patently designed to reduce competition and permit service station dealers to raise their margins at consumer expense. The Department of Justice has recognized this and opposes such laws. Many oil companies—large and small—together with independent wholesalers are actively opposing this type of legislation. But where are the consumer groups? We do not see any of them opposing this legislation even though many have been briefed on it and understand the issue. Why? Is it so hard to oppose laws that shield selected businesses from the discipline of competition at consumer expense simply because large oil companies might be on the same side of the issue as you are? I hope not!

Another even more blatant case is the one billion dollar a year subsidy program the Department of Energy is running under the guise of protecting certain small refiners. Many of these so-called "small refiners" are Fortune 500 companies with assets of many hundreds of millions of dollars. We as consumers are unwittingly paying this subsidy in the price of products we buy. But as far as I am aware, no consumer groups have protested it. Again, why? Can a subsidy provided to one part of an industry at the expense of consumers be in the consumers' interest simply because it might also be hurting large oil refiners?

We could go on with this litany. We could talk about the broader subjects of the overall cost increases and adverse energy supply consequences that inevitably fall upon consumers when the price of government overregulation and protection finally has to be paid. But time doesn't permit.

CONSUMERS PAY FOR IT ALL

The greatest illusion of all is that somebody *else* pays for the things that government gives us as consumers. Ladies and gentlemen, nobody else pays. Consumers and individual taxpayers—and that is all of us—pay for everything.

All costs of regulation on industry, *all* costs of subsidies, *all* costs of government bureaucracy are inevitably passed on to us in higher prices and taxes. No amount of government legerdemain can stop that. So let's recognize that every protection or government intervention that we ask for, or tolerate, is going to be paid for *totally* by us as consumer-citizens.

If all of us wake up to that one simple but immutable fact, perhaps we will find both the courage—and the wisdom—to work together to solve our problems rather than going to "big brother" in Washington to do it for us.

The basic questions are: "Have business and consumer groups come of age?" "Are we mature enough to cooperate when our interests coincide even though we may be in opposition on other issues?" I certainly hope so. Because real progress will only come if we do have the maturity, the wisdom, and the courage to work together.

B Governmental Regulation

38 REGULATION: ASKING THE RIGHT QUESTIONS

Peter H. Schuck

In recent years, a vast literature on regulation has emerged, a literature to which many professional disciplines have contributed. Historians have chronicled the circumstances under which existing regulatory systems were established. Political scientists have described (often incorrectly) the political and institutional dynamics of regulation. Lawyers have analyzed the legal rules that govern the procedures and substantive policies of regulatory agencies. Economists have measured the economic performance of regulated industries and the costs and benefits associated with regulatory activities. And politicians, whose intellectual effusions fill countless volumes of their professional journal (the *Congressional Record),* have debated the merits of regulation in general and of regulatory proposals in particular.

Very little of this analysis, however, bears upon the question that policy makers most need to answer: How well is a regulatory program likely to be *implemented* in the real world? To be sure, economic theory has analyzed "market failure" (i.e., market conditions, such as external effects, inadequate consumer information, the "free rider" problem, inadequate tort remedy, monopoly, etc., which may justify regulatory intervention on efficiency grounds), and the efficiency and distributional consequences of particular regulatory proposals or programs ("cost-benefit analysis"). But the "market failure" and "cost-benefit" criteria are *minimal* ones, necessary but not sufficient to justify a regulatory intervention. Virtually all markets, after all, are imperfect to some degree,

---

Reprinted, with permission, from *National Journal* 11, April 28, 1979, pp. 711–717.

especially consumer markets in which, among other market flaws, the information possessed by consumers is often inadequate. Third party effects (called "externalities") which impose costs of activities upon persons who do not fully benefit from them (or vice versa) are also pervasive in a crowded, interdependent society, particularly one in which equity considerations (e.g., the income distribution and the fate of low-income groups in the marketplace) have increasingly come to affect the preferences of voters-consumers.

But if markets are almost always flawed, so are regulatory interventions by government. However inadequate consumer information may often be, information in the political marketplace (where there is no FTC to police claims) is probably worse. A consumer purchasing a product may know little about its performance, safety, durability, etc., but that pales in comparison to what the Consumer Product Safety Commission (CPSC) does not know but would have to know in order to prescribe a safety standard that would maximize the welfare of millions of consumers while taking into account the dynamic economic and technical realities of hundreds of firms. Much the same is true of externalities: Market transactions in an unsafe product will often harm third parties (e.g., those injured in accidents or compelled to pay higher insurance premiums) without compensation, but the potential for uncompensated, unforeseen harm to consumers, workers, stockholders and other third parties resulting from uninformed economy-wide or industry-wide regulations may be far greater. Other aspects of what might be called "regulatory failure"—for example, protracted, legalistic and expensive proceedings; a chronic tendency to lump differently-situated persons or firms into broad, unrefined regulatory categories; discouragement of long-term investment; discouragement of innovation—must also be weighed against the inevitable imperfections of the market.

Cost-benefit analyses are also invariably flawed. The reasons for this are well-known: the difficulty of identifying and quantifying many costs and benefits; the inevitably arbitrary nature of valuations of human life or health; the special difficulty of evaluating extremely low risk but catastrophic events (e.g. a meltdown of a nuclear reactor); the problem of interpersonal and intergenerational comparisons of utility; and many others. These limitations imply that cost-benefit ratios, whether favorable or unfavorable, should (like analyses of market failure) constitute only the beginning of the inquiry, not its conclusion.

To begin to address questions of regulatory *implementation,* one must first possess a theory not only of how markets work but of how regulation—whether of markets *per se* ("economic" regulation) or of other market-related phenomena, such as pollution, pensions or civil rights ("social" regulation)—works. Such a theory must be grounded not only in a knowledge of economics but in a knowledge of law, of politics and of history; in short, it must be interdisciplinary in nature. Perhaps for that reason, no such theory yet exists. And given the complexity, diversity and value-laden nature of the phenomena to be explained, any such theory is not likely to be a rigorous one. Nevertheless, this article suggests some modest hypotheses as a starting point.

Most of the propositions that follow must be qualified by the condition "other things being equal" in the regulatory world, of course, this condition is never really met. Nevertheless, such generalizations can help us to identify additional criteria or points of reference that can stimulate policy makers to think critically about the likely effects of regulation in real world situations, and decide what form or forms the regulation ought to take. These criteria will be grouped into five general categories relating to: (1) the structure of the market or other phenomenon to be regulated; (2) the informational needs of the regulator; (3) the objectives of the regulation; (4) the enforceability of the regulation; and (5) the political support for the regulation.

THE STRUCTURE OF WHAT IS TO BE REGULATED

The relevance of the structure of the market or other regulated activity to the probable efficacy of regulation extends well beyond the possibility of market imperfection.

Number of Regulatees

Other things being equal, the more numerous the firms, people or processes that must be regulated, the less likely it is that regulation will be effective. This generalization, while perhaps more true of what Charles Schultze has termed "command-and-control" regulation, tends to be true of "incentives" regulation as well. First, if scarce regulatory resources must be spread over a large number of entities, inspection and monitoring become sporadic, thereby diminishing the credibility of regulatory sanctions. The Occupational Safety and Health Administration (OSHA), for example, purports to regulate some five million workplaces. Although OSHA devotes four-fifths of its staff to enforcement, its inspections during 1976 covered fewer than 2 per cent of the workplaces. A probability of inspection for the average workplace of only once in several decades, coupled with very low fines for violations

($37.49 on average in 1976), means that the regulatory sanction is unlikely to be an important factor in and of itself. While private enforcement of a regulatory standard could supplement agency resources (e.g., the anti-fraud provisions of the Securities Act), private remedies are normally not authorized where the administration of a complex regulatory scheme is delegated to a regulatory agency.

Second, the number of entities may be so great as to make it difficult or impractical for the regulator even to *identify*, much less regulate, them all. The jurisdiction of several federal civil rights laws, for example, extends to all recipients and sub-recipients of "federal financial assistance;" no one has ever compiled a list of them, but it would probably include a half million or more entities. Similarly, the FCC has licensed some 13 million CB operators using about 25 million transmitters; with an enforcement staff of 100. It can only respond to the most extreme violators, such as transmissions involving criminal conduct. Finally, as the number of regulated entities increases, their diversity tends to increase as well, creating difficulties to which we now turn.

Diversity of Regulatees

As an artifact of law, regulation manifests what are perhaps the basic tensions of law: the inescapable conflict between uniformity and diversity, between rule and discretion, between certainty and uncertainty, and between the "rough justice" of broad categories and justice tailored to the equities of individual situations. Regulation almost invariably opts for the former of each of those dualities, for several reasons: limited resources; the importance to economic enterprise of predictability; the danger to effective regulation of delay and stale data; and the sheer enormity of the regulatory task.

The experience of the Federal Power Commission furnishes a dramatic example of this phenomenon. When the FPC undertook regulation of producer rates for natural gas in 1954. It began by determining "just and reasonable" rates for each of the more than 3,000 individual producers. By 1960, the sheer number of backed-up rate proceedings had swamped the Commission, and it was compelled to simplify the process drastically by lumping all producers together into fewer than a dozen "areas." Each producer in a given area was required to sell gas at or below the same "area rate," regardless of the cost and profit profile of the particular producer. Because even area data were difficult and expensive to compile, "area rates" were themselves determined by the Commission on the basis of area or nationwide *averages*, further attenuating the relationship between an area rate and the economic profile of any particular firm. Even area-rate regulation, however, proved too complex—the Southern Louisiana area rate was not affirmed by the Supreme Court until 1974—and the Commission in 1974 issued a single "national rate" applicable to all but the smallest producers. Within six months, this "single" rate had been increased by almost 20 per cent, and had been repeatedly encumbered with regulatory exceptions, exclusions and amendments.

To an even greater extent that its predecessors, the national rate was an artificial construct, bearing about as much resemblance to the economic profiles of the individual producers as the "average American" does to the diverse society that he or she is said to exemplify. In 1978, Congress enacted a *statutory* rate, but in order to provide flexibility found it necessary to provide for some 17 different rate categories. Many similar examples from the area of "social" regulation (such as FDA's attempts to regulate large numbers of over-the-counter drugs for safety and efficacy) could also be adduced.

Regulators cannot reasonably be faulted for adopting such "rough justice" strategies, given the regulatory tasks Congress sets for them and the meager (relative to such tasks) appropriations Congress votes for them. Nevertheless, its inevitable result is that people or firms in radically dissimilar circumstances are treated as if they were alike, producing competitive distortions and gross inequities. The use of the "base year" concept in price regulation, for example, ensures that some firms will enjoy substantial pricing latitude while others will be severely constrained, depending upon how each firm happened to fare in the base year and how typical that year was for each. Similarly, the notion that the small firm is simply a large firm in miniature ignores the very real differences between them with respect to mode of operations, access to capital, accounting systems and many other aspects of economic activity. Yet most regulatory requirements do not—and, as a practical matter, probably cannot—fully take account of such differences. Indeed, when an agency tries to do so, the administrative problems can be immense; one ERISA provision elicited more than 220,000 individual requests for exemption, some taking more than a year to process.

Where a regulator has jurisdiction over only one or a relatively small number of firms in an industry—for example, state public service commission regulation of public utilities, FCC regulation of interstate telephone service, or some state hospital cost review commissions—the problem of creating competitive inequities through regulation is reduced somewhat (although not entirely, since regulated firms must compete with unregulated firms in capital and other markets). The problems of acquiring adequate information, political support and other resources, however, will remain formidable ones, as the FCC's chronic difficulty in regulating AT&T demonstrates.

The Dynamism of the Particular Market

Some activities (say, telecommunications) are more subject to rapid technological, economic, or other changes than others (say, the practice of law). In general, regulation is most problematical when it is attempting to employ "command-and-control" techniques to regulate firms, industries or activities that are relatively dynamic.

Any regulatory system will tend to develop a political momentum (or inertia) reflecting the power of those groups that have or acquire vested economic, bureaucratic, ideological or political interests in the maintenance of the regulatory *status quo*. Whether it be the interest of trucking interest (and their unions) in cartelization under the auspices of the ICC; of small refiners in regulation of oil prices; of environmental groups in enforcement of anti-pollution laws; or of the congressional small business committees in the enforcement of the Robinson-Patman Act, these commitments make it quite difficult for a regulatory system to respond to changes in its environment. Thus, when rapid technological transformations or dramatic perturbations in the potential competitive situation occur, they create strong pressures for fundamental adjustments which the regulated firms (and their allies) strongly resist. That resistance may be successful (as with the banking industry's use of regulation to prevent competition across state lines) or unsuccessful (as with airline deregulation, the relaxation of certain FCC controls over specialized telecommunications services, and the demise of "fair trade" laws), depending upon a number of political and economic factors. The banking industry, for example, consists of a large number of firms distributed in every congressional district; it tends to be well-connected politically at the local level; it can play the several bank regulatory agencies off against one another; and it is often protected from competition even within the borders of its own state. But even when regulation does adjust to the new technological and competitive realities, it tends to do so only after considerable delay (or "regulatory lag").

A second reason why regulation, especially the "command-and-control" variety, does not sit easily in the saddle of change has less to do with regulatory politics than with the nature of legal rules. Many, perhaps most, regulatory standards are "input," "design," or "process" standards; they prescribe what one must do (or, in the case of credentialling, be) or how one must go about doing it. Yet the technical reality which they describe changes (or should change) constantly; indeed, the very essence of innovation is to alter the nature or mix of inputs and processes to deliver a product or service to consumers more efficiently. For that reason, a "performance" standard is less subject to this objection. Unfortunately, as discussed below, there are limits on the extent to which performance standards can be, or ought to be, employed. And even a performance standard is often undermined by technological change and advances in learning. Many of the "consensus" standards which OSHA adopted in 1971, for example, were performance standards, yet many of these had been rendered obsolete long before 1971, either because the state of the engineering art permitted equally effective but less costly standards or because the state of knowledge concerning the health and safety effects of certain equipment, processes and substances had changed. Nevertheless, many of these are still on the books due to the laborious and controversial process required to develop new ones.

The Existence of Countervailing Interests

While the economic interests of consumers will sometimes coincide with those of regulated firms, they often will not. The interests of polluters, for example, will usually diverge from those of persons living nearby. In such situations, the ability of regulation to protect affected third parties will depend to a considerable extent upon countervailing interests with a stake in challenging and countering the assumptions, data and policy arguments regulated firms press upon their regulators. In some cases, such adversariness inheres in the regulatory program. Regulation of the collective bargaining process by the National Labor Relations Board, for example, systematically pits well-defined, well-organized economic interests—management and labor—against each other. This is sometimes true under OSHA as well. In some cases, the structure of a regulated industry naturally generates some degree of adversariness. For example, the International Trade Commission presides over a process in which pressures by domestic industries for protection through trade restrictions are sometimes (though not always) countered by importers and manufacturers favoring liberalized trade. In still other cases, environmental, consumer or other "public interest" groups may help fill the void; EPA, the FTC and the CPSC, among others, have encouraged this approach. Two formidable forces—the regulatory agencies themselves and congressional committees—have (in recent years, at least) often attempted to perform this adversarial function, with varying success. Taken all together, these countervailing interests have helped to subvert the conventional wisdom about the inexorable, irreducible pro-industry bias of regulation, especially (but not exclusively) in the case of "social" regulation.

Even when one of these countervailing forces is operating in a regulatory system, of course, inequalities in information, technical skills, political support and other resources will advantage one interest or another; in the nature of the case, it is difficult to see how it could ever be otherwise. Nevertheless, a regulatory system in which adversariness, through one or another of these mechanisms, is a reality is more likely to generate policies that take into account the wide variety of interests implicated by important regulatory decisions.

THE INFORMATION NEEDS OF REGULATORS

One of the principal justifications for regulation is the market failure that results from inadequate consumer information. Yet regulation does not obviate the need for such information; it simply shifts the locus of that need from the consumer to the regulator, while vastly increasing the quantity, quality and types of information needed.

The Availability of Information

Regulators ordinarily need a great deal of information in order to make sound regulatory decisions—information concerning costs; benefits; consumer preferences; quality-cost trade-offs; effects of alternative decisions on the environment; employment and competition; and on many other subjects. Almost invariably, much of that information is in the exclusive possession of the regulated industry and some of that (e.g., cost data or trade secrets) may be legally protected against disclosure to the public. Nevertheless, the extent to which regulation-relevant information is already in the public domain or can be obtained through legal process by the regulator does vary. The Equal Employment Opportunity Commission (EEOC), for example, has access to most of the occupational, salary and other such information it needs to construct a *prima facie* case of employment discrimination against a firm, and the CPSC can obtain much data on the incidence and cost of consumer injuries, the engineering of regulated products and the cost of proposed safety requirements. On the other hand, the FPC (and its successor) was almost wholly dependent upon producers of (and drillers for) natural gas for the basic information upon which its rate formula was based despite the fact that the industry data were demonstrated to be highly questionable. Access to needed information, of course, does not assure that it will be used either intelligently or fairly, but an agency that cannot even obtain it is almost certain to make poorly-supported decisions.

Finally, "economic" regulation often undermines the valuable information implicit in costs and prices; this may be intentional (as with Regulation Q, which in effect mandates that small savers subsidize homeowners) or not (as with "regulatory lag" in public utility regulation). On the other hand, much "social" regulation is designed to enhance the availability and value of cost and price information by making such information reflect the full, "true" costs of doing business.

The Quality of Information

The quality of information, of course, is related to its availability to the extent that it is open to challenge by someone other than those who have supplied it. Beyond the question of its availability to the regulator, however, its quality may vary considerably depending upon a number of factors. Data may be "soft" due to the primitive state of scientific knowledge (e.g., the environmental and health effects of certain chemicals at various levels of exposure), or to the irreducibly subjective nature of the phenomenon being regulated (e.g., the relationship between staffing ratios and "quality" day care). It may be suspect by reason of the self-interested character of its source (e.g., the American Gas Association's data on gas reserves); or the incapacity of third parties to evaluate it either as a legal matter (e.g., confidential wage and price data submitted by industry to the Council on Wage and Price Stability) or as a practical matter (e.g., data submitted to USDA under the incredibly complex program of dairy price supports). And it may be stale due to the protracted nature of many regulatory proceedings (e.g., one proposed merger of a major railroad gained final ICC approval only after 12 years, by which time the line was bankrupt).

The quality of regulatory information, moreover, may be affected by the distribution of the benefits and costs of a regulatory proposal. Robert Reich has pointed out that cost-benefit analysis is more likely to be demanded and supplied by both opponents and proponents of a proposed regulation in those instances (e.g., much environmental and safety regulation) in which its costs are highly concentrated and its benefits are widely dispersed, than in those instances in which the reverse is true. Other things being equal, the quality of information available to the regulator as a result of those analyses is likely to be better than in their absence.

The Quantity of Information

Regulation through economic incentives tends to require far less information on the part of the regulator than regulation through "command-and-control" techniques. Since regulatory information of high quality is often difficult to come by, that is no small virtue. A regulator designing an effluent tax, for example, need not know in detail the technology or the cost profiles of firms; he need only know the benefits that particular reductions in effluent level will generate and then set the tax accordingly. Moreover, if experience suggests that the tax is too high or too low, its level can be adjusted far more easily than can a regulation which mandates certain specified inputs or processes and on which firms have relied through large investments in plant or machinery. A performance standard shares some of these attributes of incentives, but because it does not (as the tax does) give a firm the freedom to pollute at any level it wishes (so long as it is willing to pay the social cost), the regulator cannot rationally set the level of the standard without knowing what the cost of compliance will be to firms. On the other hand, *enforcing* "incentive" regulations may require more information than enforcing input, design or process requirements, a possibility discussed below.

THE NATURE OF THE REGULATORY OBJECTIVE

The particular task that Congress sets for the regulatory agency will not necessarily control its future behavior, for the agency is inevitably transformed over time from an instrument of legislative policy into an institution with an organic life and purposes of its own. Moreover, most regulatory statutes are exceedingly ambiguous (and sometimes even contradictory) in defining the regulatory objectives. Thus, the CPSC must eliminate "unreasonable risks of injury," the ICC must set "just and reasonable" rates; and civil rights statutes typically proscribe "discrimination" without defining it. And particular regulatory objectives, such as occupational health and safety, are ordinarily mitigated by other regulatory objectives (such as "feasibility") with little or no guidance given as to how these values should be traded off against one another. Nevertheless, an agency's formal objectives are important in establishing a regulatory "mood;" they define the outer boundaries of its principal mission and other institutions, especially the courts, will be called upon to enforce that mission once it begins to stray. Two dimensions are especially important to a regulation's efficacy: the substantive content of its objectives and the direct measurability of their achievement.

The Content of the Objective

Some regulatory objectives are more easily achieved than others. To a great extent, the strengths and limitations of regulatory agencies correspond to the strengths and limitations of law itself. Thus, regulatory agencies, like the law, tend to be better at regulating procedures and the flow of information than at regulating market characteristics (e.g., the price, quality and health and safety effects) which require at the margin a tradeoff of important economic and social values. That is certainly not to deny that regulating such characteristics is often essential in order to protect the public. It is only to say that this kind of regulation tends to be far more difficult—and errors far more costly to society—than regulating information and procedures. To be sure, the distinction between these types of regulatory objectives will not always be clear-cut: The proper functioning of markets depends upon information and procedures, and both are themselves commodities which are often marketed (as the durability of *Consumer Reports* and labor arbitration demonstrate); moreover, the regulation of procedures and information generates costs and often implicates important values and interests. But it remains the case that what the SEC, NLRB, Commodity Futures Trading Commission and Federal Elections Commission (FEC) attempt to do tends to be quite different from—and far more manageable than—what the ICC, OSHA, EEOC and energy regulators attempt to do.

The most important differences relate to what Dahl and Lindblom have called the "problem of calculation" and the "problem of control." The quantity, type and quality of data that the SEC needs to determine what kinds of information investors should have for the efficient functioning of the securities markets; that the NLRB needs to determine what is an appropriate bargaining unit or whether an unfair labor practice has been committed; or that the FEC needs to determine whether a particular activity by a candidate constitutes a campaign "expenditure," are very different from that which the ICC needs to calculate "just and reasonable" rates for competing modes of transportation; OSHA needs to devise health and safety standards that will protect workers while not unduly jeopardizing their jobs; the EEOC needs to determine whether employers are engaging in discrimination or merely reacting to labor market conditions that confront them; or the Department of Energy needs to price and allocate scarce gasoline supplies. The information required for the former tasks, while often imperfect, tends nonetheless to be manageable, available and reasonably stable over time; moreover, it possesses few of the infirmities of information discussed earlier. In contrast, the latter tasks tend to require enormous quantities of information; much of this is obsolete by the time it is ready to be used, much is impossible to come by at any reasonable cost, and that which is available will often be of low quality.

If the problem of calculation is especially formidable with respect to regulation of price, quality and other market characteristics, the problem of control is no less so. Compliance with the SEC's disclosure requirements, the NLRB's procedures, or the FEC's strictures is relatively easy to monitor. Consequently, there is less likelihood of competitive distortions, black markets or other forms of evasion. In the case of "economic" and much "social" regulation, however, non-compliance is more difficult to detect, for several reasons: the economic incentives on the part of buyers and sellers to evade requirements are especially great; what constitutes compliance is far more ambiguous; and there tend to be fewer countervailing interests capable of enforcing compliance. To establish that a firm failed to make certain financial disclosures to the public or failed to follow prescribed procedures is one thing; to establish that it discharged pollutants in excessive quantities, sold a substance that is carcinogenic, discriminated in hiring or engaged in an anti-competitive merger, is quite another. Institutional investors, labor unions or opposition candidates are well positioned to try to police the former; ordinary consumers, workers or small businesses will have little incentive or opportunity to police the latter.

The Ability to Measure Performance

The extent to which regulatory objectives are in fact achieved can be measured more directly with respect to some objectives than others. OSHA, for example, can gauge the extent to which it has improved occupational *safety* far more readily than it can with respect to occupational *health*. Thus, the number and/or severity of industrial accidents per man-year is a reasonable measure of the former, for an "accident" is a relatively well defined phenomenon whose cause is usually (though not always) ascertainable. (Even here, of course, the accident rate clearly is affected by factors other than OSHA, as evidenced by the recent increase in lost work days and serious industrial accidents). Many occupational diseases, however, possess neither of these attributes; their symptoms are generalized, may not even appear for a generation or more and have uncertain causes.

The extent to which performance can be measured directly is often a matter that the regulator cannot control; as the example of occupational disease suggests, it may be inherent in the particular regulatory task. In this case, the regulator will usually be obliged to devise operational substitutes for the regulatory objective, proxies the achievement of which *can* be measured directly. These proxies generally take the form of "input" requirements (e.g., that only licensed physicians may perform certain tasks), "process" requirements (e.g., that certain procedures be undertaken) or "design" requirements (e.g., that certain types of machinery be used). Even when "outcome" or "performance" requirements are available, they may be impractical because of the administrative difficulties of actually measuring or enforcing them. It is far easier, for example, to enforce affirmative action requirements (at least in the first instance) by counting the proportion of minority employees in a firm than by attempting to evaluate its subjective "good faith" in seeking such employees. Similarly, an OSHA Inspector can easily measure the distance between a cutting machine and a guard rail, but measurng the safety performance of such a machine directly would require that the inspector wait until after the damage had been inflicted, thereby defeating the regulatory objective.

In many cases, however, performance or outcome standards or economic incentives are preferably. EPA, for example, is increasingly attempting to regulate the amount of permissible affluent rather than regulating the pollution control technology; similarly, HEW has devised new outcome-oriented performance measures for the Head Start program. Such standards are superior in several respects. First, they prescribe only the desired result, leaving to the informed discretion of the regulatee how best to achieve that result. This division of responsibility recognizes the comparative advantages of both regulator and regulatee, and increases the likelihood that the most efficient solutions will be devised. (On the other hand, the regulatee may select a solution that is efficient but may nevertheless be deemed objectionable. Thus, firms may require workers to wear uncomfortable personal protection devices rather than install more expensive engineering controls). Third, they avoid involving regulators in the minutiae of industrial engineering, management science, applied chemical research and the like, except to the extent necessary to prescribe the desired outcome. Finally, they provide measures against which the performance of both regulator and regulatee can be judged because the measures relate directly to the real purposes of the regulation, rather than to some imperfect proxy. Indeed, regulators and regulatees often resist performance standards for this very reason (although the stated complaint will often be not that performance measures are objectionable *per se*, but that the particular standard chosen is not an appropriate measure of the regulatory objective).

THE ENFORCEABILITY OF REGULATIONS

The disposition of people to obey a legal requirement depends upon many factors (including the costs of compliance, the clarity of its meaning and the extent to which it is perceived to be reasonable or just), but a critical one is the anticipated cost of non-compliance. For this reason, the enforceability of a regulatory scheme is an important determinant of its real-world effectiveness.

There may well be few legal requirements for which some loophole or evasion cannot be devised by a regulatee with both a strong incentive to do so and a creative lawyer to help; even under ordinary circumstances, regulations often cannot be effectively enforced. Nevertheless, some regulations are more readily enforceable than others; enforceability depends upon a number of factors, many of which relate to points made earlier. First, the resources of the regulator will often simply be inadequate to the tasks of identifying non-compliance and mobilizing the administrative apparatus, especially when the regulatees are numerous and not highly visible. Federal day care regulations have long gone unenforced for this reason (among others); it is simply impossible to identify, much less monitor or inspect, the tens of thousands of formal and informal day care arrangements subsidized by federal dollars. Second, a regulation's ambiguity, often desirable for policy or political reasons, may be so great as to preclude enforcement, either as a matter of law (as a federal appeals court recently found with respect to Department of Energy pricing regulations) or as a matter of fairness (as with the federal day care regulations). Third, certain regulations penalize what the price system rewards, thereby realizing the often considerable potential for black markets in the prohibited activity, discrediting the regulation itself and calling into question the fairness of selective enforcement. The regulation of marijuana, the rationing of gasoline and state taxation of cirarettes are examples. Finally, enforcement may not be feasible for political reasons, another way of saying that many people find the prohibited activity profitable or otherwise desirable.

THE POLITICAL SUPPORT FOR REGULATIONS

Regulation is not simply a legal, administrative and technical phenomenon; it is ultimately and inescapably a political one as well. Our decentralized, fragmented political system assures that no important regulatory program can be put in place without the mobilization of significant political resources. Once established, a regulatory agency must find sources of continuing political support in order to retain the integrity of its authorizing legislation, obtain adequate appropriations, pursue its own policy priorities, control the management of its internal affairs and sustain its enforcement efforts. While the apparent immortality of virtually all regulatory agencies attests to their success in developing such support, agencies do vary considerably in the strength and durability of that support. For example, the older agencies primarily concerned with "economic" regulation of particular industries long achieved notable success in conventional political terms, yet some, such as the CAB, FCC and ICC, have seen their autonomy and support erode under the impact of new political forces and coalitions. Others, such as the FTC, SEC and the bank regulatory agencies, have received ever more authority and influence. Even among the newer agencies charged with "social" regulation, political strength is highly variable: EPA and the Food and Drug Administration have demonstrated great ability to resist incursions on their autonomy and authority, while the CPSC and the Office of the Civil Rights have been more vulnerable.

Although there is no simple explanation for these differences, certain generalizations seem plausible enough. It seems clear, for example, that regulation significantly benefitting a well-organized constituency dispersed among all congressional districts while spreading the costs over a large number of people in ways that are not highly visible, will tend to generate substantial political support; regulation that distributes benefits and costs in the opposite way will not. Certainly, the political strength of the agencies engaged in "economic" regulation can be explained in such conventional political terms. (What is more difficult to explain in such terms is the growing strength of their opponents.) Many "social" regulators also derive their support from relatively well organized and widely dispersed interests (such as environmental groups and labor unions) and their allies in Congress, the agencies and the media. Still, it remains intriguingly unclear why, for example, some health and safety regulators, such as FDA, EPA and the National Highway Traffic Safety Administration, manage to sustain public support for their activities while others, such as the CPSC, do not. Such differences may reflect factors such as the political skills of the agency's leadership which cannot be systematically analyzed. Whatever their cause, however, these differences are highly relevant to the ability of each agency to achieve the regulatory tasks that are set for them or that they set for themselves.

CONCLUSION

The criteria that have been discussed do not exhaust those that are relevant to deciding whether, or to what extent, or in what form, to regulate. Certainly, there is nothing arcane or particularly technical about them; Indeed, once one reflects upon them, they appear quite obvious. Yet with a few exceptions, such criteria are rarely discussed in public debates concerning regulation. Indeed, even the current mood of skepticism concerning regulation, as manifested in the Administration's regulatory reform proposals, has failed to accord much significance to these questions, preferring instead to focus upon the more systematic use of cost-benefit analysis (a matter which, as discussed above, should be regarded only as a threshold inquiry, only rarely decisive).

It is important that we attempt to understand why this should be so. One answer—that it is in the interest of powerful political forces that these questions not be seriously addressed—begs the most important questions and is, in any event, almost tautological. A more useful explanation may be that our political system has come to be dominated by two views: that a public policy is to be justified less by its consequences than by the motivation animating its proponents, and that concerns about implementation in the *real* world of regulations spawned by the *political-bureaucratic* world are niggling details that can safely be deferred until after the regulations have been signed. If this explanation is correct, then the remedy can come, if at all, only through a change in public views as retracted by the political process. Questions, after all, are not likely to be asked unless people truly desire the answers.

39 SOME DIFFICULTIES IN MEASURING THE COSTS AND BENEFITS OF REGULATION

Richard B. Ross

THE OBJECTIVES OF REGULATION

Two underlying rationales for regulation are: (1) to correct market failures occasioned by such factors as monopoly of supply, inadequate information in the marketplace, and costs that fall on society instead of the producer, such as pollution; and (2) to regulate the economy for social goals, such as the redistribution of income, allocation of scarce resources, and stable prices (Hughes, Verkuil, and Williams, 1978, pp. 9–10).

A slightly different, although compatible view is provided by political scientists. Politics, Lasswell (1958) said, can be defined as "who gets what, when and how." Consequently, regulation may be seen as another means of allocating benefits. Administrative determination of who gets what, when and how is substituted for market and/or legislative determination. Regulation differs from other administrative methods of benefits allocation in at least the following way: It *expressly* takes something away from someone—usually the regulated—in order to give something to someone else—the presumed beneficiary of the regulation.

With the understanding that regulation concerns who gets what and

---

Reprinted with permission from G. David Hughes and E. Cameron Williams (eds.), *The Dialogue That Happened* (Boston: Marketing Science Institute, 1979), pp. 56–70.

how they get it, one can characterize the objectives of regulation affecting marketing. There appear to be four different types of objectives, as shown in Table 39–1.

The first type of objective is predicated on classical economic theory. Regulation in this area relies on the model of rational decision-makers who, given adequate information, will make the best decisions for themselves. Thus, the primary benefit of such regulation is reasonably clear: better decisions by the product's purchasers or users. The method for obtaining the benefit is also reasonably clear: somehow providing more or better information. Many regulations of the Federal Trade Commission (FTC) and some of other regulatory bodies, such as the Food and Drug Administration (FDA), display this model. Examples would include regulations issued under the Magnuson-Moss Warranty Act, the proposed franchise disclosure rule, the FTC's advertising substantiation program, the warnings required on cigarette advertising, and all labeling requirements.

The second type of objective is based on protecting the product user from illness, injury, or death by imposing product standards. This regulatory approach goes back to the muckrakers and Upton Sinclair's exposé of conditions in the meatpacking industry and requires specific action by the regulated firm in the manufacture of the product. The activities of the FDA and Consumer Product Safety Commission are heavily in this area. The motor vehicle safety regulations of the National Highway Traffic Safety Administration (NHTSA) fall under this objective, too. The justification for this approach is that the individual con-

TABLE 39–1. OBJECTIVES OF REGULATION

TYPE OF OBJECTIVE	PRIMARY BENEFICIARY	PRIMARY BENEFIT	METHOD FOR OBTAINING BENEFIT
I	Prospective purchaser or user of a product	Better decisions	More/better information
II	Product user	Elimination of hazardous products and/or their consequences	Product standards
III	Society	Attainment of agreed-upon social goals	Mandated product modifications
IV	Society and/or individual consumers	Improvement in public welfare	Controlled business practices

sumer cannot tell if the product is unsafe until after purchase and use; by then it is too late.

While the first two types of objectives of regulation have existed for some time, the third type is relatively new. Society, rather than the individual, is the primary beneficiary of the third type. The benefit is the attainment of agreed-upon social goals. The mechanism is mandated product modifications that force the consumer to behave in what is defined as a socially responsible way. That is, regulation of the industry is simply a convenient way of regulating the individual consumer for the benefit of society as a whole.

Examples of this regulatory approach include NHTSA's motor vehicle fuel efficiency standards, which are designed to reduce fuel consumption by limiting the consumer's choice of cars to those which are relatively fuel efficient; the appliance energy efficiency standards of the Department of Energy, which will limit the consumer's choice to relatively energy efficient appliances; and the prohibition by the "Environmental Protection Agency" (EPA) of the sale of leaded gasoline to cars that require unleaded fuel.

The fourth and last type of objective is more difficult to describe because it encompasses a variety of regulations, some of them quite recent, some much older. The primary beneficiary of such regulation is the individual consumer or society, although it is not clear which. The primary benefit seems to be an improvement in what might be termed the public welfare. The method for obtaining the benefit is control of business practices.

Not surprisingly, this area is one in which there tends to be more controversy than others. It includes, on the one hand, requiring businesses to take actions to correct market imperfections. An example of this type is the Holder-in-Due Course Rule, which is designed to prevent the seller of a shoddy retail product sold on an installment basis from transferring the installment loan to a third party, such as a bank, and then having both the retailer and the bank avoid responsibility for product defects. Other examples are Equal Credit Opportunity, Fair Credit Reporting, and proposals to prohibit so-called red-lining of neighbors by mortgage financing institutions. Another example of this type, which will be discussed in more detail later, is the FTC's Product Availability Rule which, in essence, requires supermarkets to have advertised items available on the shelves.

A second thrust of this type of objective controls business practices in a different way by restricting the dissemination of certain information. The clearest example is the ban on television cigarette advertising. The present proposal by the FTC staff to prohibit advertising on children's programs is another example.

In contrast to the other three types of objectives, the underlying rationale of this fourth class is not entirely clear. It seems somehow to relate to the belief that the government has an obligation to make life fairer. Thus, buried somewhere in the history of these regulations is the argument that certain groups of persons are maltreated by the normal functioning of the market. So, for instance, Equal Credit Opportunity regulations are necessary to insure that women and minorities are not discriminated against in access to credit. The Product Availability Rule is necessary to protect inner-city dwellers from being ripped off by supermarkets that entice them to shop by advertising specials that are not available in any reasonable quantity. And, currently, a ban on advertising on children's television shows is deemed necessary because children do not have the maturity to judge advertising claims and, consequently, advertising to them is *per se* unfair and deceptive. In this vein, one should remember that the ban on television cigarette advertising was also justified on the basis that such advertising unfairly influences children and teenagers through the manipulation of symbols which are important to them.

Some typology of regulatory objectives—whether this one or not—is necessary as a first step in assessing the costs and benefits of regulation for two reasons:

1. It appears likely that cost-effectiveness analysis is more useful in evaluating regulations than cost-benefit analysis (Stern et al., 1977, p. 50). Cost-effectiveness analysis involves determining the extent to which a rule has achieved its objectives. Hence, one needs to know what the objectives were; that determination is significantly simplified if objectives can be categorized.
2. As will be discussed in more detail later, final determination of the wisdom of adopting, modifying, or eliminating a regulation frequently, if not always, turns on value judgments (e.g., see Hughes, Verkuil, and Williams, 1978, p. 21). These judgments can be enhanced when the objectives of the regulation are classified.

MEASUREMENT MODELS OF REGULATORY IMPACT

. . . Since the purpose of a regulation is to induce change of some kind, it is possible to formulate the Measurement Model as a "Before" and "After" design in which there are three variables.

The regulatory variable is that which is directly being manipulated by the regulation—say, product standards for packaging under the

TABLE 39-2. THE MEASUREMENT MODEL AS A BEFORE/AFTER DESIGN

	BEFORE	AFTER
Regulatory variable	no	yes
Primary benefit	+	+++
Cost	+	++

Poison Prevention Packaging Act. The change from "Before" to "After" may be from zero to one—nothing to something; or it might be qualitative or quantitative in nature.

The primary benefit is the criterion variable. This variable is what the regulation is supposed to change—say, the number of injuries and deaths.

The cost is the by-product of attaining the primary benefit via manipulation of the particular regulatory variable as specified in the regulation. The notion behind regulation, generally unarticulated, is that (a) this cost will be less than the benefit and/or (b) it will fall on groups other than the primary beneficiaries of the regulation.

Thus, as illustrated in Table 39-2, the regulatory variable changes from "no"—not having a regulation—to "yes," having one. In consonance with that change is the change in the level of the criterion variable—from there being some of it to there being more of it. Finally, there is a change in cost—from some to more. But the cost in the "After" state is less than the benefit—and so, the regulation is a good one.

This, then, is a measurement model which is useful for analysis and which adequately represents the measurement model of decision-makers. The model is not perfect by any means. However, it has the advantage of being meaningful to those whose feelings about the research results are important. Moreover, as will be seen, even with such a crude model the difficulties in assessing costs and benefits are formidable.

RESEARCH PROBLEMS

The six cells of Table 39-2 represent difficulties in measurement. These are not merely the difficulties of inadequate "Before" data or insufficiently powerful measurement methodologies. Our experience has indicated that such difficulties can, to a reasonable extent, be overcome through proper research design. Rather, the difficulties are more fundamental, having to do with the ways in which the issues are conceptualized in the research and in the regulation itself.

The Regulatory Variable

Several examples will illustrate the problems that are associated with the regulatory variable.

The action being regulated may not be clear in the regulation. The FTC Product Availability Rule calls for grocery stores to have advertised items available in sufficient quantities to meet expected demand. What is being regulated? Grocery store inventories of advertised items? Or the advertising of such items? Is the expectation that grocery stores will build up adequate inventories of items they advertise or is the expectation that they will only advertise items for which they have adequate inventories? In other words, how is the regulated industry's behavior expected to change? To spend more on inventories or to modify advertising practices to correspond better to the level of inventories?

The most appropriate unit of analysis may not be clear. In the Product Availability Rule case, how is the regulatory variable to be operationalized? Is the appropriate unit of analysis the store, so that big stores and small stores are expected to have the same rate of availability? Or is it product exposure, so that a big store which has a 5% rate of unavailability is really "harming" more consumers than a small store with the same rate? Or is it by product category, so that a product, such as meat, which is purchased by nearly everyone, bears more weight in the assessment of availability than a product, such as yeast, which is purchased by few consumers? Clearly, different "availability" rates will result from how the action being regulated is operationally defined.

Measurement of change in the regulatory variable also presents difficulties and not simply in the sense that "Before" data are not always available. Take the case of the FTC's advertising substantiation program which requires advertisers to have substantiation for advertising claims before using those claims. Assume that adequate "Before" and "After" data are obtainable because large companies keep good records of their operational procedures. Thus, one can tell whether the procedures used in the development of advertising have changed. Given that, what if one finds:

- No change in procedures? That is, if the amount of substantiation is the same today as it was before active implementation of the substantiation program by FTC? There would, apparently, be no benefit and no cost, except for FTC staff salaries and perhaps litigation expenses of companies accused of violations. But is this true? Is it not possible that although procedures—the regulated variable—have not changed, the psyche of the regulated has? That discrete decisions concerning the adequacy of substantiation for a claim are different now than before? In other words, is it not possible that mere existence of regulation changes the action being regulated—a sort of Heisenberg principle of regulation?

- A change in procedures? That is, if the amount of substantiation is different today than it was before? Does one ascribe the change to the regulatory effort? Or, is the change in the regulatory variable caused by other factors, such as the network rules for advertising clearance or just a general change in community and business attitudes about what is acceptable in advertising. That is to say, we are used to the notion that it is difficult to ascribe change in a criterion varible—the benefit—to a particular cause, such as a regulation. What is being suggested here is that it may be equally difficult to ascribe change in the regulatory variable itself to the regulation.

Benefits

The next set of difficulties have to do with the primary benefit—the criterion variable.

- First, there is the question of simply identifying what the primary benefit is supposed to be. In the case of automobile fuel efficiency standards, is the primary benefit an increase in average miles per gallon for the automobile fleet? Or, is it not really a decrease in the total energy consumed by motor vehicles? We would argue that regulation of average fleet mph is the regulatory variable, while reduction in energy use is the primary benefit. If the latter is the correct benefit, then one can deal with the question of whether or not the regulation actually achieves its objective; if the former is the benefit, then *ipso facto* the regulation achieves the benefit simply by being complied with.
- Then we have the problem of operationally defining the primary benefit:

  A primary benefit of the Product Availability Rule is clearly lower search costs for consumers. Is this defined as fewer trips after the rule than before? Or as fewer unnecessary trips? And, if the latter, how is "unnecessary" to be defined?

  In rules with Type I objectives—better consumer decisions—the difficulty in defining the benefit in a manner that permits reasonable measurement is appreciable. How is a "better decision" identified?

Measuring change in the benefit variable and ascribing it to the rule is a problem that probably requires little comment. However, to illustrate the complexity of the matter, consider what should be a fairly clear case: automobile fuel efficiency standards. Yet it is not all clear that with the regulation less fuel is being used—or, if so, how much of the reduction, if any, is attributable to the standards. It may very well be that more fuel efficient vehicles simply mitigate the effects of higher priced gasoline—consumers may be driving the same number of miles as before because the new cars allow them to do so at the same or only marginally higher costs. *Without* the rules it is possible that fewer miles would be driven because aggregate annual gasoline costs could be sufficiently high so as to encourage conservation.

Costs

It has been noted that measures of costs must go beyond enforcement and compliance to include the total costs to society of producing a product under a given regulatory regime in comparison with what the costs would have been at the same output level at a base regulatory regime (Harbridge House, 1977, pp. IV-9). This formulation, while unquestionably correct, tends to obscure some important issues.

- First, many decision-makers have tended not to care very much about costs.
- Second, really a subpart of the first part, this formulation focuses on allocative costs. In fact, the political process is more concerned with distributive costs.
- Third, intangible costs are easily lost sight of when one focuses on physical elements, such as production and output.

In this context, allocative costs are new costs created by regulatory action, such as the salary of the employee hired to complete the required forms. Distributive costs, on the other hand, are existing costs which are transferred from one group to another, such as when the tax burden is shifted as a result of special credits for senior citizens.

Virtually, all research on regulatory costs is concerned with the notion of allocative efficiency. Yet, few rules are adopted or unadopted because they affect the efficiency of the economy. This concept of "costs" as understood by decision-makers is simply not relevant to most rule-making.

Market Facts recently interviewed a number of decision-makers about factors which might influence their attitudes toward certain regulations. Each one dismissed out of hand costs in the allocative sense as being of little or no interest. This formal study simply confirms what we have learned informally in dealings with most agencies on most issues. There are, happily, some exceptions, but the irrelevance of allocative costs tends to be the rule.

When decision-makers think about costs, they tend to think of distributive costs. This tendency follows perfectly from the concept of rule-making as another form of politics and the definition of politics as who gets what when.

Distributive costs become more or less relevant to decision-makers depending upon:

- Which groups the cost is being distributed to—i.e., whose ox is being gored.
- The type of objective which the rule is supposed to achieve.

In the present environment, costs distributed to big business have little impact on decision-makers. Costs to small business, consumers, or specific groups of consumers are likely to get more attention. But this concern varies with the type of objective of the rule.

Rules with Type II objectives—elimination of hazardous products or their consequences—appear to be least sensitive to complaints that they produce costs for certain groups. Rules with Type III objectives—attainment of agreed-upon social goals—also appear relatively insensitive to issues of distributive costs.

On the other hand, rules with Type I and Type IV objectives—better decisions and improvements in public welfare—appear more amenable to inclusion of distributive costs in decision-makers' calculations.

Distributive costs can become very important when they are borne by the intended beneficiaries of the rule. Thus, for example, the Product Availability Rule was originally motivated, in part, by a perceived need to protect inner-city residents from supermarket advertising of items that were not readily available. It is now hypothesized that the rule may have had the unintended effect of decreasing the quantity of advertised items particularly appealing to minority groups because of the requirement that advertised items be generally available in all stores in a market area.

This discussion of allocative and distributive costs is to illustrate the point that if research on the impact of regulation is to be actionable, it must address questions meaningful to decision-makers, not researchers. Frequently, this requirement means dealing with distributive costs even though they are not as "objectively" important as allocative costs.

Another area which requires attention is the need to establish the extent of compliance with a regulation before regulatory costs are calculated. Without compliance there can be only enforcement costs. It cannot be taken for granted that simply because a regulation is issued, very many firms out there in the world (a) know about it and/or (b) do what it requires, either fully or in part.

Determining the extent of compliance, if any, can be a monumental undertaking when the rule covers an industry or industries with many firms. The problem is less difficult for Type II and III rules where the characteristics of the product are regulated. For Type IV regulations, where business practices are controlled, the difficulty of determining levels of compliance is especially acute. To illustrate the problem, consider what would be involved in determining the extent to which there is compliance with the regulation requiring display of warranty information on the sales floor.

Intangible costs present another area of difficulty. The problem of dealing with intangibles is usually associated with the measurement of benefits. However, this same problem or similar problems are present in the measurement of costs. Intangible costs are not easily amenable to market measures. Putting a dollar value on more product information or fewer deaths or injuries is both technically difficult and of doubtful utility, since decision-makers are likely to view such measures as questionable.

Intangible costs, like intangible benefits, may be divided into two groups, broadly labeled the psychological and the physical.

Consider these examples of intangible, psychological costs:

- The advertising substantiation program is directed at improving consumer information. It has been theorized, however, that one by-product of the program might be the ''chilling'' of advertised speech. That is, advertisers might not make certain claims which are, in fact, true and useful for the consumer to hear about because of fear—misplaced or not—that such claims would result in FTC action, with resultant bad publicity and possibly expensive litigation costs for the firm. Clearly, *decreasing* consumer information is just as much a cost as increasing it is a benefit.
- The proposed ban on the use of saccharin is designed to save lives by protecting the public from hazardous products. Yet, for users of saccharin who have serious weight control needs, such a ban would presumably impose a psychological penalty

Consider these examples of physical costs:

- The saccharin regulation impacts on people, such as the obese, for whom saccharin serves a clear physical need. Banning it presumably imposes a cost on them of increased risk of heart disease.
- Child-resistant containers are required for most drugs by the U.S. Consumer Product Safety Commission. These containers are fre-

quently hard to open for average people and occasionally next to impossible for the elderly or infirm. Although exempt containers are available, many of those who need them probably don't have them. If medication cannot be used when needed because an elderly consumer cannot get the regulated container open, there would appear to be a physical cost imposed by the rule.

- If there is compliance, it is sometimes difficult to determine whether or not the complying adjectives, and their cost, were or would have been undertaken by the regulated firm anyway. For instance, if firms substantiate their advertising for other reasons, how much cost, if any, can be ascribed to the FTC?

Finally, there is the difficulty of quantifying economic cost. Most research in the field has noted the difficulty of determining the aggregate economic cost of a regulation. Beyond this difficulty, however, is the problem of estimating the effects of such cost on consumer prices. This is an important issue for the following reasons:

- Consumer prices do mean something to decision-makers, whereas aggregate costs often do not.
- In industries with large volume, simply dividing aggregate cost by the number of units produced is likely to yield a very small price increment per unit.
- Both consumers and decision-makers are apt to feel that the "protection" offered by the regulation is worth that small incremental cost, regardless of how effective or ineffective the regulation is.
- The impact of a regulation on consumer prices can be considerably more complex—and greater—than simple division of aggregate cost by aggregate production (or sales) would indicate. For example, regulations which create high fixed costs will tend to increase disproportionately the production cost, and eventually, price of small-volume producers of the product. This increase is paid for by consumers preferring the product of the small producer. Although consumers in general might feel that the "average" cost of the regulation is not worthwhile, *these* consumers might not feel that way about their higher cost.
- Similarly, higher costs of production and higher prices for small producers can lead to loss of market share for them, greater industry concentration, and, in the long, run, higher prices to consumers as the industry becomes less price competitive.

How does one measure other intangible costs or benefits of a similar nature? It hardly seems reasonable to ignore them simply because it is difficult to translate them into dollar values. As costs, they represent a burden to society or parts thereof. As benefits, they often represent the very rationale for the rule. The case for accounting for these intangible costs or benefits is further enhanced when it is recognized that there are psychological scaling techniques which can accommodate at least some of the problems.[1] The fact is that decision-makers do not issue or evaluate regulations solely on their economic merits. Addressing only economic issues when rigorously studying the impact of regulation allows noneconomic issues to be accounted for by proponents or opponents of regulation in a haphazard and one-sided manner. This situation can hardly lead to better regulation.

Summarizing Benefits and Costs

After the individual costs and benefits are measured, the results must be summarized so that they will be intelligible to someone other than the researcher. Two methodologies have been applied to this problem:

1. Cost-Benefit Analysis
2. Cost-Effectiveness Analysis

Cost-benefit analysis is used to produce a ratio of benefits to costs and so, in one arithmetic term, to compress neatly the net value of the regulation. The method suffers from three defects (Stern et al., 1977, p. 48):

- The effects of the regulation on the attitudes and conduct of organizations and individuals must be isolated when, in fact, there are rarely data to enable this.
- Intangible benefits and costs must be converted into dollar values. This effort can be a dubious undertaking.
- The methodology assumes that "society" has a homogeneous utility function rather than recognizing that there are distributive costs and benefits.

Cost-effectiveness analysis suffers from none of these drawbacks. This method is simply an assessment of how well the regulation met its own stated objectives. The results may be examined for individual segments of society (Stern et al., 1977, p. 49).

It seems clear that the cost-effectiveness approach is to be preferred in the study of regulation. This appears to be true even when it is possible to eliminate the first two objections to cost-benefit analysis: i.e., there are data for assessing the effects of regulation on organizations and individuals, and intangible benefits and costs can be placed on a common scale.

The third objection to cost-benefit analysis, the assumption of a

[1] Psychological scaling techniques for quantifying utilities have been used by the author in work for the FTC. Similar techniques are described by Hughes (1977).

homogeneous utility function, is the most telling. In the real world, utilities for the benefits of a regulation and disutilities for its costs are not homogeneous. Nor is the impact of costs and benefits homogeneous. Rather, different segments of society, different organizations, and different individuals are impacted differently.

The formulation and evaluation of rules by decision-makers is a process which attempts to accommodate diverse interests. Cost-benefit analysis attempts to reach an *optimal* solution based on notions of efficiency. Decision-makers in rule-making are seldom interested in optimal solutions. Rather, they are interested in solutions that satisfy as many parties to the issue as possible or, at least, dissatisfy as few as possible.

Hence, the great advantage of cost-effectiveness analysis: it can describe the effects of a regulation on each party by a variety of meaningful terms; monetary values, consumer satisfaction, numbers of injuries, etc. Decision-makers can then do their own mental calculus of the importance of each and all of these effects.

The result is a summary of the impact of the regulation that is a value judgment. It is, in the end, a political judgment, and that is the most appropriate kind, because the regulatory process is from the beginning to the end a political process.

REFERENCES

HARBRIDGE HOUSE, INC., "Applied Research on the Benefits and Costs of Public Regulation of the Copper Wire Industry," Vol. 1, Technical Report submitted to the RANN Division, National Science Foundation, August 1977.

HUGHES, G. DAVID, "Monetizing Utilities for Product and Service Benefits," in A. G. Woodside, J. N. Sheth, and P. D. Bennett (eds.), *Consumer and Industrial Buying Behavior* (New York: North Holland, 1977), pp. 179–189.

HUGHES, G. DAVID, PAUL VERKUIL, and CAMERON WILLIAMS, "The Mounting Private Costs of Public Policy in Marketing," Report No. 78–103, Marketing Science Institute, Cambridge, Mass., May 1973.

LASSWELL, HAROLD G., *Politics: Who Gets What, When, and How* (New American Library, 1958).

STERN, LOUIS W. et al., "The Evaluation of Consumer Protection Laws: The Case of the Fair Credit Reporting Act," Report No. 77–114, Marketing Science Institute, Cambridge, Mass., November 1977.

STIGLER, GEORGE J., "The Theory of Economic Regulation," *Bell Journal of Economics and Management Science,* Spring 1971.

40 MEASURING THE COST OF REGULATION

R. Lee Brummet

The methods of cost/benefit or cost/effectiveness analysis and "bottom line accountability" using "net benefit" as the final criterion have been proposed to determine the social desirability of a regulation and its various alternatives. While these methods may place different emphases on objectives, they all depend upon an assessment of cost.

The topic of this volume and the originating workshop was "the mounting private costs of public policy." In the workshop discussions, the assumption that cost is increasing to a level of "mounting" proportions was never seriously questioned, although the magnitude of these costs was suggested only within a range of, say, $50 billion to $200 billion a year—a range not likely to call forth an ecstatic reaction from an independent expert cost accountant or analyst. The potential for intelligent and effective use of regulation is surely dependent in large part on the degree of accuracy in assessing the cost involved. The purpose of this brief exploration is to suggest a framework for approaching the subject of cost assessment and to identify some studies that are underway to measure the costs of regulation.

Although *private* costs of regulation were emphasized in the announced theme of the workshop, interest and concern for the subject need not and perhaps should not reflect a private-sector bias or be limited

---

Reprinted with permission from G. David Hughes and E. Cameron Williams (eds.) *The Dialogue That Happened* (Boston: Marketing Science Institute, 1979), pp. 80–83.

In a brief exposition of its work in measuring federal regulatory costs, the Dow Chemical Company has indicated its willingness to share its methodology and its experience if interested parties will write to Joe Bevirt, Dow Chemical Company, 2020 Dow Center, Midland, Michigan 48640.

to costs incurred in that sector only. An evaluation of economic and social welfare should ultimately deal with all costs and all benefits of regulation, considering the sector incidence of costs only as it relates to timing and the distributional aspects of such costs and benefits. Thus, this chapter will take a somewhat broader view of costs.

A FRAMEWORK FOR COST ASSESSMENT

Cost assessment always involves a sequence of identification and measurement. The two processes interact to complicate the effort. Yet the logic of the sequence is persuasive. Economists and other social scientists provide expertise in cost identification and conceptualization, while accountants, and a somewhat different set of other social scientists, provide expertise in cost measurement. Both roles are essential and formidable and they must be considered in tandem. This task is possible at a very basic level in the form of an approach or a framework for consideration. So let us consider both the identification and classification of costs and the measurement technology available or appropriate to such classifications. The following classifications are appropriate, although not exhaustive:

I. Public sector costs—costs of enactment, enforcement, monitoring, and reenactment of legislation and regulation
II. Private sector costs
    1. Cost of compliance
    2. Cost of compliance assurance
III. Social costs—externalities
    1. Cost of suboptimal resource allocation
    2. Cost of loss of productivity
    3. Cost of decreased capital formation
    4. Cost of dampening of innovation.
    5. Cost of developing new required management skills
    6. Cost of suboptimal industry structure through discouraging of smaller firms.

The first category, the public sector costs, may be assessed in a reasonably objective manner by identifying the portions of our federal budget committed to the various regulatory areas. Some allocations may extend across multiple agencies or departments, and some agency budgets may include nonregulatory activities. Nevertheless, the identification process, or cost calculation, is relatively straightforward. We know, for example, the amounts included in the federal budget for the Departments of Agriculture; Commerce; Health, Education and Welfare; Housing and Urban Development; Interior; and other agencies significantly involved in policy determination and regulation. A more complete analysis would include some portion of the costs of the legislative and judicial branches of the federal government. The total of these amounts should provide an adequate assessment of explicit costs incurred in the public sector. These figures may be arrayed longitudinally to show trends.

A still more exhaustive analysis must include the social costs related to these public-sector outlays. It would require determination of the incidence of taxation and the higher order effects of inflationary and deflationary impacts. It would also require the use of less objective measures that would inevitably be vulnerable to question. Stopping short of the complete "social cost" impact assessment, we can nevertheless obtain a useful first approximation.

The second category of costs is the private sector costs. In the area of compliance, we may identify the added costs of complying with standards set by OSHA for employee safety, by the FDA for product quality, by the EPA for pollution abatement and solid waste disposal, by the EEOC for additional employment costs, by ERISA for worker benefits, and the like. Most of these costs may be identified through normal cost-accounting procedures. Certain direct costs may be captured and somewhat arbitrary, but nevertheless usual cost-accounting procedures may be applied in the identification of related overheads. A major problem will be to determine the portions of these costs that are incremental in relationship to the related regulation. This determination must involve some presumption of the behavior that would be expected under an environment that does not exist. This problem is no different, however, from that of determining the assumed cost of alternative regulatory approaches which are not taken, and should not be so severe as to make the effort impracticable.

The second type of costs incurred in the private sector are those needed to insure compliance. These are largely costs of investigation, internal control, and paperwork connected with the filing of reports on actions taken by a given company or industry. These costs were considered in some depth by the recent Commission on Federal Paperwork. It is clear that they are significant. It is also clear that a reasonably accurate assessment of the magnitude of these costs is possible. The methodology for calculating such costs is basic and involves the identification of direct costs and the allocation of cost pools to objectives served. A central problem concerns the appropriateness of incremental versus total cost concepts. The choice must be viewed in connection with the particular regulatory setting. If the regulation and its enforcement mechanism is clearly temporary, the incremental approach may be justified on an assumption of excess capacity of the firm to fulfill the compliance assurance requirements. If, however, the setting is one of long-range compliance and monitoring, a full-cost assumption would be appropriate.

The third category of possible costs is much easier to conceptualize than to measure. The list given could be expanded, but it is of adequate length to illustrate the possibilities. Opportunities for assessment of these impacts include: (1) estimation in monetary terms; (2) estimation of the existence of the impact and whether it is material or immaterial, with a possible ranking of relative magnitudes; or (3) narrative-type explanations of the nature of the impact, with no effort to quantify it with a cardinal measure, or to rank it on an ordinal scale.

It is difficult if not impossible to justify the first of these approaches. Although some may wish to express their assessments in such a way, any proof of validity would surely be questionable. The second kind of assessment, while not subject to convincing documentation, may be less vulnerable and, if considered in a framework of needed consensus, may be useful. The third approach is surely worthy of consideration. It allows for interpretation on the part of the user of the information. Indeed, it may provide some needed leeway for the political process to exert itself.

Our suggested cost categories and measurement approaches may be summarized as follows:

Cost Categories	Measurement Approaches
Cost incurred in the public sector	Explicit identification of budgeted and actual expenditures from records of the public body or agency.
Cost incurred in the private sector	Explicit identification of direct costs of compliance and compliance assurance plus some allocation of indirect costs.
Social costs or externalities	Ranking of magnitudes of cost impact or narrative-type explanation of the nature of the impact in specific areas to assist the user in making a subjective assessment.

There are some studies currently underway to measure the costs of government regulation to specific organizations in the private sector. It may be possible to develop a summation of all of these costs, or develop cost figures for a representative sample of companies in the various industries, to make some reasonable extrapolation of total cost to the private sector. Numerous corporations are studying the costs to them of federal regulations. Dow Chemical Company has reported some results. . . .

DOW CHEMICAL COMPANY STUDY

Dow Chemical Company estimated that its costs due to federal regulation were $147 million in 1975 and $186 million in 1976. The study for 1977 is nearing completion and it is clear that these costs have increased at an increasing rate since the end of 1976. These estimates are based on an intensive study of the costs related to the impact of federal laws and regulations from more than 70 agencies, which range from specific equipment requirements for pollution control to determination of acceptable wording for new product use labels. Dow reports that "these regulatory impact studies were designed and conducted to:

- examine and evaluate the impact of Federal regulatory activity,
- develop regulatory costs data on which to base realistic guidelines,
- reduce regulatory costs where they are excessive,
- provide data that would be useful to government,
- increase public understanding of the problem,
- share methods and results so other companies and industries might assess their regulatory cost."

Dow identifies costs of regulation by product or product family, business group, location, and government program involved. The study procedures include classifications for operating costs of administration, research, manufacturing and distribution, and marketing, as well as capital costs for laboratories, equipment, and land. While the assumption that capital costs and operating costs are additive for a given year may be subject to question, one may point out that a continuing regulatory involvement will make necessary additional capital costs each year, and that the replacement of these capital costs with appropriate depreciation figures will not materially affect the results in the long run. It might be noted further that the impact of inflation might indeed cause the depreciation figures to distort the results more than distortions caused by "lumpiness" in capital expenditures.

An interesting aspect of Dow's study is the classification of regulatory costs into the categories of necessary, questionable, and excessive. Of the $186 million cost in 1976, Dow claims $14 million to be questionable, and $69 million to be excessive. These figures are interesting and perhaps useful, but they necessarily reflect some subjective assumptions about the behavior of the company under a different regulatory setting; they must be considered only as the company's self-perception. Different levels of bias, including the possibility of zero bias, may be assumed by the user. it is surely worth noting, however, that Dow considered $103 million of regulatory costs, or 55% of the expected total, for 1976 to be "appropriate."

41 CRYING WOLF

Joan Claybrook

For over a year, I have observed the rising corporate assault on government regulation, particularly regulation designed to spur business to advance health and safety. In widely circulated advertisements, in letters to shareholders, in pamphlets, speeches, testimony and trade association materials, the federal government is accused of creating unnecessary regulations that cause inflation, retard innovation, destroy jobs, and divert capital investment from "productive" pursuits. Readers will have noticed these corporate attacks on "Big Government," "Bureaucratic Bungling," "Overregulation" and, of course, "The Undermining of the Free Enterprise System." But they will not have noticed much in the way of a response from the regulators. In my opinion, it is our duty as public servants to speak up—because these charges can generate unwarranted loss of respect of legitimate government action. They can demoralize those who are trying to improve conditions within industries, and they can undermine efforts to develop the technological basis for life-preserving progress for workers, consumers, and the environment.

Here is the current corporate view as it appears to me.

- If inflation rages, Washington is the cause and only Washington can provide the cure.
- If there is unemployment, Washington is its taproot and the obstacle to its reduction.
- If there is disease-producing pollution, it is a necessary by-product of a technological society, and Washington's pressure to curb it interferes with "progress."

Reprinted, with permission, from *Regulation 2* (November–December 1978), pp. 14–16.

- If there is serious job-related disease and injury, laws that require investment to prevent such damage to society are not "productive"—as though improving the health of a nation does not add to its wealth.
- If filth, adulterants, and harmful additives are found in meat and poultry products, the solution is not to clean up the industry but to campaign against the Department of Agriculture and the Food and Drug Administration.
- If a company or industry is not doing well, it is Washington's fault for not providing additional "incentives," such as tax preferences or U.S. Treasury checks.

Corporations, in short, are engaged in a massive drive to blame the federal government for what really is the fault of business. At last reading, after all, the American economy was still overwhelmingly in corporate hands—from the land that produces the minerals, foods, and fibers, to the factories that manufacture the goods, to the office buildings that house the capital and managerial resources. Not only is that true but also the corporate economy plays a strong role in deciding how public revenues and resources are to be used. Yes, business regulates government quite frequently, and when it does, curiously enough, it seeks certain kinds of "Big Government" goodies. In short, Uncle Sam is fine when he plays Uncle Sugar. How many trucking or airline companies have been ready to shoulder the old-fashioned rigors of market pricing and entry by supporting proposals to put the regulators of these industries out of business? It is compellingly clear that many corporations welcome government when it is a subsidizer of last resort, lender of last resort, guarantor of last resort, insurer of last resort, and cartel-defender of last resort. But when Uncle Sugar becomes Uncle Sam, people-protector of last resort, the corporate tiger bares his teeth and snarls.

In regulating for health and safety, government assumes what I believe to be one of its most basic functions, promoting the general welfare. Too many companies or industries refuse to recognize both the multiple hazards of their technology and the government's legitimate interest in the public's health and safety—despite extensive pesticide and other chemical plant tragedies, food-borne diseases, contaminated drinking water, and the overall degradation of our environment.

Now, the auto industry is not one of those that still opposes the *principle* of government safety regulation. For example, John Riccardo, Chrysler Corporation's chairman, declared recently that "the need for reasonable regulation of the automobile, in the areas of safety, clean air, and energy conservation, is well established and deserves our full support." Henry Ford II was even more charitable, in retrospect, saying on "Meet the Press" (in 1977): "We wouldn't have had the kinds of safety built into automobiles that we have had unless there had been a Federal law. We wouldn't have had the fuel economy and the emission control unless there had been a Federal law.''

These remarks point the way to understanding the domestic auto industry's relationship to federal regulation. The industry fights proposed regulations that it later candidly or grudgingly approves. The Big Three auto companies fought California's and later Washington's modest air-pollution control efforts. They still fight auto safety legislation such as the proposed requirement for passive restraint systems, and they resist major vehicle recalls. The point is clear: their credibility is not high. It is not merely the way things turned out that reflects adversely on their credibility, but also the way some of the foreign auto companies have shown up the Big Three. The story of Honda and its stratified charge engine (imported into Japan from the United States and refined) is an example. So is the story of Volvo (ranking twenty-seventh in passenger car sales in the United States)—first with shoulder harnesses, among the first developmentally with air bags and crash safety, and now selling the least polluting vehicle on California's Air Resources Board list (Saab is number two).

Given this background and the fact that business is booming for the domestic auto companies, it is dismaying to hear once again that government is undermining the free enterprise system. It is particularly dismaying that, in the last year, some of the industry's top officials have charged government regulations with impeding growth, stifling innovation, putting workers on the streets, and hampering the industry's ability to compete internationally. If, under these regulations, foreign companies can compete here, why is it our companies cannot?

In January 1978, Chrysler's John Riccardo called air bags a product of ''overregulation'' that will cost $250 to $300 per car, and claimed the overall result of federal regulation would be a $1,000 per car ''rip-off'' to consumers in the middle of the next decade. In March 1978, Lee Iacocca, then president of Ford Motor Company, spoke of the ''threat'' of regulation that was ''seriously retarding scientific progress, contributing to inflation, damaging competition, costing American workers their jobs and crippling American business in the world marketplace.'' Thomas Murphy, chairman of General Motors, in a letter to President Carter, has declared that in the early 1980s the average retail price of a car could increase by more than $800 because of federal regulations—something he thinks inflationary as well as likely to produce widespread buyer resistance.

Of course, most industry comments ignore the benefits of regulations, even when they do not inflate the costs—a practice analogous to a corporate annual report's giving full details on expenses but ignoring revenues. So, in 1975 and again in 1977, in attempting to quantify safety benefits, the National Highway Traffic Safety Administration (NHTSA) carried out studies on the societal costs of motor vehicle accidents, costs such as income foregone, medical care, insurance administration, legal expenses. These costs were estimated at $38 billion annually for 1975 and $43 billion for 1977, the rise coming largely in insurance (up 44 percent in the two years) and hospital and medical costs (up over 20 percent). The figures include only the more readily quantifiable economic losses and do not fully measure the tragedy of death and injury, the disruption of family life, the trauma of witnessing a child's pain, or the mental stress of caring for once active and productive members of society now confined to wheel chairs. But if our regulations do reduce accidents, there are measurable benefits aplenty from them, even without trying to quantify the unquantifiable. Moreover, a supporting index for the necessity of automobile safety regulation may be found in the number of vehicles recalled for safety-related defects. Since 1966, about 5 million vehicles have been recalled each year for correction of defects that pose safety hazards. The fact that the procession of recalled vehicles continues unabated indicates a certain laxity of quality control on the industry's part. It is a certainty that, in the absence of the highly visible federal regulatory presence, a majority of the 65 million vehicles recalled since 1966 would be on the road with their defects unremedied.

In the area of fuel economy, the need for regulation is likewise evident. The oil shortage of 1973-74 has taught us what could happen if this country continued to rely heavily on foreign sources for oil. Motor vehicles account for about 40 percent of the nation's petroleum consumption. Conservation there is an absolute necessity, given that alternative means of transportation for most individuals are still far in the future and that drastic changes in driving patterns seem unlikely. Regulating average vehicle fuel economy is the best present means to achieve this end.

We at NHTSA estimate the costs of all our proposed regulations. However, since the standards are set in terms of performance rather than hardware or design, individual manufacturers are generally free to choose from a number of options to meet a standard—which means that their costs may vary substantially, according to the options they choose and the degree to which they may exceed the requirements of the standard. Nevertheless, it is the manufacturers themselves (who supply wholesale price information to the Bureau of Labor Statistics) who are the prime source of data on the costs of implementing our regulations. On the basis of their data and other available information, the Department of Transportation estimates the average cost to consumers of safety features contained in a model year 1978 automobile at about $250—approximately half the amount claimed by some auto makers and roughly 5 percent of the total vehicle price. Considering the payoff—the General Accounting Office estimated in 1974 that vehicle safety standards had saved some 28,000 lives over the years from 1966 to 1974—safety requirements are one of the car buyer's best investments.

In a 1976 survey of automobile manufacturers, the NHTSA asked the following question: "For each safety standard presently implemented for passenger cars, what will be the reduction in retail price if that standard is revoked. . .?" Although the manufacturers' responses varied widely (overall reductions ranged from $12 to $385), the sales-weighted average was $80. Yet in response to another question, some manufacturers claimed our standards added $368 to a vehicle's price.

Auto industry executives have been particularly critical of regulations promulgated but not yet effective. These include an upgraded bumper standard, passive restraints, and fuel economy standards for passenger cars and for light trucks and vans. Yet the estimated addition to the price of a passenger car because of these standards will be only about $300 by 1984 (in 1977 dollars), and this will be offset by a more than threefold direct out-of-pocket saving to the consumer in fuel economy, plus reductions in highway casualties. It does not appear to be disadvantageous to the consumer to pay $300 more for a 1984 car than for a 1977 car if that amount would save the consumer $890 over the life of the vehicle. Indeed, because of the heavy travel by newer vehicles, the $300 could be recouped through decreased operating expenses within two years of a vehicle's purchase. And for trucks and vans, the fuel economy standards in particular will result in consumers' spending 6 cents to save a gallon of gasoline that would have cost them at least 65 cents (given our assumptions on vehicle use).

National opinion surveys show that the American people, by a wide margin, support government health and safety standards. In a Harris poll of Spring 1978, Americans were asked to rate the importance of nine proposed improvements in the nation's transportation system. Improving auto safety finished far in front—with 83 percent of those polled rating that quest as "very important." Given the size of the job, that popular support provides a good climate for developing what has been called the socially responsible automobile.

But even if it did not—even if the climate were truly poisoned by industry exaggerations of the pernicious effects of government—the benefits of health and safety regulation and of fuel efficiency standards could still, in our view, outweigh the costs. And if the free enterprise system in this country is undermined when we force auto makers to do what the people want and what foreign companies increase their sales by doing, then perhaps our enterprise is itself subject to bureaucratic bungling. Perhaps our corporations are like the shepherd boy who cried "wolf" because he grew tired of tending to his proper business. But this much is clear—it is time for us to answer back.

A. BUSINESS RESPONSES

1. Suppose you were advising a food products manufacturer who was interested in identifying basic consumer problems and concerns. How would you design a research program to help him? What would be the role of consumer surveys? What would be the best way to obtain information from his managers? What other information sources should be used? How would your consumer audit differ if the firm were a retail drug chain?
2. What impact will an association certification or seal of approval have on consumer buyer decisions? Give examples. What are the shortcomings of certification programs? One trade association developed a standard of five-ply construction for ½-inch plywood, which became institutionalized in building codes, making it difficult to introduce three-ply materials even though they are superior. Comment. How might the tire industry set up a grading scheme that the customer can understand?
3. One author concludes that the automobile industry either cannot or will not attempt self-regulation and that safety standards must be set by the government. Comment.
4. Will the National Advertising Review Board be effective at resolving complaints about deceptive advertising? The board is planning to broaden its concern to include issues of taste. How do you think it will perform in that regard? How would you measure its performance?
5. Develop and defend a position on each of the retailer action situations described by Dornoff and Tankersley.
6. Since most retailers will refund the purchase price of any item returned, there is no consumer recourse problem in retailing. Comment.
7. How would you evaluate the effectiveness of the consumer programs at Stop & Shop and Penney's if you were the president of those organizations? If you were a consumer activist? Be specific. What measures would you use?
8. How would you prepare a suggested code of conduct for service station automobile repair if you were an industry trade association? Of what value, if any, would such a code be?

9. Analyze the common interests identified by Sitter. Why is business-consumer cooperation either nonexistent or very low-profile?

B. GOVERNMENTAL REGULATION

10. Would the regulation of motor vehicles and tires (see Chapter 32 for a description of efforts by the National Highway Traffic Safety Administration) be relatively easy or difficult given the criteria suggested by Schuck?
11. Consider Question 10 for child care centers (say, the number of instructors per child and the amount of square feet per child). For air pollution.
12. What is the command and conform approach to regulation and how does it differ from incentive regulation? Give an example of both. Regulation can be based upon standards for inputs, processes, or outputs. Give an example of each.
13. Consider the FTC product availability rule, which calls for grocery stores to have advertised items available in sufficient quantity to meet demand. Address the research problems set forth by Ross: specification of the regulatory variable, measurement of benefits, and determination of costs. Use the cost assessment structure suggested by Brummet and identify the types of costs involved in the FTC product availability rule.
14. Answer Question 13 for a state bottle bill that would provide for a substantial deposit on all soft drink and beer containers (including nonreturnable containers).
15. What is the difference between cost-effectiveness analysis and cost-benefit analysis? When would cost-benefit analysis be more appropriate?
16. Should companies analyze their costs in complying with regulations, as Dow has done? Will such analysis influence legislation? How could Dow and other firms make such efforts effective at influencing legislation?
17. Claybrook argues that regulation of the automobile industry has been cost-effective and implies that criticism from the industry has been short-sighted and ill-advised. Do you agree?
18. It has been suggested that regulation of the automobile and other industries has improved quality and boosted consumer confidence and that without such regulation the American producer

would be in even worse shape with respect to Japanese and German competitors. Comment.

19. Design an empirical test to evaluate a consumer information program to rate local auto repair establishments. Also design a mandatory state program to inspect automobiles to determine whether they are emitting excess pollutants.

INDEX